Ethical Standards in the Public Sector

A Guide for Government Lawyers, Clients, and Public Officials

Patricia E. Salkin
Editor

Section of State and Local Government Law
American Bar Association

Cover design by Catherine Zaccarine.

The materials contained herein represent the opinions of the authors and editors and should not be construed to be the action of either the American Bar Association or the Section of State and Local Government Law unless adopted pursuant to the bylaws of the Association.

Nothing contained in this book is to be considered as the rendering of legal advice for specific cases, and readers are responsible for obtaining such advice from their own legal counsel. This book and any forms and agreements herein are intended for educational and informational purposes only.

© 1999 American Bar Association. All rights reserved.
Printed in the United States of America.

03 02 01 00 99   5 4 3 2 1

Ethics, lawyers, and the public sector / Patricia E. Salkin, editor.
     p. cm.
   ISBN 1-57073-663-4
    1. Government attorneys—United States.   2. Legal ethics—United
States.   I. Salkin, Patricia E.
   KF299.G6E87   1999
   174' .3'0973—dc21   99-12692
                                                            CIP

Discounts are available for books ordered in bulk. Special consideration is given to state bars, CLE programs, and other bar-related organizations. Inquire at Book Publishing, ABA Publishing, American Bar Association, 750 North Lake Shore Drive, Chicago, Illinois 60611.

www.abanet.org/abapubs

SUMMARY OF CONTENTS

Foreword xi
About the Editor xiii
About the Authors xv
Preface xxi

Chapter 1
Ethics, Lawyers, and the Public Sector: A Historic Overview 1
John D. Feerick

Chapter 2
Who Is the Client of the Government Lawyer? 13
Jeffrey Rosenthal

Chapter 3
**Postemployment Restrictions on Government Employees:
Closing the "Revolving Door"** 28
George F. Carpinello

Chapter 4
**Doing the Right Thing? Financial Disclosure Filing Requirements
for Government Employees** 44
Barbara Smith

Chapter 5
**The Pitfalls and Pratfalls of Regulating Honoraria, Royalties,
and Travel Reimbursements** 71
Thea Hoeth

Chapter 6
Pro Bono and the Government Lawyer 84
Kathleen Waits

iii

Chapter 7
Considering Ethics at the Local Government Level 127
Mark Davies

Chapter 8
Whistleblower Law and Ethics 156
Robert T. Begg

Chapter 9
Gift Giving in the Public Sector 240
Richard Rifkin

Chapter 10
Conflicts of Interest 245
Hugh B. Weinberg

Chapter 11
Enforcement of Local Ethics Law 260
Joan R. Salzman

APPENDIX A
Select Articles Recently Published by the ABA Section
on State and Local Government Law 293

APPENDIX B
State Ethics Commissions/Agencies 311

APPENDIX C
Select Bibliography 315

CONTENTS

Foreword xi
About the Editor xiii
About the Authors xv
Preface xxi

Chapter 1
Ethics, Lawyers, and the Public Sector: A Historic Overview 1
John D. Feerick
   Early History 2
   Federal Efforts 3
   State Efforts 7
   The Future of Government Ethics Legislation 10

Chapter 2
Who Is the Client of the Government Lawyer? 13
Jeffrey Rosenthal
   Private Sector Practice 14
   To Whom Are Legal Responsibility and Allegiance Owed? 14
   Identifying Potential "Clients" Hypothetically 15
   The Public as the Client 16

Chapter 3
Postemployment Restrictions on Government Employees:
Closing the "Revolving Door" 28
George F. Carpinello
   The Ban on Appearances before a Former Employee's Agency
      ("The Agency Ban") 29
     What Services Are Prohibited? 30
     What is Considered a Former Employee's Agency? 31
     Applicability to Partners and Associates of Former Employees 33
     Applicability of the Ban to Representation of, or Further Employment
       with, the Government 33

The Ban on Involvement in Matters Handled While in Government
(The "Matter Ban") 35
How Involved Must the Employee Have Been in the Matter? *35*
What Postemployment Activities Are Covered? *36*
How Is the "Matter" Defined *36*
Restricting the Use of Confidential Information 38
Using One's Public Position to Obtain Private Employment 38
The Limitations Imposed by Professional Codes of Responsibility 39

Chapter 4
Doing the Right Thing? Financial Disclosure Filing Requirements
for Government Employees 44
Barbara Smith
Current Requirements 46
What's Next? 48
Should Consultants Be Required to Disclose? 48
Privatization Implications 48
Results of Nationwide Survey 49
Survey Respondents *49*
Excerpt from "A Model Law for Campaign Finance, Ethics
& Lobbying Regulation" .... .65

Chapter 5
The Pitfalls and Pratfalls of Regulating Honoraria, Royalties,
and Travel Reimbursements 71
Thea Hoeth
"*What* Are You Going to Say?" 71
What Constitutes an "Honorarium"? 73
Payment for Certain Activities *73*
Travel, Meals, Accommodations, and Admissions to Speech-Related Events *73*
What is the Subject Matter of the Speech, Writing, or Appearance? ... 74
What Exceptions Are There to Limits on Honoraria
for Work-Related Activities? 74
Payment to the Government Entity *74*
Payment to a Charitable Organization *74*
Provision of or Reimbursement for Travel, Meals, Accommodations,
or Other Hospitality *75*
Does It Matter Who Is Offering the Honorarium? 76
Should the Same Rules Apply Equally to All in Public Service? 77
Salary Level and/or Position Responsibilities *77*
Distinguishing among Branches of Government; Elected versus
Appointed Officials *78*
Some Honoraria May Be Subject to Case-by-Case Reviews 78
What Are Appropriate Penalties for Transgressions? 78
The Use of Public Resources for the Preparation of a Speech, Article, or Talk Should
Automatically Disqualify the Individual for Receipt of an Honorarium *79*

Teaching *79*

Establish a Monetary Threshold *79*

Administrative Considerations *79*

United States v. National Treasury Employees Union et al. (NTEU) . . . 79

Background *79*

The Litigation *80*

The Aftermath *81*

Conclusion 82

Chapter 6
Pro Bono and the Government Lawyer 84
Kathleen Waits

Introduction 84

Defining Pro Bono and Why We Need It 85

Getting a Government Pro Bono Program Started—
    The Importance of Leadership and Support from the Top 86

How Much Control over the Pro Bono Program
    Does the Government Office Want? 87

Common Obstacles to Government Pro Bono—And How to
    Overcome Them 88

Conflicts of Interest *89*

Use of Government Work Time and Resources *90*

Avoiding the Appearance of Impropriety *92*

Other Issues—Malpractice Coverage, Miscellaneous Litigation Expenses,
    Occupational Taxes *94*

Inherent Limitations on Appropriate Government Pro Bono Cases *94*

What Can Government Lawyers Do If a Pro Bono Program
    Neither Exists Nor Is Likely? 95

Institutionalizing Government Pro Bono 96

The Personal and Institutional Rewards of Pro Bono 96

Conclusion 97

Appendix 6A: State Statutes: Attorney General Pro Bono
    Involvement 105

Appendix 6B: State of Maryland Attorney General's Office
    Pro Bono Representation Program 111

Appendix 6C: Department of Justice Policy Statement
    on Pro Bono Legal and Volunteer Services 117

Appendix 6D: Contact People 126

Chapter 7
Considering Ethics at the Local Government Level 127
Mark Davies

Introduction 127

Sources of Local Government Ethics Laws 129

State Constitution *130*

State Statutes *130*

Local Laws Other Than Ethics Laws *131*
Agency Regulations *131*
Common Law *131*
Code of Ethics 132
Generally *132*
Prohibited Interests *133*
Use of Public Office for Private Gain *134*
Moonlighting *135*
Appearances, Representation, and Contingent Compensation *136*
Gifts *136*
Compensation by Private Entities for Municipal Work *137*
Confidential Information *138*
Political Activities *138*
Superior-Subordinate Relationships *139*
Preemployment Restrictions *139*
Payment for a Municipal Position *140*
Postemployment (Revolving Door) *140*
Inducement of Violations *141*
Avoidance of Conflicts of Interest *142*
Whistleblower Protection *142*
Restrictions on Private Citizens and Companies 142
Generally *142*
Inducement of Ethics Violations and Influencing Officials *142*
Appearances by Officials's Outside Employers *143*
Disclosure 144
Transactional Disclosure *144*
Applicant Disclosure *145*
Annual Disclosure *145*
Enforcement 146
Generally *146*
Stages of the Enforcement Process *147*
Penalties *148*
Administration 149
Confidentiality 150
Conclusion 151

Chapter 8
Whistleblower Law and Ethics **156**
Robert T. Begg
The Controversial Nature of Whistleblowing 157
The At-Will Employment Doctrine 159
Statutory Protection for Public Sector Whistleblowers—
    Why Is There a Need for Whistleblower Protection
    in the Public Sector? 160
Federal Statutory Protections for Whistleblowers 161

Federal Whistleblower and Antiretaliation Provisions
  outside the Merit System 165
Statutory Whistleblower Protection at the State Level 168
  Generally *168*
  Protected Conduct *169*
  Communications *170*
  Retaliation and Remedies *171*
Financial Incentives for Whistleblowing 172
Common-Law Protections for Whistleblowers 174
Professional Ethics Codes as Sources of Public Policy 177
Special Issues Encountered by Lawyers 178
The In-House Counsel's Dilemma 179
The Law Firm Corollary to the In-House Counsel Dilemma 185
Whistleblowing and the Federal Government Lawyer 188
Conclusion 193
Appendix 8A: State Whistleblower Provisions 205

Chapter 9
Gift Giving in the Public Sector 240
Richard Rifkin
  What Is the Right Rule? 240
  Developing a Relationship through Gifts 241
  Why Not a Total Bar? 241
  How to Distinguish among Gifts 242
  Guidelines 243
  Conclusion 243

Chapter 10
Conflicts of Interest 245
Hugh B. Weinberg
  Introduction 245
  Prohibited Interests 246
  Prohibited Conduct Generally 247
  Waivers and Orders Allowing Otherwise-Prohibited Interests 250
  Working for Not-for-Profit Organizations and Other
    Volunteer Activities 252
  Representing Private Interests before the Government 253
  General Practice of Law 255
  Conclusion 257

Chapter 11
Enforcement of Local Ethics Law 260
Joan R. Salzman
  Advice versus Enforcement 261
  Complaints 263

Who Investigates? 264
Jurisdiction over Former Government Employees 266
Confidentiality 268
Probable Cause, Petition, and Answer 269
Discovery 271
Trial 271
Settlement 273
"Commingling" of Adjudicative and Prosecutorial Functions 273
Penalties 275
Cooperation with Other Law Enforcement Agencies 276
Conclusion 277
Penalties for Violations 284
Appendix 11A: Disposition of *COIB v. Sergio Matos* 288
Appendix 11B: Draft Allocution for Guilty Plea to Violation
       of Chapter 68 of the City Charter 292

APPENDIX A
Select Articles Recently Published by the ABA Section
    on State and Local Government Law **293**
Redlich, Norman and David R. Lurie, "Federal Governmental
    Attorney-Client Privilege Decisions May Prove Significant
    to All Government Lawyers" *Local Government Law Weekly*
    (Oct. 23, 1998) 294
Salkin, Patricia E., "Ten Effective Strategies for Counseling
    Municipal Clients on Ethics Issues." *State and Local Law News,*
    vol. 22, No. 1 (Fall 1998). 296
Arey, Patrick K., "'Pay to Play:' The Debate Continues,"
    State and Local Law News, Vol. 21, No. 4 (Summer 1998). 300
Salkin, Patricia E., "Municipal Ethics Check for the Land-Use
    Lawyer," *State and Local Law News,* Vol. 20, No. 4
    (Summer 1997). 306

APPENDIX B
State Ethics Commissions/Agencies **311**

APPENDIX C
Select Bibliography **315**

APPENDIX D
Resources **321**

FOREWORD

Special thanks to Barbara Smith of the New York State Ethics Commission for her editorial assistance. Also, a big thank you to Albany Law School student Sara Osborn, who helped to organize the chapters and the style of the publication, and to the staff of the Government Law Center, especially Lisa Buscini and Michele Monforte, who supported this effort. The authors have my personal thanks for writing and editing their work over what seemed like a long period of time. The Council of the American Bar Association State and Local Government Law Section deserves recognition for providing and encouraging resources for the public sector bar to raise unique issues surrounding ethical considerations in this sector.

ABOUT THE EDITOR

Patricia E. Salkin

Patricia E. Salkin is associate dean and director of the Government Law Center of Albany Law School. She teaches a course in government ethics at Albany Law School and is a member of the Steering Committee for the Council on Government Ethics Laws. She currently co-chairs the ethics committee for the ABA Section on State and Local Government Law and is the section's designee to the ABA's Ethics 2000 initiative. At the state level, she is a member of the Executive Committee of the Municipal Law Section of the New York State Bar Association. She is a frequent lecturer and writer on topics dealing with government ethics at the state and local levels.

ABOUT THE AUTHORS

Robert T. Begg

Robert T. Begg is associate dean and director of the library at Albany Law School. He also teaches a course in the legal profession at the law school. He joined the faculty of Albany Law School in 1983 after serving as director of the law library and professor of law at Pettit College of Law of Ohio Northern University. He is a graduate of Slippery Rock College (B.S.), the University of Oregon School of Law (J.D.), and Rutgers University (M.L.S.).

George F. Carpinello

George F. Carpinello is a member of the firm of Barrett Gravante Carpinello & Stern L.L.P. and is resident in the firm's Albany office. He practices in the area of general litigation, antitrust, constitutional, municipal, and commercial law. He was formerly a professor of law and director of the Government Law Center of Albany Law School. He is Chair of the New York State Advisory Committee on Civil Practice, past Chair of a statewide panel studying New York's physician discipline process, past Chair of the Judicial Administration Committee of the New York State Bar Association and past president of the Legal Aid Society of Northeastern New York. He is a graduate of Princeton University and Yale Law School.

Mark Davies

Mark Davies has served as executive director and counsel of the New York City Conflicts of Interest Board since 1994. Before that he was the executive director of the New York State Temporary State Commission on Local Government Ethics, where he drafted proposed major revisions to New York State's ethics law for local government officials. He also served as a deputy counsel to the

xv

New York State Commission on Government Integrity. During fifteen years of private practice he specialized in litigation and municipal law. He is a member of the executive committee of the New York State Bar Association's Commercial and Federal Litigation Section and editor of their newsletter, and is the Chair of the Ethics and Professional Responsibility Committee of the Municipal Law Section of the association. He has lectured extensively on civil practice and on ethics and has authored numerous publications in those areas. He is also the directing editor and revision author of West's *McKinney's Forms for the CPLR* and is the directing editor and lead author of West's *New York Civil Appellate Practice*. Mr. Davies graduated from Columbia College and Columbia Law School and is an adjunct professor of law at Fordham and New York Law Schools.

John D. Feerick

John D. Feerick has served as dean of Fordham University School of Law since July 1982. He practiced law from 1961 to 1982 at the firm of Skadden, Arps, Slate, Meagher & Flom, as a partner from 1968 to 1982, developing its labor and employment law practice. During his tenure as dean he has served in a number of public positions, among them chairman of the New York State Commission on Government Integrity and special New York State attorney general. He currently cochairs the Ethics Committee of the Dispute Resolution Section of the ABA and previously chaired a joint committee of the ABA, American Arbitration Association, and SPIDR that developed a set of ethical standards for mediators of disputes. He has been a mediator and arbitrator of many labor disputes, some involving high-profile parties such as the New York City Transit Authority, the NFL, and the NBA. Dean Feerick currently serves as president of Citizens Union Foundation; as Chair of the Executive Committee of the American Arbitration Association, the oldest dispute resolution group in the United States; Chair of the Fund for Modern Courts, which studies the improvement of the administration of justice in New York courts; and Chair of the Standards Review Committee of the ABA Legal Education Section, which proposes accreditation standards for American law schools. He also chaired the New York State Committee to Review Audiovisual Coverage of Court Proceedings. He is the author of several books, scores of articles, and was nominated for a Pulitzer Prize. He is a graduate of Fordham College and Fordham Law School, where he served as editor-in-chief of its law review.

Thea Hoeth

Thea Hoeth is a native of Schenectady, New York. She attended Catholic elementary and secondary schools; was graduated cum laude from St. Lawrence University in Canton, New York; and received her J.D. from Albany Law School of Union University, Albany, New York. She was a partner in the Albany law firm of Adams, Hoeth & Justice, P.C., then held a number of positions in New York State government, including the cabinet-level post of executive director of the Office of Business Permits and Regulatory Assistance, deputy director of state operations, and special assistant to the governor for management and productivity. From 1981 to 1984 she served as executive director of the New York State Ethics Commission. She teaches legal ethics as an adjunct professor at the Sage Colleges in Albany, New York, and is currently the executive director of the Volunteer Center of the Capital Region. She is a member of the Women's Bar Association of the State of New York, having served in various statewide and local offices in the 1980s. She is a member of the board of directors of the Albany-Schenectady League of Arts.

Richard Rifkin

Richard Rifkin is currently Deputy Attorney General for the State of New York. He served as executive director of the New York State Ethics Commission from March 1994 until February 1999. From 1979 until 1994 Mr. Rifkin served in the office of Attorney General Robert Abrams, first as deputy first assistant attorney general and later as counsel to the attorney general and first assistant attorney general. Before his service in the attorney general's office, Mr. Rifkin was counsel to the borough president of the Bronx. From 1966 through 1973 he was a lawyer in private practice in New York City, associated with the firms of Hale, Grant, Meyerson, O'Brien & McCormick and Hoffinger & Stuart. He was also staff counsel to Assemblyman Leonard Price Stavisky from 1970 to 1973. He is a graduate of Washington and Jefferson College and Yale Law School and is admitted to the bar in New York and Washington, D.C. He is a member of the Chief Administrative Judge's Advisory Committee on Civil Practice and is a member of the Association of the City of New York, where he serves on the Committee on Government Ethics, and the New York State Bar Association.

Jeffrey Rosenthal

Jeffrey Rosenthal became first assistant counsel to the Governor's Office of Regulatory Reform in August 1995. Before his appointment he served as Amsterdam City Court judge. He was the first lawyer in New York State to serve two counties (Montgomery and Fulton Counties) simultaneously as assistant district attorney. He is the legal advisor, training coordinator, and member of the steering and executive committees of the Montgomery Youth Court, a student peer review court that adjudicates minor family court cases. He has served as a board member of the Amsterdam Industrial Development Agency and from 1979 until his current appointment maintained a general practice of law. He has been a legal advisor to the Tri-County Mediation Center and has been a lecturer in criminal law and procedures in the police officers recruit training program. He received a B.A. from Alfred University and a J.D. from Vermont Law School.

Joan R. Salzman

Joan R. Salzman is the director of enforcement at the New York City Conflicts of Interest Board (the NYC Board). She has served in that capacity since 1995, having begun city service as associate counsel for enforcement at the NYC Board in 1994. Ms. Salzman has written and lectured extensively on enforcement of ethics laws and conflicts of interest. Her work has appeared in *The New York Law Journal* and the *The Chief Leader,* New York City's civil service weekly newspaper. Ms. Salzman has also written or co-written several of the NYC Board's educational videotapes, including two mock ethics trials, all in conjunction with New York City's Crosswalks Television. She is a graduate of Yale College (1979) and Harvard Law School (1982). Before her government service, Ms. Salzman was in private practice as a litigator. She served as the secretary of the New York City Bar Association Committee on Municipal Affairs from 1986 to 1989 and is currently a member of the city bar association Committee on Government Ethics.

Barbara Smith

Barbara Smith serves as counsel to the New York State Ethics Commission and has done so since its founding in 1989. The State Ethics Commission has jurisdiction over state officers and employees and has authority to interpret and enforce the Public Officers Law ethics provisions. Before her position with the ethics commission, Ms. Smith served as first assistant counsel at the New York State Department of Economic Development. She is a graduate of Albany Law School and a member of the New York State Bar Association's Committee on Attorney Professionalism and the subcommittee on attorneys in public service.

Kathleen Waits

Kathleen Waits is associate professor of law at the University of Tulsa College of Law. She has also taught at Albany Law School, American University, and the University of Florida. She teaches courses in contracts, professional responsibility, remedies, and domestic violence. She has written on government ethics issues, including articles on pro bono and the client of government lawyers. Professor Waits has also worked in the public sector as a lawyer for the U.S. Department of Labor. She is a graduate of Harvard Law School.

Hugh B. Weinberg

Hugh B. Weinberg currently serves as deputy counsel for the New York City Department of Homeless Services. Previously he had spent seven years with the New York City Conflicts of Interest Board, the last four of which he served

About the Authors   xix

as deputy counsel. While there, he supervised and participated in editing opinions, conducting proceedings concerning ethics violations, preparing educational materials, and helping to conduct training sessions. Mr. Weinberg has written and spoken frequently about government ethics issues, and is still a member of the Government Ethics Committee of the Association of the Bar of the City of New York.

PREFACE

This book is a compilation of essays, articles, and research put together in 1997. It is intended to help government lawyers begin to focus on some of the ethical considerations that arise in the practice of law in the public sector. It is not intended to provide answers to each scenario for every jurisdiction. Just as "all politics is local," so too are our ethical standards, rules, and regulations that govern the conduct of state and local government officials and their lawyers. This book does, however, provide a solid overview of many of the complexities of public sector ethics. The chapters that follow contain practical insights to help lawyers and their public sector clients choose the most ethical course of conduct.

Not only must government lawyers be concerned with standards of ethics and professionalism that govern the practice of law, but they also must be conversant with myriad federal, state, and local laws that may govern their own conduct in the public sector and that clearly govern the conduct of the officials to whom they provide legal advice. Legal research on government ethics issues can be challenging at times, overwhelming, and often frustrating. For example, at the state level, in addition to the statutory law, every state has an ethics commission that issues opinions. Some of these opinions are easier to access than others as more and more state agencies are beginning to put their opinions on-line over the Internet and in other commercial electronic formats. In addition to these sources, many individual state agencies have adopted unique regulations governing specific ethics issues for employees of the agency. This is an often overlooked source of information. Furthermore, upon request, a state attorney general may issue an opinion regarding an ethics question involving individuals, conflicts between agencies, and lawyer-client relationships. This is not to suggest, however, that all state-level ethics opinions are published or even made available to the public. For example, in some cases, opinions and letters from legislative ethics committees are deemed confidential and are conveyed only to the member requesting the advice.

At the local government level, responding to government ethics questions can be even more challenging. While state statutes in many jurisdictions

xxi

address issues of official conduct at the local level, these laws are often scattered and not comprehensive. In a number of cases, state law merely enables municipalities to adopt their own codes with little or no guidance. A majority of the states provide no targeted state-level technical assistance to municipalities with respect to government ethics issues, and in only a minority of states does the state-level ethics commission have concurrent jurisdiction over localities. Further complicating the search for guidance on local ethics questions is the disparate quality and lack of consistency of locally crafted ethics laws, the lack of published information from local ethics boards (where they even exist), and even things as simple as locating a copy of the local ethics law believed to have been enacted in the past.

There is perhaps no greater responsibility and challenge confronting public sector lawyers than that of upholding the public trust and integrity in government, both through personal conduct and through counseling government clients on the appropriate course of conduct. A keen sense of awareness of the unique ethics issues facing the public sector, combined with a proactive strategy to protect the good reputation of government officials is a necessity. Ethics education and training for the public sector should begin with programs developed by the government lawyer. The modest training programs that may be available in some jurisdictions are rarely enough, and in many places, no formalized training exists.

Although many of the issues that confront public officials remain somewhat thematically related over the years, such as gifts, honoraria, and financial conflicts of interest, new issues are constantly arising and demanding that government lawyers stay on top of recent developments. For example, the American Bar Association launched Ethics 2000, an initiative designed to revisit the Model Rules of Professional Responsibility (presenting opportunities and possibly creating new concerns for government lawyers). In addition, the recent U.S. Supreme Court ruling in the *Lindsey* case raises new concerns for government lawyers and their public official clients in terms of the lawyer-client privilege and confidentiality. Finally, in the last couple of years, the issue of "pay to play," or the giving of campaign contributions by lawyers to individuals seeking elected public office, with the intent that the money was given to secure legal work, has been the subject of debate within the American Bar Association and the New York State Bar Association. These three issues alone could reshape the way in which government lawyers conduct themselves at the turn of the century.

While the challenges may be great and the issues diverse and at times not easily answered, there are a variety of places where government lawyers may go to seek assistance. The American Bar Association's Section on State and Local Government Law, as well as the Division for Government and Public Sector Lawyers, may be consulted for resource material. The Council on Government Ethics Laws is a national umbrella organization for federal, state, and local ethics agencies (as well as elections, campaign finance, and lobbying entities). The Government Law Center of Albany Law School provides training and technical assistance on ethics issues for the public sector workforce, as do many national and state municipal associations. State and local ethics agencies offer another avenue for support, as well as departments within the office of attorney general and comptroller. The Internet provides increasing information on government ethics issues as web sites from ethics agencies and other governmental entities go on-line, publishing opinions and recent developments in the law.

The authors of the various chapters and articles contained herein represent some of the best minds addressing government ethics issues today. Enjoy the thoughts, ideas, and suggestions herein, and continue to represent honesty and integrity in our great system of government and governance.

Patricia E. Salkin

To Sydney, Jordan, and Howard
. . . it's finally finished.

CHAPTER ❦ 1

Ethics, Lawyers, and the Public Sector: A Historical Overview

John D. Feerick*

Government is a trust, and the officers of the government are trustees; and both the trust and the trustees are created for the benefit of the people.
—Henry Clay, Speech at Ashland, Kentucky,
March 1829

This chapter provides background on the historical developments in government ethics from the debates at the Constitutional Convention of 1787 through federal and state efforts at the end of the twentieth century.

Representing one's fellow citizens in our form of democratic government is a formidable challenge. Our society demands much of those who accept the role of public servant. Beyond the sacrifice of private sector luxuries and opportunities and the time commitment that must be pledged, the men and women who serve the public are held to a higher degree of scrutiny in their public, and perhaps too often, their private lives. Theodore Roosevelt noted that "[t]he first requisite on the citizen who wishes to share the work of our public life . . . is that he shall act disinterestedly and with a sincere purpose to serve the whole commonwealth." The dedication of public servants to serve the public good is a tribute not only to them but to our system of representative democracy.

---

* I am very much in the debt of Joseph Sponholz, Esq., for his help in the preparation of this chapter. I also wish to acknowledge, with appreciation, the assistance of Michele Falkow of the Fordham Law School Library. In large measure, this introduction reflects views I expressed in speeches and writings on behalf of the New York State Commission on Government Integrity, which I was privileged to chair from 1987 to 1990.

The use of law as a means of assuring that public officials meet high ethical standards is rooted in the Constitution of the United States.[1] One cannot read the debates at the Constitutional Convention of 1787 and the state ratifying conventions without concluding that the Framers were concerned about the potential for the abuse of power. In addition to constituting a civil government, the Constitution treats very carefully the exercise of governmental power through a system of self-government, separation of powers, and checks and balances. Indeed, in a few instances the Constitution specifically deals with subjects of conflicts of interest. For example, article I, section 6, provides:

> No Senator or Representative shall, during the Time for which he was elected, be appointed to any civil Office under the Authority of the United States, which shall have been created, or the Emoluments whereof shall have been increased during such time; and no Person holding any office under the United States, shall be a Member of either House during his Continuance in Office.

Article I, section 9, provides that "no Person holding any Office of Profit or Trust under them, shall, without the Consent of the Congress, accept of any present, Emolument, Office, or Title, of any kind whatever, from any King, Prince, or foreign state." Plainly, these clauses illustrate that the Framers recognized the potential for conflicts of interest in a democratic government and the necessity for provisions to protect government integrity. As James Madison pointedly stated in *The Federalist* papers:

> If men were angels, no government would be necessary. If angels were to govern men, neither external nor internal controls on government would be necessary. In framing a government which is to be administered by men over men, the great difficulty lies in this; you must first enable the government to control the governed; and in the next place oblige it to control itself. A dependence on the people is, no doubt, the primary control on the government; but experience has taught mankind the necessity of auxiliary precautions.[2]

Early History

The "experience" to which Madison referred in *The Federalist* papers certainly included the first great city states, when individuals began to consider their relationship with others in an organized society. For example, Aristotle said in one of his lectures on ethics, "Justice can only exist between those whose mutual relations are regulated by law. This is why we do not permit man to rule, but the law. . . . "[3] Similarly, the public servants of Athens took an oath in which they pledged to promote respect for the laws and to make their city greater, better, and more beautiful than it was when they received it:

> We will never bring disgrace to this our city by any act of dishonesty or cowardice, nor ever desert our suffering comrades in the ranks; We fight for

the ideals and the sacred things of the city, both alone and with many; We will revere and obey the city's laws and do our best to incite to a like respect and reverence those who are prone to annul or set them at naught; We will strive unceasingly to quicken the public sense of public duty; That thus, in all these ways, we will transmit this city not only less, but greater, better and more beautiful than it was transmitted to us.[4]

In many ways, the Athenian Oath captured all of the ideals of public office as a public trust. It spoke of public servants as trustees in three significant ways: as fiduciaries of those whom they serve, as proxies of delegated political power, and as holders of the common interest to be preserved for the generations to come. Through such roles public servants serve the common good, and for these reasons the integrity of public servants must be assured. In our country, various mechanisms have been implemented to safeguard the integrity of public servants. One distinguished student of the subject has noted that "ethics laws in this country have proceeded not from a comprehensive view of the rights and duties of public officials but largely in reaction to specific scandals, and until recently on a piecemeal basis."[5]

Threshold requirements for integrity in public office were adopted by the First Congress in the creation of the United States Treasury. The act provided:

> And be it further enacted, That no person appointed to any office instituted by this act, shall directly or indirectly be concerned or interested in carrying on the business of trade or commerce, or be owner in whole or in part of any sea-vessel, or purchase by himself, or another in trust for him, any public land or other public property, or be concerned in the purchase or disposal of any public securities of any State, or of the United States, or take or apply to his own use, any emolument or gain for negotiating or transacting any business in the said department, other than what shall be allowed by law; and if any person shall offend against any of the prohibitions of this act, he shall be deemed guilty of a high misdemeanor, and forfeit to the United States the penalty of three thousand dollars, and shall upon conviction be removed from office, and forever thereafter incapable of holding any office under the United States. . . . [6]

This provision, pervasive in its approach to preventing conflicts of interest, revealed the concern of our initial representatives that public officials left unchecked could, even unwittingly, fall prey to unscrupulous practice. Unfortunately, as government has grown in size and complexity to meet the needs of an expanding society, so too have concerns over governmental integrity.

Federal Efforts

In more recent times, various organizations and bodies have attempted to evaluate the status of government ethics laws and develop safeguards to insure the integrity of our public officials. For example, in 1960, the Association of the Bar of the City of New York made public the results of a two-year study by the Special Committee on the Federal Conflict-of-Interest Laws, chaired by Roswell B. Perkins. The committee's judgment was severe. It concluded that existing restraints were "obsolete, inadequate for the protection of the Government, and a deterrent to the recruitment and retention of executive talent and some kinds of needed consultative talent."[7] The committee found that the statutory law at that time, most of which was at least a century old, was incapable of dealing with the modern, complex problems of government. The committee pointed to several areas that the antiquated laws had failed to address, including the expansion of civil service positions, the blending of the public and private sectors in American society, and the modernization of economic life. It said that government had "failed to provide a rational, centralized, continuing and effective administrative machinery to deal with the [aforementioned] problem."[8] It found that there was a hodgepodge of uncoordinated and uninterpretable statutes and regulations that made conformance impractical. Accordingly, it recommended that Congress take thirteen steps to ameliorate the state of conflict of interest regulation.

The first group of suggestions related to the structure of conflict of interest laws. The committee called for Congress to recognize conflict of interest problems and treat them as important, complex, and independent subjects of attention and concern in the management of government. It suggested that "[t]he present scattered and uncoordinated statutes relating to conflicts of interest . . . be consolidated into a single unified Act, with a common set of definitions and a consistent approach . . ." and that "[a]rchaic provisions should be repealed."[9] It said that only if Congress identified and isolated potential problems could the status of governmental ethics be improved and that only a unified act could provide the general law of conflict of interest an enforceable and more rational format. The committee also recommended that Congress expand the scope of existing restraints to include all matters in which the public deals with federal government. It defined a "transaction involving the government" as "'any proceeding, application, submission, request for a ruling or other determination, contract, claim, case or other such particular matter' which will be the subject of Government action."[10]

The committee's second group of recommendations focused on the need to recruit effective public officials. It proposed that in order to encourage participation in public office, "the statutes should permit the retention by Government employees of certain security-owned economic interests, such as continued participation in private pension plans."[11] It also stated that "it is safe, proper and essential from the viewpoint of recruitment, [that] the statutes should differentiate in treatment between regular employees and citizens who serve the Government only intermittently, for short periods, as advisors and consultants."[12] By doing so, the committee felt, more knowledgeable and skilled private citizens would participate in the management of the government.

A third group of recommendations addressed the structure and enforcement of a modern conflict of interest act. The committee said that violations should be addressed by administrative remedies rather than by criminal penalties. This approach was designed to combat the reluctance of government officials to pursue expensive, time-consuming and often overly harsh criminal sanctions, and to restore the deterrent power of conflict of interest laws. Furthermore, in order to centralize and simplify the current regulatory scheme, the committee proposed that an administrator be appointed by the president to oversee the implementation and enforcement of the act. Through this mechanism, the committee believed that clear overall responsibility for ethical conduct would be placed on the president and that appropriate attention would be given to the critical importance of the act. The committee also suggested that the president be given the power to create a second and third tier of regulations in administrative agencies so that the responsibility for the day-to-day enforcement of the statutes and regulations would rest upon the agency heads.

The fourth group of committee recommendations focused on the need to perceive and take proactive steps to combat conflicts of interest in government. The committee suggested that preventative measures, such as an orientation program for new government employees, be undertaken; that there be more effective prohibitions on the conduct of persons outside the government; and that Congress initiate a study of conflicts of interest of members and employees of the legislative branch.

The work of the Perkins committee contributed significantly to a growing perception that the government was in dire need of ethics reform. As suggested by the committee, the Kennedy administration took steps to broaden the administrative scope of the rules of ethics[13] by ordering all administrative agencies to issue regulations on conflicts of interest. Moreover, by executive order, President Kennedy set standards for the heads and assistant heads of departments and agencies, full-time members of boards and commissions, and members of the White House staff.[14] President Johnson took similar steps during his presidency, signing Executive Order 11222, which dictated rules governing the acceptance of gifts, outside employment, the safeguarding of confidential information, and the avoidance of financial conflicts.[15]

Despite these actions, there remained no single federal ethics law. This void, coupled with increased public concern over the integrity of public officials in the wake of the Watergate scandal, led in the late 1970s, to major legislative ethics initiatives and laws at both the federal and state levels.

In 1977, the House and Senate Judiciary Committees began debate on a comprehensive plan to assure governmental integrity. The Senate Judiciary Committee explained in its report:

> During the extensive hearings this committee held . . . [after the Watergate scandal], there was little if any dispute about two crucial facts: (1) The Department of Justice has not in the past allocated sufficient Departmental

6 ETHICS, LAWYERS, AND THE PUBLIC SECTOR

resources to handle official corruption cases and cases arising out of the
federal election laws; and (2) That the Department of Justice has difficulty
investigating and prosecuting crimes allegedly committed by high-ranking
Executive Branch officials because the department as an institution is
poorly equipped to handle cases involving senior Executive Branch officials.[16]

The committee went on to say:

The solution to these problems is not merely the enactment of more criminal laws. It is essential that the President, the Attorney General and other
top officials in the Department of Justice be men of unquestioned integrity.
However, it is also essential that we have a system of controls and institutions which makes the misuse and abuse of power difficult, if not impossible.[17]

The result of these congressional efforts was the adoption of the Ethics in
Government act of 1978, a thorough and comprehensive system of conflict of
interest prevention. The act proceeded along a number of lines. It contained
detailed conflict of interest provisions, including regulation of the postemployment area. It set forth wide-ranging financial disclosure requirements for
members and employees of the legislative, executive, and judicial branches of
government.[18] It created an Office of Government Ethics (OGE) and authorized the president to appoint an administrator to oversee the new regulatory
system. The OGE would guide the agencies and departments of the executive
branch in administering the financial disclosure system, issue regulations on
standards of conduct and advisory opinions on questions of ethics, and provide for the education of employees about the rules.[19]

In 1979, Congress made several clarifying changes to the act. These
included a definition of "executive branch" to include independent regulatory commissions; an amendment to open to public scrutiny reports made by
the three branches with relation to the act; and a change to make clear that
the act preempted state and local disclosure laws. In 1983, the Act of 1978 was
reevaluated by Congress and resulted in several changes relating to the reau-
thorization of the OGE. However, as the Senate Judiciary Committee indicated: "The OGE has, in its almost five-year history, performed its statutory
duties thoroughly and responsibly, and thus should be reauthorized for five
more years."[20]

Federal ethics in government regulations underwent a total reorganiza-
tion in 1989 under the Ethics Reform Act of 1989.[21] As described by the
House Judiciary Committee, the act

consolidated the ethics laws applicable to all three branches of government; expanded the post-employment restrictions for employees of the
Executive Branch and extended such restrictions to the legislative branch;

revised the financial disclosure rules for senior government officials; authorized "certificates of divestiture" for incoming political appointees who sell assets in order to avoid conflicts of interest; changed certain aspects of the laws pertaining to the acceptance of gifts, outside earned income, and outside employment; banned the receipt of honoraria by federal employees; and added civil penalties to the arsenal of political sanctions for violations of the criminal ethics laws. . . . [22]

Thus, essentially, the 1988 act reflected the original goal of the Ethics in Government Act of 1978: a cohesive, thorough, and workable set of ethics regulation for public employees. The most recent version of the act is the Office of Government Ethics Authorization Act of 1996, which extended for three years the authorization and appropriation for OGE and made several minor changes to the gift acceptance authority of public officials and the limitation on postemployment activities.

State Efforts

As the federal government undertook to deal comprehensively with the subject of government ethics, so did the states. In 1976, the National Municipal League undertook to give leadership to this effort by creating an ethics project to provide information and to evaluate existing state statutes. In 1979 it proposed a model state Conflict of Interest and Financial Disclosure Law to provide guidance, noting in the introduction:[23]

> The committee began its work with one basic premise, which was that the only conflicts of interest which could be regulated under this law were those which concerned finances. Having a conflict of interest is not, in and of itself, evil, wrong or even unusual. Conflicts may be ethnic, cultural, emotional, nostalgic, regional, financial or philosophical. Conflict of interest laws are concerned with financial conflicts which set apart an individual office holder from most of the general public.

It added:

> Conflict of interest provisions are designed to prevent public officials and employees from gaining financial profit from their official actions (other than government salaries), or from helping family or friends to profit unfairly because of inside information or preferential treatment. At the same time, the provisions can take some outside pressure off by making certain practices illegal instead of merely unethical. This is particularly true when the provisions are combined with those for financial disclosure and when the existence of conflicts or potential conflicts becomes a matter of public record.

Unfortunately, the history of ethics legislation at the state level mirrors that of the federal level in terms of its slow and long evolution, spurred usually by scandal. Each state can point to some scandal that focused the issue and led to a governmental response. In New York, for example, Charles Evans Hughes was an early champion of ethics reform. He received his start in public life in 1905 when he investigated—on behalf of the legislature—corruption in both the public utilities industry and the insurance industry. At that time, several political bosses ran New York State politics and divided the patronage spoils among themselves and their allies. These politicians received ample support from heads of business in the state and the bosses reciprocated with legislative favors. Hughes faced a difficult challenge; the bosses did everything they could to stymie his efforts. Nevertheless, he proved to be an extremely talented investigator. He was often able to elicit admissions from witnesses that the witnesses themselves never thought they would divulge, thereby exposing the link between the large insurance companies and the entrenched political establishment.

It was Hughes's very success in investigating the insurance industry that led him to face a personal dilemma that tested his own commitment to the highest ethical standards. In the heat of the investigation, the political bosses looked for a way to end the threat that he posed. In order to remove his influence from the investigation, they arranged for him to receive the Republican nomination for mayor of New York City. He knew nothing about the nomination before it happened. In fact, he and his wife were enjoying a rare night out at the theater as a temporary break from his work. When they returned home, a small group of political leaders paid him a visit to persuade him to accept the nomination. They stressed loyalty to the party banner and the danger posed by the Democratic incumbent's victory.

Hughes recognized that he faced an ethical dilemma: Should he accept the mayoral nomination with its possibilities of personal advancement and service to the community, or should he reject it because it would destroy his investigative committee's credibility? The decision was not an easy one. He did not respond to the offer immediately and apparently spent a few days wrestling with the issue. In the end, he placed the public trust above his personal ambitions for public office. In turning down the offer, Hughes said: "In this dilemma I simply have to do my duty as I see it. In my judgment, I have no right to accept the nomination. A paramount public duty forbids it."[24]

As it turned out, taking the ethical path did nothing to keep Hughes out of public office. He was elected governor of New York in 1907 and later he would be a presidential candidate and chief justice of the United States Supreme Court. As governor, Hughes provided persistent, vigorous leadership in the area of ethics reform. One success he had was in establishing a pair of independent public service commissions to free government from the earlier regulatory commissions controlled by old guard politicians and business interests. His idea became a blueprint for the modern public service commission in this country.

A second success in promoting ethical government was a statute to authorize the governor to carry on investigations or to appoint a commissioner to conduct investigations of the administration of various departments and institutions of government. The statute became known as the Moreland Act.

Difficulty in securing effective ethics legislation was more recently highlighted by the work of the New York State Commission on Government Integrity. In 1987, this Moreland Act Commission was created by an executive order of Governor Mario Cuomo in response to widespread scandals in New York. The commission's mandate was exceedingly broad: to investigate laws and practices in the state and municipal governments of New York that foster corruption and the appearance of impropriety and to make recommendations for needed reforms. During its several-year tenure, the commission conducted investigations, held public hearings and laid out an ethical framework worthy of emulation throughout the country. It published its agenda in reports, in a volume,[25] and in the form of a booklet entitled, "Restoring the Public Trust: A Blueprint for Government Integrity." [26]

Among the subjects identified by the commission as important for any modern-day framework of government ethics were the following: conflicts of interest regulation, campaign finance reform, ballot access laws, open meetings, patronage prohibitions, whistleblower protections, procurement reform, and training and educational programs. Throughout its many reports, the commission emphasized the importance of legislating ethical standards for governmental employees in order to promote public confidence in government, protect the public sector from pressures by the private sector, provide guidance to public officials, reduce the temptation of some to abuse their trust, and to articulate a moral standard for the entire community. As Justice Brandeis wrote, "our Government is the potent, the omnipresent teacher. For good or for ill, it teaches the whole people by its example . . . If the Government becomes a law breaker, it breeds contempt for law; it invites every man to become a law unto himself; it invites anarchy."[27]

One issue of paramount concern to the commission was municipal ethics. Although in 1987 New York passed an Ethics in Government Act covering statewide employees, the act had little application to local government. More than 95 percent of the municipalities of the state were left completely unaffected by the act, continuing to be controlled by vague regulations passed 25 years ago. As the commission wrote in its report, "the result [of these laws] has been a confusing and often contradictory patchwork of unenforced and unenforceable ethics codes. New York needs a set of minimum ethical standards for *all* public officials, a statement that certain behavior is simply not acceptable for a government servant, no matter where he or she works and lives."[28] The logic of having one uniform and coherent set of standards is simple: not only does a uniform set of ethical regulations make it easier for the vast majority of dedicated and well-intentioned public actors to understand the ethical minimums, but it makes the regulations uniformly enforceable statewide.

The committee sought to provide leadership by proposing a Municipal Ethics Act that would set uniform ethical standards for municipal officials.

10   ETHICS, LAWYERS, AND THE PUBLIC SECTOR

The commission wrote that "the standards are intended only as a minimum; localities can adopt more stringent legislation where they feel it is appropriate to do so." Unfortunately, the commission's recommendations, and that of the subsequent Miller commission,[29] have not been acted upon, with New York remaining rooted in a pre-Watergate view of municipal ethics.

Both the Commission on Government Integrity and the Miller commission found that in addition to ethical regulations, there was a clear need for disclosure requirements for local officials. Similar to statewide officials, local officials should be required to disclose meaningful information about their finances. With this in mind, the commission proposed three solutions. First, that there be a requirement of applicant disclosure for individuals making bids for municipal businesses; second, that municipal officials be required to disclose annually all personal financial interests; and third, that transactional disclosure be required for situations where an official's actions may be personally profitable, in which case the official would take no action. These three disclosure requirements, the commission noted, would provide the public with much-needed information about municipal candidates and serve to discourage conflicted or self-interested action by officials.

The commission also made recommendations on other subjects, including placing restrictions on employment after leaving government and strengthening enforcement mechanisms, especially at the regional and local levels. As Raymond O'Connor, a councilman from Wilton, New York, stated to the commission: "Having this type of legislation within our town, we think lends greater credibility and integrity to the people serving within the community."[30]

New York is not alone in finding considerable resistance to the idea of ethics reform. Efforts similar to that of the Commission on Government Integrity have taken place in a number of states in recent years, with more tangible results in some states.[31]

The Future of Government Ethics Legislation

It is of paramount importance that governmental ethics be constantly evaluated and reexamined as long as we view public office as a public trust.

Public servants must enact strong laws governing official conduct and enforce those laws with vigorous prosecution and stiff penalties. In addition, they must find ways to establish clear, *internal* codes of conduct and police themselves for violations of such codes in advance of and not simply in reaction to scandal. A major role for existing government ethics commissions and agencies is to define strong ethical codes for present societal needs, monitor existing law on a continuing basis, close loopholes, and give force to sanctions.

Here professional associations and educational institutions have significant roles to play. In addition to promoting values, they can foster dialogue and provide the disinterested judgment necessary for a proper exploration of the subject of government ethics. It is far too great a burden to place on public servants alone the development of appropriate standards.

In government today, we need to renew the hope of young people that one does not have to be unethical to succeed in politics. There is a constant need to reaffirm and give meaning to the concept that public office is a public trust. Opportunities and incentives that pit self-interest against integrity must be reduced or eliminated. Leaders in all walks of life have a responsibility to help in this endeavor. Honest government officials labor under constraints unparalleled by those imposed upon the rest of us. When the burdens become too great, and there is no visible moral support from the communities at large, officials may fall prey to pressures that not infrequently come from the private sector. In the areas of campaign financing and procurement particularly, the potential for corruption of the public sector by private interests is great. If business leaders insist upon institutional codes and continued dialogue about the ethical implications of various kinds of contact between business people and government officials, they will contribute to an atmosphere that will diminish the likelihood of both government and private unethical behavior. Hopefully, we can clarify gray areas so the process is not full of traps. It is a sad state of affairs when distinguished public servants can describe the present political system as a "dangerous business," but that is not the fault of politicians alone.

In addition to its examination of so many critical areas of government ethics, this volume provides useful guidance and practical tips for identifying and avoiding ethical conflicts. It will be a valuable resource for lawyers, government officials, and members of the public alike for a long time to come. I salute the organizers of the volume, especially Dean Patricia Salkin, for the contribution it is bound to make to the process of civilization. As Elihu Root observed in 1926:

> There are no worse enemies of all attempts at improving the machinery of government, in any field, state, municipal, national, international, than the people who are always in a hurry, who are dissatisfied if results are not reached today or tomorrow, who think that if they cannot on the instant see a result accomplished, nothing has been done. The process of civilization is always a process of building up brick by brick, stone by stone, a structure which is unnoted for years but finally, in the fruition of time, is the basis for greater progress. I think it makes but little difference what part of that process a man contributes his life to. I think it makes but little difference whether a man gives his life and his service to laying the foundation and building up the structure, or whether he is the man that floats a flag on the battlements and cries, Victory![32]

Notes

1. *See generally,* Daniel Koffsky, *Coming to Terms with Bureaucratic Ethics,* 11 J.L. & Pol. 235 (1995).

2. The Federalist No. 51 (James Madison).

12   ETHICS, LAWYERS, AND THE PUBLIC SECTOR

3. ARISTOTLE, NICHOMACHEAN ETHICS, Book V (J.A.K. Thompson, ed., Penguin Books, 1959).

4. THE ATHENIAN OATH, *reprinted in* THE ETHICS FACTOR HANDBOOK (International City Management Association 1988).

5. Davies, *U.S.-German Public Ethics Laws,* 18 GA. J. INT'L & COMP. L. 319, 324 (1988).

6. An Act to Establish the Treasury Department, ch. 12, § 8, 1 Stat. 65, 67 (1789).

7. REPORT OF THE ASSOCIATION OF THE BAR OF THE CITY OF NEW YORK COMMITTEE ON THE FEDERAL CONFLICT-OF-INTEREST LAWS (Roswell B. Perkins, Chairman, February 23, 1960). *See also Congress and the Public Trust,* REPORT OF THE ASSOCIATION OF THE BAR OF THE CITY OF NEW YORK SPECIAL COMMITTEE ON CONGRESSIONAL ETHICS (1970).

8. *Id.*

9. *Id.*

10. *Id.*

11. *Id.*

12. *Id.*

13. Koffsky, *supra* note 1, at 245.

14. *Id.* (describing Exec. Order No. 10939, 26 Fed. Reg. 3951 (1961)).

15. *Id.*

16. S. REP. No. 170, 95th Cong., 1st Sess. (1977), *reprinted in* 1978 U.S.C.C.A.N. 4216, 1977 WL 9629 (leg. hist).

17. *Id.*

18. 18 U.S.C. § 207 (1977).

19. Koffsky, *supra,* note 1, at 250 (quoting 1978 U.S.C.C.A.N. 4246–47).

20. S. REP. No. 98-59 (1983), *reprinted in* 1983 U.S.C.C.A.N. 1313.

21. P.L. 101–94 (1989).

22. H.R. REP. No. 104-595(I), at 3, *reprinted in* 1996 U.S.C.C.A.N. 1356, 1358.

23. NATIONAL MUNICIPAL LEAGUE, MODEL STATE CONFLICT OF INTEREST AND FINANCIAL DISCLOSURE LAW (1979).

24. MERLON J. PUSEY, CHARLES EVANS HUGHES 148 (1951).

25. *See* GOVERNMENT ETHICS REFORM FOR THE 1990s: THE COLLECTED REPORTS OF THE NEW YORK STATE COMMISSION ON GOVERNMENT INTEGRITY (Fordham University Press, 1991).

26. New York State Commission on Government Integrity, *Restoring the Public Trust: A Blueprint for Governement Integrity,* 18 FORDHAM URB. L.J. 173, 180 (1990–91).

27. Olmstead v. United States, 277 U.S. 438, 485 (1928) (dissenting).

28. *Id.* at 205.

29. State of New York Temporary State Commission Local Government Ethics, *Final Report,* 20 FORDHAM URB. L. J. 1 (1993).

30. New York State Commission on Government Integrity, *supra,* note 26 at 204.

31. More specific information about the states is on file with the Council on Government Ethics Laws (COGEL), located at the Center for Governmental Studies, 10951 West Tico Boulevard, Suite 120, Los Angeles, CA 90064, Attention: Robert Stern, (310) 470-6590.

32. *See* T. SCHICK, THE NEW YORK STATE CONSTITUTIONAL CONVENTION OF 1915 AND THE MODERN STATE GOVERNOR 133 (1978).

CHAPTER ❦ 2

Who Is the Client of the Government Lawyer?

*Jeffrey Rosenthal**

This chapter explores the difficult issue of identifying exactly who is the client of the government lawyer. Although some advise that it is the government lawyer's duty to obtain just results, rather than paying strict servitude to one client, government lawyers struggle with client confidentiality and other ethical dilemmas in attempting to determine the duty owed to the chief elected official, a legislative body, boards, other ranking government lawyers, the government as a whole, and the public at large. This question is faced by all government lawyers, whether working at the federal, state, or local level.

The question for the lawyer in performing routine functions—providing research, litigation support, legislative or regulatory initiatives—is to whom the legal responsibility and allegiance is owed. Unlike the lawyer engaged in private practice, whose client is clearly recognizable, the government lawyer does not *necessarily* represent a single client and, as a result, the client of the government lawyer is not so easily identified. Dilemmas concerning whom the government lawyer is representing and potential conflicts of interest[1] will arise for the government lawyer for which no parallels or comparisons with the private lawyer can be drawn.[2] Emphasis is placed on the word "necessarily," since, as this discussion reveals, the government lawyer may arguably owe ethical responsibilities to a number of "clients," in the same or related matters, but the lawyer engaged in private practice generally owes his or her allegiance to a single client in a matter. The purpose of this chapter is, first, to identify a number of possible clients of the government lawyer and, second, based on ethical considerations applicable to all lawyers and common sense, determine who is the true client and to whom the concomitant responsibilities are owed.

---

* The views expressed in this article are those of the writer and are not intended to represent those of the Governor's Office of Regulatory Reform or the State of New York.

Private Sector Practice

The lawyer in a private law firm is instructed that a certain client of the firm has a particular problem that needs to be addressed, for example, a dispute between parties to a contract or a contested divorce. The supervising lawyer provides a factual outline of the circumstances that are relevant to the client's case. He or she may provide a cursory analysis of salient legal issues and the desired outcome pertinent to the task to which the lawyer is assigned. The lawyer reviews the file to identify the issues necessary to conduct research of the applicable statutes and case law. As the private lawyer eagerly commences to go about his or her work assignment the ultimate responsibility readily comes into focus. The research, document preparation, and specific work hours can be attributed to a specific client. Ethical considerations are directed toward thorough and proper advocacy of the particular client's interests. While undertaking his or her work assignment the lawyer's responsibility to the client—to advocate, within legal and ethical boundaries, the desired outcome on behalf of such client—remains the driving force of the assignment. Parallels to cases that support the client's position will be developed; cases that do not support the desired outcome will be distinguished. The responsibilities of the private lawyer are directed toward developing a strategy that will best serve that client's interests.

To Whom Are Legal Responsibility and Allegiance Owed?

The lawyer employed by a government agency[3] does not undertake his or work with a specific client's interests in mind in the same sense as the private practitioner does. The government lawyer, generally speaking, is assigned, for example, to draft legislative initiatives, address regulatory issues, or provide litigation support or general legal advice for matters pertinent to the agency. The lawyer may be supervised by a senior counsel member, another policy or program staff member, or the agency head. The latter two agency members are likely nonlawyers. Thus, the first difference is that the hierarchy and chain of command in the private law firm is more likely comprised of all lawyers, whereas such is not the case for an agency. Further, the private lawyer is employed by a law firm that has as its foundation legal representation of the interests of the clients who retain the law firm for such purposes. The government lawyer is employed by the agency, which has as its purpose the implementation of an enabling statute enacted by Congress or a state or local legislature, as well as fulfilling the goals of the executive branch, for example, president, governor, mayor, and so on, of which the agency is a part.[4]

For example, an enabling statute such as the New York Environmental Conservation Law provides the general purposes for which the New York Department of Environmental Conservation (DEC) is established and the general policies to be implemented.[5] Generally speaking, the responsibility of the DEC, as set forth in statute enacted by the legislative body, is to promote the public health and welfare by protection and most efficient and effective use of the state's natural resources. The DEC lawyer, in commencing his or her routine duties, begins to recognize that there are differing interests that can be advocated and goals achieved in fulfilling the legislative mandate, depending upon who is deemed to be the client. Initially, the lawyer must discern what the general requirements in the various statutory provisions are. Specific implementation of those provisions must, however, be accomplished amidst various and, oftentimes, competing interests, for example, environmental or health advocacy groups, businesses, industries, developers, local governments or municipalities, and neighborhood associations, each of which will, undoubtedly, have different views as to how the overall goals prescribed in statute are to be implemented. Individual legislators or legislative committees will maintain views as to how the statute is to be implemented. The agency head, counsel, and staff members may have differing views or interpretations of the statutory mandates and the best means of implementing those requirements, and may have differing views or interpretations amongst themselves. The chief elected official, the governor, also may have his or her own goals and policy considerations in implementing statutory requirements. Lastly, judicial opinions may exist that interpret and otherwise give meaning to the statutory mandates. The underlying ethical considerations, that is, to preserve, advocate and advance the interests of the "client" remain constant. The specific interpretation given to the enabling statute, as well as the approach, direction and advice of the lawyer will depend on whose interests are to be preserved, advocated, and advanced.

Identifying Potential "Clients" Hypothetically

It has been stated that the dilemma in identifying the client of the government lawyer rests in the very dynamics and tension amongst the three branches of government itself and the role that the lawyer plays within such framework.[6] One writer offers a hypothetical wherein the lawyer is assigned to work on a project for which the goal is antithetical to what the lawyer perceives to be in the pubic interest. Additionally, the project may violate a decision of the Supreme Court involving a case that concerned issues similar to those that the lawyer faces in the assignment, or it may not be authorized by the enabling statute enacted by Congress. The author advances two potential arguments to be made in articulating the role and responsibility of the government lawyer. First, he recognizes, but rejects, the argument that a government lawyer, as an advocate of a government agency, has a special responsibility to advance the "public interest." The article points out the impossibility of concluding that the government lawyer represents the public interest as "[i]t is commonplace that there are as many ideas of the 'public interest' as there are people who think about the subject."[7] The article continues:

> If attorneys could freely sabotage the actions of their agencies out of a subjective sense of the public interest, the result would be a disorganized, inefficient bureaucracy, and a public distrustful of its own government. More

fundamentally, the idea that government attorneys serve some higher purpose fails to place the attorney within a structure of democratic government. Although the public interest as a reified concept may not be ascertainable, the Constitution establishes procedures for approximating that ideal through election, appointment, confirmation, and legislation. Nothing systematic empowers lawyers to substitute their individual conceptions of the good for the priorities and objectives established through these governmental processes."[8]

The public interest in this argument is cast in subjective terms of what the lawyer himself or herself has identified to be in the public interest, not what might be considered to be the public interest as established by one or more of the branches of government.

Addressing this latter notion of the public interest, the author suggests a second possible argument that the agency lawyer works for the government as a whole, a notion that "assumes that the public interest is determined through the constitutional processes of government."[9] In the hypothetical the dilemma is that, by undertaking efforts to implement the program, the lawyer may not be fulfilling his or her responsibility to the government as a whole since, to do so, might violate established judicial decisions or exceed statutory authorization. He concludes that the idea that the government lawyer represents the government as a whole "fails to situate the attorney within a system of separation of powers and checks and balances."[10] In making such conclusion, however, the article does not examine how the processes of government within each of the branches may be viewed as determinative of the public interest.

The Public as the Client

In attempting to identify who is the client, it is helpful to explore some postulates that might be advanced that the public interest is determined by such branches of government, and in exercising professional judgment the lawyer's responsibility is to follow such public interest. For example, it might be argued that, since the enabling statute has been enacted by the duly elected legislators, the "public interest" is expressed in the statute as the embodiment of universally held beliefs or goals. Therefore, the role of the lawyer is to interpret the statute and provide legal advice that best fulfills the public interest as expressed in such statute. However, such an approach ignores several things. First, it is implausible to characterize the enabling statute as the expression of some collective, universally agreed upon, public interest. A statute does not reflect the embodiment of the views of every citizen, since legislation results, not from a universally agreed-upon good or public interest, but from the personal ideals or agendas of the governor, legislators and of their constituents, lobbying efforts of different interest groups, negotiation and compromise, and is also driven, in large measure, by budget and political considerations. A legislator may support a proposed piece of legislation, not because he or she necessarily wants to advance the principles enunciated in such legislation, but rather because it serves his or her purposes of having a different piece of legislation supported by another legislator. A statute most often establishes only broad policies, not the specific details of implementing those policies. While everyone can agree, for example, that having clean water or clean air are in the public interest, specific requirements and methods to achieve these goals may not be so easily agreed upon. The statute authorizes an agency within the executive branch of government to interpret and implement the policies that have been articulated only in general terms. Thus, a more logical interpretation is that the public interest as expressed in a statute, such as the New York Environmental Conservation Law, is the result of the legislative process, not the expression of universally agreed-upon environmental goals or desired outcomes.

In the last analysis, however, whether the public interest established through legislation is considered to be the embodiment of universal agreement or the result of the legislative process, to conclude that the lawyer is bound to represent such public interest would juxtapose the lawyer between this "public interest" client and the agency heads or supervisors by whom the lawyer was hired and to whom the lawyer is immediately responsible. Their interpretation of the "public interest" may differ from the meaning that the lawyer gives to the statute and, moreover, the views of the agency head, supervisors, or other policy makers of the agency also may conflict with one another. The view that the government lawyer is duty bound to advocate only such interest presupposes that the lawyer possesses the ability to interpret the statute consistently with and on behalf of such public interest on every occasion, and do so for every issue that may arise. This also assumes that the lawyer is ethically bound to advocate for what he or she perceives as the public interest, not only ignoring the wishes or direction of supervisors or other agency superiors who have been appointed to determine policy issues, but also sacrificing the right of the client to be independently represented by agency counsel.[11]

In the same exploration of identifying the client of the government lawyer in the context of the separate branches of government, it can be argued that the lawyer is obliged to follow judicial interpretations and other legal precedent of an enabling statute. If a particular statute is the expression of public interest, then, it necessarily follows, a court decision is the conclusive interpretation of that law and, therefore, the ultimate guidepost of public interest. Such an approach assumes that the agency lawyer is thereby provided definitive guidance regarding the meaning of the statute and, thus, the advice to give to the agency head or other agency policy makers in fulfilling the agency's statutory obligation. However, this interpretation of the lawyer's responsibility is too simplistic and assumes, as in the case of determining a statute's meaning, that every lawyer will interpret the court's precedents the same.

Comparing the agency lawyer's role to that of the private lawyer demonstrates the weakness of such an argument. Should the private lawyer be guided blindly by court decisions, the interests of the individual client would undoubtedly take a back seat to the "objective" interpretation of the court precedent. It would be unnecessary for the private lawyer to thoroughly scrutinize and distinguish case law from the facts and circumstances underlying his or her client's case. The lawyer's role would necessarily be relegated to reading relevant case law and advising the client what the outcome of his or her case would be. Although the lawyer should bring to bear on the client's decision to pursue a certain course of action his or her professional judgment regarding what the probable outcome, based on judicial precedent, will be, the lawyer, nevertheless, is bound to proceed in accordance with the client's desires.[12] Otherwise, the ethical responsibility to advocate the client's case "zealously within the bounds of the law" would surely be a rather hollow obligation.[13]

The fact that neither legislative enactments nor judicial opinions should be considered absolute statements is supported by Ethical Consideration 7-2 of the ABA Model Code of Professional Responsibility, which recognizes that statutes and court decisions are not definitive. "The limits and meaning of apparently relevant law may be made doubtful by changing or developing constitutional interpretations, inadequately expressed statutes or judicial opinions, and changing public and judicial attitudes."[14] Both legislative enactments and judicial opinions are only expressions of an ever-changing public interest. Moreover, court decisions turn, more often, on a particular set of facts, rather than larger fundamental principles. Just as the "public interest" cannot be said to be expressed absolutely in any statute, it cannot be concluded—for purposes of identifying the government lawyer's client—that court decisions provide definitive statements of what constitutes the public interest, never subject to different interpretation or legitimate challenge. The frailty in such an argument is demonstrated by the fact that legislators oftentimes do disagree with a court's decision and pass or amend statutes to override a judicial decision. Furthermore, Ethical Consideration 7-22 of the code recognizes that a lawyer has a responsibility to challenge judicial interpretations when appropriate for the proper representation of a client. "Respect for judicial rulings is essential to the proper administration of justice; however, a litigant or his lawyer may, in good faith and within the framework of the law, take steps to test the correctness of a ruling of a tribunal."[15] And the fact that legislators do indeed amend or pass laws in response to court decisions underscores two things that exclude the public interest as client argument. First, that the courts can give interpretations to statutes different from that given by the legislators who enacted such statute is evidence itself that the "public interest" may not be clearly expressed in a particular statute. The fact that legislators and the courts harbor differing interpretations only begs the question whether the public interest is expressed in the statute itself or in the court decision that interprets such statute. Second, when the legislators amend a statute in response to judicial opinion, such action, it would have to be opined, remedies the original legislation, which may not have been the reflection of the public interest after all, at least as intended by the legislators, since the court's interpretation differs from what the legislators intended. Such a paradigm illustrates the circuitous nature of proffering the public interest as client argument insofar as it being expressed in statute or by the courts: if the courts should again interpret the amended statute in a manner other than what the legislators intended, the legislators would amend the statute yet again; subsequent litigation could cause the courts to interpret the legislative enactment and, if such interpretation were again in conflict with what the legislators intended, would cause additional amendments to the statute. This process could continue ad infinitum.

Assuming at some point judicial opinions that interpret a given statute are in harmony with the views of the legislators, newly elected legislators would, no doubt, have a different view of the "public interest" and would go about the process of amending those same statutes and, thus, the process of judicial review and legislative response would commence anew. Bearing in mind that the agency lawyer does not advocate the legislators' interests in formulating laws nor assist the court in deciding the issues surrounding those laws, it can be concluded that neither the legislative nor judicial branch of government is the "client" of the government agency lawyer. Therefore, to the extent that the "public interest" has been articulated either by the legislators' enactment of a statute or the court's interpretation of that statute, such "public interest" cannot be said to be the government lawyer's client.

Identifying the client of the government lawyer also is difficult when examined in the context of the executive branch of government. Although there is a paucity of definitive statutory authority or case law that articulates who is the client of the government lawyer,[16] the application of general tenets and ethical considerations of a lawyer's responsibility to his or her client provides guidance. Viewed with common sense and framed with such general tenets and ethical considerations, who the client is becomes more clear. It is first helpful to recognize certain facts surrounding the government lawyer's employment, as well as the dynamics in the operations of a government agency itself. Although an agency is part of the executive branch of government, day-to-day operations of the agency are not overseen or controlled by the governor; further, the agency lawyer is rarely hired directly by the chief executive, unless perhaps the lawyer is counsel to the governor.[17] More often, the lawyer is employed by a particular agency, one of many constituting the executive branch. As previously discussed, the agency is charged with the responsibility of fulfilling the mandates of an enabling authorization; the role of the lawyer is to give advice to the personnel who make up the agency to properly implement such enabling authorization. The enabling authorization may arise in a statute enacted by the state legislature or by executive order of the governor. If the authority is provided in statute, the purposes may be set forth in provisions of the statute; if such authority emanates from an executive order, the preamble clauses or paragraphs will identify the purposes and goals for which the agency has been established.[18]

Recognizing that the agency's responsibility is to implement the general policies provided in its enabling authorization, the question arises as to how and in what manner the agency will implement such responsibilities. In the examples given, the government lawyer is concerned with providing advice to superiors as to how the statute or executive order must be implemented and what considerations he or she must keep in mind in providing the advice. As this relates to the central question of who is the client of the government lawyer, the issue is complex, even recognizing that the client is limited to the executive branch of government. Here the question is whether the agency lawyer's client is the governor, that is, the chief officer of the executive branch, an individual or individuals within the agency that employs the lawyer, or the specific agency itself.

An argument can be advanced that the governor is the ultimate client of the government agency lawyer. He or she, as the chief elected official, speaks for the government on behalf of all citizens and appoints the various heads of the executive branch agencies who, in turn, directly or through designees of the agency, hire the agency lawyer. Therefore, the argument could be advanced that all government employees owe their ultimate allegiance to the governor. For the government lawyer this would mean that the governor is the client to whom ethical responsibilities are owed. Such an argument, however, ignores, as indicated above, that most government lawyers are hired by the separate agency head and undertake routine responsibilities relative to the particular agency, not the governor. Furthermore, it ignores the fact that agency heads, usually appointed by the governor, are charged with implementing, consistent with the enabling legislation, the policy goals of the governor. In the example of the DEC, the agency undertakes the responsibility of implementing and enforcing the Environmental Conservation Law, mindful of the environmental policies or goals enunciated by the governor. Furthermore, the governor has his or her own legal staff from whom advice is sought. If every government lawyer's client is the chief elected officer, it follows that there would be no need for each agency to have counsel separate from the governor's staff counsel. Giving advice on the proper implementation of a statute would be a simple task of ascertaining what the Governor's desires or interpretation are and proceeding accordingly. This view, as in the previous examples regarding the legislative or judicial branches, places the government lawyer in a position of having to maintain two loyalties—one to the governor and another to the agency head or other superior in the agency who hired the lawyer. Notwithstanding that the agency heads are usually appointed by the governor and thereby expected to have similar policy goals, there may be situations when the governor and a particular agency head do, in fact, have a difference of opinion respecting the manner in which a particular statute should be implemented or enforced. In such a case, if the government agency lawyer bears allegiance to the governor, the interests of the agency head—the lawyer's immediate supervisor—would be sacrificed.[19] In recognizing that a government lawyer does not represent the "public interest," as expressed either through legislators or the courts, or the governor, the task of identifying the client of the agency lawyer is narrowed.

However, questions remain as to whether the client is the "agency" as an entity itself or individuals within the agency. The examination must begin by understanding the general operations of a state agency. As discussed, the overall agency policy goals will be articulated by the agency director, commissioner, or similarly titled agency head.[20] A larger agency may have divisions or bureaus within the agency that are charged with the responsibility of implementing specific aspects of an enabling authorization and headed by their own bureau or division chief. Again, in the example of the DEC, there are separate divisions charged with implementing and enforcing air quality standards, water quality standards, and the like. While the division or bureau chiefs may have a role in determining policy for the particular division or bureau, those policies must yield to the goals as determined for such division or bureau by the agency head, since he or she is ultimately responsible for the conduct of the agency. Since division or bureau chiefs employed by an agency are ultimately accountable to the agency head, it can be assumed that it would be unlikely that they would seek to implement or enforce provisions of an enabling authorization in a manner antithetical to the desires of such agency head. If such a circumstance should arise, the agency lawyer should adhere to the wishes of the agency head, not the separate division or bureau chief.

Federal Ethical Consideration 5-1 of Canon 5 of the American Bar Association Code of Professional Responsibility as adopted by the Federal Bar Association in 1973 provides guidance that the government lawyer represents the agency by whom he or she is employed:

> The immediate professional responsibility of the federal lawyer is to the department or agency in which he is employed, to be performed in light of the particular public interest function of the department or agency. He is required to exercise independent professional judgment which transcends his personal interests, giving consideration, however, to the reasoned views of others engaged with him in the conduct of the business of government.

The federal ethical consideration does not make clear whether the language "department or agency" is meant to identify the same governmental organization with different commonly used names or suggests a responsibility of the lawyer to a department—division or bureau—within an agency, when employed within such department. Practically speaking, both "department" and "agency" should mean the same larger governmental organization, for the reasons outlined above. However, if responsibility to a department within an agency is intended, the ethical consideration fails to address the issue, mentioned above, of the lawyer's obligation when there is a conflict between the department head and the agency head. And if this is the intended interpretation, the lawyer could be forced to advocate interests that would undermine the interests of the agency, as determined by the person responsible for the agency. It is submitted that, in such a case, the lawyer has an obligation to express to the department chief his or her conclusion that the department chief's desires are not consistent with those held by the agency head and discourage the department chief from proceeding in such a manner. In the event that the department chief is insistent that the lawyer proceed, he or she must advise that the intended course of action must be disclosed to and discussed with the agency head. While such approach would undoubtedly be difficult or uncomfortable, the lawyer's obligation to the agency, as ultimately spoken for through the agency head, must remain paramount.

Additionally, the federal ethical consideration, although instructive, may be of limited assistance, as it attempts to superimpose an obligation, in fact the ability, that the government lawyer can exercise independent judgment while being ever keenly aware of the "public interest function" of the agency. To the extent that its guidance is to suggest that, for example, the United States Environmental Protection Agency's (EPA) public interest function is to implement environmental legislation—however it may be interpreted—then it provides direction that the agency lawyer's responsibility is limited to matters concerning the EPA, but not other agencies. If its meaning is to suggest a broader obligation to a universal "public interest," then, as previously discussed, its guidance is less helpful.

In further support of the above, the Federal Bar Association has stated that the federal government lawyer's client "is the agency where he is employed, including those charged with its administration insofar as they are engaged in the conduct of the public business."[21] Opinion 73-1 more clearly provides the proper approach for the government agency lawyer, as it identifies the agency as the overall client and recognizes the fluidity of individuals who make up an agency and, therefore, the changing interests of the agency to be preserved and advocated, as established by such individuals. In recognizing that an agency can speak only through its administrators, that is, those authorized to make policy for the agency, this approach more closely approximates the role of the private lawyer who must advocate the interests of the individual who hires the lawyer to do so. When the private practitioner represents a client, there is no infusion of some greater obligation to which the lawyer owes his or her allegiance. Opinion 73-1 does not attempt to impose such a responsibility. Although the federal ethical consideration and Opinion 73-1 are applicable to the federal government lawyer, parallels can be drawn for the government lawyer of a state agency. Additionally, one state has adopted ethical rules applicable to government lawyers.[22] Within the comments to the Hawaii code is the recognition that the government lawyer faces issues in identifying his or her client, not encountered by the private lawyer: ". . . defining precisely the identity of the client and prescribing the resulting obligations of such lawyers may be more difficult in the government context. Although in some circumstances the client may be a specific agency, it is generally the government as a whole." However laudable the effort to clarify the ethical obligation owed, the guidance may be of limited utility. First, the comment assumes, as previously discussed, that it is possible to articulate the interests of the agency entity independently of the individuals who make up the agency. Second, although the comment does remove the notion that the agency lawyer represents a "public interest" superior to any other consideration, it nevertheless clouds the ability to identify the client by casting the ethical responsibility owed in terms of an overall government good, as amorphous a concept as the public interest.[23] If, however, the "government as a whole" can be interpreted to place the lawyer's ethical obligation in the context of the tension between the branches of government, with the recognition that it is through this tension that the democratic process is best served, then the effort to characterize the lawyer's ethical responsibility is of some value.[24] That is, in advocating exclusively on behalf of the agency, with the recognition that the legislature will advocate for its own interests and the court system will independently exercise its role, the fundamental operation of the checks and balances in democratic government will be advanced.[25]

A government agency also has been likened to that of a corporation. Similar to the view that the corporate lawyer represents the corporate entity, but not the officers, directors, or shareholders, one court has concluded that the government lawyer represents the agency by which he or she is employed and not the agency head or other employees.[26] The majority of case law concerning the issue of the corporate lawyer's client has generally been addressed to the issue of the attorney-client privilege pertaining to communications between the corporate lawyer and certain individuals within the corporation. And the issue has arisen generally when an individual who has conferred with the corporate lawyer engages in conduct antithetical to the interests of the corporation. The question has become whether the lawyer is bound to honor the attorney-client privilege of confidentiality of the information received from the client. It has been held that when the individual's conduct is at odds with the lawful corporate interests then the attorney-client relationship does not exist and the lawyer is not bound to maintain confidentiality; in fact, he or she is bound to disclose the information so as to preserve and protect the corporate interests. The conclusions concerning the representation of the corporate entity and not the individuals within the entity parallel the conclusion that the government lawyer represents the agency by whom he or she is employed, but not the individuals themselves within the agency. Citing an opinion of the New York State Bar Association Committee on Professional Ethics, an article by Josephson and Pearce provides support to the conclusion that the agency by whom the government lawyer is employed is owed the ultimate ethical obligation, and not a larger concern such as the "government" or "public interest."[27] Although specifically concerned with issues regarding governmental lawyer conflicts and questions of dual representation when conflicts arise between the individual clients, the article provides:

> When a governmental body is organized into a number of separate departments or agencies, such department or agency, and not the parent governmental unit, should be treated as the client for purposes of the rule which forbids the concurrent representation of one client against another.

Additionally, while the private lawyer's ultimate ethical responsibility is to safeguard the interests of the corporate entity,[28] the private lawyer also can be representing individuals who constitute the corporation, when and as long as

24   WHO IS THE CLIENT OF THE GOVERNMENT LAWYER?

those interests are not in conflict with one another. The ABA Model Rules of Professional Conduct recognizes this possible duality of representation.[29] The comment to Rule 1.13 makes its provisions applicable to the government lawyer. Such "duality" of representation is consistent with the discussion herein of the role that the government lawyer fulfills in advocating the interests of the agency, as spoken for through its agency head and other agency policy makers.

The conclusion to be drawn from the above is that the government lawyer is ethically bound to represent the agency by whom he or she is employed, recognizing that the agency speaks through—and its specific interests are formulated by—the individuals within the agency who are authorized to do so.

Particular policies or goals in the implementation of the agency's enabling authority will necessarily be the expression of and articulated by these individuals. It is the government lawyer's responsibility to preserve and advocate the interests of the agency, as so expressed by these individuals within the agency. As long as the expressions, acts, or desires are not clearly unlawful, the government lawyer has the obligation, both ethically and practically, to advance those interests. Similar to the role of the private lawyer, the government lawyer may not second-guess the feasibility or viability of advancing arguments in support of those interests to the ultimate detriment of arguing in favor of them, nor should the government lawyer substitute his or her personal judgment whether such interest should be advanced.[30] The government lawyer must exercise professional judgement in pointing out the strengths and weaknesses in pursuing the agency head's desired course of action. However, as in the case of the private lawyer, the government lawyer is ethically bound to pursue the course chosen by the agency head. A caveat, however, is necessary that the government lawyer must carefully scrutinize the position or argument to be advanced and discern by whom such position or argument is being proffered. The lawyer must not advance a position being articulated by an agency staff member who is not in the role of making policy or setting agency goals, unless it is evident that the position or argument is consistent with and will advance the interests of the agency as articulated by those in the position of making policy or defining agency goals. Further, the government lawyer still must be mindful that he or she, as a public servant, is faced with obligations that the private lawyer is not. The government lawyer carries the obligation to fulfill his or her responsibilities to the agency in a manner that is not clearly inconsistent with lawful requirements. Federal Bar Association Ethics Opinion 73-1 provides:

> [T]he government, over-all and in each of its parts, is responsible to the people in our democracy with its representative form of government. Each part of the government has the obligation of carrying out, in the public interest, its assigned responsibility in a manner consistent with the Constitution, and the applicable laws and regulations. In contrast, the private practitioner represents the client's personal or private interest. . . . [W]e do not suggest, however, that the public is the client as the client concept is

usually understood. It is to say that the lawyer's employment requires him to observe in the performance of his professional responsibility the public interest sought to be served by the government organization of which he is a part.[31]

In this context the responsibility to the public interest is parallel to the ethical responsibility of a public prosecutor, not simply to seek a conviction, but rather to see that justice is served.[32] Similarly, such responsibility mirrors the obligation of all lawyers to strive to maintain the integrity of the legal profession and improve the legal system.[33] Additionally, with the conclusion that the government lawyer represents the agency by which he or she is employed, the arguments that the lawyer is bound to advance the public interest or the government as a whole also can more reasonably be understood. The public interest is that which results from separation of powers amongst the legislature, the courts, and the executive branch. The government lawyer promotes the public interest when he or she advocates the agency client's interests; by doing so, the proper functioning of the government as a whole is fulfilled.

One final point of this discussion concerns the lawyer's ethical obligation to preserve inviolate the confidences of a client.[34] It is well settled that the attorney-client privilege against the disclosure of confidential communication is held by the client, not the lawyer. The chapter herein has purposely avoided basing the discussion regarding the identification of the government lawyer's client on issues of confidentiality. To have taken such approach would have served only to limit the scope of the inquiry into the lawyer's responsibility to the client. Rather, the effort has been made to show through the various codes of ethics and professional responsibilities that the government lawyer's client can, in the first instance, be identified and second, that ethical responsibilities, including the obligation to preserve confidences, are equally applicable to private and government lawyers. Government lawyers are no less obligated than private practitioners to proceed on behalf of their clients in a manner that best serves the client's interests. In doing so, the government lawyer has a responsibility when providing advice, preparing documents, and otherwise advocating the client's case to ensure that he or she undertakes such efforts in a way that safeguards against unnecessary, inappropriate, or unintended disclosure of information or documents. While some have argued that the attorney-client privilege has no place in the operation of good government,[35] it is submitted that the same principles that foster free and full communication between the private client and his or her lawyer, among them, knowing that such communication will be protected, is no less compelling for agency heads to rely upon in discussing the government agency's business. Government lawyers must be aware, however, that, unlike lawyers in the private sector, the work product they produce and the advice they provide may be subject to the discovery of others that are adversaries of their client, unless they are vigilant in protecting against such disclosure. Not only are government lawyers subject to the exceptions to the attorney-client privilege, but also government agencies may be subject to disclosure of potentially sensitive government information through specific statutes.[36] Therefore, when representing their clients, government lawyers must be guided by the canons or rules of ethics, just as private sector lawyers must; but, because of the nature of government structure, agency lawyers must also be mindful of responsibilities that the private lawyer does not face.

Since the government agency lawyer is ultimately representing the agency by whom he or she is employed, as spoken for by the agency head, it is such individual who is authorized to assert or waive the privilege, but only on behalf of the agency. Therefore, an important caveat is necessary. Should the agency head resign or otherwise terminate service and be replaced with a different individual, it is the new agency head that speaks on behalf of the agency and thus will be able to assert or waive the privilege. Both the lawyer and the agency head must be aware that once the agency head no longer serves as such, that agency head does not have the right to assert the attorney-client privilege. Given this limitation, the lawyer must provide representation in a manner lawfully and ethically to preserve the best interests of the agency irrespective of those who are its heads.

Notes

1. This chapter discusses issues regarding the identification of the government lawyer's client itself and not issues pertaining to conflicts of interest that can arise for government lawyers who may potentially have to advocate conflicting interests of different government clients at the same time. For a discussion of such topic see, for example, William Josephson and Russell Pearce, *To Whom Does the Government Lawyer Owe the Duty of Loyalty When Clients Are in Conflict?*, 29 How. L. J. 539 (1986)

2. *See, e.g.,* Catherine J. Lanctot, *The Duty of Zealous Advocacy and the Ethics of the Federal Government Lawyer: The Three Hardest Questions,* 64 S. CAL. L. REV. 951, 967 (1991).

3. The term "agency" will be used throughout to mean any governmental agency, unity, authority, department, bureau, division, or other body of the executive branch of the state, federal, or local municipal government.

4. Although this chapter more specifically addresses the role of a government lawyer employed by an agency within the executive branch of state government, parallels to lawyers employed within the judicial or legislative branches of government are indicated where appropriate. In addition, questions concerning who the client is are equally difficult in all levels of government—local, regional, state, and federal.

5. New York Environmental Conservation Law §§1-0101, 3-0101 (McKinney 1984).

6. Geoffrey P. Miller, *Government Lawyers' Ethics in a System of Checks and Balances,* 54 U. CHI. L. REV. 1293 (1987).

7. *Id.* at 1294, 1295.

8. *Id.* at 1295.

9. *Id.*

10. *Id.* at 1296.

11. MODEL CODE OF PROFESSIONAL RESPONSIBILITY Canon 1, Ethical Consideration 1-1(1980) as adopted by New York State Bar Association, January 1, 1970 [hereinafter Code, Canon, or Ethical Consideration, respectively].

12. Code, Canon 7, Ethical Consideration 7-5.

13. Code, Canon 7.

14. *Id.,* Ethical Consideration 7-2.

15. *Id.,* Ethical Consideration 7-22.

16. *See, e.g.,* Hawaii Professional Conduct Rule 1.13 (1996) [hereinafter Hawaii Code], discussed below, which attempts to identify the government lawyer's client and define the ethical responsibility owed.

17. This discussion assumes that the lawyer is employed by an agency within the executive branch of government, but not the executive chamber itself. However, the conclusions drawn herein are equally applicable to government lawyers employed within the executive chamber, in which case the governor should be considered the "agency head."

18. *See, e.g.,* N.Y. Exec. Order No. 20, Governor George E. Pataki, Nov. 30, 1995, N.Y. Comp. Codes R. & Regs. Tit. 9, establishing the Governor's Office of Regulatory Reform, which has as its purpose, among other things, the "careful examination [of proposed regulations] to assure that they faithfully execute the laws of the State without unduly burdening the State's economy and imposing needless costs and requirements on the businesses, local governments and citizens of this State."

19. Code, Canon 1, Ethical Consideration 1-1.

20. Hereinafter, for convenience, director, commissioner, or other agency head shall be referred to singularly to mean the senior-most individual within a state agency.

21. Federal Bar Association Professional Ethics Committee; The Honorable Charles Fahy, Chairman. *The Government Client and Confidentiality: Opinion 73-1,* 32 F.B.A.J. 71 (1973) [hereinafter Opinion 73-1].

22. Hawaii Code, *supra* note 16, Notes and Comment: Government Agency [7].

23. Miller, *supra* note 6, at 1296.

24. *Id.*

25. *Id.*

26. *See, e.g.,* Dooley v. Boyle 140 Misc. 2d 177, 531 N.Y.S.2d 161 (N.Y. Supreme Court, 1988); *cf.* United States v. American Tel. & Tel. Co. 86 F.R.D. 603 (D.D.C. 1979); Lori A. Barsdate, *Attorney-Client Privilege for the Government Entity,* 97 Yale L.J. 1725 (1988); Josephson and Pearce, *supra* note 1.

27. Josephson and Pearce, *supra* note 1, at 547 citing N.Y. State Bar Association Committee on Professional Ethics, Op. 501 (1979); see, however, Miller, *supra* note 6, at 1298, to the contrary that the government agency lawyer does owe ethical responsibility to the executive branch as a whole.

28. Code, Canon 5, Ethical Consideration 5-18 (1986); Barsdate, *supra* note 26, at 1731.

29. Model Rules of Professional Conduct Rule 1.13(a), (e) (1983); *see also,* E.F. Hutton v. Brown, 305 F. Supp. 371 at 388 (S.D. Tex. 1969).

30. Code, Canon 5, Ethical Consideration 5-1.

31. Barsdate, *supra* note 26, citing Federal Bar Association Ethics Committee, *The Government Client and Confidentiality:* Opinion 73-1.

32. Code, Canon 7, Ethical Consideration 7-13, as adopted by New York State Bar Association, January 1, 1970.

33. Code, Preamble and Preliminary Statement; Canon 8.

34. Code, Canon 4.

35. *See, e.g.,* Barsdate, *supra* note 26.

36. *See, e.g.,* New York Public Officers Law §89 (McKinney 1988).

CHAPTER ❦ 3

Postemployment Restrictions on Government Employees: Closing the "Revolving Door"

George F. Carpinello

This chapter explores special considerations that arise for public sector lawyers when they leave public service, specifically with respect to postemployment restrictions. While there are easily identifiable federal and state statutes on point, at the local government level practitioners must also consult local ethics laws and applicable case law. Furthermore, lawyers would be wise to weigh relevant postemployment restrictions prior to accepting employment and/or contracts for service with governmental entities.

A number of ethical issues arise when a public employee leaves public service. One concern is that employees not use confidential information they have gained while working for the government to their private advantage or the private advantage of others. Second, public employees might use their acquaintance with former colleagues as an opportunity to curry special favor, on behalf of a private interest, from their former agency. Additionally, public employees might be influenced in the performance of their job by the prospect of future employment. In carrying out their duties, public employees may seek to favor a potential future employer. Finally, a high degree of mobility between the regulators and the regulated may create the appearance of impropriety in the eyes of the public and give the impression that the government entities are captives of the industries they regulate.[1]

This chapter discusses the various rules that have been adopted by government at the state, local, and national level to regulate postemployment activity. Those rules fall into four categories. The first type is a ban on appearances before one's former agency for a relatively limited period of time (the "agency ban"). The second is a prohibition, often indefinite, on a former government employee's involvement in any matter the employee worked on as a government official (the "matter ban"). The third is a prohibition on the use, for personal advantage, of any confidential information obtained by an individual while in government employment. Finally, many states and municipali-

28

ties prohibit government employees from seeking future employment from private entities appearing before their agency.

In addition to state and federal statutory controls on postemployment activities of former government employees, government lawyers are bound by various provisions of the Model Rules of Professional Conduct or the Code of Professional Responsibility, as adopted by their jurisdiction, from becoming involved as a private lawyer in matters in which they were involved as a government official.

All of these restrictions are discussed below in more detail.

The Ban on Appearances before a Former Employee's Agency ("The Agency Ban")

Many states prohibit former employees from appearing, on behalf of a private party, before their former agency for a period of one to two years after the termination of their employment. New York and Florida, two of the strictest states, have enforced a two-year ban.[2] The federal government has imposed a one-year ban on senior government officials from appearing before their former agencies and a ban for very senior officials, such as the vice president, cabinet level officers, and other officers appointed by the government, from appearing before *any* agency of the government for a period of one year.[3] A one-year ban on most government employees from appearing before their own agency is quite common.[4]

These restrictions are both criminal and civil statutes and can provide serious sanctions. For example, the federal statute is a criminal statute, and violators are subject to up to five years' imprisonment, a $50,000 civil penalty, and any other remedies available to any other person.[5] Like the federal regulation, Ohio's statute is also criminal, and violation of it constitutes a misdemeanor in the first degree.[6] New York's statute subjects its violators to a civil penalty of up to $10,000 or upon referral by the ethics committee to the appropriate prosecutor, punishment as a Class A misdemeanor.[7]

The purpose of these regulations is obviously to create a cooling-off period between the time an employee leaves government service and the time he or she reappears before the agency as an advocate for private interests. While it is questionable that a truly influential government official would lose that influence within a one- or two-year period, the inability to lobby former colleagues for that period of time often induces former government officials to opt for private positions that entirely avoid any potential conflict.

For certain public officials, especially lawyers, a one- or two-year ban can cause considerable hardship. For example, a lawyer involved in any area subject to pervasive state regulation, such as environmental or public utility law, would have difficulty leaving government service and entering into private practice, where the bulk of such practice would require an appearance before the lawyer's former agency. This hardship can be especially acute when the lawyer leaves involuntarily because of a workforce reduction. In such a case, the lawyer obviously is not entering into private practice to take advantage of

30 POSTEMPLOYMENT RESTRICTIONS ON GOVERNMENT EMPLOYEES

his or her state connections; he or she has no choice but to enter private practice. New York, in recognition of this fact, enacted temporary legislation exempting some employees terminated in downsizing from the application of the agency ban.[8]

The agency ban most routinely applies to executive branch officials. However, some states and the federal government have enacted restrictions on former legislators. For example, the federal government prohibits a member of Congress, or certain legislative congressional staffers from lobbying Congress for a one-year period.[9] Similarly, New York and California prohibit former legislators from lobbying the state legislature for two years[10] and one year, respectively.[11] New York also applies the ban to legislative staffers, but only nominally. For them, the ban ends upon the end of the two-year legislative session. Thus, a senior legislative staffer could leave the legislature on December 31, 1996, and assume a lobbying position with a private firm on January 1, 1997. Moreover, this applies only to a matter with which that person was directly concerned and in which he or she directly participated during the period of service or employment. Thus, there is nothing to prohibit staffers from leaving the employ of the legislature, immediately commencing employment as lobbyists, and lobbying their former bosses, as long as they do not lobby on matters in which they were personally involved. The different treatment between executive and legislative branch employees led to a constitutional challenge to New York's revolving door legislation.[12] The challenge, however, was unsuccessful—the court finding was that there were presumably rational reasons for the legislature to draw a distinction between the two branches of the government.[13]

Some states have also enacted restrictions on former judges. For example, the New York court of appeals has prohibited former members of the court of appeals from appearing before the court for a period of two years after leaving the court.[14] Additionally, restrictions have been placed upon the employees of judges, such as their law clerks or law secretaries. These restrictions, whether found in statute form or in rules adopted by individual judges, restrict former law assistants' appearances before their former court for a certain period of time after they leave their position as clerk.[15] Some rules also prohibit former law clerks from practicing in connection with any case that was pending during the time of their clerkship.[16] See discussion of the "matter ban" on page 35.

What Services Are Prohibited?

The agency ban applies to appearances on *any* matter before one's former agency. (Compare with the "matter ban" discussed on page 35.) Moreover, it does not depend upon the employee's motivation or whether or not he or she will contact acquaintances in the agency. However, rules vary considerably among the states as to what form of contact or activity is prohibited. For example, the federal government prohibits the making of any communication to, or appearance before, the employee's former agency with the intent to influence that agency.[17] However, a former employee can offer "behind-the-scenes advice and assistance" to those dealing directly with the agency.[18] Similarly, Rhode Island prohibits a former employee from representing any person before the employee's former agency.[19] New York City prohibits "any communication, for compensation, other than those involving ministerial matters."[20]

New York State, in contrast, prohibits former employees from appearing or practicing before their former agency *or* receiving compensation for any services rendered on behalf of any person "in relation to any case, proceeding or application or other matter before such agency."[21] Because the statute is in the disjunctive, a former employee who does not appear or practice before the agency, but aids in the preparation of a matter that is presented to the agency and receives compensation for such preparation, violates the statute.[22] The former employee therefore cannot submit to his or her former agency permit and grant applications, contract proposals, and/or any work that contains the individual's professional stamp or seal.[23] Former employees may give general advice to their new employer as to the requirements of their former agency or prepare a general report that could be used by potential funding applicants to their former agency, but they may not be involved in preparing a specific application that would be submitted to the agency.[24] "If the former employee can reasonably assume that his/her work product will reach the individual's former agency," the former employee would be appearing before that agency and would violate the statute.[25] Indeed, even the making of a Freedom of Information Act request to one's former agency, whether compensated or not, is barred by New York's revolving door provisions.[26]

Florida, in contrast, limits its two-year ban to actual "representation" before an agency, which means "actual physical attendance on behalf of a client in an agency proceeding, the writing of letters or filing of documents on behalf of a client, and personal communications made with the officers and employees of any agency on behalf of a client."[27] Thus, it appears that behind-the-scenes work by a former employee would not come within the scope of the ban. However, the Florida Commission on Ethics has cautioned that representation includes any contact with the agency that might influence agency action in a matter that is not purely ministerial.[28] Acting as a mediator in cases that may go before one's former agency is not representation because the former official is not representing either of the parties to the mediation before the agency.[29]

What Is Considered a Former Employee's Agency?

Ambiguities often arise as to the scope of the "agency" before which the former employee cannot appear. Ambiguities in the federal revolving door laws created considerable controversy and provided an opportunity for loopholes through compartmentalization of individual agencies or departments. For example, because the Office of the President was divided into a number of

32   POSTEMPLOYMENT RESTRICTIONS ON GOVERNMENT EMPLOYEES

agencies, former top aides of President Reagan were allowed to lobby former colleagues because those colleagues were designated as employees of different agencies than the employee lobbying them. This was eventually resolved by legislation that prohibited the breaking up of the Executive Office of the President to separate agencies.[30]

However, current federal law still provides that a former employee may make appearances before unrelated bureaus or agencies within the same department.[31] Further, federal law gives the Office of Government Ethics authority to designated various agencies or bureaus as separate and distinct for purposes of the agency ban.[32]

New York law does not provide for any compartmentalization of agencies. However, ambiguities may nonetheless arise as to whether an employee is lobbying his former agency or department. For example, the New York Ethics Commission has held that a former executive branch employee and assistant counsel to the governor could appear before the much larger Executive Department since the Executive Chamber is not statutorily a part of the Executive Department.[33] New York also has held that an official could be considered to be an employee of more than one agency if the official performs substantial and continuous work for an agency other than the one to which he or she is officially assigned. Moreover, technical or statutory designations between agencies or bureaus are ignored when the official exerts substantial control beyond official lines of authority.[34] At the same time, the commission has applied the ban only to a former employee's particular office or bureau, and not to the whole department, where that office or bureau operated independently, with its own power of appointment and funding separate from that of the department.[35]

Ambiguities also arise from changes in agency structure. For instance, an employee's former agency may merge with another agency, resulting in an entirely different entity. Florida has defined "agency" as the "lowest departmental unit within which [the former official's] influence might reasonably be considered to extend."[36] The Florida Commission on Ethics held that the restricted agency was not the entire entity, as it stood postmerger. Rather, the former employee was restricted only from the department of the new agency with which he or she worked before the merger.[37] The federal Office of Government Ethics has held that the one-year ban does not apply at all to postemployment appearances of former employees of the Civil Aeronautics Board (CAB) before the Department of Transportation (DOT) even though CAB had been merged into DOT.[38] New York has taken a case-by-case approach. In one case, where two agencies were entirely merged and their staffs intermingled, employees from both predecessor agencies were barred from appearing before the entire merged entity.[39] However, where the functions of two merged agencies were distinct, the Commission limited the ban on a former official to only the types of matters that would have been submitted to the official's former agency.[40]

Because the goal of the one- and two-year bans is to reduce the former employee's influence with his or her own agency, these bans generally do not apply to appearances before a court.[41] Thus, former employees are generally free to litigate against their former agency in a court of law and to enter into settlement discussions with their former agency.[42] It should be noted, however, that, with regard to matters with which a former employee was personally involved, employees are generally prohibited from any involvement in that matter on behalf of a private entity, even in a court of law. See discussion of the "matter ban" on page 35.

Applicability to Partners and Associates of Former Employees

An important consideration for any lawyer leaving government service is whether any ban on future government work would apply to other members of the former employee's new firm.

Generally, most states and the federal government have construed the statute to be limited solely to the individual lawyer and not to apply to the entire firm.[43] It should be noted, however, that the rule may very well be different with regard to appearances on particular matters with which the lawyer was involved in during government service.[44] See discussion of the "matter ban" on page 35.

In this area as well, New York has taken a relatively strict stand. Although the New York statute does not prohibit a former employee's firm from appearing before that employee's former agency, the ethics commission has emphasized that if the firm is "so identified with the individual, for example, utilizes his name as its organizational name or he is the only principal [of the entity]," all appearances would be prohibited under New York's statute.[45] Moreover, if a former government employee's partner or associate appears before that former employee's agency, that employee may not receive any of the "net revenue" derived from that representation.[46]

If a former employee's new role includes responsibility over all aspects of the entity with which he or she is employed, he or she may not avoid the ban by delegating responsibilities to others. Thus, the Ohio Ethics Commission prohibited a member of that state's public utilities commission from becoming the consumer counsel, who must appear before that board. The employee could not avoid the ban by delegating such matters to a subordinate because the counsel would be required by law to be involved in all matters before the agency.[47]

Applicability of the Ban to Representation of, or Further Employment with, the Government

A recurring issue in the interpretation of the various states' statutes is the question of whether the agency ban applies to service on behalf of another government. The federal government expressly allows bureau officers to contact their former agency on behalf of the United States government.[48] New York also excludes from the reach of the statute former officials who appear before their former agencies carrying out official duties as elected officers or employees of any other level of government.[49] However, a former state employee who is a paid consultant to a municipality or is retained as a paid private lawyer by the municipality is not exempt from the ban.[50] Other states have broader provisions allowing any representative activities on behalf of other governments.[51]

In what appears to be an unreasonably strict interpretation of the statute, the New York Ethics Commission has held that an agency may not even hire its own former employee as a consultant for a period of two years after public service.[52] Obviously, in such cases, former employees are not attempting to use their influence with the agency on behalf of a private entity. The only private gain would be their own compensation, which would not appear to be significantly different from their receipt of a salary as public officials. Nonetheless, the commission apparently was concerned about sweetheart deals between an agency and its former officials in which the employee would leave the agency and then perform the same work at a much higher rate of pay. Ohio and Indiana, in contrast, expressly allow a former public official to be retained by, or to represent, the agency with which he or she was previously employed.[53]

The City of New York Conflicts of Interest Board has allowed a former employee to be retained by the employee's agency as a consultant, but refused to allow a private firm that hired the former government official from itself being retained by the agency for the purpose of utilizing the services of the former public official. In such a case, the board concluded, the firm would be obtaining a contract solely by virtue of its hiring of a former government employee.[54] The federal Office of Government Ethics, in contrast, has held that a former employee's new employer could be retained for the purpose of employing the former official to complete work on a manual for the employee's former agency. The Office found that none of the concerns that motivated Congress to pass the revolving door rules were implicated.[55]

A closely related question is whether or not the prohibition on postemployment appearances before one's former agency applies to representation of employees as a union or collective bargaining representative. In a recent advisory opinion, the New York City Conflicts of Interest Board held that the city's postemployment restrictions technically applied to a former employee who, while employed with the agency, acted as the union representative and who, upon leaving government service, continued to act as a union representative in collective bargaining with the former agency. Nonetheless, the Board, finding that the former employee's continued representation as a union official did not create a conflict of interest, granted a waiver from the provisions of the statute.[56]

The Ban on Involvement in Matters Handled While in Government
(The "Matter Ban")

Many states, localities, and the federal government have a ban that prohibits former employees from becoming involved in any matter with which they had a personal involvement during their employment.[57] It differs from the agency ban in two important respects. First, the ban usually prohibits *any* postgovernment involvement in any matter handled while in government. It is not limited to appearances before the employee's former agency.[58] It usually prohibits appearances before all agencies, courts, and the legislature.[59] Second, the ban is often, but not always, of indefinite, or "lifetime," duration.[60] The reason for the ban is obvious: a government official, having represented the government on a particular matter, should not be able to "switch sides" and represent a private party in the same matter. The danger that confidential information gained as a public employee could be used in such situations for private advantage is manifest.

Indeed, former government lawyers who work in states having relatively shorter matter bans or no bans at all should be aware that professional codes of responsibility severely restrict their ability to represent a private client on matters handled while in government. See discussion of professional codes of responsibility below. Moreover, the Ohio Ethics Commission, in applying that state's matter ban, advised a former public servant that, although the disqualification applied only for a period of twelve months, "disqualifying yourself from participation in such matters beyond the twelve-month period imposed by [the statute] would help to avoid an appearance of impropriety."[61]

Some governments, such as the federal government and the California state government, apply the ban only to matters in which the respective government has a direct or substantial interest.[62] Thus, former federal employees can be involved in litigation relating to matter that they worked on in the government if their former agency had no interest in the litigation.[63] Others, such as the New York state government, have no such limitation.[64]

How Involved Must the Employee Have Been in the Matter?

The federal government imposes a permanent restriction on representation of a particular matter in which the former employee participated personally while in government service. Substantial participation "requires more than official responsibility, knowledge, perfunctory involvement, or involvement on an administrative or peripheral issue."[65] The statute requires a direct relationship and "contemplates a responsibility requiring the official to become personally involved to an important, material degree, in the investigative or deliberative processes."[66] However, federal law also imposes a two-year ban on postgovernment involvement in any matter that a former government employee had "under his or her official responsibility" within a period of a year as part of his or her termination.[67]

36 POSTEMPLOYMENT RESTRICTIONS ON GOVERNMENT EMPLOYEES

In New York, the statute applies to any matter that the employee was directly concerned with and in which he personally participated.[68] Personal participation includes participation through "decision, approval, recommendation, investigation or other similar activities."[69] "[M]ere acquaintance with or knowledge of a fact or circumstance is insufficient to trigger the lifetime bar."[70] Advisory opinions have held that the mere presence in a room when a particular matter is discussed does not constitute personal participation[71] and suggest that the former official must have had some official role effecting the outcome of the matter.[72] However, the New York State Ethics Commission has also taken the position that a very senior official, such as an agency head, will be deemed to have participated personally in major policy decisions made by his or her close, senior staff, even though he or she actually had no personal involvement.[73] Ohio includes within the term *personal participation* the supervision or general oversight of other personnel and their work on the particular matter.[74]

What Postemployment Activities Are Covered?

The previous section dealt with the question of how involved with a matter the former employee had to be while in government for the ban to apply. This subsection deals with the degree of *postemployment* involvement necessary for the ban to apply. As with the agency ban, New York State prohibits the former employee from appearing or communicating before any state agency on the matter or receiving compensation for any services related to the matter.[75]

The City of New York has taken a similar view. That city's one-year ban on appearance before an official's former agency prohibits only communications "for compensation" with the agency. In contrast, the city's matter ban applies to a former official's appearance "whether paid or unpaid" before the agency, or the receipt of compensation "for *any* services rendered" (emphasis added) in relation to the matter in which the party was formerly involved in as a public official.[76] The federal government, in contrast, bans only representation before agencies or courts of the United States and does not prohibit behind-the-scenes activities.[77]

Ohio has interpreted its regulations in a similar way. To "[r]epresent a client or act in a representative capacity" has been interpreted to mean "any written or oral communication, formal or informal, including preparation of communications even if the former officer does not sign the communication." It includes both formal advocacy and informal lobbying. However, if the former officer "merely consulted with the attorneys or other personnel who prepared the documents, letters, or notes [which were submitted to the agency] the prohibition would not apply."[78]

How Is "Matter" Defined?

A significant question of interpretation that arises in these regulations is the definition of the term "matter." Matter can include almost any action, including administrative proceedings, legislation, rule promulgation, negotiation, or contracts. Many states, such as Ohio, however, draw a distinction between cases, proceedings, and applications, which are included in the ban, and the promulgation of rules, regulations and statutes which are not.[79] A discrete administrative proceeding or contract is generally of limited duration, and the issues raised are usually applicable only to the parties before the agency. It is appropriate in such circumstances to prohibit a former public official from becoming involved in *that* proceeding or application at any time after leaving public service. A statute, rule, or regulation, in contrast, is generally applicable to a wide class of parties and individuals, and it seems unreasonable and unduly burdensome to prohibit a former employee from having any involvement with a particular law, rule, or regulation for the rest of his or her professional career.

The New York City Charter does not, by its terms, include legislation within the scope of the matter ban.[80] However, the Conflicts of Interest Board has interpreted the provision to include legislation with which a former employee has been involved, but only during the particular legislative session. Once the session has ended and a similar or exact bill is introduced in a subsequent session, the new bill would be considered a different matter and the former employee would be free to become involved in that legislation in a private capacity.[81]

In contrast, the New York State Ethics Commission[82] has taken the position that legislation can constitute a matter and that bills introduced in the same or even different legislative sessions may constitute the same matter if they affect the same or substantially the same population or issues. "This can be true even when the form in which the issue is presented is not identical."[83] Additionally, the commission has held that a former government employee involved in development of legislation was barred upon leaving state service from any involvement in the promulgation of regulations based upon that legislation.[84] Indeed, the commission has gone so far as to caution a former government employee who was involved in drafting legislation relating to the personal income tax to refrain from any postemployment involvement in any legislation involving the income tax without first seeking approval from the commission on a case-by-case basis.[85]

The federal Office of Government Ethics has held that legislation can be a matter for purposes of Section 207(a), the federal matter ban, but that former employees would rarely be barred from appearing before the government on that same legislation because 207(a) also requires that the former official's involvement with legislation, while in the government, has to "involve a particular party or parties." The office found that such a situation would usually arise only in the context of private relief bills or bills establishing grant programs "for which only one known organization was eligible."[86]

In the area of contracts, the matter ban usually would apply to any subsequent involvement with the contract, including providing services under that contract or negotiating any change in the contract.[87] Moreover, for purposes

38   POSTEMPLOYMENT RESTRICTIONS ON GOVERNMENT EMPLOYEES

of the ban, a contract remains the same matter (and is therefore subject to the ban), even though it may have been amended in a number of respects or assigned to a new party.[88]

To determine whether two matters are in fact the same matter, the federal Office of Government Ethics looks at whether the matters "involve the same basic facts, the same unrelated parties, related issues . . . [and the] same confidential information." They also look at the amount of time elapsed and the continuing existence of an important federal interest.[89]

Restricting the Use of Confidential Information

The third type of revolving door statute prohibits the use of confidential information that is gained during the course of public employment for an employee's personal benefit or gain. For example, Florida's statute provides that a public employee cannot disclose or use "information not available to members of the general public . . . for his or her personal gain or benefit."[90] These statutes not only prohibit the use of information for the former employee's own benefit, but also prohibit its use for the gain of any other person, including a relative, business associate, friend, or acquaintance.

A "gain" or "benefit" can include different things, such as selling information to an interested party, or using this information to acquire future clients or to acquire a contract. Additionally, an employee could benefit by using his position as a public employee to seek potential employment offers. See discussion below.

Using One's Public Position to Obtain Private Employment

Many states and municipalities expressly prohibit a public officer or employee from accepting or soliciting, or using one's position to secure, a promise of future employment with any party that is regulated by, doing business with, seeking to do business with, or having any matters before the agency that the public official serves, unless the public officer withdraws from the matters affecting the interest of that party.[91]

If a federal employee hires a search firm to secure future employment, the employee must remove himself or herself from all matters involving the financial interest of any perspective employer whom the employee knows has been contacted by the search firm. The Office of Government Ethics has declined to endorse a procedure whereby the search firm "screens" the employee from any knowledge of the initial contacts made by the firm. The office noted that the employee may have constructive knowledge of which firms are contacted, and that, in any event, the procedure creates an appearance of impropriety.[92]

A corollary provision is a ban on a former public official profiting from any public contract that is authorized by the official or by a body of which he or she was a member while in public employment.[93] The Ohio Ethics Commission interpreted this provision to prohibit a former agency lawyer from recommending that the agency hire private counsel, and then obtaining a position as that private counsel.[94] Similarly, a former official could not, for a period of one year, assume the directorship of an entity that received a substantial grant approved by the former official.[95] Ohio, however, allows a former public official to obtain a contract authorized while he was in office, if the contract is let by competitive bidding and the public official made the lowest and best bid.[96]

The Limitations Imposed by Professional Codes of Responsibility

Rule 1.11 of the ABA Model Rules of Professional Conduct expressly prohibits a lawyer from representing a private client in connection with a matter in which the lawyer participated "personally and substantially" as a public officer or employee, unless the government agency expressly consents to such representation. Moreover, no lawyer in a firm with which that lawyer is associated may undertake or continue representation of such a matter unless the disqualified attorney is screened[97] from any participation in the matter and written notice is given to the government agency so that the agency can ascertain whether there has been full compliance with this rule. The lawyer is also barred from receiving any direct compensation from the firm for such work, even if performed by others. This requirement is necessary to avoid disqualification of the other lawyers in the firm.[98] Similar prohibitions are contained in the Model Code of Professional Responsibility adopted by New York. See, for example, D.R. 9-101(B)(1).[99]

The model rules also prohibit any lawyer who has obtained confidential information about a person, acquired while the lawyer was in public service, from representing a private client whose interests are adverse to that person in any matter in which the information could be used to a material disadvantage to that person. Furthermore, the law firm with which that lawyer is associated is prohibited from such representation unless the disqualified lawyer is screened from participation and receives no fee from such representation.[100]

Similarly, the rules prohibit a lawyer who is in public service from participating in a matter in which the lawyer participated personally and substantially while in private practice or nongovernment employment unless "under applicable law no one is, or by lawful delegation may be, authorized to act in the lawyer's stead in the matter."

Finally, the rules also prohibit any government lawyer from negotiating for private employment with any person who is involved as a party or as a lawyer for a party in a matter in which the lawyer is participating personally and substantially.

Notes

1. *See, e.g.,* New York City Conflicts of Interest Board Advisory Op. No. 95-1 (the purpose of postemployment restrictions is "among other things, to prevent former public servants from exploiting public office for personal gain, subordinating the interests of the City to those of a

40   POSTEMPLOYMENT RESTRICTIONS ON GOVERNMENT EMPLOYEES

perspective employer, or exerting undue influence on government decision-making"). *See also* Fla. Advisory Op. CEO 91-49 (postemployment restriction designed to "prevent influence peddling and the use of public office to create opportunities for personal profit once officials leave office"); N.Y.S. Formal Ethics Op. 92-20 (the purpose of the revolving door provision is to "preclude the possibility that a former State employee may leverage his or her knowledge, experience and contacts gained in State service to his or her advantage or that of a client, thereby securing unwarranted privileges, consideration or action").

2. N.Y. Pub. Off. Law § 73(8)(a)(i) (McKinney 1988 and Supp. 1997); Fla. Stat. § 112.313(9)(c)(3),(4) (1996). *See also* La. Rev. Stat. § 42.1121(B) (1996).

3. 18 U.S.C. § 207(c)(1),(d). This provision applies to federal employees as specified in 5 U.S.C. § 5312-15, which include, generally, the numerous federal secretaries and deputy secretaries (of state, etc.), the chairpersons of the federal commissions, directors and members of federal boards, and other more specific executive positions.

4. For similar statutes in Arkansas, Indiana, California, and Hawaii, *see* Ark. Code Ann. § 19-11-709(b)(2) (1995); Ind. Code Ann. § 4-2-6-11(a)(2) (Mitchie 1996); Cal. Gov't. Code § 87406(c) (Deering 1996); Haw. Rev. Stat. § 84-18(c) (1996).

Pennsylvania's revolving door statute has been interpreted not to apply to former state lawyers. 65 Pa. Cons. Stat. Ann. § 403(g). Pennsylvania case law holds that the Pennsylvania Supreme Court has exclusive jurisdiction to promulgate conduct rules for state lawyers. Therefore, the restrictions as set forth in the statute would not apply to a lawyer who was performing duties within the practice of law and would not prohibit a former public lawyer from appearing before his or her former agency or office. *See* Pennsylvania Pub. Util. Bar Ass'n v. Thornburgh, 434 A.2d 1327 (1981).

5. 18 U.S.C. § 216.

6. Ohio Rev. Code § 102.99 (1996).

7. N.Y. Pub. Off. Law § 73(14).

8. N.Y. Pub. Off. Law § 73(8)(b)(i).

9. 18 U.S.C. § 207(e)(1).

10. N.Y. Pub. Off. Law § 73(8)(a)(iii).

11. Cal. Gov't. Code § 87406(b). *See also* Ha. Rev. Stat. § 84-18(b) (Hawaii prohibits lobbying for one year).

12. N.Y. Pub. Off. Law § 73(8)(a)(iii).

13. Forti v. New York State Ethics Comm'n, 75 N.Y.2d 596, 554 N.E.2d 876, 555 N.Y.S.2d 235 (1990).

14. *See* NY CLS Standards & Admin. Policies, N.Y. Comp. Codes R. & Regs. tit. 22 § 16.1 (1996). *See also* LA R USDCTED General Order No. 90-3 (1996) (Louisiana U.S. District Court Order) (which provides that for two years after a judge vacates the bench, the present judges shall recuse themselves in any case before them in which the former judge appears).

15. U.S. Ct. of App., 1st Cir., Rule 46 (a law clerk may not "appear at the counsel table or on brief in connection with any case heard during a period of one year following separation from service with the court"); Missouri Rules of Ct., Rule 82.05(a) (a former law clerk "shall not appear at counsel table or sign any filing in any case before this Court for a period of six months after leaving this Court's employment").

16. U.S. Ct. of App., 1st Cir., Rule 46; U.S. Dist. Ct. Rules D.C., Gen. Rule 119; U.S. Dist. Ct. Rules W.D. Mo., Rule 31.

17. 18 U.S.C. § 207(c)(1).

18. OGE Inf. Adv. Letter 81-35.

19. R.I. Gen. Laws § 36-14-5(e)(2), (4) (1998).

20. N.Y.C. Charter ch. 68 § 2601(4); *See also* § 2604(d)(4).

21. N.Y. Pub. Off. Law § 73(8)(a)(i).

22. *See* N.Y.S. Formal Ethics Op. 89-7. New York goes so far as to prohibit a former employee from appearing or working on a matter before an agency that involves or seeks input from the former employee's agency. *See Id.* However, where the former employee has no reason

to know or anticipate that his or her former agency will be involved, and there is no statute, law, or policy requiring involvement, there is no violation of the statute. *Id.*

23. N.Y.S. Formal Ethics Op. 94-6.

24. N.Y.S. Formal Ethics Op. 94-18, 90-3.

25. N.Y.S. Formal Ethics Op. 94-6.

26. N.Y.S. Formal Ethics Op. 89-7.

27. Fla. Stat. § 112.312(22).

28. Fla. Advisory Op. CEO 91-49.

29. *Id.*

30. *See* 18 U.S.C. § 207(h)(2) as added by Public Law 101-194, the Ethics Reform Act of 1989, which specifically provides that "no agency or bureau within the Executive Office of the President may be designated . . . as a separate department or agency."

31. 18 U.S.C. § 207(h).

32. 18 U.S.C. § 207(h)(1).

33. N.Y.S. Formal Ethics Op. 89-3.

34. N.Y.S. Formal Ethics Op. 95-33.

35. N.Y.S. Formal Ethics Op. 95-1.

36. Fla. Advisory Op. CEO 91-49.

37. Fla. Advisory Op. CEO 94-029. Another advisory opinion went on to say that the restricted duties were "those duties or segments of the former agency where one's influence would naturally extend and which the former employee should be prohibited from exploiting." Fla. Advisory Op. CEO 96-018.

38. OGE Inf. Adv. Letter 85-5.

39. N.Y.S. Formal Ethics Op. 93-11.

40. N.Y.S. Formal Ethics Op. 96-7.

41. Ohio Ethics Op. 93-014, 87-001; R.I. Gen. Laws Ann. § 36-14-5(e)(4).

42. *See* N.Y.S. Formal Ethics Op. 95-28.

43. N.Y.S. Formal Ethics Op. 90-14.

44. Cal. Ethics Op. 1993-128.

45. N.Y.S. Formal Ethics Op. 89-12, 94-6 and 90-14.

46. N.Y.S. Formal Ethics Op. 94-6; 90-14.

47. Ohio Ethics Op. 93-011.

48. 18 U.S.C. § 207(a)(1),(2); *see* OGE Inf. Adv. Letter 91-29.

49. N.Y. Pub. Off. Law § 73(10).

50. N.Y.S. Formal Ethics Op. 89-7; *and see* Op. 93-15 (matter ban does not apply to a lawyer who works for a municipality pro bono).

51. *See* Cal. Gov't. Code § 87406(e) (the restrictions shall not apply to an employee "of another state agency, board, or commission if the appearance or communication is for the purpose of influencing legislative or administrative action on behalf of the state agency"); N.Y.C. Charter ch. 68 § 2604(d)(6) (the ban does not apply to "positions with or representation on behalf of any local, state or federal agency").

52. N.Y.S. Formal Ethics Op. 89-9, 91-9. The commission has held, however, that the former employee may serve in an unpaid capacity. N.Y.S. Formal Ethics Op. 93-3.

53. Ohio Rev. Code § 102.03(A)(6); *see* Ohio Ethics Op. 92-005; 91-009; 91-005; Ind. Code Ann. § 4-2-6-11(f) (Mitchie 1998).

54. N.Y.C. Conflicts of Interest Board Advisory Op. No. 95-1. *See also* N.Y.S. Formal Ethics Op. 95-31. Similarly, the New York State Ethics Commission has held that an agency cannot "outsource" work by hiring private companies that, in turn, hire recently departed former employees from the agency. *See* N.Y.S. Formal Ethics Op. 95-31. The New York legislature provided some relief from this ban by allowing temporary workers who perform some clerical duties to work for an outsource firm within two years of their departure. N.Y. Pub. Off. Law § 73(8)(f).

55. OGE Inf. Adv. Letter 81-29 (interpreting the federal "matter" ban).

42   POSTEMPLOYMENT RESTRICTIONS ON GOVERNMENT EMPLOYEES

56. N.Y.C. Conflicts of Interest Board Advisory Op. 96-1. *See also,* N.Y. Pub. Off. Law § 78(7)(e).

57. 18 U.S.C. § 207(a)(1); N.Y. Pub. Off. Law § 73(8); Ark. Code Ann. § 19-11-709(b)(1); LA Mun. Code § 49.5.11(A); Cal. Gov't. Code § 87401.

58. *See* 18 U.S.C.§ 207(a)(1),(2); Ohio Rev. Code § 102.03(A)(1); Ohio Ethics Op. 87-001 (which defines representation as any formal or informal appearance before any public agency, and Ohio Rev. Code § 102.03 includes as a public agency "all courts"); N.Y. Pub. Off. Law § 73(8)(a)(ii). N.Y.S. Formal Ethics Op. 93-13 (ban applies to involvement "anywhere," including appearances before Congress).

59. The New York Ethics Commission has held that the state's law would prohibit a former state official who, as an official, lobbied Congress for legislation aiding businesses converting from defense work, from lobbying Congress on behalf of those businesses to amend that legislation. In the case before it, however, the commission found that the employee was not barred because he was not sufficiently involved in the matter while working for the state. N.Y.S. Formal Ethics Op. 93-13.

60. Examples of the lifetime bans are the federal rule, 18 U.S.C. § 207(a)(1); Massachusetts, Mass. Gen. Laws. Ann. 268A § 5(a); Connecticut, Conn. Gen. Stat. Ann. § 1-84b(a); New York, N.Y. Pub. Off. Law § 73(8)(a)(ii); N.Y. City Charter ch. 68 § 2604(d)(4). Examples of shorter bans are Alabama (two years), Ala. Code 36-25-13(e); Ohio (one year), Ohio Rev. Code 102.03; Louisiana (two years), La. Rev. Stat. § 1121(B) and Delaware (two years), Del. Code Ann. 29 § 5805(d).

61. Ohio Ethics Op. 92-005.

62. 18 U.S.C. § 207(a)(1). Cal. Gov't. Code § 87401. *See also* Ala. Code § 36-25-13 (state must be a party or have a direct and substantial interest).

63. OGE Inf. Adv. Letter 82-2.

64. N.Y. Pub. Off. Law § 73(8)(a)(ii).

65. United States v. Josten, 1989 WL 112310, at *2 (N.D. Ill Sept. 14, 1989).

66. *Id.*

67. *See* 18 U.S.C. § 207(a)(2)(B).

68. N.Y. Pub. Off. Law § 73(8)(ii).

69. N.Y.C. Conflicts of Interest Board Advisory Op. 96-7.

70. N.Y.S. Formal Ethics Op. 90-16. The opinion went on to remark, "presence at a meeting where an issue is discussed and the former employee did not vote on the issue, although others did, does not rise to the level of personal participation." *See also,* N.Y.S. Formal Ethics Op. 89-3.

71. N.Y.S. Formal Ethics Op. 95-7.

72. N.Y.S. Formal Ethics Op. 95-16.

73. N.Y.S. Formal Ethics Op. 92-20.

74. Ohio Ethics Op. 93-0011; 91-009; 91-005.

75. N.Y. Pub. Off. Law § 73(8)(a)(ii).

76. Compare N.Y.C. Charter chs. 68 § 2604(d)(2) and § 2601(4) *with* 2604(d)(4).

77. 18 U.S.C. § 207(c); OGE Inf. Adv. Letter 91-29.

78. Ohio Ethics Op. 86-001.

79. Ohio Rev. Code § 102.03(A); *see also,* Ohio Ethics Op. 91-009.

80. N.Y.C. Charter ch. 68 § 2604(d)(4).

81. N.Y.C. Conflicts of Interest Board Advisory Op. No. 95-23.

82. N.Y.S. Formal Ethics Op. 92-20.

83. N.Y.S. Formal Ethics Op. 92-20. However, each year's budget is a separate matter as is each separate application for a rate increase by the same utility. N.Y.S. Formal Ethics Op. 95-32.

84. N.Y.S. Formal Ethics Op. 93-2.

85. N.Y.S. Formal Ethics Op. 94-6.

86. OGE Inf. Adv. Letter 87-3.

87. *See generally* Ohio Ethics Op. 89-009.

88. OGE Inf. Adv. Letter 91-24.

89. *Id.*

90. FLA. STAT. § 112.313(g) (1995). For examples of similar state statutes, *see* R.I. GEN. LAWS § 36-14-5 (1995); OHIO REV. CODE § 102.03(B); N.Y.C. Charter ch. 68 § 2604(d)(5).

91. *See, e.g.,* OHIO REV. CODE § 102.03(7)(D) ("no public official or employee shall solicit or accept anything of value"); Ohio Advisory Ops. 82-002, 87-004 and 89-010; FLA. STAT. § 112.313(2); 18 U.S.C. § 208 (officer or employee cannot participate in matter involving the financial interest of an entity with which the employee "is negotiating or has arrangement concerning any prospective employment"); N.Y.C. Charter ch. 68 § 2604(d)(1) ("no public servant shall solicit, negotiate for or accept any position . . . with any person or firm who or which is involved in a particular matter with the city"); R.I. GEN LAWS § 36-14-5(g). *But see* ARK. CODE ANN. § 19-11-709(e)(1) (1995) "this section is not intended to preclude a former employee from accepting employment with private industry solely because his employer is a contractor with this state").

92. OGE Inf. Adv. Letter 92-17.

93. OHIO REV. CODE § 2921.42(A)(3).

94. Ohio Ethics Op. 92-005.

95. Ohio Ethics Op. 87-004.

96. OHIO REV. CODE § 2921.42(A)(3).

97. Valid screening requires that the former employee (1) receives no part of the compensation from the matter; and (2) provides prompt, written notice to the appropriate agency. MODEL RULES OF PROFESSIONAL CONDUCT Rule 1.11; *see also* Fla. Advisory Op. CEO 72-41.

98. Although a lawyer is prohibited from receiving a fee from such representation, the comment to the rule explains that a lawyer is not prohibited from receiving a salary or a partnership share "established by prior independent agreement." The rule only prohibits a lawyer from receiving a fee which is directly related to the matter from which the lawyer is disqualified.

99. *See also* California Business and Professions Code § 6131(b), which makes it a misdemeanor for a current or former prosecutor, after having aided in the prosecution of any matter, to directly or indirectly advise in relation to or take any part in the defense of that matter. In interpreting this provision, the California State Bar concluded that a former district attorney could join a law firm that was retained to represent a defendant who was prosecuted by the former district attorney as long as the firm established an elaborate screening procedure to assure that the district attorney was screened from any involvement in the defense. *See* Cal. Ethics Op. No. 93-128.

100. *See generally* Armstrong v. McAlpin, 625 F.2d 433 (2d Cir. 1980) *en banc vacated on other grounds,* 449 U.S. 1106 (1981).

CHAPTER ❦ 4

Doing the Right Thing?
Financial Disclosure Filing Requirements
for Government Employees

Barbara Smith

This chapter features a national survey of state and local financial disclosure laws as well as a reprint of the provisions applicable to financial disclosure from the Model Law for Campaign Finance, Ethics and Lobbying Regulation published by the Council on Government Ethics Laws. The chapter concludes by raising the issue of disclosure in the growing area of privatization.

Whatever one may think of the intrusiveness of financial disclosure laws, they are widespread . . . and reflect the not unreasonable judgment of many legislatures that disclosure will help reveal and deter corruption and conflicts of interest.[1]

The government employee, then, must be prepared to subordinate his or her right to privacy to the greater good of an informed public. Financial disclosure filing requirements for state government employees have become fairly commonplace in the post-Watergate era. After surviving early challenges based upon constitutional rights, financial disclosure is now routine, particularly at the state government level. This chapter traces the highlights of litigation challenging financial disclosure requirements and reviews how different states approach the issues.

Ethics in government is difficult to legislate. Critics say no law can make an individual do the right thing, and that may be so. However, financial disclosure is commonly perceived as an effective means to prevent potential conflicts of interest and corruption, to inform the public, and to increase its confidence in government. Over time, disclosure initially required only from candidates and elected officials has been broadened to include senior appointed officials, and, finally, certain civil servants.

While constitutional attacks on financial disclosure statutes cite many rights, the more successful cases focus on the right of privacy. Many relate their privacy claims to the 1965 Supreme Court decision of *Griswold v. Con-*

necticut,[2] which initially recognized the right of privacy under the Ninth Amendment.

In an early challenge to a financial disclosure statute based on the assertion of privacy rights, the Supreme Court of California held unconstitutional a statute requiring every public officer and every candidate to place on public record a statement describing his or her investments and those of his or her spouse, on the ground that requiring the release of such information violated the individual's right of privacy.[3] Since the law required officials to disclose private information that did not affect the duties or functions of their particular offices, the court held it to be unconstitutionally overbroad. Further, the court was troubled by the requirement that civil servants were subjected to the same scrutiny as that for elected officials. However, in a subsequent case the same court upheld the revised law, which required disclosure of only those interests that would materially affect the decisions filers made in their official state capacity.[4]

In 1975, the U.S. Supreme Court, expanding its interpretation of the right of privacy under the Fourteenth Amendment, firmly established within the "confidentiality" branch of the right of privacy the principle that individuals have a protected interest in "avoiding disclosure of personal matters."[5]

A number of decisions addressing the constitutionality of financial disclosure requirements for government employees link the expectation of privacy to the rank of the employees. In *Nixon v. Administrator of Gen. Servs.*[6] the Supreme Court recognized that Nixon, "having placed himself in the public spotlight," had a lower expectation of privacy than someone who had not entered public life. As one commentator has noted, "[l]ower courts also subscribe to the public status standard for determining reasonable expectation of privacy. See, e.g., *Lehrhaupt v. Flynn*, 140 N.J.Super. 250, 261; 356 A2d 3542 (N.J. Super. Ct. App. Div. 1976) (by accepting public employment, officials move toward status of a public citizen and must subordinate privacy to the public's right to know); *Fritz v. Gorton*, 83 Wash.2d 275, 294; 517 P.2d 911, 923 (1974), (candidates or public officers who enter the limelight invite greater scrutiny of their public lives); *In re Kading*, 70 Wis.2d 508, 526, 235 N.W.2d 409, 417 (1975) (those who willingly place themselves in the public arena are subject to reasonable scrutiny and exposure)."[7]

In *Plante v. Gonzalez*,[8] Florida State senators challenged the constitutionality of the state's financial disclosure law on the grounds that it violated their right to privacy. The Fifth Circuit upheld mandatory financial disclosure for public officials as constitutional, considering the low expectation of privacy that public officials should have.

In *Barry v. City of New York*,[9] the Second Circuit Court of Appeals upheld a New York City financial disclosure law that required the filing of annual financial reports from most elected and appointed officials, candidates for city office, and civil service employees having an annual salary equal to or exceeding $30,000. The court determined that lower echelon employees are not immune from corruption, and therefore, found no reason to differentiate

46 FINANCIAL DISCLOSURE REQUIREMENTS FOR GOVERNMENT EMPLOYEES

among classes of employees. In upholding the filing requirement, the court appeared convinced of the protection afforded by the screening provision contained in the law, which provides that if a covered employee designates certain information as private, it cannot be publicly disclosed unless a board of ethics determines that the information is not highly personal, is relevant to the employee's duties, and involves an actual or potential conflict of interest. See *Developments in the Law—Public Employment,* 97 Harvard L. Rev. 1611, 1668 (1984). Critics have charged that the standards to exempt material are vague and seem inadequate to protect the filers' legitimate expectation of privacy.[10]

In upholding New York State's 1987 financial disclosure statute, which required detailed disclosure even from lower echelon employees, the New York Supreme Court held "that in matters of financial disclosure, government employees and public officials, due to the significant governmental interest in ensuring the integrity and honesty of government and in fostering public confidence in the same, have a diminished expectation of privacy as compared to their counterparts in private industry."[11]

The government employee, then, must be prepared to subordinate his or her right to privacy to the greater good of an informed public.

Current Requirements

To support this chapter with information, a survey of all of the states was undertaken in 1996 seeking information regarding who must file financial disclosure statements, what must be revealed, what enforcement there is for noncompliance, how the information is reviewed and by whom.[12] (See table of survey results for complete data.) Officials in 38 states and New York City responded to the questionnaire, and 12 states filed no response. Of the responding jurisdictions, 36 had disclosure laws covering executive branch officers only, while 31 had measures covering both officers and employees; 32 required disclosure from legislators, while 21 required filings from both legislators and legislative employees; 22 required disclosure from judges, with 14 requiring disclosure from judges and judicial branch employees. Of the 39 respondents, 24 noted laws requiring financial disclosure from municipal officers, with 18 noting disclosure from municipal officers and employees.

Individuals are required to file based upon either their particular position (for example, agency heads and deputies) or the duties of the position. Job duties that would require filing include, for example, negotiating, authorizing or approving contracts, leases, permits or licenses; purchasing, selling, or leasing real property, goods, or services; obtaining grants of money or loans; and/or the adoption or repeal of a rule or regulation having the effect of law. In six states and New York City, individuals who earn in excess of an arbitrary salary threshold are required to file.

Ten states have a process by which an individual may seek a waiver from the filing requirement. Examples of grounds upon which a waiver may be granted include not performing the acts that require filing (New York, Iowa,

New York City); a legally recognized privilege (such as physician-patient) (California); undue hardship for spousal disclosure (Illinois); serious health problems (Ohio); and information that might jeopardize security/safety (Ohio).

What information is reported varies widely from state to state. (But, see the Model Code.) Generally, thirty-two respondents required details that include the filer's income from outside activities, investments, real property owned, and certain gifts. Twenty-two states require such information from spouses, and fifteen require that information concerning dependents or members of the household. Information on political party office holding is not often reported, as only eight of the respondents require that.

Twenty-four respondents reported they have the authority to penalize individuals for failure to file, late filing, or deficient filing. "Late" penalties vary from $5 per day in Oregon to $100 per day in Oklahoma. Many states noted average penalties in the $200 range for late filing. Interestingly, Indiana, Iowa, and Maine indicated that the authority is rarely used for late filers, since few or no filings are ever late. The fines steepen considerably for failure-to-file violations; many states report average penalties of $1,000 or $2,000. Willful or intentional failure to file is a misdemeanor or infraction prosecutable in seven states. With respect to deficient filings, at least two states allow a grace period in which the individual may correct his or her statement without monetary penalty. Other states assess monetary fines or refer deficient filings or failure-to-file cases to prosecutors for action. Notwithstanding penalties assessed by state ethics boards, individual state agencies usually retain the authority to undertake disciplinary proceedings against employees who do not meet their filing requirements. The range of penalties includes suspension of pay (Minnesota, Oregon) or forfeiture of office (New York City, New Jersey, North Dakota).

Twenty of the respondents indicated that, once all the information is collected, they review the forms for completeness or conduct a "desk audit"; fifteen replied that no audit was performed. Fifteen respondents reported investigations did arise from the information provided on the financial disclosure statements, but they represented only 1 or 2 percent of total investigations.

Among the respondents, all of the jurisdictions make the information on the financial disclosure statements available to the public, and all but Indiana, New York State, and New York City make copies available.[13] The total approximate number of filers from the reporting jurisdictions was about 446,000.[14] The press most frequently reviews financial disclosure statements, with law enforcement agencies and other state agencies also often reviewing the forms. It would seem the initial concerns of reporting individuals—that the information would be put to an "improper use," for example, by unscrupulous salesmen or that they should be embarrassed by revealing details to the public about their financial status—are largely unfounded.

In response to a question regarding the value of financial disclosure, six respondents thought it was very valuable, four said it was somewhat valuable; and fourteen others noted it was not very valuable. Those dissatisfied with the reporting requirements usually cited the lack of specific information required.

What's Next?

While most states seem comfortably entrenched in requiring financial disclosure from public officers and employees, there are still efforts at reform. For example, at the local government level, the Temporary State Commission on Local Government Ethics in New York State has championed a broad-based municipal ethics reform.[15] "The public has been sold a bill of goods on lengthy annual financial disclosure forms. They do little more than collect dust, while driving good people, particularly volunteers, out of local government. What we really need is transactional disclosure: disclosure (and recusal) when a conflict actually arises."[16] Clearly, the Temporary State Commission supported the move away from lengthy, complicated disclosure to transactional disclosure. With transactional disclosure, officials charged with authority to act upon a matter must disclose their financial interest and usually recuse themselves from participating further on the matter.

Whether the concept of transactional disclosure catches on will probably depend on state legislatures' views of the purposes to be served, but it seems to be an uphill battle. The conundrum of what appropriately should be disclosed was addressed in *Snider v. Shapp* where the court opined:

> [w]e think it plain that to limit disclosure to financial interests that relate only to government activities or to the functions and duties of a particular officeholder would not guarantee the absence of a conflict or enhance the confidence of the people in an honest and impartial government.[17]

Should Consultants Be Required to Disclose?

Another frontier appears to be whether states will require financial disclosure reporting from a limited category of consultants. The Model Law on Ethics, Conflict of Interest, and Personal Financial Disclosure proposed by the Council on Government Ethics Laws suggests that a consultant should file a "statement of economic interests no later than twenty-one (21) days after entering into a contractual relationship with the state or a political subdivision if the consultant, or a member of the household of the consultant has an economic interest in an entity: (1) whose bid was evaluated by the consultant and who was subsequently awarded the contract by the state or the political subdivision that contracted with the consultant; or (2) who was awarded a contract by the consultant." Kansas has enacted a financial disclosure filing requirement for private consultants under contract with any Kansas State agency to evaluate bids for public contracts or to award public contracts.[18]

Privatization Implications

Another cutting-edge suggestion is to require financial disclosure statements from individuals rendering certain services under privatization contracts with state agencies. As more and more states downsize and transfer traditional state functions to the private sector, the question of public accountability must be addressed. What mechanism is there to insure ethical conduct by the workers performing the privatized function? Ideally, the state's ethics codes would address the ethical standards to be met. Failing that, perhaps some limited financial disclosure would provide the desired measure of accountability.

In the end, one reflects on the efficacy of the financial disclosure filing requirement. Has it increased the public's confidence in government? That nebulous concept is not as easily measured as the statistics in the foregoing survey. What is certain is that there is a vast quantity of information reported, which largely goes unread by the public whose trust it was meant to earn. Very few cases have developed from the information reported, although a number of states indicate that those few cases were very significant ones. Perhaps the results of the survey support and underscore the conclusion that government employees are trustworthy, conduct themselves in a manner befitting their position, and deserve the respect of citizens-at-large.

Results of Nationwide Survey

Survey Respondents

Alabama Ethics Commission
Nevada Commission on Ethics
State of Alaska Public Offices Commission
New Hampshire Office of Secretary of State
Arizona Secretary of State
New Jersey Executive Commission on Ethical Standards
California Fair Political Practices Commission
Connecticut State Ethics Commission
New York State Ethics Commission
Delaware State Public Integrity Commission
New York City Conflicts of Interest Board
State of Florida Commission on Ethics
North Carolina Board of Ethics
Georgia State Ethics Commission
North Dakota Secretary of State
Illinois Board of Ethics
Ohio Ethics Commission
Indiana State Ethics Commission
Oklahoma Ethics Commission
Iowa Ethics and Campaign Disclosure Board
Oregon Government Standards and Practices Commission
Kansas Commission on Government Standards and Conduct
Pennsylvania State Ethics Commission
Kentucky Executive Branch Ethics Commission
Rhode Island Ethics Commission
Louisiana Ethics Administration
South Carolina State Ethics Commission

50   FINANCIAL DISCLOSURE REQUIREMENTS FOR GOVERNMENT EMPLOYEES

Maine Commission on Governmental Ethics and Election Practices
South Dakota Secretary of State
Utah Lieutenant Governor's Office, Director of Elections
Massachusetts State Ethics Commission
Virginia Secretary of the Commonwealth
Maryland State Ethics Commission
Vermont Secretary of State's Office; Elections
Michigan Department of Civil Service
West Virginia Ethics Commission Board of Ethics
Wisconsin Ethics Board
Minnesota Ethical Practices Board
Wyoming Secretary of State

Notes

1. Slevin v. City of New York, 712 F.2d at 1560.

2. 381 U.S. 479 (1965).

3. City of Carmel-by-the-Sea v. Young, 2 Cal. 3d 259, 466 P.2d 225, 85 Cal. Rptr. 1 (1970)

4. County of Nevada v. MacMillen, 11 Cal. 3d 662, 552 P.2d 1345, 114 Cal. Rptr. 345 (1974)

5. Whalen v. Roe, 429 U.S. 589, 599–600. The Whalen case charged that New York State's Controlled Substances Act, which required disclosure of names and addresses of persons obtaining certain prescription drugs, violated their privacy interests. In upholding the statute, the Court cited the Act's safeguards against public disclosure of the collected information, the limited access to the information, and the destruction of records after five years.

6. 433 U.S. 425 (1977).

7. Sharon Obel Thompson, *Public Employees Financial Disclosure Law Requiring Detailed Disclosure from Low-Echelon Employees Not Unconstitutional:* Barry v. City of New York 712 F.2d 1554, 62 WASH. U. L.Q. n. 85.

8. 575 F.2d 1119 (1978).

9. 712 F.2d 1554 (2d Cir.), *cert. denied,* 464 U.S. 1017 (1983).

10. *See,* Thompson, *supra* note 7.

11. Watkins v. NYS Ethics Comm'n, 147 Misc. 2d 350, 554 N.Y.S.2d 955 (1990), citing Kaplan v. Board of Educ. of the City Sch. Dist. of the City of New York, 759 F.2d 256 (2d Cir. 1985). *See,* 97 HARV. L. REV. 1611 (1984), *Developments in the Law—Public Employment,* footnote 105: "Courts have generally made short shrift of constitutional challenges not based directly or indirectly on privacy." *See, e.g.,* Duplantier v. United States, 606 F.2d 654, 666–68 (5th Cir. 1979) (separation of powers), *cert. denied,* 449 U.S. 1076 (1981); United States v. Hansen, 566 F. Supp. 162, 169–71 (D.C. 1983) (speech and debate clause); Slevin v. City of New York, 551 F. Supp. 917, 924–927 (S.D.N.Y. 1982) (first, fourth, and fifth amendments), *aff'd in part and rev'd in part on other grounds sub nom.* Barry v. City of New York, 712 F.2d 1554 (2d Cir.), *cert. denied,* 104 S. Ct. 548 (1983). See generally Note, *The Constitutionality of Financial Disclosure Laws,* 59 CORNELL L. REV. 345 (1974) (discussing privacy, free expression, and self-incrimination). See, also, 62 WASH. U. L.Q. 337, footnote 16, discussing privacy protections based on the first, third, fourth, fifth, and ninth amendments within specific contexts. See also, 73 MICHIGAN L. REV. Note: *Fighting Conflicts of Interest in Officialdom: Constitutional and Practical Guidelines for State Financial Disclosure Laws,* March 1975.

12. One oft-heard criticism for financial disclosure from government employees is that it discourages individuals from joining state (or government) service. Whether and to what extent that choice has been made for that reason is not known. In a decision upholding a financial disclosure filing requirement for certain town officials in New Jersey, the Court recog-

nized the concern but dismissed it: "[t]here is no doubt that the preparation of the disclosure statement necessarily involves a considerable burden in the expenditure of time and effort on the part of the involved public officials. Perhaps the nature of the information requested may be embarrassing to some officeholders or may have a chilling effect upon those aspiring to those offices. Nevertheless, such objections have no force when compared with the paramount right of the public to an honest and impartial government." Lehrhaupt et al., v. Flynn, 140 N.J. Super. 250, 356 A.2d 35 (1976).

13. New York's rule, which allowed inspection and handwritten notes to be taken from financial disclosure statements, but which prohibited photocopying, was challenged and upheld as striking a balance between public disclosure and the right to personal privacy. "The limitation on reproduction prevents wholesale invasion into deeply personal data and seeks to limit improper use of the information, a difficult task once that information has left respondent's offices as a photocopy, photograph or other mechanical reproduction . . . While the minimal limitation does not seriously restrict public access where there is a specific interest, it does reflect sensitivity to privacy and provides a safeguard against widespread dissemination of the contents of the filings which could have a commercial value totally unrelated to the governmental function served by its compilation." John v. NYS Ethics Comm'n, 178 A.D.2d 51, 581 N.Y.S. 2d 282 (3d Dep't 1992).

14. A summary of similar information was published in *The Blue Book: A Compilation of Campaign, Ethics, and Lobbying Reform Laws,* prepared by the Council on Government Ethics Laws, edited by Carla Bailey. Compare the 1996 total of 446,000 filers with the total filings anticipated in 1979 of 109,619! As observed in Slevin v. City of New York, 551 F. Supp. 917, the figure of 109,619 "greatly understates the total persons affected, since 13 jurisdictions did not respond [to that survey], since most filings cover more than one person . . . In addition to these state and local laws, the federal government's disclosure requirements are extensive, and apply to thousands of employees and their families." [fn 1] "Financial disclosure laws thereby potentially invade the privacy of millions of Americans as individuals and in their marital and family relations."

15. The Temporary State Commission on Local Government Ethics was created by chapter 813 of the Laws of 1987 and sunset December 31, 1992.

16. In Search of a Wise Law: Municipal Ethics Reform: A Report of the Temporary State Commission on Local Government Ethics and a Joint Proposal of the Temporary State Commission on Local Government Ethics and the Local Government Advisory Board, March 20, 1991.

17. In *Snider v. Shapp,* elected members of school districts challenged the constitutionality of the Public Officials Ethics Act, which proscribed certain conduct involving conflicts of interest and required candidates for public office, elected officials, and certain appointed officials to file financial disclosure statements.

18. Kan. Stat. Ann. §46–247.

Alabama – Kentucky

Who Must File Financial Disclosure?

	Ala.	Alaska	Ariz.	Calif.	Conn.	Del.	Fla.	Ga.	Ill.	Ind.	Iowa	Kans.	Ky.
Executive branch officers	Y	Y	Y	Y	Y	Y	Y	Y	Y	Y	Y	Y	Y
Executive branch employees	Y	N	N	Y	Y	Y	Y	Y	Y	Y	Y	Y	Y
Legislators	Y	Y	Y	Y	Y	Y	Y	Y	Y	Y	Y	Y	—
Legislative branch employees	Y	N	N	Y	N	N	Y	—	Y	N	Y	Y	—
Judges	Y	Y	Y	Y	N	Y	Y	—	Y	Y	N	N	—
Judicial branch employees	Y	N	N	Y	N	N	Y	—	Y	N	N	N	—
Municipal officers	Y	Y	Y	Y	N	N	Y	Y	Y	N	N	Y	—
Municipal employees	Y	N	N	Y	Y	N	Y	N	Y	N	N	Y	—
Do lower echelon employees file the same financial disclosure statement as upper echelon employees?	Y	Y	N (1)	N	N	N	N	N	Y	N	Y	Y	Y
Salary threshold Ala.—$50,000; Mass.—$36,720; Md.—$31,631; New York City—$64,200; N.C.—$30,000; N.Y.—$58,198	Y	N	N	N	N	N	N	N	N	N	N	N	—
Must individuals file based on job responsibilities?	Y	N	N	Y	Y	Y	Y	N	Y	Y	Y	Y	Y
Must individuals file based on job title?	Y	Y	N	—	Y	Y	—	Y	—	—	Y	Y	
If the individuals had responsibility for the negotiation, authorization, or approval of the following, would they have to file?													
• Contracts, leases, franchises, revocable consents, variances, permits, or licenses?	Y	N	N	Y	Y	—	Y	—	Y	Y	—	Y	Y
• Purchase, sale, rental, or lease of real property, goods, or services, or a contract therefor?	Y	N	N	Y	Y	—	Y	—	Y	Y	—	Y	Y
• The obtaining of grants of money or loans?	Y	N	N	Y	Y	—	Y	—	Y	N	—	Y	Y
• The adoption or repeal of any rule or regulation having the force and effect of law?	Y	N	N	Y	Y	—	—	—	Y	N	—	N	Y
Other duties: Ala.—investing public funds, Calif.—investing public funds, government decision makers; Conn.—government decision makers; Ill.—adjudicators; Iowa—expending public funds; Kans.—policy makers, some consultants		—	—				—	—		—			—

52

Alabama - Kentucky

	Ala.	Alaska	Ariz.	Calif.	Conn.	Del.	Fla.	Ga.	Ill.	Ind.	Iowa	Kans.	Ky.
Is there a process for seeking a waiver from the filing requirement?	N	N	N	Y	Y	N	N	N	Y	N	Y	N	N
Grounds	—	—	—	(2)	(3)	—	—	—	(4)	—	(5)	—	—
How many people under your agency's jurisdiction have to file financial disclosure statements?	25,000	2000	200	100,000	1500	300	39,165	6000	10,000	600	750	6000	1400

What Must Be Reported

	Ala.	Alaska	Ariz.	Calif.	Conn.	Del.	Fla.	Ga.	Ill.	Ind.	Iowa	Kans.	Ky.
Source, type, and amount of income received by filer?	Y	Y (6)	Y (6)	Y over $250	Y (6)	Y (6)	Y	N (7)	Y	Y (6) (8)	Y $1000	Y (6) $2000	Y (6)
• By filer's spouse?	Y	Y (6)	Y (9)	Y	Y (6)	N	N	N	Y	Y (6)	N	Y	Y (6)
• By filer's dependents?	Y	Y (6)	Y (9)	N	Y (6)	N	N	N	Y (9)	N	N	—	Y (6)
Source of gifts and their value received by filer?	Y	Y (6)	Y	Y	N	Y	Y	N	Y	Y	N	Y	Y (6)
• By filer's spouse?	Y	Y (6)	Y (9)	N	N	—	N	N	Y	Y	N	Y	—
• By filer's dependents?	Y	Y (6)	Y (9)	N	N	—	N	N	Y	Y	N	N	—
• Or reported only if over a certain dollar value?	—	Y over $100	$500+	$50	N	$250	$100	N	$50	Y	N	$500	Y
Source of anything received from a lobbyist by filer?	Y	Y	N	N	N	Y	N	N	N	Y	N	N	—
• By filer's spouse?	Y	Y	N	N	N	—	N	N	N	N	N	N	—
• By filer's dependents?	Y	Y	N	N	N	—	N	N	N	N	N	N	—
Type and value of property owned by filer?	Y	Y (6)	Y (9)	Y over $1000	Y (6)	Y	Y	Y (6)	Y	Y	N	Y (6) $5000	Y (6)

Key

(1) Elected officials only
(2) Legally recognized privilege
(3) "Impossibility"
(4) Undue hardship pertaining to spousal disclosure
(5) Forbidden duties not performed
(6) Not amount or value
(7) Only honoraria
(8) Different disclosure for judges and legislators
(9) If in household
(10) In limited circumstances
(11) Many
(12) Under current law
(13) Civil penalties after hearing
(14) Discipline
(15) Recommend action to governor
(16) Withhold salary until filed
(17) Criminal prosecution
(18) 90 days to amend without penalty
(19) Others audit
(20) Full audit
(21) Desk audit
(22) At random
(23) Public
(24) Lawyers
(25) Law enforcement agencies
(26) Other state agencies
(27) Political opponents
(28) Informs public
(29) Sources of outside income, debt owed
(30) More specific information re assets, debts and dollar categories
(31) Governor and gaming board only
(32) Local only
(33) Governor's appointees
(34) Over $1000
(35) Only legislators
(36) Over $5000
(37) Governor only
(38) 1 to 10 days—$50; 21 to 39 days—$200; over 30 days—$500
(39) Cross section
(40) Unknown
(41) Press
(42) A financial statement of assets, liabilities, and net worth; more information on spouses and children; possibly eliminate ranges of value and estimate within $500
(43) Amounts
(44) Candidates only
(45) Serious health problems, security, safety
(46) From public agencies
(47) Forfeiture of compensation/loss of authority
(48) Spouse and dependent information
(49) Debt; real and personal property disclosure
(50) Public information

Alabama – Kentucky

	Ala.	Alaska	Ariz.	Calif.	Conn.	Del.	Fla.	Ga.	Ill.	Ind.	Iowa	Kans.	Ky.
• By filer's spouse?	Y	Y (6)	Y (9)	Y	Y (6)	—	N	N	N	Y	N	Y (6)	Y (6)
• By filer's dependents?	Y	Y (6)	Y (9)	Y	Y (6)	—	N	N	Y	Y	N	N	Y (6)
Description and amount of payment received from the sale, lease, or rental of personal property by filer?	Y	N	N	Y 250+	Y 1000+	Y	Y	N	N	N	Y	Y	Y (6)
• By filer's spouse?	Y	N	—	Y	Y	—	N	N	N	N	N	Y	Y (6)
• By filer's dependents?	Y	N	—	N	Y	—	N	N	N	N	N	N	Y (6)
Identity of every business or entity in which the filer or a family member of the filer held securities valued over $1,000?	Y	Y	Y	Y	Y $5000+	Y $5000	Y	Y $20,000+	Y $1000	Y $10,000	N	Y $5000	Y $10,000
Listing of creditors owed in excess of $500 (other than for a credit card) of the filer?	Y	Y	Y +$1000	Y	Y $10,000	Y $1000	Y $1000	Y	Y	Y	N	N	Y
• By filer's spouse?	Y	Y	Y (9)	Y	Y	if joint	—	N	N	N	N	—	Y
• By filer's dependents?	Y	Y	Y (9)	N	Y	if joint	—	N	Y	N	N	—	Y
The amount of debt outstanding?	Y	Y (10)	N	Y	N	N	—	N	Y	N	N	—	—
The interest rate charged?	Y	Y (10)	N	Y	N	N	—	N	Y	N	N	—	—
Listing of position held by the filer as an officer of any political party or political organization?	Y	Y	N	N	N	N	—	N	N	N	N	Y	—
For how many years has financial disclosure reporting by state officers and employees been in effect?	21	21	—	21	18	13	22	(11)	28	22	2	22	4 (12)
Enforcement													
Does your agency have authority to penalize individuals who file after the date when the financial disclosure statements are due?	Y	Y	N	Y	Y	N	(13) (14)	Y	Y	Y	Y	Y	Y
If yes, what is the average penalty assessed?	$10/day	$100	—	$10/day	$500	—	—	$1000	(15)	$10/day	—	—	(16)
Does your agency have authority to penalize individuals who fail to file any statement?	Y	Y	N	Y	Y	N	—	Y	Y	Y	Y	Y	Y
If yes, what is the average penalty assessed?	(17)	(14) (17)	—	$2000	$2000	—	—	$1000	(15)	(17)	—	—	$2000
Does your agency have authority to penalize individuals who file a deficient statement?	Y (18)	Y	N	Y	Y	N	—	Y	Y	Y	Y	Y	Y
If yes, what is the average penalty assessed?	—	$150	—	$2000	$200	—	—	$1000	(15)	$10/day	—	—	—

Alabama - Kentucky

	Ala.	Alaska	Ariz.	Calif.	Conn.	Del.	Fla.	Ga.	Ill.	Ind.	Iowa	Kans.	Ky.
Are there any other enforcement measures that can be taken against late filing, false filing, or failure to file?	(14) (17)	N	(17)	(14) (17)	(14)	(17)	N	N	(14)	(14)	(17)	Y	(13)
Audits or investigations													
Does your agency audit all the financial disclosure statements received or a representative cross section?	Y (19)	Y (20)	N	Y (21)	Y (21)	Y (21)	N	Y (22)	Y (21)	Y (21)	N	Y (21)	(22)
Has information reported on financial disclosure statements lead to investigations of conflicts of interest?	Y	N	N	Y	Y	—	—	N	Y	N	N	Y	Y
If yes, please characterize the percentage that do.	10%	—	—	few	< 1%	—	—	—	few	1%	—	1%	1%
How many staff members devote some or all of their time to processing financial disclosure statements?	7	1	1	5	5	2	—	—	3	—	3	2	2
Public Information													
Are financial disclosure statements available for public inspection?	Y	Y	Y	Y	Y	Y	Y	Y	Y	Y	Y	Y	Y
If they are available for the public, do you make copies available?	Y	Y	Y	Y	Y	Y	—	Y	Y	N	Y	Y	Y
Who most often requests to view financial disclosure statements?	All	(23) (27)	(23)	(23)	(23) (25)	(23) (25)	—	(23)	(23) (25)	(23)	(23)	(23) (26)	(23) (25)
Policy Issues													
How valuable is the information reported on financial disclosure statements to uncovering conflicts of interest?	—	—	—	(28)	Very	Not very	—	Somewhat	Very	Not very	Not very	Somewhat	Not very

Key

(1) Elected officials only
(2) Legally recognized privilege
(3) "Impossibility"
(4) Undue hardship pertaining to spousal disclosure
(5) Forbidden duties not performed
(6) Not amount or value
(7) Only honoraria
(8) Different disclosure for judges and legislators
(9) If in household
(10) In limited circumstances
(11) Many
(12) Under current law
(13) Civil penalties after hearing
(14) Discipline
(15) Recommend action to governor
(16) Withhold salary until filed
(17) Criminal prosecution
(18) 90 days to amend without penalty
(19) Others audit
(20) Full audit
(21) Desk audit
(22) At random
(23) Public
(24) Lawyers

(25) Law enforcement agencies
(26) Other state agencies
(27) Political opponents
(28) Informs public
(29) Sources of outside income, debt owed
(30) More specific information re assets, debts and dollar categories
(31) Governor and gaming board only
(32) Local only
(33) Governor's appointees
(34) Over $1000
(35) Only legislators
(36) Over $5000
(37) Governor only

(38) 1 to 10 days—$50; 21 to 39 days—$200; over 30 days—$500
(39) Cross section
(40) Unknown
(41) Press
(42) A financial statement of assets, liabilities, and net worth; more information on spouses and children; possibly eliminate ranges of value and estimate within $500
(43) Amounts
(44) Candidates only
(45) Serious health problems, security, safety

(46) From public agencies
(47) Forfeiture of compensation/loss of authority
(48) Spouse and dependent information disclosure
(49) Debt: real and personal property
(50) Public information

Alabama - Kentucky

	Ala.	Alaska	Ariz.	Calif.	Conn.	Del.	Fla.	Ga.	Ill.	Ind.	Iowa	Kans.	Ky.
If different information were required to be reported, would the statements be more useful?	—	N	—	N	Y	—	—	Y	N	N	Y	N	Y
What information would you think necessary?	—	—	—	—	Value	—	—	(29)	—	—	(30)	—	—
Would you agree that the best attribute of financial disclosure is its deterrent value? A—Strongly agree; B—Agree; C—Strongly disagree	—	A	C	B	B	—	A	(28)	C (28)	B	B	B	A

Louisiana - North Dakota

Who Must File Financial Disclosure?

	La.	Maine	Md.	Mass.	Mich.	Minn.	Nev.	N.H.	N.J.	N.Y.	N.Y. City	N.C.	N. Dak.
Executive branch officers	Y (31)	Y	Y	Y	Y	Y	Y	Y	Y	Y	Y	Y	
Executive branch employees	Y (31)	Y	Y	Y	Y	Y	Y	N	Y	Y	Y	Y	
Legislators	N	Y	Y	Y	—	Y	Y	Y	—	Y	Y	Y	
Legislative branch employees	N	N	Y	Y	—	Y	Y	N	—	Y	Y	Y	
Judges	N	N	Y	Y	—	N	Y	N	Y	Y	N	N	
Judicial branch employees	N	N	N	Y	Y	N	Y	N	Y	Y	N	N	
Municipal officers	N	N	N	N	Y	Y	Y	N	Y	Y	Y	Y	
Municipal employees	N	N	N	N	Y	Y	Y	N	Y	Y	Y	Y	
Do lower echelon employees file the same financial disclosure statement as upper echelon employees?	—	N	Y	Y	—	N	Y	—	N	Y	Y	Y	
Salary threshold Ala.—$50,000; Mass.—$36,720; Md.—$31,631; New York City—$64,200; N.C.—$30,000; N.Y.—$58,198	N	N	N	Y	N	N	N	N	N	Y	Y	Y	
Must individuals file based on job responsibilities?	N	Y	—	N	Y	Y (32)	N	N	N	Y	Y	N	N
Must individuals file based on job title?	Y	—	Y	Y	Y	Y	Y	Y	Y	Y	Y	Y	Y (33)
If the individuals had responsibility for the negotiation, authorization, or approval of the following, would they have to file?													
• Contracts, leases, franchises, revocable consents, variances, permits, or licenses?	N	N	Y	Y	Y	Y	—	—	—	Y	Y	N	
• Purchase, sale, rental, or lease of real property, goods, or services, or a contract therefor?	N	N	—	N	Y	—	—	—	—	Y	Y	N	

Louisiana - North Dakota

	La.	Maine	Md.	Mass.	Mich.	Minn.	Nev.	N.H.	N.J.	N.Y.	N.Y. City	N.C.	N. Dak.
• The obtaining of grants of money or loans?	N	N	—	N	Y	—	—	—	—	Y	Y	N	N
• The adoption or repeal or any rule or regulation having the force and effect of law?	N	N	—	N	Y	—	—	—	—	Y	Y	N	N
Other duties:	—	—	—	—	—	—	—	—	—	—	—	—	—
Is there a process for seeking a waiver from the filing requirement?	N	N	Y	N	N	N	N	N	N	Y	Y	N	N
Grounds	—	—	Bds only	—	—	—	—	—	—	(4) (5)	(4)	—	—
How many people under your agency's jurisdiction have to file financial disclosure statements?	10	186	9000	4500	—	3410	6000	424	2000	17,000	12,000	944	2500
What Must Be Reported													
Source, type, and amount of income received by filer?	Y	Y	N	Y	N	Y (6)	Y (6)	Y (6)	Y	Y (34)	Y	Y	Y (6)
• By filer's spouse?	Y	Y	—	N	N	N	Y (9)	N	Y	Y (34)	Y	N	Y (6)
• By filer's dependents?	Y	Y	—	N	N	N	Y (9)	N	Y (6)	N	Y	N	N
Source of gifts and their value received by filer?	N	Y	—	Y	N	N	Y	Y (1)	Y	Y (34)	Y	Y	N
• By filer's spouse?	N	N	—	N	N	N	N	N	Y	Y (34)	Y	N	N
• By filer's dependents?	N	N	—	N	N	N	N	N	Y	Y (34)	Y	N	N
• Or reported only if over a certain dollar value?	—	$300	$25	N	N	N	$200	N	$1000	$1000	Y	$50	N
Source of anything received from a lobbyist by filer?	N	Y	Y	Y	N	N	N	Y (35)	N	N	Y	N	N

Key

(1) Elected officials only
(2) Legally recognized privilege
(3) "Impossibility"
(4) Undue hardship pertaining to spousal disclosure
(5) Forbidden duties not performed
(6) Not amount or value
(7) Only honoraria
(8) Different disclosure for judges and legislators
(9) If in household
(10) In limited circumstances
(11) Many
(12) Under current law
(13) Civil penalties after hearing
(14) Discipline
(15) Recommend action to governor
(16) Withhold salary until filed
(17) Criminal prosecution
(18) 90 days to amend without penalty
(19) Others audit
(20) Full audit
(21) Desk audit
(22) At random
(23) Public
(24) Lawyers
(25) Law enforcement agencies
(26) Other state agencies
(27) Political opponents
(28) Informs public
(29) Sources of outside income, debt owed
(30) More specific information re assets, debts and dollar categories
(31) Governor and gaming board only
(32) Local only
(33) Governor's appointees
(34) Over $1000
(35) Only legislators
(36) Over $5000
(37) Governor only
(38) 1 to 10 days—$50; 21 to 39 days—$200; over 30 days—$500
(39) Cross section
(40) Unknown
(41) Press
(42) A financial statement of assets, liabilities, and net worth; more information on spouses and children; possibly eliminate ranges of value and estimate within $500
(43) Amounts
(44) Candidates only
(45) Serious health problems, security, safety
(46) From public agencies
(47) Forfeiture of compensation/loss of authority
(48) Spouse and dependent information
(49) Debt; real and personal property disclosure
(50) Public information

Louisiana - North Dakota

	La.	Maine	Md.	Mass.	Mich.	Minn.	Nev.	N.H.	N.J.	N.Y.	N.Y. City	N.C.	N. Dak.
• By filer's spouse?	N	N	N	Y	N	N	N	N	N	N	Y	N	N
• By filer's dependents?	N	N	N	Y	N	N	N	N	N	N	Y	N	N
Type and value of property owned by filer?	Y	N	Y	Y	N	Y (6)	Y (6)	N	Y	Y (34)	Y	Y (36)	Y (6)
• By filer's spouse?	Y	N	N	Y	N	N	Y (6)	—	Y	Y (34)	Y	N	Y (6)
• By filer's dependents?	Y	N	N	Y	N	N	Y (6)	—	Y (6)	N	N	N	N
Description and amount of payment received from the sale, lease, or rental of personal property by filer?	Y	N	Y	Y	N	N	N	N	N	Y (34)	Y	Y $5000	Y (6)
• By filer's spouse?	Y	N	N	N	N	N	N	—	Y	Y (34)	Y	N	Y (6)
• By filer's dependents?	Y	N	N	N	N	N	N	—	Y	N	N	N	N
Identity of every business or entity in which the filer or a family member of the filer held securities valued over $1,000?	Y	N	Y	Y	N	Y $2500	N	N	Y	Y	Y	Y $10,000	N
Listing of creditors owed in excess of $500 (other than for a credit card) of the filer?	Y	N	Y	Y	N	N	N	N	Y	Y $5000	Y $5000	Y $5000	N
• By filer's spouse?	Y	N	—	Y	N	N	N	—	Y	Y $5000	Y $5000	N	N
• By filer's dependents?	Y	N	Y	Y	N	N	N	—	Y	N	N	N	N
The amount of debt outstanding?	Y	N	Y	Y	N	N	N	—	N	Y	Y	N	N
The interest rate charged?	N	N	Y	N	N	N	N	—	N	N	N	N	N
Listing of position held by the filer as an officer of any political party or political organization?	N	N	Y	Y	N	N	N	—	N	Y	Y	N	N
For how many years has financial disclosure reporting by state officers and employees been in effect?	16 (37)	10	—	18	1	22	11	2	20	8	18	19	15
Enforcement													
Does your agency have authority to penalize individuals who file after the date when the financial disclosure statements are due?	N	N	Y	Y	N	Y	N	N	N	N	Y	N	N
If yes, what is the average penalty assessed?	—	—	—	(38)	—	$5 to $100	—	—	—	—	$100 to $1000	—	—
Does your agency have authority to penalize individuals who fail to file any statement?	N	N	Y	Y	Y	Y	Y	N	N	Y	Y	N	N

Louisiana – North Dakota

	La.	Maine	Md.	Mass.	Mich.	Minn.	Nev.	N.H.	N.J.	N.Y.	N.Y. City	N.C.	N. Dak.
If yes, what is the average penalty assessed?	—	$100 (17)	—	$500	(14)	$5 to $100	(17)	—	—	$1000 to $10,000	$100 to $1000	—	—
Does your agency have authority to penalize individuals who file a deficient statement?	N	N	Y	Y	Y	N	Y	N	N	Y	Y	N	N
If yes, what is the average penalty assessed?	—	(17)	—	(38)	(14)	—	(17)	—	—	—	—	—	—
Are there any other enforcement measures that can be taken against late filing, false filing, or failure to file?	—	(17)	(14)	N	—	(17)	(17)	—	(14)	(14) (17)	(14) (17)	N	(17)
Audits or Investigations													
Does your agency audit all the financial disclosure statements received or a representative cross section?	N	—	(39)	Y	—	N	Y (20)	—	All	Y (21)	Y (22)	N	N
Has information reported on financial disclosure statements lead to investigations of conflicts of interest?	N	N	Y	Y	N	Y	Y	N	Y	Y	Y	N	—
If yes, please characterize the percentage that do.	—	—	< 5%	—	(40)	≤ 1%	5%	—	5%	1%	small	< 1%	—
How many staff members devote some or all of their time to processing financial disclosure statements?	—	(40)	6	4	(40)	4	2	2	7	8	10	1	1
Public Information													
Are financial disclosure statements available for public inspection?	Y	Y	Y	Y	Y	Y	Y	Y	Y	Y	Y	Y	Y
If they are available for the public, do you make copies available?	Y	Y	Y	Y	Y	Y	Y	Y	Y	N	N	Y	Y

Key

(1) Elected officials only
(2) Legally recognized privilege
(3) "Impossibility"
(4) Undue hardship pertaining to spousal disclosure
(5) Forbidden duties not performed
(6) Not amount or value
(7) Only honoraria
(8) Different disclosure for judges and legislators
(9) If in household
(10) In limited circumstances
(11) Many
(12) Under current law
(13) Civil penalties after hearing
(14) Discipline
(15) Recommend action to governor
(16) Withhold salary until filed
(17) Criminal prosecution
(18) 90 days to amend without penalty
(19) Others audit
(20) Full audit
(21) Desk audit
(22) At random
(23) Public
(24) Lawyers
(25) Law enforcement agencies
(26) Other state agencies
(27) Political opponents
(28) Informs public
(29) Sources of outside income, debt owed
(30) More specific information re assets, debts and dollar categories
(31) Governor and gaming board only
(32) Local only
(33) Governor's appointees
(34) Over $1000
(35) Only legislators
(36) Over $5000
(37) Governor only
(38) 1 to 10 days—$50; 21 to 39 days—$200; over 30 days—$500
(39) Cross section
(40) Unknown
(41) Press
(42) A financial statement of assets, liabilities, and net worth; more information on spouses and children; possibly eliminate ranges of value and estimate within $500
(43) Amounts
(44) Candidates only
(45) Serious health problems, security, safety
(46) From public agencies
(47) Forefeiture of compensation/loss of authority
(48) Spouse and dependent information
(49) Debt; real and personal property disclosure
(50) Public information

Louisiana - North Dakota

	La.	Maine	Md.	Mass.	Mich.	Minn.	Nev.	N.H.	N.J.	N.Y.	N.Y. City	N.C.	N. Dak.
Who most often requests to view financial disclosure statements?	(41)	(41)	(41)	(41)	(40)	(26)(27)(40)	(25)(26)(27)(41)	(41)	(25)(41)	(25)(41)	(23)(25)(41)	(41)	(23)(27)(41)

Policy Issues

	La.	Maine	Md.	Mass.	Mich.	Minn.	Nev.	N.H.	N.J.	N.Y.	N.Y. City	N.C.	N. Dak.
How valuable is the information reported on financial disclosure statements to uncovering conflicts of interest?	—	Not very	Very	—	(40)	—	Very		Somewhat	Not very	Very	Not very	Not very
If different information were required to be reported, would the statements be more useful?	—	Y	—	—	(40)	—	Y	N	N	(40)	Y (42)	—	Y (43)
What information would you think necessary?		(29)	—	—	(40)	—	Donor info	—	—	—	—	—	
Would you agree that the best attribute of financial disclosure is its deterrent value? A—Strongly agree; B—Agree; C—Strongly disagree	B	B	A	B	(40)	—	B	B	B	B	B	B	C

Ohio - Wyoming

Who Must File Financial Disclosure?

	Ohio	Okla.	Oreg.	Pa.	R.I.	S.C.	S.D.	Utah	Vt.	Va.	W.V.	Wis.	Wyo.
Executive branch officers	Y	Y	Y	Y	Y	Y	Y	N (44)	N (44)	Y	Y	Y	N (44)
Executive branch employees	Y	Y	Y	Y	N	Y	N	N	N	Y	Y	Y	N
Legislators	Y	Y	Y	Y	Y	Y	Y	N	N	Y	Y	Y	N
Legislative branch employees	Y	Y	Y	Y	N	Y	N	N	N	Y	Y	Y	N
Judges	Y	Y	Y	Y	Y	N	Y	N	N	Y	Y	Y	N
Judicial branch employees	Y	Y	Y	Y	N	N	N	N	N	Y	Y	Y	N
Municipal officers	Y	N	Y	Y	Y	Y	Y	N	N	Y	N	Y	N
Municipal employees	N	N	Y	Y	N	Y	Y	N	N	Y	N	N	N
Do lower echelon employees file the same financial disclosure statement as upper echelon employees?	N	Y	Y	N	N	Y	—	N	N	Y	Y	N	N
Salary threshold Ala.—$50,000; Mass.—$36,720; Md.—$31,631; New York City—$64,200; N.C.—$30,000; N.Y.—$58,198	N	N	N	N	N	N	N	N	N	N	N	N	N
Must individuals file based on job responsibilities?	N	Y	Y	Y	N	Y	N	N	Y	Y	N	N	N

Ohio - Wyoming

	Ohio	Okla.	Oreg.	Pa.	R.I.	S.C.	S.D.	Utah	Vt.	Va.	W.V.	Wis.	Wyo.
Must individuals file based on job title?	Y	—	—	—	—	—	—	—	—	—	—	—	
If the individuals had responsibility for the negotiation, authorization, or approval of the following, would they have to file?													
• Contracts, leases, franchises, revocable consents, variances, permits, or licenses?	N	Y	N	Y	N	—	N	N	N	Y	N	—	N
• Purchase, sale, rental, or lease of real property, goods, or services, or a contract therefor?	N	Y	N	Y	N	—	N	N	N	Y	N	—	N
• The obtaining of grants of money or loans?	N	Y	N	Y	N	—	N	N	N	Y	N	—	N
• The adoption or repeal or any rule or regulation having the force and effect of law?	N	Y	N	Y	N	—	N	N	N	Y	N	—	N
Other duties:	—	—	—	—	—	—	—	—	—	—	—	—	—
Is there a process for seeking a waiver from the filing requirement?	Y	N	N	N	N	N	N	N	N	N	Y	Y	N
Grounds	(45)	—	—	—	—	—	—	—	—	—	Blind trust	—	—
How many people under your agency's jurisdiction have to file financial disclosure statements?	10,200	5000	—	150,000	5500	10,000	150	0	0	20,000	2500	2000	0
What Must Be Reported													
Source, type, and amount of income received by filer?	Y	Y (6)	—	Y (6)	Y (6)	Y (46)	Y (6)	N	N	Y	Y (6)	Y (6)	N
• By filer's spouse?	N	N	—	N	Y (6)	Y	Y (6)	N	N	Y	Y (6)	Y (6)	N
• By filer's dependents?	N	N	—	N	N	Y	Y (6)	N	N	Y	N	Y (6)	N

Key

(1) Elected officials only
(2) Legally recognized privilege
(3) "Impossibility"
(4) Undue hardship pertaining to spousal disclosure
(5) Forbidden duties not performed
(6) Not amount or value
(7) Only honoraria
(8) Different disclosure for judges and legislators
(9) If in household
(10) In limited circumstances
(11) Many
(12) Under current law
(13) Civil penalties after hearing
(14) Discipline
(15) Recommend action to governor
(16) Withhold salary until filed
(17) Criminal prosecution
(18) 90 days to amend without penalty
(19) Others audit
(20) Full audit
(21) Desk audit
(22) At random
(23) Public
(24) Lawyers
(25) Law enforcement agencies
(26) Other state agencies
(27) Political opponents
(28) Informs public
(29) Sources of outside income, debt owed
(30) More specific information re assets, debts and dollar categories
(31) Governor and gaming board only
(32) Local only
(33) Governor's appointees
(34) Over $1000
(35) Only legislators
(36) Over $5000
(37) Governor only
(38) 1 to 10 days—$50; 21 to 39 days—$200; over 30 days—$500
(39) Cross section
(40) Unknown
(41) Press
(42) A financial statement of assets, liabilities, and net worth; more information on spouses and children; possibly eliminate ranges of value and estimate within $500
(43) Amounts
(44) Candidates only
(45) Serious health problems, security, safety
(46) From public agencies
(47) Forfeiture of compensation/loss of authority
(48) Spouse and dependent information
(49) Debt; real and personal property disclosure
(50) Public information

Ohio - Wyoming

	Ohio	Okla.	Oreg.	Pa.	R.I.	S.C.	S.D.	Utah	Vt.	Va.	W.V.	Wis.	Wyo.
Source of gifts and their value received by filer?	Y	N	—	Y	Y	Y	N	N	N	Y		Y	N
• By filer's spouse?	N	N	—	N	Y	Y	N	N	N	—	Y	Y	N
• By filer's dependents?	N	N	—	N	Y	Y	N	N	N	—	N	Y	N
• Or reported only if over a certain dollar value?	$75	N	—	$200	Y	—	N	N	N	Y	$100	Y	N
Source of anything received from a lobbyist by filer?	Y	N	—	N	N	N	N	N	N	N	N	N	N
• By filer's spouse?	N	N	—	N	N	N	N	N	N	N	N	N	N
• By filer's dependents?	N	N	—	N	N	N	N	N	N	N	N	N	N
Type and value of property owned by filer?	Y	Y (6)	—	N	Y	Y	N	N	N	Y	N	Y	N
• By filer's spouse?	N	N	—	N	Y	Y	N	N	N	Y	N	Y	N
• By filer's dependents?	N	N	—	N	Y	Y	N	N	N	Y	N	Y	N
Description and amount of payment received from the sale, lease, or rental of personal property by filer?	N	N	—	N	Y (6)	Y	N	N	N	Y	N	Y	N
• By filer's spouse?	N	N	—	N	Y (6)	Y	N	N	N	Y	N	Y	N
• By filer's dependents?	N	N	—	N	Y (6)	Y	N	N	N	Y	N	Y	N
Identity of every business or entity in which the filer or a family member of the filer held securities valued over $1,000?	Y	Y $5000	Y	Y 5% FMV	Y	Y $10,000	N	N	N	Y	N	Y $5000	N
Listing of creditors owed in excess of $500 (other than for a credit card) of the filer?	Y	N	N	Y $5000	Y	Y (10)	N	N	N	Y	N	N	N
• By filer's spouse?	N	N	N	N	Y	Y	N	N	N	Y	N	N	N
• By filer's dependents?	N	N	N	N	Y	Y	N	N	N	Y	N	N	N
The amount of debt outstanding?	N	N	N	N	N	Y	N	N	N	N	N	Y	N
The interest rate charged?	N	N	N	Y	N	Y	N	N	N	N	N	N	N
Listing of position held by the filer as an officer of any political party or political organization?	N	N	N	N	Y	N	N	N	N	N	N	N	N
For how many years has financial disclosure reporting by state officers and employees been in effect?	23	—	21	17	18	20	—	0	0	2	7	20	0

Ohio - Wyoming

Enforcement

	Ohio	Okla.	Oreg.	Pa.	R.I.	S.C.	S.D.	Utah	Vt.	Va.	W.V.	Wis.	Wyo.
Does your agency have authority to penalize individuals who file after the date when the financial disclosure statements are due?	Y	Y	Y	Y	Y	Y	N	N	N	N	Y	Y	N
If yes, what is the average penalty assessed?	$100	$100/day	$5/day	$25/day	$50	$100	—	—	—	—	Y	$25	—
Does your agency have authority to penalize individuals who fail to file any statement?	Y	Y	Y	Y	Y	Y	N	N	N	N	Y	Y	N
If yes, what is the average penalty assessed?	$250	$2000 to $50,000	$500 to $1000	$25/day	$100	$100 to $600	—	—	—	—	—	—	—
Does your agency have authority to penalize individuals who file a deficient statement?	Y	Y	Y	Y	Y	Y	N	N	N	N	Y	Y	N
If yes, what is the average penalty assessed?	(17)	(17)	0	$25/day	$75	—	—	—	—	—	—	—	—
Are there any other enforcement measures that can be taken against late filing, false filing, or failure to file?	N	N	(47)	Y (17)	N	—	Y (17)	N	N	Y (17)	—	N	—

Audits or Investigations

	Ohio	Okla.	Oreg.	Pa.	R.I.	S.C.	S.D.	Utah	Vt.	Va.	W.V.	Wis.	Wyo.
Does your agency audit all the financial disclosure statements received or a representative cross section?	Y (26) (21)	Y (39)	Y (22)	—	N	Y (39)	N	N	N	N	N	N	N
Has information reported on financial disclosure statements lead to investigations of conflicts of interest?	Y	N	N	Y	Y	Y	(40)	N	N	N	N	N	N
If yes, please characterize the percentage that do.	≤1%	—	—	—	<5%	≤1%	(40)	N	N	—	—	—	N

Key

(1) Elected officials only
(2) Legally recognized privilege
(3) "Impossibility"
(4) Undue hardship pertaining to spousal disclosure
(5) Forbidden duties not performed
(6) Not amount or value
(7) Only honoraria
(8) Different disclosure for judges and legislators
(9) If in household
(10) In limited circumstances

(11) Many
(12) Under current law
(13) Civil penalties after hearing
(14) Discipline
(15) Recommend action to governor
(16) Withhold salary until filed
(17) Criminal prosecution
(18) 90 days to amend without penalty
(19) Forbidden duties not performed
(20) Only honoraria
(21) Full audit
(22) Desk audit
(23) At random
(24) In limited circumstances

(25) Law enforcement agencies
(26) Other state agencies
(27) Political opponents
(28) Informs public
(29) Sources of outside income, debt owed
(30) More specific information re assets, debts and dollar categories
(31) Governor and gaming board only
(32) Local only
(33) Governor's appointees
(34) Over $1000
(35) Only legislators
(36) Over $5000
(37) Governor only

(38) 1 to 10 days—$50; 21 to 39 days—$200; over 30 days—$500
(39) Cross section
(40) Unknown
(41) Press
(42) A financial statement of assets, liabilities, and net worth; more information on spouses and children; possibly eliminate ranges of value and estimate within $500
(43) Amounts
(44) Candidates only
(45) Serious health problems, security, safety

(46) From public agencies
(47) Forfeiture of compensation/loss of authority
(48) Spouse and dependent information
(49) Debt; real and personal property disclosure
(50) Public information

Ohio - Wyoming

	Ohio	Okla.	Oreg.	Pa.	R.I.	S.C.	S.D.	Utah	Vt.	Va.	W.V.	Wis.	Wyo.
How many staff members devote some or all of their time to processing financial disclosure statements?	5	5	2	10	1	4	1	0	0	2	1	1.5	0

Public Information

	Ohio	Okla.	Oreg.	Pa.	R.I.	S.C.	S.D.	Utah	Vt.	Va.	W.V.	Wis.	Wyo.
Are financial disclosure statements available for public inspection?	Y	Y	Y	Y	Y	Y	Y	—	—	Y	Y	Y	—
If they are available for the public, do you make copies available?	Y	Y	Y	Y	Y	Y	Y	—	—	Y	Y	Y	—
Who most often requests to view financial disclosure statements?	(23) (25) (41)	(23) (24) (25) (26) (41)	(27) (41)	(23) (25) (27) (41)	(25) (41)	(27) (41)	(26)	—	—	(23) (41)	(41)	(27) (41)	—

Policy Issues

	Ohio	Okla.	Oreg.	Pa.	R.I.	S.C.	S.D.	Utah	Vt.	Va.	W.V.	Wis.	Wyo.
How valuable is the information reported on financial disclosure statements to uncovering conflicts of interest?	Somewhat	Not very	Very little	Not very	Not very	Not very	(20)	—	—	Very	It isn't	—	—
If different information were required to be reported, would the statements be more useful?	N	Y	Y	—	Y	Y	—	—	—	N	—	N	—
What information would you think necessary?	—	(48) (49)	(30)	—	(30)	(30) (49)	—	—	—	—	—	—	—
Would you agree that the best attribute of financial disclosure is its deterrent value? A—Strongly agree; B—Agree; C—Strongly disagree	B	A	B	C (50)	C	B	—	—	—	B	—	A	—

Key

(1) Elected officials only
(2) Legally recognized privilege
(3) "Impossibility"
(4) Undue hardship pertaining to spousal disclosure
(5) Forbidden duties not performed
(6) Not amount or value
(7) Only honoraria
(8) Different disclosure for judges and legislators
(9) If in household
(10) In limited circumstances
(11) Many
(12) Under current law
(13) Civil penalties after hearing
(14) Discipline
(15) Recommend action to governor
(16) Withhold salary until filed
(17) Criminal prosecution
(18) 90 days to amend without penalty
(19) Others audit
(20) Full audit
(21) Desk audit
(22) At random
(23) Public
(24) Lawyers
(25) Law enforcement agencies
(26) Other state agencies
(27) Political opponents
(28) Informs public
(29) Sources of outside income, debt owed
(30) More specific information re assets, debts and dollar categories
(31) Governor and gaming board only
(32) Local only
(33) Governor's appointees
(34) Over $1000
(35) Only legislators
(36) Over $5000
(37) Governor only
(38) 1 to 10 days—$50; 21 to 39 days—$200; over 30 days—$500
(39) Cross section
(40) Unknown
(41) Press
(42) A financial statement of assets, liabilities, and net worth; more information on spouses and children; possibly eliminate ranges of value and estimate within $500
(43) Amounts
(44) Candidates only
(45) Serious health problems, security, safety
(46) From public agencies
(47) Forfeiture of compensation/loss of authority
(48) Spouse and dependent information
(49) Debt; real and personal property disclosure
(50) Public information

EXCERPT*

A Model Law for Campaign Finance, Ethics & Lobbying Regulation

§226 Personal Financial Disclosure

§226.01 Exceptions to Reporting Requirements

This section does not require the disclosure of financial information concerning the following:

(1) A spouse legally separated from the public official or public employee.

(2) A former spouse.

(3) A gift from a family member.

(4) A campaign contribution that is permitted and reported under [the Campaign Finance Act], if required.

§226.02 Individuals Required to File

The following individuals shall file a statement of financial interests with the agency:

(1) A public official or public employee.

(2) An individual nominated to become a public official or public employee.

(3) An individual who is a candidate to become a public official.

(4) A public member.

(5) A consultant.

Comment:

The requirement that certain classes of individuals file a statement of financial interest, identifying the official or employee's personal financial interests and that of family members, reminds these people both of what financial interests are actually held, and of the need to avoid affecting them through a personal action or inaction. Violations are also

---

*This excerpt from "A Model Law for Campaign Finance, Ethics & Lobbying Regulation" is used with the permission of the publisher, the Council on Governmental Ethics Law © 1995. For additional copies, contact COGEL, c/o Center for Governmental Studies, 10951 West Pico Boulevard, #206, Los Angeles, CA 90064.

deterred by the knowledge that a filer's financial interests have been made a matter of public record, making it easier to detect a violation. The preferred practice in states of late has been to move toward classes of individuals as a determinant of who should be required to file, rather than relying upon often misleading salary schedules as the determinant.

§226.04 Deadline for Filing Statements

The statement of financial interest must be filed for the preceding year no later than April 30 of each year, complete through December 31 of the preceding year, except:

(1) In the case of an individual nominated to be a public official, public member, or public employee, no later than 21 (twenty-one) days after the nomination.

(2) In the case of a candidate to become a public official, at the time of filing for the public office.

(3) In the case of a public employee employed after January 1, the later of April 30 or 21 days after employment.

Comment:
The April 30 deadline for filing for the preceding year may appear to be a long deadline, but was chosen to allow an individual to receive and evaluate all of the tax-related materials that he or she might need to fully complete the statement of economic interests, and to review his or her federal and state income tax returns for items that might otherwise have been overlooked on the disclosure form.

§226.06 Filing Entity for Consultant Statements

A consultant shall file a statement of economic interests no later than twenty-one (21) days after entering into a contractual relationship with the state or a political subdivision if the consultant, or a member of the household of the consultant, has an economic interest in an entity:

(1) whose bid was evaluated by the consultant and who was subsequently awarded the contract by the state or the political subdivision that contracted with the consultant; or

(2) who was awarded a contract by the consultant.

§226.08 Amounts to Be Reported

(1) Where an amount is reported, a filer must report information in the following category amounts unless otherwise indicated:
 (A) $1,000—$9,999
 (B) $10,000—$24,999
 (C) $25,000—$49,999
 (D) $50,000—$99,999

(E) $100,000—$149,999
(F) $150,000—$249,999
(G) $250,000—$499,999
(H) $500,000—$999,999
(I) $1,000,000 and above.

Comment:

This section requires identification of specific amounts and interests. An alternative, minority view expressed is that the value of a statement of financial interests is found in the identification of financial interests, not identification of a person's wealth or lack of wealth. In this view, a person ought not to have personal financial interests in a business or other entity that the official or employee affects by official action or inaction, and the added information that the investment was valued at between, e.g., $10,000 and $24,999, rather than a greater amount, does not exonerate a public official or public employee, nor make a conflict less noteworthy.

In this view, the value of an investment (or income or indebtedness) is not helpful to identification of conflicting interests and is a deterrent to an individual's candid completion of a statement of financial interests. This alternative recommends that a public official or public employee merely identify those entities in which the official or employees, or member of their families, have invested more than a specified sum (e.g., $5,000) or from which the family derived more than a specified amount of gross income (e.g., $500) during the reporting period.

§226.10 Agency Handling of Disclosure Statements

(1) The Agency must grant a reasonable extension of time for filing a statement of financial interests. The extension may not exceed thirty (30) days, except in cases of illness or incapacitation.

(2) A statement of financial interests becomes a public record available for copying when received by the Agency. A statement may be reviewed and copied at the office of the Agency during ordinary business hours.

(3) A statement of financial interests must be retained by the Agency for a period of five (5) years after filing in a form, including microfilming, that will facilitate document retention, except that:

(A) Upon the expiration of three (3) years after an individual ceases to be a public official, the agency shall, unless the former public official otherwise requests, destroy any statements of financial interests or copies of such statements filed by the former public official and any copies in the possession of the Agency.

(B) Upon the expiration of three years after any election at which a candidate for election as a public official was not elected, or a nominee for public office or public employee is not confirmed in the position, the Agency shall destroy any statements of financial interest or copies of such statements filed by him or her as a candidate,

68   CONSIDERING ETHICS AT THE LOCAL GOVERNMENT LEVEL

(i) unless the individual is otherwise required to file a statement; or

(ii) unless the individual otherwise requests.

Comment:

There is some sentiment for retention of disclosure statements by the Agency for an indefinite period of time.

§226.12 Information Required

(1) A statement of financial interests must contain full and complete information concerning the following:

(A)   The name, business or governmental address, and work place telephone number of the filer.

(B)   The source, type, and amount or value of income received from a governmental entity by the filer and the filer's spouse and dependents.

(C)   The source, type, and amount of income in cash or in-kind received by the filer and the filer's spouse, and dependents.

(D)   The source, payee, type, date, and exact amount of gifts, including food, lodging, or entertainment:

(i) received by a filer and filer's spouse and dependents; and

(ii) in excess of fifty dollars ($50) in a calendar year.

(E)   The source, payee, type, date, and exact amount of anything of value received from a lobbyist or lobbyist's principal, including a notation of the word "lobbying" to identify gifts received by the filer, or filer's spouse and dependents from a person engaged in lobbying activities or any lobbyist organization.

Comment:

This provision does not sanction receipt by an official or employee of anything of value from a lobbyist or a lobbyist's principal that is otherwise prohibited under the Lobby Regulation Act.

(F) (i) The description (commercial, residential, or rural), value, and location of all real property owned during the calendar year by a public official, public employee, or consultant, and the official's or employee's immediate family members, and the same information for options to purchase such real property;

(ii) the amount received from the sale, lease or rental of real property; the name of the person the payment was received from; and

(iii) an identification of all commercial tenants, lobbyists, and lobbyist's principals (but not individuals who are not lobbyists or lobbyist's principals) from which income of [$1,000 or more] including rent or purchase money was derived during the reporting period.

If the sale, lease, or rental of real property involves a state, county, or municipal instrumentality of government, a copy of the contract, lease, or rental agreement must be attached to the statement of financial interests.

(G) the description, location, and amount of payment received from the sale, lease, or rental of personal property during the preceding calendar year by a public official, or public employee, and the official's or employee's immediate family members, and an identification of all lobbyists and lobbyists' principals from which income of [$250 or more] was derived during the reporting period.

If the sale, lease, or rental of personal property involves a state, county, or municipal instrumentality of government, a copy of the contract, lease, or rental agreement must be attached to the statement of financial interests.

(H) the identity of every business or entity in which the public official or public employee, or a family member of the public official or public employee held securities valued at [should range from $1,000 to $5,000] or more during the reporting period.

(I) A listing by name and address of:

(i) each creditor to whom the public official, public employee, or consultant, and the official or employee or consultant's immediate family members owed a debt in excess of five hundred dollars [$500] at any time during the calendar year, other than for a credit card or retail installment contract, and the original amount of the debt and amount outstanding; and

(ii) the rate of interest charged the public official, public employee, or consultant, and the official or employee or consultant's immediate family members.

If a discharge of the debt has been made, the date of the transaction must be shown.

(J) The amount and listing by name and address of all clients represented by the public official, public employee, or consultant, and the official's or employee's immediate family members before a state, county, or municipal regulatory Agency for a fee, reward, gift, or other compensation in excess of [$250] during the preceding calendar year.

Comment:

The disclosure of names of clients by attorneys as a requirement of governmental financial disclosure laws has been upheld in some states, including California. At least one other state, Wisconsin, permits such disclosure under a rule of the state's supreme court.

(K) Every officership, directorship, trustee, or other fiduciary relationship held in a business during the disclosure period, the term of office, and the annual compensation.

(L) The amount and identity of every creditor interest in an insolvent business held during the disclosure period having a value of five hundred dollars ($500) or more.

(M) The amount of every loan made to someone by the public official or public employee and their immediate family members in an amount of five hundred dollars ($500) or more, the original amount of the loan and amount outstanding, rate of interest, payment schedule, and the name and address of the person to whom the loan was made.

(N) State professional or occupational permits or licenses held.

(O) The name of a lobbyist who is:

(i) an immediate family member of the public official or employee;

(ii) a partner of the public official or employee of an immediate family member;

(iii) an officer or director of the public official or public employee's employer, or employer of the public official or public employee or an immediate family member; or

(iv) a business associate of a public official or public employee or member of the public official's or public employee's immediate family.

(2) The information shall be filed on a form prescribed by the Agency.

CHAPTER ❦ 5

The Pitfalls and Pratfalls of Regulating Honoraria, Royalties, and Travel Reimbursements

Thea Hoeth

This chapter identifies many of the issues that arise in relation to the acceptance of honoraria, royalties, and travel reimbursements. It illustrates how some jurisdictions deal with these topics, offers practical insights into definitions, and highlights key considerations government lawyers need to raise with their clients.

"What *Are You Going to Say?*"

Mention the word "honoraria" to Stan Lundine, former member of Congress from western New York State and the state lieutenant governor from 1986 to 1994, and he will likely tell you the following story:

In the early 1980s, when congressional salaries were lower than today, and it was permissible for members of Congress to accept honoraria, I refused them, unlike most of my colleagues. In fact, one of my colleagues told me, "You're not being ethical. You're being a sucker." I decided to construct a rule by which I could accept honoraria and not compromise myself. I would accept no honoraria from banks or anyone else directly affected by matters that came before the house banking committee on which I served.

One evening, as I was preparing to leave my home to speak before a group not disqualified by my self-imposed rule, my eight-year-old son asked me why I had to go out that evening. "I have to give a speech," was my answer. "Why do you have to give a speech?" asked my son. "Well, because some people expect me. They are going to pay me, and we need the money." My son's interest was piqued at the mention of money. He asked, "How much are they going to pay you?" "A thousand dollars." "A thousand dollars?!" My son's eyes nearly popped out of his head. "*What* are you going to say?"

72 REGULATING HONORARIA, ROYALTIES, AND TRAVEL REIMBURSEMENTS

I asked myself that question all the way to the speech and all the way home. What, indeed, was I going to say that was worth a thousand dollars? That night I decided never to accept another honorarium.[1]

As we know from the headlines of the late 1980s, many of Congressman Lundine's colleagues did not have the benefit of his eight-year-old's insight. His perfectly legal practice of accepting an occasional honorarium paled in comparison with what his peers were doing. It was common practice for his colleagues and their often equally powerful staffers to supplement their salaries quite handsomely by giving speeches to constituents or others who were interested in what was happening that session on a bill.

Common Cause has estimated that in 1988 House and Senate members accepted $9 million in speaking fees.[2] During tax reform negotiations earlier in the decade, the staff director of the United States Senate Finance Committee reportedly received nearly $38,000 for speeches "and turned down much more."[3]

Of course, not every offer or acceptance of an honorarium by a public officer or employee is problematic. An honorarium can be a legitimate way of acknowledging knowledge, time, and effort. The public workforce is, after all, made up of millions of individuals with countless talents, ideas, and skills. The Supreme Court has said that an absolute ban on honoraria not only unreasonably limits federal workers, but deprives the world of hearing and reading what they have to say.[4]

However, as with financial disclosure, conflicts of interest, and gifts, nearly any time anything of value is given, paid, or loaned to a public employee or official, he or she needs to ask certain questions:

1. Am I being offered this because of my official government position?
2. Is anything expected in return, either explicitly or implicitly? Will I feel obligated in any way if I accept?
3. How will acceptance appear to the public? To those I supervise? To those my agency regulates?

At worst, an honorarium can be a payment for something far more valuable than a speech—access to, or the favor of, a government employee. It can be an improper gift or an unacceptable campaign contribution. The desire to acquire honoraria can lead to the inappropriate use of public resources and can tempt public servants to spend time and energy pursuing those outside payments rather than fulfilling their official responsibilities. Accompanying all of these potentials is that of the impression of impropriety that can result from the acceptance of an honorarium. These concerns lead governments to regulate the conditions under which honoraria may be accepted.

According to the 1993 compilation by the Council on Government Ethics Laws, by 1992 the overwhelming majority of states had addressed the issue of the receipt of fees or honoraria in some fashion, whether by law, regulation, executive order, or agency ruling.[5] The enactments may serve as useful models if your jurisdiction is considering adopting or amending standards concerning the acceptance of honoraria or travel reimbursements. Invaluable because of their comprehensiveness and many examples are the federal regulations, "Standards of Ethical Conduct for Employees of the Executive Branch."[6] These regulations are the bulk of what has survived the Supreme Court's invalidation of the broad ban on honoraria imposed by the Ethics Reform Act of 1989 in *United States v. National Treasury Employees Union*. That case is discussed at the end of this chapter.

What Constitutes an "Honorarium"?

Payment for Certain Activities

In federal regulations, compensation for activities treated as honoraria includes "any form of consideration, remuneration or income, including royalties, given for or in connection with the employee's teaching, speaking or writing activities."[7]

In its advisory materials to government officials and employees, the California Fair Political Practices Commission sets out a more expansive, yet concise, list of the kinds of activities the state's codes and regulations regard as honoraria.

> An "honorarium" is any payment made in consideration for any speech given, article published, or attendance at any public or private conference, convention, meeting, social event, meal, or like gathering.
>
> A "speech given" means a public address, oration, or other form of oral presentation, including participation in a private seminar, or debate.
>
> An "article published" means a nonfictional written work: 1) that is produced in connection with any activity other than the practice of a bona fide business, trade or profession; and 2) that is published in a periodical, journal, newspaper, newsletter, magazine, pamphlet, or similar publication.
>
> "Attendance" means being present during, making an appearance at, or serving as host or master of ceremonies for any public or private conference, convention, meeting, social event, meal, or like gathering.

Exceptions to the definition include payment for dramatic, musical, or other artistic performances or the publication of plays, screenplays, and income from personal services provided in connection with a bona fide business, trade, or profession, including teaching. All income may be reportable on the individual's statement of economic interests.[8]

Travel, Meals, Accommodations, and Admissions to Speech-Related Events

Sometimes included and sometimes excluded from definitions related to honoraria are reimbursements for travel, meals, accommodations, and admissions to conferences. Such payments are discussed in the following section.

What Is the Subject Matter of the Speech, Writing, or Appearance?

Whether the speech or appearance is related to the speaker's government position should be a threshold question. Most jurisdictions that choose to address the issue ban or limit the acceptance of honoraria only for talks, appearances, or writings related to one's official position or responsibilities. The regulations enforced by the federal Office of Government Ethics prohibit covered individuals from receiving compensation "from any source other than the Government for teaching, speaking or writing that relates to the employee's official duties," including any matter to which the employee is or has been assigned in the past, or any ongoing policy, program, or operation of the employee's agency.[9]

Honoraria are generally allowed for speeches or appearances not related to one's government work, unless some other disqualifying factor is present.

What Exceptions Are There to Limits on Honoraria for Work-Related Activities?

Payment to the Government Entity

Some jurisdictions, such as South Carolina and California,[10] allow the honorarium to be paid into the general fund of the speaker's government or agency.[11] The city charter of Phoenix is silent on the topic of honoraria, but employees are referred to language that prohibits the receipt of "fees, perquisites, emoluments, rewards or compensation aside from the salary as fixed by the law. All fees in connection with official duties shall be paid into the City Treasury daily."[12]

The rationale for such exceptions must be that any mischief that could be caused by an individual's receiving payment is eliminated, or at least significantly mitigated, if payment is made to a governmental entity. To reduce the possibility or appearance of institutional preferences in favor of generous hosts, it seems advisable to establish review and reporting procedures and a requirement that such funds be directed to general funds, as opposed to specific programs' coffers.

Payment to a Charitable Organization

Another exception is allowing the payment to be made directly to a charitable, educational, civic, religious, or similar tax-exempt not-for-profit organization. The California rule here is also instructive. It provides that the donation cannot be extracted as a condition for making the speech; it may not be claimed by the speaker as a tax deduction; the recipient of the donation must not know the identity of the speaker; and the donation may not have any reasonably foreseeable effect on the speaker or any member of his or her family.[13]

Provision of or Reimbursement for Travel, Meals, Accommodations, or Other Hospitality

A common occurrence, whether or not considered an alternative to an offer of a monetary honorarium, is payment for a public employee's travel, meals, accommodations, or admission to a conference the individual attends in his or her official capacity. This typically occurs in the context of conferences, conventions, and seminars sponsored by trade and professional organizations, advocacy groups, unions, and the like. Because these entities frequently have business before government, such as contracts, or litigation, or interest in legislation or other decision making, one might anticipate ethics provisions would disallow the offer.

But the value of convening with members of such entities is indisputable. "There are sound reasons for public officials to speak at industry gatherings or be questioned by business executives. It helps keep them in touch with conditions in those industries and pays political dividends for the official."[14] Equally indisputable is the inability if most governments to finance their employees' attendance at such events. In view of this dilemma, many jurisdictions that disallow the payment of fees to individuals for speeches related to their official duties will allow the speaker's travel, accommodations, and meals in relation to the event to be paid for by the sponsoring organization.

In an advisory opinion inspired by the federal regulations,[15] the New York State Ethics Commission allows the practice in the executive branch thus:

> [A] State officer or employee may receive or accept meals, entertainment or hospitality . . . from a disqualified source . . . when the appearance, attendance, presence or participation of the State officer or employee is for a State agency purpose and relates to his or her official duties.
>
> Attendance at events at which the activities are substantially recreational in nature shall not be considered to be for a State agency purpose or related to an employee's official duties.
>
> [U]nder no circumstances may travel or lodging be included.
>
> When a State agency determines that an employee's attendance at an event is for a State agency purpose because it will further agency programs and operations, the employee may accept . . . free attendance at all or part of a widely attended gathering of mutual interest to a number of parties. A gathering is "widely attended" if it is open to members from throughout a given industry or profession, or if those in attendance represent a range of persons interested in a given matter.
>
> "Free attendance" may include waiver of all or part of a conference or other fee or the provision of food, refreshments, entertainment, instruction and materials furnished to all in attendance as an integral part of the event.
>
> When others in attendance will generally be accompanied by spouses, the State agency may authorize the State employee to accept a sponsor's invitation to all or a portion of the event at which the employee's free attendance is permitted. Travel expenses, lodging, entertainment collateral to

the event, or meals taken other than in a group setting with all others in attendance may not be included as part of a gift, either to the employee or the employee's spouse.

For a State agency to find that an agency purpose is served by a State employee accepting free attendance at a widely attended event, the agency should conclude that its interest in the employee's participation outweighs the likelihood that such participation will actually or apparently improperly influence the employee in the performance of his or her official duties. A number of factors should be considered, including: the nature of any pending matter affecting the donor's interest, the importance of the event to the agency, the significance of the state officer or employee's role in the event, the timing of the event, the identity of other expected participants and the monetary value of the gift.[16]

Under certain circumstances, New York will allow reimbursement for travel expenses from professional organizations and boards of which the individual's agency is a dues-paying member even if other, disqualifying factors exist.[17]

South Carolina's statute allows a public official or employee to accept such event-related amenities from a lobbyist if the activities are reasonably and directly related to state or local economic development efforts. In such case, prior written approval of the governor or pertinent legislative leader is required. Furthermore, a disclosure of the payment is required if the individual is required to file a statement of economic interest. The law provides for confidential filings to the state ethics commission if release of the information could jeopardize such a project.[18]

In California, when an individual who is speaking or participating on a panel is allowed to receive lodging and subsistence expenses, only those expenses related to the day immediately preceding and the day immediately following the day of the speech may be accepted.[19]

Does It Matter Who Is Offering the Honorarium?

Even if the subject matter of the speech or the appearance is totally unrelated to the speaker's official position, the source of the honorarium may render it inappropriate. Does the donor have or seek a contract with the speaker's government entity? Is the donor regulated by the speaker's entity? Does the donor lobby or attempt to influence the actions or policies of the government entity? Is the donor a party to any litigation involving the speaker's agency? Can the donor benefit in any action or deferral of action on the part of the speaker or the speaker's agency?

An affirmative answer to any of these questions typically triggers prohibitions or limitations of varying degrees. For example, New York State's regulations prohibit executive branch officers and employees from accepting honoraria from any of the donors described above even if the speech or attendance at the meeting or seminar for which the payment is offered is unrelated to the individual's public service.[20] The Massachusetts rule for executive branch employees is substantially the same, but if the source of a payment for a non-work-related speech has business dealings with the speaker's agency, "public written notice to one's appointing official may be necessary."[21]

Massachusetts legislators, however, may accept honoraria from any source, including those representing interests before the legislature, but only if the engagement or speech is "legitimate," meaning that it

1. is formally scheduled in advance of the legislator's arrival;
2. is before an organization that normally has outside speakers; and
3. is more than perfunctory.

Further, "the totality of the circumstances must be examined using basic common sense" to assure that the payment was not an illegal gratuity or could give that impression. This review includes considering whether

1. it is usual for the organization to offer honoraria,
2. the amount of the honorarium was reasonable,
3. the honorarium was reported, and
4. the organization has clearly demonstrated a substantial interest in legislation that the legislator is, or has recently been, in a unique position to affect either because the legislator is a member of the leadership or is on the committee considering it.[22]

Should the Same Rules Apply Equally to All in Public Service?

Categorical exceptions are administratively attractive but should be founded on some rational basis. Factors such as whether the speaker or author is full- or part-time, paid or unpaid are pertinent to ethics regulation only if they help identify persons for whom it makes sense to apply a different standard.

Salary Level and/or Position Responsibilities

As in other areas of ethics regulation, it is common, and I believe defensible, to establish a higher standard of behavior for those who are policy makers and/or who earn salaries above a certain level or who occupy high-ranking positions. As leaders in their organizations, decision makers, and the most visible representatives of the government to the public, these individuals must exhibit the highest standards of behavior. Furthermore, because of the authority they wield, the opportunities for mischief abound.

The State of Ohio does not allow individuals who are in a financial disclosure category, except for local elected officials making less than $16,000 per year and presidents and trustees of public colleges, to accept honoraria.[23] New York State has more stringent reporting and approval requirements for those in policy-making positions.[24] On the federal front, Executive Order

78   REGULATING HONORARIA, ROYALTIES, AND TRAVEL REIMBURSEMENTS

12731 prohibits honoraria for any outside activity by presidential appointees and full-time noncareer positions. The income of other high-ranking (above grade GS-15) federal employees is limited to 15 percent of an estimated salary level.[25]

Distinguishing among Branches of Government; Elected versus Appointed Officials

It is not uncommon for a jurisdiction's rules governing the acceptance of honoraria (whether or not honoraria are explicitly addressed) by members of the legislative branch to differ from those applicable to officers and employees of the executive branch. Some reasons for this might be inferred.

First, many legislatures, especially those of municipalities, are part-time. Some may even be unpaid. Thus, it is understood that many, if not most, legislators hold other jobs, or run businesses, or engage in other income-producing activities. A general code of conduct that allows outside activities only if they do not conflict with the individual's public duties may be adequate to address honoraria situations.

Further, it can be argued that a less stringent standard for elected officials is not inappropriate as they, unlike appointed individuals, are most immediately accountable to the public.

Some Honoraria May Be Subject to Case-by-Case Reviews

The city of Los Angeles, which prohibits its elected officials from accepting honoraria, allows full-time city officials to receive them, but only upon the prior written approval of the head of the individual's department. If that manager decides the source of the payment is "restricted," the prior written approval of the city ethics commission is required.[26]

For any preapproval system to be useful, decisions must be rendered in a timely fashion. To help everyone, requiring submission of a request within a stated number of days or weeks before delivery of the speech or the article makes sense.

What Are Appropriate Penalties for Transgressions?

This question is best answered by reference to penalties for violations of other ethics provisions in a given system. At a minimum, however, the return of an inappropriate payment and, depending upon the circumstances, disciplinary action are appropriate. The federal law provides for a civil penalty of up to the greater of $10,000 or the amount of the compensation the individual received from the prohibited conduct in addition to return of the payment, unless the recipient acted in good faith reliance upon advice of the Office of Government Ethics.[27]

The Use of Public Resources for the Preparation of a Speech, Article, or Talk Should Automatically Disqualify the Individual for Receipt of an Honorarium

The city of Los Angeles defines such resources to include time off, personal assistance, equipment, and copiers.[28]

Teaching

Worth special mention is that teaching is typically excluded from the definitions of honoraria. The federal regulations define teaching for which payment may be received as relating to a course involving multiple presentations offered as part of the regularly established curriculum of a recognized school or institution of higher learning. The prohibition against receiving compensation for teaching that relates to the employee's official duties does not, in the federal scheme, preclude compensation for teaching within the individual's discipline or area of expertise based on his or her educational background or experience.[29]

Establish a Monetary Threshold

Administrative convenience may suggest that only those honoraria that exceed a minimum dollar value, however small, should be prohibited under some of the circumstances addressed earlier. Common Cause has warned that annual or "per appearance" limits should be established at a level that prevents honoraria fees from becoming a major source of personal income or the primary motivation of public appearances."[30]

Administrative Considerations

Additional issues the administrators of any limitation on honoraria may wish to consider include:

1. Whether there will be a mechanism for the preapproval of speeches and written materials. Whether this is feasible will depend on the resources available. The reasonableness of the service is indisputable.
2. Reporting of income from honoraria, including the provision of transportation, lodging, meals, and so on. Devotees of the "sunlight-is-the-best-disinfectant" school of ethics might argue that the more that is disclosed, the less that needs to be banned. Many jurisdictions impose reporting requirements in addition to limitations.

United States v. National Treasury Employees Union et al. (NTEU)

Background

Some would say that, far more than any urge to reform, it was the desire for salary increases that moved Congress to enact the Ethics Reform Act of 1989, which included the across-the-board ban on honoraria. Salaries for top positions in all three branches of government had been stagnant for many years, and the 1989 Report of the Quadrennial Commission on Executive, Legislative, and Judicial Salaries related the practice of accepting honoraria to the erosion of salary levels by inflation since 1969. Endorsing that commission's recommendations for addressing those two issues was the President's Commission on Federal Ethics Law Reform.

The act awarded a 25 percent salary increase for members of Congress, federal judges, and top-level executive branch employees and imposed a number of ethics provisions, most far-reaching of which was an almost absolute ban on honoraria in all three branches of federal government.[31] The ban on honoraria applied regardless of the subject matter of the speech or the identity of the party offering the payment.

The Litigation

Almost as soon as the act took effect in January 1991, two unions and several individual midlevel executive branch career civil servants who had accepted honoraria in the past commenced a lawsuit to enjoin its enforcement against them. By subsequent stipulation, the case was deemed brought on behalf of every employee below grade GS-16 who, but for the new law, could receive honoraria.

The United States District Court for the District of Columbia concluded that the statute violated the First Amendment and therefore was unenforceable in relation to all executive branch employees.[32]

Affirming the lower court's invalidation of the ban as it applied to executive branch employees, the District Court of Appeals found significant the lack of nexus between the employee's job and either the subject matter of the prohibited speech or the payer of the honorarium, and the lack of evidence of corruption among lower level employees occasioned by their acceptance of honoraria from such activities.[33]

The Supreme Court, affirming so much of the decisions below that found the ban unconstitutional, commenced its analysis with reference to the line of cases starting with the familiar *Pickering v. Board of Education of Township High School District*[34] The Court crafted the balancing tests to be applied whenever the government imposes restraints on the speech of public employees. The court declared that the burden the government bears in balancing the interests of a public employee as a citizen against the interests of the state as an employer in promoting the efficiency of its public service varies depending on the nature of the speech. In the case of the honoraria ban, the Court found that the government had not sustained its burden. The types of speech for which the new law would ban honoraria included addresses to public audiences that do not occur in the workplace and do not relate to their government employment. Furthermore, unlike restraints the Court has upheld, the law in question "chills potential speech before it happens."[35]

The law's prohibition of the acceptance of money for speech was tantamount to a restriction on speech itself, especially for lower paid employees, the Court determined. And, from the perspective of the potential audiences for all the banned activity, the Court fretted that the ban might thwart a future Herman Melville or Nathaniel Hawthorne, both of whom wrote some of their best works while working for the Customs Service.[36]

Rejecting the government's argument that administrative convenience justifies a broad prospective ban rather than one that requires individual nexus determinations, the Court cited a 1991 amendment that allows series of speeches, articles, or appearances unless directly related to the individual's official duties. Similarly inconsistent with the claim of governmental efficiency, the Court held, were the government's own implementing regulations, which allowed artistic and athletic performances, reading a part in a play, delivering a sermon, and teaching.

In what dissenting Chief Justice Rehnquist called an O. Henry ending, the majority affirmed the invalidation of the ban only as it applied to executive branch employees below grade GS-16, the class of individuals who brought the suit. Reticent to engage in judicial legislation, the Court refused the government's request that it craft an acceptable nexus test.

In two separate dissents, four justices called the majority's remedy as overbroad as the statute since it will allow the receipt of honoraria by those giving speeches on work-related topics. The proper remedy, they argue, would be to invalidate the law only as to those below grade GS-16 who seek honoraria for speeches unrelated to their government employment.

The Aftermath

In an opinion issued in early 1996, the Department of Justice Office of Legal Counsel called the entire honoraria ban effectively "eviscerated" by the Supreme Court's decision and concluded that the honoraria prohibition cannot be enforced against any government employee, including employees of the legislative and judiciary branches and high-level executive branch officials.[37] As the Office of Government Ethics will hasten to tell you, however, the decision did not address and therefore left intact the body of regulations found at 5 C.F.R. 2635, cited in numerous instances earlier in this chapter. Those provisions impose limitations and outright bans on certain activities that relate to one's government job and duties.

As the case relates to employees in other jurisdictions, one commentator on *NTEU* is sanguine about the future of honoraria regulation, predicting that "as long as the government employer is able to justify its restraints on expression in a sufficient manner, and also demonstrate that its interest clearly outweighs any burden imposed on its employees, then its restraint will pass judicial scrutiny."[38] The author does not, however, suggest how to pass those tests.

Far more concerned about the reach of the case is George Brown, professor of law at Boston College Law School and Chair of the Massachusetts State Ethics Commission. Calling the Court's lack of deference to Congress "perhaps *NTEU*'s most disturbing legacy," he expresses grave concerns about the case's implication not only for all ethics legislation, but for kindred enactments such as the Hatch Act and campaign finance laws.

Ethics laws are so important, he argues, that, in any constitutional balancing test, they merit more weight than the Court afforded the federal honoraria ban. The Court's approach in *NTEU* threatens, for example, revolving door laws because they prohibit future communications. Similarly, rules instructing employees to avoid the appearance of impropriety may be deemed void for vagueness. Whereas the Court may have been right that a prospective ban on speech is not ideal, Brown warns that the alternative, case-by-case reviews, is unwieldy. The more important virtue of a preannounced rule is that it gives the public the reassurance it needs that its government is above suspicion.

There is no doubt Brown is very concerned that the Court has given the wrong answer to "[the] big question in ethics regulation today [which] is whether to tighten existing rules even further, . . . to convince the public that government really can police itself, or to relax them based primarily on a desire not to enmesh public employees in a sea of legalism."

Conclusion

Is the Supreme Court the champion of individual liberties or a group of antireformists? You be the judge. What is clear is the Court's warning to drafters of ethics standards that they should take care to relate, either empirically or logically, the risk of abuse of public office to limitations on constitutionally conferred liberties.

Notes

1. Author's conversation with Mr. Lundine, November 25, 1996.

2. STEINBERG & AUSTERN, GOVERNMENT ETHICS AND MANAGERS: A GUIDE TO SOLVING ETHICAL DILEMMAS IN THE PUBLIC SECTOR, 45 (1990).

3. CODY & RICHARDSON, HONEST GOVERNMENT: AN ETHICS GUIDE FOR PUBLIC SERVICE, 96 (1992).

4. United States v. National Treasury Employees Union, 115 S. Ct. 1003 (1995).

5. COUNCIL ON GOVERNMENT AND ETHICS LAW, BLUE BOOK: CAMPAIGN FINANCE, ETHICS, LOBBY LAW & JUDICIAL CONDUCT, Table 29A (9th ed. May 1993).

6. 5 C.F.R. Part 2635.

7. *Id.,* §2635.807(a)(2)(iii).

8. CAL. CODE §89502; CAL. CODE REGS. tit. 2, §18931.

9. 5 C.F.R. §26350807(a).

10. S.C. CODE § 8-13-715.

11. California Political Reform Act: Government Code §§ 81000–91015; 2 CAL. CODE REGS.

12. City of Phoenix Charter ch. III §9.B.

13. CAL. CODE REGS. § 18932.5.

Notes 83

14. CODY & RICHARDSON, *supra* note 3, at 55.

15. 5 C.F.R. §2635.204(g)(1).

16. New York State Ethics Commission Advisory Op. No. 94-16.

17. New York State Ethics Commission Advisory Op. No. 91-8.

18. S.C. CODE §2-17-90.

19. CAL. CODE §§89500 et. seq.; CAL. CODE REGS. 18950 et. seq.

20. 19 N.Y. COMP. CODES R. & REGS. part 930.

21. Massachusetts State Ethics Commission Fact Sheet No. 12.

22. Massachusetts State Ethics Commission Advisory No. 2.

23. Ohio Ethics Law: Revised Code § 102.03 (H).

24. 19 N.Y. COMP. CODES R. & REGS. part 930.

25. 5 C.F.R. §2636.304.

26. City of Los Angeles Ethics Ordinance §49.5.9.

27. 5 U.S.C. app. 104(a)(8).

28. City of Los Angeles Ethics Ordinance §49.5.9.

29. 5 C.F.R. §2636.203 (a)(8).

30. A Model Ethics Law for State Government (1989).

31. Pub. L. No. 101–94, 103 STAT. 1717 (1989) codified on scattered sections of 2, 5, 18, and 38 U.S.C.

32. 788 F. Supp. 4 (D.D.C. 1992).

33. 990 F.2d 1271 (D.C. Cir. 1993).

34. 391 U.S. 563 (1968).

35. 115 S. Ct. at 1014.

36. 115 S. Ct. at 1014.

37. "Illegality of Government Honoraria Ban Following *U.S. v. National Treasury Employees Union*," memorandum from Walter Dellinger, assistant attorney general, to the attorney general (Feb. 26, 1996).

38. Judy M. Lin, *United States v. National Treasury Employees Union and the Constitutionality of the Honoraria Ban: Protecting the First Amendment Rights of Public Employees,* U. RICH. L. REV., 1555, 1589 (1995).

CHAPTER ❦ 6

Pro Bono and the Government Lawyer*

Kathleen Waits

This chapter discusses the issues and responsibilities surrounding the establishment of pro bono programs in government law offices. Practical advice and references to programs across the country are offered in an effort to focus attention not only on the need for government lawyers to engage in pro bono activities, but to assist public law offices in the creation of programs that work.

Introduction

It can be done; it has been done; it is being done right now. When considering pro bono by government lawyers, these are the most important words to remember. It is indeed possible for a government office to establish a pro bono program for its attorneys and staff. There are government pro bono programs that have been running successfully for a number of years. And, under the right conditions, it can even be *easy* to establish a credible, effective program of pro bono representation by government lawyers. For example, in Maryland "[i]t was less than six months between the time the [state] Attorney General proposed the idea and the time we were accepting our first cases. This was despite the fact that we had a committee of twelve lawyers working on the project."[1]

Anyone interested in starting a pro bono program in a government law office need not reinvent the wheel. Although local conditions and laws may affect the details of a pro bono plan, there are many places where government pro bono programs are up and working today. For example, an October 1996 chart from the American Bar Association (ABA) indicates that twenty jurisdictions already have official policies permitting government lawyer pro bono,[2] while six more states had policies "in progress."[3]

---

*This chapter was written in March 1997.

84

There are plenty of models that the interested government lawyer or public law office leader can use in developing a plan tailored to his or her local situation. This chapter will focus on two working, but very different, models for government pro bono: the Maryland Attorney General's Office and the United States Department of Justice.[4]

This chapter will consider voluntary pro bono by government lawyers.[5] The focus will be on how to get a pro bono program started in a government law office. Various problems that must be addressed before government lawyers can engage in pro bono representation, including conflicts of interest and the use of government resources, will be highlighted.

This chapter will also address strategies that might be helpful in establishing a government pro bono program, as well as how an individual government attorney might become involved in pro bono work even if his or her office doesn't have an official pro bono program.

Defining Pro Bono and Why We Need It

"Pro bono" means different things to different people. Some define it to include any work done for free by the lawyer, even cases where the lawyer expected to be paid and was not, or where the lawyer reduced his or her fee after the fact.[6] Others say that pro bono includes any kind of free or reduced-fee public service activity by lawyers. Under this definition, service as a board member for any philanthropic organization, such as a church or the Red Cross, would qualify, even if the lawyer does no legal work for the organization.

Other definitions of pro bono focus on the unmet legal needs of the poor. This is what the ABA has done in Model Rule of Professional Conduct 6.1. This rule states an aspirational goal of 50 hours of pro bono per lawyer per year. Rule 6.1(a) then says that a "substantial majority" of these hours should consist of the lawyer's providing "legal services without fee or expectation of fee to (1) persons of limited means or (2) [to] charitable, religious, civic, community, governmental and educational organizations in matters which are designed primarily to address the needs of persons of limited means."[7]

As used in this chapter, "pro bono" work is defined as direct or indirect unpaid legal services to the poor. The focus will be on direct legal representation of poor people by government lawyers. Most existing pro bono programs in government law offices concentrate on individual representation. Further, it is direct legal representation of poor people that is likely to raise the most serious issues for government lawyers. Few problems arise when government lawyers are involved in nonlegal work for various "do-good" causes.[8]

This chapter will also assume that all lawyers, including government lawyers, should at least have a chance to be involved in pro bono services for poor people. The unmet legal needs of the poor are enormous and have been exhaustively studied and described elsewhere.[9] In addition, the legal profession has long supported voluntary pro bono programs and expressed an aspirational duty for all lawyers to be involved in pro bono services. Although the model rules recognize that pro bono work by government lawyers may not always be *possible*,[10] few people have suggested it is not *desirable*.[11] The ABA is on record that pro bono service by government lawyers should not be prohibited or discouraged.[12] A well-designed voluntary pro bono program for government lawyers can realistically hope to gain widespread support from many constituencies, including government and private lawyers, political leaders, and the general public.

Getting a Government Pro Bono Program Started—The Importance of Leadership and Support from the Top

Leadership is critical to getting any job done. It is no different with government pro bono. Surely the fastest way to get a pro bono program going is to have support and leadership from the head of the government legal office. If the attorney general, departmental general counsel, or city/county attorney puts a high priority on establishing a pro bono program, it is likely to happen. The head of the office may be able to issue ethics opinions that remove certain barriers. For instance, a sympathetic state attorney general might issue regulations or opinions containing helpful interpretations of various statutes or defining appropriate "public service" for government lawyers as including limited amounts of pro bono.[13] Chief lawyers at local levels may also be able to interpret ordinances and other regulations in a favorable manner. Further, if legislative, regulatory, or ordinance change is needed, the chief legal officer can be a powerful lobbyist.

More importantly, the office head can set a "can-do" tone for the development of a pro bono program. Government offices are, by their nature, very hierarchical. Even the most recalcitrant bureaucrat will hesitate to throw up groundless obstacles when the boss has made it clear that he or she wants to see a pro bono program adopted as soon as possible. In addition, the chief lawyer can ensure that the people who are setting up the pro bono program have any necessary institutional support. Leadership from the top can ensure that all necessary steps—whether it is meetings that must be held or questions that must be answered—occur expeditiously. Finally, enthusiasm is contagious. If the office leader is excited about pro bono, his or her subordinates may be as well.

Successful government pro bono programs often start with strong leadership from the top. For instance, the Maryland program undoubtedly developed so rapidly because of the leadership of state Attorney General Joseph Curran.[14] Similarly, programs at the federal level got a boost in February 1996 when President Clinton issued Executive Order 12988, which said that "All Federal agencies should develop appropriate programs to encourage and facilitate pro bono legal and other volunteer service by government employees . . . including attorneys."[15] Attorney General Janet Reno's support and interest facilitated the establishment of the pro bono program at the United States Department of Justice.[16]

If the office head is not immediately receptive to the idea of pro bono, an interested lawyer or group of lawyers can look to other ways to get the leader involved. Perhaps the state bar can be brought in as an ally.[17] Perhaps the office leader just needs to be assured that other, similar government offices have adopted pro bono programs.

Strategic thinking is also important to avoid or go around likely road-blocks. For example, if the legislature or city council is likely to oppose pro bono, they should be consulted only if absolutely necessary. It might be that a pro bono program can be established without their approval. Note that both the Maryland and U.S. Department of Justice programs were established administratively, without legislative action. In other locations, powerful people in the legislature may support pro bono and can be enlisted as allies if the executive branch is less enthusiastic.

As an example, consider the question of whether government pro bono is barred by a statute, regulation, or ordinance that requires that government employees work "full-time" for the government.[18] If the executive branch favors pro bono, then the attorney general or other executive branch officer might issue an opinion stating that a "full-time" government lawyer is still permitted to devote small amounts of time to pro bono during normal business hours.[19] On the other hand, if the relevant legislative body is amenable, then the law could be amended to expressly provide for pro bono.[20]

The politics of establishing a pro bono plan can indeed be frustrating. But, as with all politics, persistence can pay off.[21]

How Much Control over the Pro Bono Program Does the Government Office Want?

A government law office must examine many details before it can establish a pro bono program. However, policy makers might want to consider as a preliminary matter how much centralized control the office wants to exercise over the pro bono work done by staff lawyers. The Maryland attorney general's program chose a high level of centralized control. In contrast, the U.S. Department of Justice chose a very decentralized program.

A key feature of the Maryland program (see Appendix 6B), is that all pro bono work is funneled through a central point in the attorney general's office.[22] The central intake point keeps track of the status of cases to ensure that clients are receiving adequate representation and cases are not falling through the cracks. Maryland's procedures provide for informing the central administrator when a case is closed.[23]

Under the Maryland program, lawyers are not supposed to go out on their own and accept pro bono cases. Instead, cases come from a specified group of referring agencies, particularly the state's volunteer lawyer service organization.[24] These agencies, among other things, generally prescreen clients for financial eligibility.[25] Maryland also limits the types of cases that the program will accept for referral. As discussed in the next section, this helps avoid conflict of interest problems.

In contrast with the Maryland program, the U.S. Department of Justice (DOJ) system is quite decentralized (see Appendix 6C). Under the DOJ program, there is no centralized source for pro bono referrals or supervision. Although there is a department "pro bono program manager," decisions about pro bono rest with the heads of the various components of DOJ and with individual supervisors.

The individual DOJ lawyer is not limited to any particular kind of pro bono work. So long as the individual lawyer abides by the department's conflict of interest, prior approval, and other rules, he or she can search out pro bono opportunities on his or her own. There is no central registry for pro bono work by department lawyers and no reporting requirements on what pro bono work is in progress or completed.[26]

If a particular government legal office is comfortable with "letting a thousand flowers bloom," a decentralized system could work. A decentralized system makes sense if the types of conflict of interest that might arise are largely self-evident. Further, the office head must be comfortable with the lawyers and supervisors who will be making the decisions about which pro bono cases to accept.

A decentralized system may make more sense at a federal agency or in a small county or municipality than at the state government level. Because most federal agencies enforce laws that have little or no relevance to the lives of poor people, it may be relatively easy for a federal lawyer to avoid conflict of interest problems.[27] On the other end of the spectrum, conflicts of interest may present few problems in a municipal or county lawyer's office because the office may be very small and have a limited range of legal issues presented to it.

A more centralized and rigid system may be wiser for statewide law offices and large local offices, such as those in big cities. These offices often represent agencies that have frequent contact with poor people. Lawyers in one branch of the office may not realize all the potential conflicts presented. The conflict of interest and other problems may therefore be serious enough—and complex enough—to call for a centralized system. For example, the Maryland attorney general's office has some 300 lawyers;[28] the office represents "the Governor, the General Assembly, the judiciary, all departments, state boards, and most state commissions. Various enforcement units, including consumer protection, antitrust and securities are also part of the office. The Attorney General also handles all criminal appeals in the state."[29] In this setting, a "decide conflicts on your own" system might have been difficult. It is important to remember that despite its broad subject matter jurisdiction, Maryland was able to formulate a workable, conflict-of-interest–free pro bono system.

Common Obstacles to Government Pro Bono—And How to Overcome Them

Two major, recurring obstacles must be overcome for a pro bono program to get off the ground and succeed. Conflicts of interest has already been mentioned. The second is use of government resources, including lawyer and support staff time and government equipment, for pro bono representation.

Conflicts of Interest

All lawyers must avoid conflicts of interest.[30] However, special concerns arise when government lawyers undertake pro bono representation. First, the government has a broad involvement in people's lives, including (or perhaps especially) poor people.

Government involvement is not always obvious, particularly in the beginning of a case. Therefore, a public lawyer could agree to represent a pro bono client, only to later discover that his or her main client—the government—has a significant, conflicting interest in the matter. The result could be disastrous for all concerned: The pro bono client might have to start over with new counsel if the government lawyer must withdraw. The pro bono lawyer and the pro bono program could be embarrassed.[31]

A lawyer must be sensitive to conflicts both at the beginning and throughout the representation. However, most government pro bono programs look for ways to provide pro bono services while avoiding even the possibility of conflicts.

Limiting which cases a government pro bono program will accept is one way to deal with possible conflicts problems. This prophylactic approach requires some up-front time and analysis but can pay off in the long run. A public law office might consider investigating whether there are certain types of cases where poor people need legal services but where the risk of conflicts with the governmental client is minimal.

This is what the Maryland attorney general's office did when it set up its program. The organizing committee first contacted legal services providers and community agencies to determine areas of need. The committee then developed a list of areas where representation was unlikely to conflict with the attorney general's regular legal work. The pro bono program then restricted the cases it would take to the specified areas. Maryland's initial list included "domestic violence cases in which an order of protection is the only relief sought"; "AIDS-related cases not involving state institutions or public assistance"; and "divorces involving no minor children and no alimony claims."[32] Later, after the attorney general's office had gained some experience with the pro bono program, the types of eligible cases were changed somewhat. Maryland's latest list of approved cases includes "divorces involving no custody disputes"; "general wills, advance directives, powers of attorney, private guardianships not involving any State agency"; "landlord/tenant cases not involving the application of the Consumer Protection Act"; and "veterans benefit appeals."[33]

The Maryland system has worked very successfully. The advance thought that went into the program's case selection has worked well. Conflict of interest problems are so rare in Maryland that the lawyer in charge of the program could hardly remember the last time a conflict issue had arisen.[34]

Once again, the U.S. Department of Justice is different. All department employees are banned from any kind of criminal representation.[35] Otherwise, DOJ does not limit its lawyers to certain specified pro bono projects, although the various components of DOJ (such as the civil division) are encouraged to preapprove certain types of cases as appropriate for their lawyers.[36] If a particular kind of pro bono case is on the preapproved list, the lawyer must only notify a supervisor before starting work on the representation.[37] Still, an individual DOJ lawyer can look for any pro bono project and ask his or her component head to approve the lawyer's participation.[38] The component head or his or her designee is required to consider conflict of interest issues before approving the pro bono activity,[39] and the individual employee is "responsible for ensuring that his or her [pro bono services]" do not present conflict of interest problems or violate other statutes and regulations.[40]

The U.S. Department of Justice system may be especially worth considering in very large, highly diversified, and geographically dispersed government law offices. While it is true that the Maryland attorney general's office has more than 300 lawyers and does a wide variety of work, its lawyers are located in only a few different places in Baltimore. It was therefore feasible in Maryland to bring together all the necessary people to devise a list of appropriate, conflict-free pro bono cases. In another office, an attempt to devise such a list might result in no pro bono program at all. People who are trying to start a pro bono program will have to decide, as a political and practical matter, whether a centralized "laundry list" of cases will work better than a decentralized, individualized system for conflicts management.

Use of Government Work Time and Resources

The taxpayers pay for government law offices, and of course the taxpayers should not pay for pro bono by government lawyers. Consequently, lawyer time used for pro bono should not be at the taxpayers' expense. Additionally, there is the question of whether the government pro bono lawyer can use the government's equipment and resources, such as computers, paper, library books, telephones, secretarial support, and even paper clips. Government pro bono programs have overcome these problems with a little forethought and creativity.

Taken to an extreme, either of these issues can inhibit and even doom a government pro bono program. For many kinds of representation, the government lawyer will usually have to do at least some pro bono work during normal business hours. Phone calls and meetings with clients and opposing counsel may be required during the day. If the matter involves litigation, the government lawyer must be able to go to court when the courthouse is open.[41]

The U.S. Department of Justice policy recognizes that pro bono work will sometimes have to be done during employees' regular working hours.[42] DOJ gives supervisors discretion to determine whether to allow individual lawyers time off during the day for pro bono activities. However, the department encourages supervisors "to be flexible and to accommodate, where feasible, the efforts of their employees to do pro bono or volunteer work."[43] Generally, the employee will have to take leave without pay or annual leave (that is, vacation time). However, administrative leave (that is, leave with pay) may be authorized for pro bono activities if the time "is directly related to the Department's mission; is officially sponsored or sanctioned by the Attorney General; or will enhance the professional development or skills of the employee in his or her current position."[44]

Though not explicitly stated in the DOJ policy, it also seems clear that some supervisors may accommodate lawyers' pro bono work through informal means, that is, without any use of leave. So long as an employee is working his full complement of required hours and is getting his regular job done, some supervisors will undoubtedly look the other way if the employee is also doing pro bono either in the office or outside it.[45] This is consistent with what reasonable supervisors, including ones in the government, do all the time with good employees who are doing also engaged in some sort of outside work.[46]

In Maryland, the attorney general's pro bono policy recognizes that many staff lawyers work much longer than the 40-hour standard set by the state. However, most of the extra time worked is not available for use as vacation time; the state imposes sharp limits on the use of compensatory time. Thus, many lawyers have large amounts of excess compensatory leave, that is, accumulated leave that cannot be used to take time off from work. Under the Maryland policy, pro bono lawyers may use excess compensatory time for pro bono activities, so long as the lawyer certifies that his workweek met the minimum hourly requirement "plus whatever additional time is needed for the lawyer to provide the kind of lawyering that this office expects."[47]

As the DOJ and Maryland experiences indicate, a lawyer can be a "full-time" government employee and still do some pro bono during regular business hours. Therefore, statutory requirements that government workers or government lawyers must be "full-time" should not prevent pro bono. Indeed, Maryland has such a law.[48] If necessary, an office trying to start a pro bono program can look for ways to overcome any problems raised by "full-time" requirements. Possibilities include attorney general opinions, office policy statements, and legislative change. The chart in Appendix A shows which states have statutory requirements for "full-time" work as well as statutes specifically authorizing pro bono by state legal employees.

In addition to lawyer time, there is the question of the use of government equipment and support services for pro bono work. An absolute prohibition on *any* use of government resources would lead to the absurd result described by Professor Lisa Lerman:

> A dutiful government lawyer who wished to call her opposing counsel during the day without [any use of government resources or time] might leave the office during the half hour allowed for lunch, with her (privately purchased) pen and pad in hand, and stand in a phone booth on the corner, hoping that her adversary would return her call to the public phone within the appropriate time. If she was fortunate enough to get through, she would have to balance her pad against the wall of the phone booth to make notes of the conversation.[49]

Luckily, functional pro bono programs recognize that most use of government computers, library books, copying equipment, phones, pens, and so on is de minimus. Therefore, pro bono lawyers should be allowed to use equipment so long as it is just part of normal "wear and tear." The focus should be on *abuse* of resources, not on minimal use.[50] Of course, if there is a real drain on resources, such as a large copying job, the pro bono lawyer should provide his or her own paper.[51]

Use of secretaries and other nonlawyer staff for pro bono presents special issues. As with office equipment and lawyer time, it would be an abuse of government resources for secretaries to do long pro bono projects during regular office hours. More importantly, secretaries are people, not machines; they should not have to do any pro bono work if they do not want to. Further, given the hierarchical nature of a law office, a secretary might feel she could not refuse to do pro bono if a lawyer asked her. For this reason, some have suggested that lawyers should not be allowed to ask secretaries to do pro bono work.[52] On the other hand, typing a brief assignment such as a short pleading, could be considered de minimus.

Each pro bono program will need to consider how to handle the support staff problem. Maryland allows secretaries and other support staff to do "limited typing of short letters or pleadings," apparently at the request of the pro bono lawyer.[53] The U.S. Department of Justice policy says that pro bono work "may not be assigned to or otherwise required of support staff."[54]

Luckily, the issue is not as critical as it once might have been. With computers, many lawyers will routinely do their own typing. Additionally, much of the pro bono work done by government lawyers will involve limited amounts of paperwork; only a short letter or pleading may be required. And much of the work can be reduced to forms and templates that, after they are developed, can be easily generated from the lawyer's computer.

Finally, it is completely proper to ask for secretarial volunteers for pro bono work. The legitimate concern about possible coercion should not prevent secretaries from volunteering their time. It would be paternalistic and elitist to assume that lawyers are the only ones interested in helping with pro bono. Thus, the best solution might be for the pro bono coordinator or committee to develop a list of support staff volunteers who are willing to help with pro bono projects.[55]

Issues surrounding the use of government time and equipment are likely to be important in any pro bono scheme. Statutory and regulatory concerns can be complex. Ideally, the committee devising the pro bono program should have at least one member who supports pro bono and who is already knowledgeable about the jurisdiction's rules on use of government resources.[56]

Avoiding the Appearance of Impropriety

To survive and thrive, a government pro bono program must consider more than just legal barriers. It must also confront other, more subtle concerns.

These might be called "appearance-of-impropriety" issues. True, the ethics rules in most states no longer contain "appearance of impropriety" as a basis for disqualification or discipline.[57] But that is beside the point for the government and the government lawyer. Government officials must always worry about not only *being* fair and lawful but about *appearing* fair and lawful. Otherwise, citizens will not respect and trust their government. Therefore, government pro bono programs should bend over backwards to ensure that the program is above reproach.

An important appearance-of-impropriety issue is making sure that everyone understands that government pro bono lawyers are acting in their individual capacity only. No one—not the pro bono client, not opposing counsel, not the court—should ever get the impression that the government is somehow representing this client. Often the best way to distinguish between the government lawyer's official work and his or her pro bono work is for no one to know that he or she works for the government. Thus, many successful pro bono programs suggest or require that meetings with clients, witnesses, and opposing counsel take place in neutral sites away from any government office.[58] The pro bono program may even arrange with bar associations and other groups to make rooms available for this purpose.[59] Similarly, government lawyers are usually prohibited from using official government office stationery for their pro bono cases.[60]

To some, special meetings rooms and stationery may seem overly cautious and formalistic. But there are important practical reasons why a government pro bono program must be very cautious about appearances. By definition, the government is involved in politics, and political winds can change rapidly. In most states there will always be people, both in and out of government, who will not look fondly on government pro bono. They may be hostile to any help for poor people, or they may believe strongly that government lawyers should work exclusively for the government.[61] Other people may be essentially neutral about pro bono but would be upset and concerned if they felt a pro bono program had been mismanaged.

What happened to the state attorney general's program in Texas can serve as a cautionary tale. The program had been running less than a year when it became the focus of a political firestorm. An assistant attorney general, Gary Bledsoe, was also head of the county Democratic Party and the Texas state chair of the National Association for the Advancement of Colored People (NAACP). Bledsoe was accused of misusing state resources by performing work for these two organizations during state working hours without adequately making up the time.[62] Bledsoe had not represented clients under Texas's pro bono program,[63] nor had he asked permission to perform pro bono work.[64] Bledsoe was ultimately cleared of charges that he had done political and personal work on state time.[65] In response to the controversy, however, the Texas attorney general abolished the office's pro bono program.[66]

Based on the published news reports, it is impossible to tell what really happened in the Texas situation. Perhaps not surprisingly, there were strong

94   PRO BONO AND THE GOVERNMENT LAWYER

partisan overtones to the entire controversy.[67] But the case should remind us that government pro bono programs are inherently vulnerable. They were usually created with the stroke of a pen; they can be destroyed just as easily. Participants and supporters must be very circumspect.

Other Issues—Malpractice Coverage, Miscellaneous Litigation Expenses, Occupational Taxes

Other barriers to pro bono are malpractice insurance and various miscellaneous expenses, such as filing fees and transcription. And in some states the pro bono practice could subject government lawyers to occupational taxes intended for the private bar.

Generally, the pro bono lawyer will not have to get his or her own malpractice coverage for pro bono work. The agency that referred the pro bono case will typically have malpractice coverage and will either automatically cover pro bono lawyers or will do so if asked.[68] Another possibility—risky but at least worth mentioning—is for the pro bono lawyer to "go bare" and not carry malpractice coverage for his or her pro bono cases.[69]

Miscellaneous costs will have to come out of the pro bono lawyer's pocket, unless an alternative is found. The referring agency might cover these expenses, or they might be waived because of the client's indigent status.[70]

Maryland has devised an ingenious solution to this problem. It created a private, nonprofit corporation to cover these expenses for pro bono lawyers in the attorney general's office.[71] Tax-deductible donations to the corporation come from various members of the attorney general's staff. This setup, in addition to providing needed funds, has another advantage. There are a number of lawyers in the attorney general's office who agree with pro bono but do not want to represent indigent clients themselves. They can express their support through donations to the corporation.[72]

Some states may have an occupational tax on lawyers. Government lawyers are typically exempt from this tax but may fear that participation in pro bono could make them liable for it. The state attorney general or commissioner of revenue might issue a ruling exempting government pro bono lawyers from the tax. This is what happened in Connecticut[73] and Florida.[74]

Inherent Limitations on Appropriate Government Pro Bono Cases

Only certain types of cases are appropriate for a government pro bono program. By necessity, government pro bono will involve one-on-one representation, involving limited, discrete client issues. Big law reform cases and even major one-on-one litigation are impossible as part of government pro bono. "Big" pro bono cases would take up too much government lawyer time and government resources. They would probably involve too many costs, such as depositions, expert witnesses, and so on. Big cases might also be too controversial, thus raising appearance-of-impropriety issues. Finally, conflicts of interest might be more likely to arise in a big case, and conflicts not apparent at the start might cause problems later.

But government lawyers can at least take on some of the burden. Ideally, private firms and private advocacy groups, which are free to devote as much time and as many resources to any kind of pro bono as they want, will take the lead in law reform and other controversial, resource-intensive cases.[75] Further, subject to some Hatch Act–type restrictions, government lawyers can be involved, after hours, in political activities. For instance, many government lawyers are active in groups such as the National Organization for Women (NOW), the NAACP, and with battered women's shelters.

What Can Government Lawyers Do If a Pro Bono Program Neither Exists Nor Is Likely?

In some government offices, it may become clear to staff lawyers that no formalized pro bono program will be adopted, at least under existing political and legal conditions.[76] What can these lawyers do?

First, they can consider whether pro bono might be possible even under existing conditions. They could take small cases and work only during their lunch hour. Or perhaps their office is one where pro bono is not officially authorized but where their supervisor will look the other way as long as pro bono lawyers get their regular jobs done and do not abuse the supervisor's good will. This is what occurred in some federal agencies before President Clinton signed the executive order officially allowing and encouraging pro bono by federal employees.[77]

If pro bono during regular working hours is not possible, committed lawyers have other options. Local bar associations and advocacy groups may sponsor nighttime legal clinics or self-help lectures. These projects typically involve one-time, informal legal advice, but no ongoing representation.

Government lawyers should also consider whether they could assist in after-hours continuing legal education and training for private pro bono lawyers. If a lawyer works in a government office that deals a lot with poor people, he or she may be able to provide invaluable training on the applicable law and on how to "work the system." So long as individual cases are not discussed, there are no conflict of interest problems if the government lawyer shares his or her expertise with the private bar.

Finally, as has already been mentioned, government lawyers have a basic citizen's right to be involved in social action. They can be on the board of a nonprofit agency whose mission they support and use their legal expertise to write by-laws and help in other ways that do not conflict with their government duties. Of course lawyers must be careful to not let their board work interfere with their official duties and must also make clear that they are acting as individuals and not government representatives.

Institutionalizing Government Pro Bono

Once a government pro bono program is started, how can we make sure it continues? Put another way, how do we institutionalize government pro bono? Frankly, it is not easy; it is virtually impossible to institutionalize *any* new program in government, particularly one that has political and antipoverty overtones. Note, however, that it is not just "liberal" politicians who may support pro bono. Some conservatives may believe that government pro bono can be part of a kind of "Thousand Points of Light" volunteerism.[78]

A critical time comes when a key political figure changes. If the attorney general, governor, or government law office head changes, will pro bono survive? Government pro bono is new enough that we do not have a lot of examples yet of successful transitions from one administration to the next. Maryland, however, provides a hopeful sign. When a new governor, Parris Glendenning, took office in January 1995, pro bono survived without a peep.[79] Of course, it did not hurt that the attorney general who had spearheaded pro bono for his staff remained in office. Further, the new governor was of the same political party and held similar political views to both his predecessor and the attorney general.

The Personal and Institutional Rewards of Pro Bono

So far, this chapter has focused on the altruistic aspects of pro bono. But pro bono, like other forms of public service, can benefit the giver as well as the receiver. The pro bono lawyer can receive numerous advantages from pro bono work. Pro bono cases often call for skills that are not otherwise used by government lawyers. For example, hearings and trials may often occur in pro bono work, in contrast to a normal government lawyer's workload, which more often involves "advice and counsel functions or major litigation that rarely goes to trial."[80] Work with individual clients can hone a lawyer's interviewing and counseling skills. This kind of skills development may be particularly useful in public law offices, which often have young and inexperienced lawyers.[81]

Working for individual, needy clients can also provide a welcome change of pace from the more abstract and impersonal issues that generally concern government lawyers. The variety provided by pro bono might even lessen burnout and potentially decrease lawyer turnover.[82]

Pro bono can also reap officewide benefits. "[E]ven those attorneys who do not participate in the pro bono program seem to have a greater pride in the office and a better feeling about it because of the program's existence."[83] The positive publicity generated by pro bono would tend to boost office morale.[84] Having a pro bono program can help in recruiting lawyers who are interested in government service but who also want to represent indigents.[85]

Conclusion

There will always be naysayers—especially among lawyers—and anyone who wants to start a government pro bono program will have to deal with them. But government pro bono programs are increasingly widespread. Further, the diversity of such programs suggests that a model can be devised—and probably already exists—to fit any office. The ABA and many concerned and experienced individuals stand ready to help anyone interested in starting a government pro bono program. In preparing this chapter, I found that nearly all people involved in government pro bono gave generously of their time and expertise. (Some contact people are listed in Appendix 6D.) So, as the Nike slogan says, all that remains is to "Just Do It."

Notes

1. John J. Capowski, *Jumping the Hurdles: Establishing Pro Bono Programs in Government Law Offices,* American Bar Association, Private Bar Involvement in Legal Services for the Poor, PBI Exchange, Vol. 9, No. 2, Spring 1991, p. 2, at p. 3, reprinted in materials for American Bar Association, Government and Public Sector Lawyers Division program, "Voluntary Legal Services and the Government and Public Sector Attorney," August 6, 1994. *See also* Colleen Schweigert, *Government Attorneys & Pro Bono: It's Easier Than You Think,* PBI Activation Exchange, July 1985, in "Info Pack," "Government Attorney Pro Bono Participation," available from American Bar Association Center for Pro Bono, 541 N. Fairbanks Court, Chicago IL 60611-3314; 312-988-5770 [hereafter ABA packet]: changing the law in North Dakota to allow government lawyers to provide pro bono "was one of the easiest projects I've been involved in so far."

2. Item no. 24 ("Government Attorney PB Policy") in "Pro Bono Profiles—State Survey Results," prepared by ABA Center for Pro Bono, October 1996, available in ABA packet, *supra* note 1. The states listed as having government lawyer pro bono policies are Alaska, Arkansas, Connecticut, Florida, Idaho, Iowa, Kansas, Maine, Maryland, Minnesota, Nevada, New York, North Dakota, Oklahoma, Oregon, Pennsylvania, South Carolina, Texas, Washington, and Wisconsin.

3. *Id.* According to the ABA chart, states with policies in progress are California, Colorado, Missouri, North Carolina, South Dakota, and Vermont.

Some of the government lawyer pro bono policies are quite restrictive, especially on the issues of lawyer time and use of government equipment, discussed on p. 84. *See, e.g.,* Florida policy, § 3, attached to July 2, 1991, letter from Patricia R. Gleason, General Counsel, Office of the Attorney General, State of Florida, to Beverly Groudine, American Bar Association, in ABA packet, *supra* note 1: "[Pro bono] service must be performed on the attorney's own time, and no department personnel, supplies or equipment may be used."

Therefore, not all the states listed by the ABA as having government lawyer pro bono policies would permit the kind of pro bono program described in this chapter.

4. Other prominent government pro bono programs include the Broward County (Florida) County Attorney's Office, *see generally* John J. Copelan, Jr., Pro Bono Service by Government Attorneys: The Broward County Experience, Paper presented at American Bar Association, Government and Public Sector Lawyers Division program, Voluntary Legal Services and the Government and Public Sector Attorney, Aug. 6, 1994, and the State of Washington, *see* Maria Elliott, *Government Attorneys Provide Pro Bono Service in Washington State,* PBI Activation Exchange, Sept. 1994, p. 8, in ABA packet, *supra* note 1 (government lawyers in Washington state have been providing pro bono service since 1981; throughout the state, there are about 100 volunteer government lawyers).

98   PRO BONO AND THE GOVERNMENT LAWYER

5. I will not consider whether government lawyers should be covered under a mandatory pro bono program. To date, no state has adopted mandatory pro bono.

If a state should adopt mandatory pro bono, at a minimum it will need to review its statutes and regulations (such as those discussed below on use of governmental resources) to determine whether government lawyers can be legally required to participate.

For arguments why government lawyers should be included in a mandatory pro bono program, *see* COMMITTEE TO IMPROVE THE AVAILABILITY OF LEGAL SERVICES, FINAL REPORT TO THE CHIEF JUDGE OF THE STATE OF NEW YORK (April 1990), *reprinted in* Victor Marrero, *Committee to Improve the Availability of Legal Services—Final Report to the Chief Judge of the State of New York,* 19 HOFSTRA L. REV. 755, 854 (1991) (hereafter Marrero Committee Report). The Marrero committee concluded that "[e]xamined closely, the particular concerns expressed by government lawyers [who sought an exemption from the Committee's mandatory pro bono proposal] are not difficult to overcome." *Id.* at 786.

6. The ABA Model Rules of Professional Conduct rejects this definition. Comment no. 4 to Model Rule 6.1 says that "services rendered cannot be considered pro bono if an anticipated fee is uncollected."

7. Model Rule 6.1(b) states that lawyers may fulfill their remaining pro bono commitment by providing legal services to various public service and charitable groups, Rule 6.1(b)(1); by providing legal services at substantially reduced fees to persons of limited means, Rule 6.1(b)(2); or through law reform activities, Rule 6.1(b)(3).

Rule 6.1 waffles on the question of whether lawyers can fulfill their pro bono obligation through monetary payments to legal services or similar organizations. The rule itself says that "[a] lawyer should aspire" to 50 hours of pro bono service per year and then says that "[i]n addition, a lawyer should voluntarily contribute financial support for organizations that provide legal services to persons of limited means." However, comment no. 9, while stating that pro bono is "the individual ethical commitment of each lawyer," goes on to say "there may be times when it is not feasible for a lawyer to engage in pro bono services." The comment then says that the lawyer may, in such cases, discharge his or her pro bono requirement through financial support of legal services organizations and states that "[s]uch financial support should be reasonably equivalent to the value of the hours of service that would have otherwise been provided."

Some believe that pro bono should be defined to focus *exclusively* on legal services that help poor people directly or indirectly. Thus, New York's Marrero committee proposed a mandatory pro bono requirement of 40 hours and limited qualifying services to:

1. Professional services rendered in civil matters, and in those criminal matters for which there is no government obligation to provide funds for legal representation, to persons who are financially unable to compensate counsel

2. Activities related to improvement of the administration of justice by simplifying the legal process for, or increasing the availability and quality of legal services to, poor persons

3. Professional services to charitable, religious, civic and educational organizations in matters which are designed predominantly to address the needs of poor persons

Marrero Committee Report, *supra* note 5, at 854.

8. *But see* p. 86, for discussion of problems caused by the high-level involvement with the NAACP by a lawyer in the Texas attorney general's office.

9. *See generally* Marrero Committee Report, *supra* note 5, at 771–79 and citations therein. The Marrero committee concluded: "The scope and dimension of the crisis of poverty and the gap between legal needs and legal services associated with them are matters of common experience and are confirmed by information, studies, documentation and statistical evidence that put the size and importance of the crisis beyond reasonable doubts." *Id.* at 772. *See also* Kimberly A. Gulley, *Equal Access to Justice: The Responsibility of the Legal Profession,* 4 KAN. J.L. & PUB. POL'Y 105, 105 (1994) and citations therein; James L. Baillie & Judith Bernstein-Baker, *In the Spirit of Public Service: Model Rule 6.1, The Profession and Legal Education,* 13 LAW & INEQ. 51, 76 n. 40 (1994) (Minnesota Symposium: Legal Education & Pro Bono).

For discussion of unmet legal needs in a particular state, *see* William P. Quigley, *The Unmet Civil Legal Needs of the Poor in Louisiana,* 19 S.U. L. Rev. 273 (1992). For a discussion of the unmet legal needs of a particular group, *see* Giovanni Anzalone, *AIDS and Mandatory Pro Bono: A Step Toward the Equal Administration of Justice,* 8 Geo. J. Legal Ethics 691, 698–701 (1995) (AIDS-infected poor people).

10. Comment no. 5 to Model Rule 6.1 states: "Constitutional, statutory or regulatory restrictions may prohibit or impede government and public sector lawyers . . . from performing the [direct] pro bono services [to poor people and agencies serving them] outlined in paragraphs (a)(1) and (2) [of Rule 6.1]. Accordingly, where those restrictions apply, government and public sector lawyers . . . may fulfill their pro bono responsibility by performing [the more general philanthropic and law reform] services outlined in paragraph (b) [of Rule 6.1]."

11. *But see* Editorial, *Pro Bono: State Lawyers Should Work for State, Not Other People,* Hous. Chron., Nov. 5, 1993, at 32 (applauding decision of Texas attorney general to cancel pro bono program). The Texas situation is discussed further on p. 86.

12. Resolution passed by ABA House of Delegates, Annual Meeting, August 1984, described at 1 ABA/BNA Law. Man. on Prof. Cond. 380 (Aug. 22, 1984).

13. For instance, Texas has a statement in the state constitution prohibiting government employees from nongovernmental work. However, "the attorney general issued an opinion stating that private individuals may benefit from the use of public funds as long as an overall public purpose is served. And, since providing legal services to indigent persons is a public service, the constitutional prohibition was not violated." Cynthia Rapp, *Volunteer Legal Services and Government and Public Sector Attorneys,* Fla. B.J., vol. 70, Feb. 1996, at 66, 67–68. See p. 86 for later problems in the pro bono program in the Texas attorney general's office.

14. Curran had served on a state advisory committee that had looked at the unmet legal needs of Maryland's poor and had found existing legal services to be woefully inadequate. As a result, Curran concluded that he would try to establish a pro bono program for the state attorney general's office. Capowski, *supra* note 1, at 2.

Curran was undoubtedly influenced by his family's history of public service. As a child, he took phone messages for his father, who was active with the St. Vincent DePaul Society, a Catholic relief agency for needy families. *Id.*

Curran also had a staff that was quite receptive to the idea of a pro bono program. In the late 1980s, when the Maryland program was established, many lawyers in the attorney general's office were former legal services lawyers. They were naturally interested in finding some way to continue to help Maryland's poor. They also had the necessary substantive legal expertise to represent poor people in areas such as divorce, landlord-tenant, etc. Many of these lawyers still had contacts with legal aid and other service providers. These contacts helped the attorney general's office establish appropriate pro bono referral mechanisms. Interview with Professor John J. Capowski, Widener University School of Law, Harrisburg (Pa.) Campus (Dec. 11, 1996) [Hereinafter Capowski interview]. Prof. Capowski was director of education and training for the Maryland office of the attorney general during the time the Maryland pro bono program was established; he was involved in both the establishment and later the administration of that program.

Curran led by deed as well. He had personally done pro bono while a legislator and in private practice. Even while attorney general, he handled some pro bono domestic violence cases. Capowski interview.

15. Exec. Order 12988, § 2, 61 Fed. Reg. 4729 (Feb. 5, 1996).

16. Interview with Nancy G. Miller, Senior Counsel and Pro Bono Program Manager, Office of Policy Development, U.S. Department of Justice (Nov. 19, 1996). (Hereafter Miller interview.)

17. This may have been what happened in Minnesota. On January 29, 1994, the House of Delegates of the Minnesota State Bar Association approved a "Model Pro Bono Policy and Procedures for Government Attorneys." The policy is contained in the ABA packet, *supra* note 1.

100 PRO BONO AND THE GOVERNMENT LAWYER

Later, the state attorney general adopted a pro bono policy (effective November 1995) that is obviously modeled on the bar association's proposal. The Minnesota attorney general's policy is also in the ABA packet, *supra* note 1.

18. See p. 84 for more discussion of this issue.

19. *See* Appendix 6A on p. 99, "State Statutes: Attorney General Pro Bono Involvement," n.*: "[T]he interpretation of these types of statutory provisions [requiring full-time work by government employees] varies widely among the states. The best way to determine the interpretation of the provision in a given state at a given time is to contact the attorney general's office. Most often, there exists some policy (either written or unwritten) on the issue of pro bono involvement by members of the staff."

20. See Appendix 6A for statutes authorizing pro bono by government lawyers, in states such as Arizona, Nevada, North Dakota, Oregon, and Washington. For further description of how easily the North Dakota statute was passed, *see* Schweigert, *supra* note 1.

21. Capowski, *supra* note 1, at 3, acknowledges that motivations and local political conditions will vary tremendously from place to place. He then advises:

If you believe the head of the office cannot be influenced directly, consider gaining support from those who can influence that person. Learn what you can about the office and its decision-making, develop a range of strategies that might be used, weigh the positive and negative consequences of those various strategies, and move ahead.

22. At first, this centralized point was the Pro Bono Coordinating Committee and its members. Later, the coordinating task was taken over by an administrative assistant who was quite familiar with the program and who had been involved in its development. Capowski, *supra* note 1, at 13. The administrative assistant was able to manage the day-to-day operation of the program quite successfully, both because the nature of the cases accepted was routinized and because the administrative aide selected was a very capable and intelligent person. Capowski interview, *supra* note 14.

23. State of Maryland, Office of the Attorney General, Policies and Procedures, § 10.2, "Pro Bono Representation Program," (Jan. 6, 1995), Appendix 6B on p. 109, § X, "Closing a Case" [hereafter Maryland policy].

Capowski, *supra* note 1, at 13, indicates that some public law offices might wish "to develop a more detailed and formal system for monitoring the progress of cases" than is used in Maryland.

24. Maryland policy, Appendix 6B on p. 105, § I, "Summary of Program."

25. Maryland policy, Appendix 6B on p. 106, § III, "Process."

26. Miller interview, *supra* note 16.

27. Capowski interview, *supra* note 14.

Note also that most commentators agree that the client of the government lawyer is his or her agency, not the entire government. *See* District of Columbia Rules of Professional Conduct 1.6(i), "The client of the government lawyer is the agency that employs the lawyer unless expressly provided to the contrary by appropriate law, regulation, or order." The comment to D.C. Rule 1.6 says, "the employing agency has been designated the client under this rule to provide a commonly understood and easily determinable point for identifying the government client."

28. Capowski interview, *supra* note 14.

29. Capowski, *supra* note 1, at 10.

30. See Model Rules 1.7 through 1.11.

31. It is even conceivable, though probably unlikely, that a conflict might go undiscovered for so long and be so severe that the government would be forced to engage private, nongovernmental counsel to represent it. That is, *other* government lawyers who work with the disqualified pro bono lawyer would be disqualified. *See* Model Rules of Professional Conduct 1.10(a): "While lawyers are associated in a firm, none of them shall knowingly represent a client when any one of them practicing alone would be prohibited from doing so by Rules 1.7, 1.8(c), 1.9 or 2.2 [the basic conflict of interest rules]."

But see Capowski, *supra* note 1, at 11: "[A] reasonable application of the conflict rule to government lawyers should require withdrawal only from the representation of the pro bono client. This is because the Model Rules encourage pro bono service, the other client is the state and the conflict most likely would be, at most, imputed. In addition, strictly applying withdrawal from both sides would defeat the existence of such pro bono programs." The Maryland policy, Appendix 6B on p. 106, § III, "Process," n.2 provides "If an unanticipated conflict of interest later arises [i.e., after the government attorney has started the representation] that makes further representation or work impossible, the Committee will refer the case or matter back to the referring organization [for assignment to new, private pro bono counsel.]"

32. Attorney General's Office, State of Maryland, "Policy Guidelines: Pro Bono Representation," Policy issued on Oct. 21, 1988; Policy revised on May 24, 1989, § C, "Cases" (on file with the author).

33. Maryland policy, Appendix 6B on p. 106, § IV, "Cases."

34. Interview with Jack Schwartz, Chief Counsel for Opinions and Advice, Office of the Attorney General, State of Maryland (Dec. 17, 1996). Occasionally, a potential conflict arises because of inadequate factual information at intake. For example, Mr. Schwartz remembered one case where an assistant attorney general had started a pro bono divorce case, believing that no children were involved. The lawyer quickly learned that the client did have children. The case was immediately sent back to the referring agency to be redirected to private pro bono counsel. There was little disruption to the client, since the government lawyer had not done any work on the case. Further, because the problem was spotted early, the government lawyer had not learned any confidential client information; indeed, no actual conflict with the attorney general's office had actually arisen. Consequently, there was no possibility that the situation might result in vicarious disqualification of the attorney general's office.

Of course, the Maryland pro bono policy regulations still state that lawyers must monitor their cases for any conflicts of interest that might develop. However, as my conversation with Mr. Schwartz indicates, late-blooming conflicts have almost never occurred.

35. U.S. Department of Justice, Office of the Attorney General, Department of Justice Policy Statement on Pro Bono Legal and Volunteer Services, March 6, 1996, Appendix 6C on p. 113, § III(B)(3) [hereinafter DOJ policy].

36. *Id.*, Comment to § III(A)(2).

37. *Id.*, § III(A)(1).

38. *Id.*

39. *Id.*, § III(B)(4)(a).

40. *Id.*, § III(B)(4)(b).

41. 41. But see p. 89 for pro bono activities that can be done outside normal business hours.

42. DOJ policy, Appendix 6C on p. 118, § V(A), states: "Department employees are encouraged to seek volunteer and pro bono legal opportunities that can be accomplished outside their scheduled working hours. However, pro bono legal or volunteer activities may sometimes occur during the working hours."

43. *Id.* The DOJ policy further states that a "supervisor's personal views regarding the substance of the [subordinate's] pro bono activity" shall not affect the supervisor's decisions about whether to allow pro bono work during regular business hours. *Id.*

44. *Id.*, Comment to § V(A).

45. The DOJ policy hints at this possibility when it urges supervisors to be flexible and then says that employees engaged in pro bono may "*also* be granted leave without pay," etc. *Id.*, § V(A) (emphasis added). This suggests that means other than official leave-taking are permitted.

46. As a personal example, during academic year 1977–78, I was a lawyer for the U.S. Department of Labor in Washington, D.C., while at the same time acting as an adjunct research and writing instructor at a local law school. I did some modest amount of my teaching work at the office. My supervisor and others in the office were fully aware of what I was doing and never

102 PRO BONO AND THE GOVERNMENT LAWYER

raised any questions about it, presumably because I was performing my regular work adequately.

47. Maryland policy, Appendix 6B on p. 107, § V, "Lawyers' Time." This section also states that the lawyer need not take leave for small amounts of pro bono time (for instance, to make a few phone calls), but that "significant blocks of time, i.e., in excess of one hour spent exclusively on a pro bono matter, should be recorded as leave." *Id.* I thank John Capowski for explaining Maryland's excess compensatory time system to me. Capowski interview, *supra* note 14.

48. Md. Code 1957, Art. 10, § 33B(k), provides that the attorney general "and the attorneys on his staff appointed by him shall devote full time to their official duties and shall not engage in the private practice of law." See Appendix 6A on p. 99.

49. Lisa G. Lerman, *Public Service by Public Servants,* 19 Hofstra L. Rev. 1141, 1220 (1991).

50. Lerman, *id.* at 1213, reports on a federal lawyer who described her office's practices before the 1996 executive order on pro bono. The lawyer told Professor Lerman, "[I]n general, people in her office do not take all the rigid rules on use of resources very seriously . . . and . . . the rules are enforced only when there is an abuse of resources."

51. *See, e.g.,* Maryland policy, Appendix 6B on p. 109, § IX (1) "Financial Details."

The Maryland rules provide that computerized legal research, such as Westlaw, can only be done with the approval of a member of a pro bono coordinating committee. Maryland policy, Appendix 6B on p. 109, § XI, "Computer Research." This rule was necessary because the Maryland Attorney General's Office pays for every minute of computer use, rather than paying a flat rate. Capowski interview, *supra* note 14.

52. Lerman, *supra* note 49, at 1223–24.

53. Maryland policy, Appendix 6B on p. 107, § VI, "Support Staff Time."

54. DOJ policy, Appendix 6C on p. 118 § V(C), "Clerical Support."

55. *See* DOJ policy, Appendix 6C on p. 118, comment to § V(C), "Clerical Support": "The Pro Bono Program Manager and Volunteer Services Program Coordinator will develop a central pool of support staff who are willing to volunteer to support pro bono legal or volunteer projects." Maryland apparently had no problem finding secretaries who were willing to volunteer for pro bono work, including for large projects that needed to be done after hours. Capowski interview, *supra* note 14.

56. In Maryland, the committee added a member who was the assistant attorney general who acted as counsel for the state comptroller. Capowski, *supra* note 1, at 11. This person's expertise proved invaluable. Capowski interview, *supra* note 14.

57. *See* comment to Model Rule 1.9, explaining why "appearance of impropriety" is no longer a basis for disqualification under the conflict of interest rules: "[D]escribing the problem of disqualification cannot be properly resolved . . . by the very general concept of appearance of impropriety." *But see* New York Code of Professional Responsibility, Canon 9, which retains the standard: "A lawyer should avoid even the appearance of professional impropriety."

58. Maryland policy, Appendix 6B on p. 107, § VII, "Identification."

59. *Id.*

60. In Maryland, the separate nonprofit corporation established to assist the pro bono program, the Public Lawyers Legal Service Program, Inc., provides stationery to pro bono government lawyers.

61. *See* Editorial, *supra* note 11.

62. Terrence Stutz & Wayne Slater, *Morales Puts Aide on Leave,* Dallas Morning News, Oct. 16, 1993, at 29A.

63. Clay Robison, *Morales Blames GOP for End to Free Legal Aid,* Hous. Chron., Nov. 4, 1993, at 25.

64. Clay Robison, *Morales Cancels Program That Offers Free Legal Aid,* Hous. Chron., Oct. 29, 1993, at 35.

65. George Kuempel & Christy Hoppe, *Grand Jury Clears Enoch, Bledsoe,* Dallas Morning News, March 12, 1994, at 33A.

66. Robison, *supra* note 64.

67. Bledsoe's supporters claimed that the investigation of him was intended to divert attention from the prosecution of Republican U.S. Senator Kay Bailey Hutchison, who had been charged with and later acquitted on ethical violations. Kuempel & Hoppe, *supra* note 65. When Texas Attorney General Dan Morales, like Bledsoe a Democrat, discontinued the pro bono program, he said he was doing so because Republican legislators were claiming that the program was illegal and he wanted to avoid further criticism of his office. Robison, *supra* note 63.

68. The Maryland policy, Appendix 6B on p. 108, § VIII, "Insurance," indicates that the malpractice insurance will be available from the referring agencies and instructs participating pro bono lawyers to contact the pro bono program's coordinating committee. DOJ policy, Appendix 6C on p. 115, § C(2), "Malpractice Coverage," says that the pro bono lawyer "should determine whether the referring pro bono program or organization has a malpractice insurance policy which covers volunteer attorneys" before meeting with or accepting a pro bono client. The comment to this section of the DOJ policy says that local bar volunteer lawyer programs and "more established referral programs" generally carry malpractice insurance for volunteer lawyers.

69. *See id.*: "Attorneys who choose to provide legal services without malpractice insurance coverage are acting at their own risk."

"Going bare" in pro bono cases is potentially dangerous, but probably less so than in private practice with middle- and upper-class clients. Though there is little information on the subject, it appears that poor clients rarely sue their legal services lawyers.

70. *See* Maryland policy, Appendix 6B on p. 106, § IV, "Cases": "Each volunteer attorney will . . . be send [sic] a proposed Motion and Order for Waiver of Court Costs that can be tailored to the particular client."

71. *Id.,* § IX (1), "Expenses," "Financial Details." Because the nonprofit corporation has limited funding, pro bono lawyers are asked to consult a member of the coordinating committee before incurring expenses of more than $100. *Id.*

72. Capowski interview, *supra* note 14.

73. Under a ruling from the Connecticut Commission of Revenue, government lawyers remained exempt from the occupational tax as long as they were performing pro bono services only. Rapp, *supra* note 13, at 67.

74. When the issue arose due to the Broward County attorney's pro bono program, the Florida attorney general issued an opinion stating that "because the program in which the attorneys were involved was a charitable organization, an occupational license was not required." *Id.*

75. The involvement of the private bar in pro bono is crucial, since Congress has banned Legal Service Corporation grantees from many law reform and similar cases. *See, e.g.,* Omnibus Consolidated Rescissions and Appropriations Act of 1996, Pub. Law 104-134, 110 Stat. 1321, § 504, prohibiting Legal Service Corporation grantees from involvement in class action suits, prisoner litigation and immigration cases, even with privately obtained money. Regulations implementing the law can be found at 61 Fed. Reg. 63749-01 (Dec. 2, 1996) and 61 Fed. Reg. 63754-01 (Dec. 2, 1996). *See also* Richard C. Reuben, *Keeping Legal Aid Alive, Programs Restructuring—Seeking Funds in Rescue Effort,* A.B.A.J., Nov. 1996, at 20 (describing efforts by legal aid offices, with mixed success, to get private lawyers to take over class action and other law reform activities).

At least one court has held that the restrictions on grantees' use of private funds were unconstitutional under the First Amendment, Varshavsky v. Perales (New York State Supreme Court, New York County, Dec. 24, 1996), Jan. 6, 1997, West's Legal News 14048, 1997 WL 2053. Several Legal Service Corporation grantees have also challenged the law in federal court in Hawaii, Legal Aid Society of Hawaii v. Legal Services Corp., (D. Hawaii, complaint filed Jan. 9, 1997), Jan. 13, 1997 West's Legal News 14363, 1997 WL 8482.

104   PRO BONO AND THE GOVERNMENT LAWYER

76. For instance, the lawyers may work in a place where both the executive and legislative authorities are opposed to pro bono. Or perhaps the existing law is very restrictive on how "full-time" government work is defined and no legislative relief is in sight.

77. *See* Lerman, *supra* note 49, at 1210–16, for several different stories of federal government lawyers doing pro bono before President Clinton's 1996 executive order. The lawyers' experiences differ sharply on issues such as taking time off, use of government resources and equipment, supervisors' reactions and approval, etc.

78. Capowski interview, *supra* note 14.

79. Schwartz interview, *supra* note 34.

80. Capowski, *supra* note 1, at 2.

81. *Id.*

82. *Id.* Capowski speculates that pro bono might "spur new insights and creativity into the routine of attorneys." *Id.*

83. *Id.* at 3. Capowski notes that some lawyers who do not participate in pro bono personally may be very supportive of pro bono by others. There can be many reasons for an individual not to participate in pro bono, such as other commitments or not feeling personally qualified to do work with indigent clients. *Id.*

84. For instance, it seems safe to assume that Broward County lawyers were proud when the office was one of five recipients of the ABA's 1996 Pro Bono Publico awards, given by the ABA Standing Committee on Lawyers' Public Service Responsibilities. The award recognizes "lawyers, law firms or institutional legal departments for direct service to the poor or for activities that increase the access of poor persons to legal assistance." The Broward County office, the only government law office to win, was "cited as a model for other governmental agencies around the country for the legislation that removed barriers to publicly employed lawyers doing pro bono work." ABA News at a Glance, no. 31, June 25, 1996.

85. Capowski, *supra* note 1, at 3.

APPENDIX ❦ 6A

STATE STATUTES: ATTORNEY GENERAL PRO BONO INVOLVEMENT*

(As of January, 1995)

Alabama   Private practice prohibited.
Ala. Code §36-15-9: "All Assistant Attorneys General of the state of Alabama are . . . hereby prohibited from engaging in the private practice of law during the time that they are such Assistant Attorneys General."

Alaska   No statute.

Arizona   Private practice prohibited, but pro bono permitted.
Ariz. Rev. Stat. Ann. §41-191(B)(2): "The Attorney General and assistants shall devote full-time to the duties of the office and shall not directly or indirectly engage in the private practice of law or in an occupation conflicting with such duties, except an Assistant Attorney General may, but in no circumstances shall be required to, represent private clients in pro bono, private civil matters under the following circumstances:" (List of eleven circumstances follows including representation must be conducted exclusively during off hours, must not interfere with performance of official duties and must not utilize resources that will result in cost to the state. See statute for complete listing.)

---

* The fact that an attorney general in a given state must devote full-time to his/her duties or is prohibited from the private practice of law does not necessarily mean that s/he cannot engage in pro bono work; the interpretation of these types of statutory provisions varies widely among the states. The best way to determine the interpretation of the provision in a given state at a given time is to contact the attorney general's office. Most often, there exists some policy (either written or unwritten) on the issue of pro bono involvement by members of the staff.

105

106 PRO BONO AND THE GOVERNMENT LAWYER

Arkansas	Private practice prohibited. Ark. Stat. Ann. §25-16-701: "the Attorney General of the state of Arkansas shall not engage in the private practice of law."
California	Private practice prohibited. Cal. Government Code §12504: "The Attorney General shall not engage in the private practice of law . . . but instead he shall devote his entire time to the service of the state."
Colorado	No statute.
Connecticut	Full time required. Conn. Gen. Stat. §35-3-124: "The Attorney General shall devote full time to the duties of the office."
Delaware	Private practice prohibited. Del. Code Ann. tit. 29, §2505(H): "The Attorney General shall devote full time to the office and shall not practice law for the term to which he is elected. He shall determine whether any of his assistants, other than those designated as full time . . . shall be excluded from the practice of law."
Florida	No statute.
Georgia	Private practice prohibited. Ga. Code Ann. §40-1612: "Neither the Attorney General nor any other attorney at law employed full time by the Department of Law shall engage in the private practice of law during his term of appointment."
Hawaii	Private practice prohibited. Haw. Rev. Stat. §4-28-10: "The Attorney General, the Attorney General's first deputy, and other deputies shall devote their entire time and attention to the duties of their respective offices. They shall not engage in the private practice of law."
Idaho	No statute.
Illinois	No statute.
Indiana	Full time required. Ind. Code Ann. §4-6-2-3: "The attorney-general shall reside at Indianapolis, and he shall keep his office in the statehouse; and he shall, on all business days, during business hours, be at said office, in person or by deputy, unless engaged in court or elsewhere in the service of the state."
Iowa	Full time required. Iowa Code Ann. §13.4: Assistant Attorneys General "shall devote their entire time to the duties of their position."

Kansas	No statute.
Kentucky	Private practice prohibited. Ky. Rev. Stat. Ann. §15.015: "The Attorney General shall not engage in the private practice of law during his term in office."
Louisiana	Private practice prohibited. La. Rev. Stat. 49:256: "The attorney general shall not engage in the private practice of law during his term of office, but shall devote his full time to the duties of the office of the attorney general."
Maine	Private practice prohibited. Me. Rev. Stat. Ann. tit. 5, §191: "The Attorney General shall devote full time to his duties and shall not engage in the private practice of law during his term of office."
Maryland	Full time required. Md. (Legal Officials) Code Ann. §33B(k): The Attorney General "and the attorneys on his staff appointed by him shall devote full time to their official duties and shall not engage in the private practice of law."
Massachusetts	No statute.
Michigan	No statute.
Minnesota	No statute.
Mississippi	Full time required. Miss. Code Ann. §7-5-17: The Attorney General must be full-time "open Monday through Friday for not less than eight hours each day." Miss Code Ann. §7-5-5: The assistant attorneys general "shall devote their entire time and attention to the duties pertaining to the department of justice. . . ."
Missouri	Private practice prohibited. Mo. Ann. Stat. §27.010: "The Attorney General shall devote his full time to the office and . . . shall not engage in the private practice of law."
Montana	No statute.
Nebraska	Private practice restricted. Neb. Rev. Stat. §84-201.02: "The Attorney General shall not engage in the private practice of law for compensation."
Nevada	Private practice prohibited, but pro bono permitted. Nev. Rev. Stats. §228.070(2): "Except as otherwise provided in NRS 7.065, the attorney general shall not engage in the private practice of law."

Nev. Rev. Stat. §7.065: "Except as otherwise provided by a specific statute, any attorney employed by the State of Nevada . . . may represent an indigent person in any proceeding if: 1. The attorney first receives the permission of his supervisor . . . 2. The interests of the indigent person in that proceeding do not conflict with the interests of the state . . . 3. The representation is provided through or in association with an organization that provides free legal assistance to indigent persons; and 4. The attorney receives no compensation for representation."

New Hampshire Private practice prohibited.
N.H. Rev. Stat. Ann. §7:6-d: "The attorney general, deputy attorney general, assistant attorneys general and all attorneys employed by the Department of Justice shall not directly or indirectly engage in the private practice of law."

New Jersey Private practice prohibited.
N.J. Stat. Ann. §52:17A-3: "The Attorney General . . . shall devote his entire time to his duties as Attorney General and shall not, while in office, engage in the private practice of law."

New Mexico No statute.

New York No statute.

North Carolina Private practice prohibited.
N.C. Gen. Stat. §114-3: "The Attorney General shall devote his whole time to the duties of his office and shall not engage in the private practice of law."

North Dakota Pro bono permitted.
N.D. Cent. Code §27-14-02: "An attorney general or assistant attorney general with the permission of the attorney general may voluntarily represent indigent clients referred by an organized *pro bono* program in addition to the regular duties of the office; . . . at no cost to the state of North Dakota."

Ohio No statute.

Oklahoma No statute.

Oregon Pro bono permitted.
Or. Rev. Stat. 180.140(6): "None of the provisions of ORS 180 prohibit the Attorney General or any of the Attorney General's full-time deputies or assistants from voluntarily representing, without compensation or expenditure of state resources, indigent clients referred by a nonprofit civil legal aid office or pro bono program."

Pennsylvania	No statute.
Rhode Island	No statute.
South Carolina	Pro bono permitted. S.C. Code Ann. §40-5-380: "An attorney employed by any executive agency of the state may, with the permission of his agency head, represent without fees indigent clients referred by a pro bono program organized, sponsored, or endorsed by the South Carolina Bar. The pro bono service must be at no cost to the state, and may not conflict with the attorney's official duties or the interests of the State. The attorney shall use compensatory or annual leave for pro bono service performed during normal working hours . . ."
South Dakota	Private practice prohibited. S.D. Codified Laws Ann. §1-11-1.1: "The Attorney General shall serve on a full-time basis and shall not actively engage in the private practice of law."
Tennessee	Private practice prohibited. Tenn. Code Ann. §8-7-104: "District attorneys general shall be prohibited from engaging in the practice of law." Tenn. Code Ann. §8-6-107: "Attorney general and reporter and his assistants shall be under the . . . restrictions . . . of the district attorneys general." Tenn. Code Ann. §8-7-201: The assistant attorney general "will devote full time to the duties as such assistant attorney general and will not actively engage in the practice of law in any civil courts of the state of Tennessee or any other state. . . ."
Texas	No statute.
Utah	Private practice prohibited, but pro bono permitted. Utah Code Ann. §67-5-10: "Attorneys in career status shall be full-time employees and shall not engage in the private practice of law and shall not receive any fee for legal services rendered to any person, corporation, partnership, or other legal entity other than the state or the county in which the person holds office or by whom the person is employed. The practice of law prohibited by this subsection does not include pro bono service."
Vermont	No statute.
Virginia	No statute.

110   PRO BONO AND THE GOVERNMENT LAWYER

Washington   Private practice prohibited, but pro bono permitted.
Wash. Rev. Code Ann. §43.10.115: "The attorney general shall not practice law for remuneration in his private capacity." (Wash. Rev. Code Ann. §43.10.120 for assistants.)
Wash. Rev. Code Ann. §43.10.130: "None of the provisions of RCW 43.10.010 and 43.10.115 through 43.10.125 shall be construed as prohibiting the attorney general or any of his full-time deputies or assistants from: (2) Performing legal services of a charitable nature."

West Virginia   No statute.

Wisconsin   Private practice prohibited.
Wis. Stat. Ann. §19.45(9): "The attorney general may not engage in the private practice of law during the period in which he or she holds that office."

Wyoming   Private practice prohibited.
Wyo. Stat. §9-1-604: "The Attorney General . . . shall not engage in any private practice."

APPENDIX ❦ 6B

State of Maryland
Attorney General's Office
Pro Bono Representation Program

I. *Summary of Program*

The Attorney General's pro bono Representation Program has been initiated as an exception to the ban on private practice currently in effect. This program is voluntary and attorneys will engage in pro bono activity in addition to their official duties. Each attorney will take all necessary steps to differentiate his or her pro bono representation from the work of the office.

In light of the public interest underlying the pro bono program, as reflected in Rules of Professional Conduct 6.1, and the program's direct benefits in terms of broadened experience for our attorneys, the office will support the program in several ways. First, cases will be referred to our pro bono Coordinating Committee (the "Committee") from the Maryland Volunteer Lawyer Service, Inc., (MVLS) and other approved referral sources. This Committee will then refer the cases to volunteer attorneys.

The office will provide reasonable secretarial support, so long as the time commitment of the support staff is limited and does not interfere with the performance of primary responsibilities to this office or to client agencies. The office will provide centralized coordination for the program, especially to screen potential conflicts of interest. The office will also sponsor training programs for volunteer attorneys in the areas of representation. Finally, the office will adjust its policy for the use of earned compensatory time to allow this form of leave to be taken by lawyers when they engage in pro bono representation.

II. *Pro Bono Coordinating Committee*

The Committee, chaired by a Deputy Attorney General, consists of attorneys from units throughout the office. (See Appendix A.) The Committee will serve as the liaison between the organizations that refer cases to the Office of the Attorney General (OAG) and the volunteer attorneys. The Committee is available to assist volunteer attorneys with questions concerning conflicts of

111

interest and will provide procedural and substantive advice on issues that arise as attorneys undertake pro bono services.

III. *Process*

The referring organizations will refer a case or matter directly to the Committee after screening the prospective client for financial eligibility. Assuming that no conflict of interest is apparent, the program's administrative assistant will contact an attorney who has indicated a willingness to participate in the program.[1] The attorney should consult the Rules of Professional Conduct, in particular Rules 1.7 and 1.10, to ensure that he or she sees no conflict of interest before proceeding with the case. The volunteer attorney should contact the Committee member listed in Appendix A, #1 if questions concerning conflicts of interest arise.[2] The referring organization and the Committee will periodically request information from the volunteer attorney concerning the status of the case or matter being handled. When a case has been completed, the volunteer attorney should notify the Committee. If the attorney leaves the OAG after completion of the case, the case file should be forwarded to the Committee. Of course, if the volunteer attorney should leave the OAG during the pendency of the case, the attorney-client relationship should continue.

IV. *Cases*

Attorneys involved in the pro bono program will provide representation and services in the following areas only:

(A) Divorces involving no custody disputes;

(B) General wills, advance directives, powers of attorney, private guardianships not involving any State agency;

(C) Landlord/tenant cases not involving the application of the Consumer Protection Act;

(D) Counseling and other legal assistance, through the Lawyers Clearing House Project to nonprofit organizations that serve low-income people (except for work related to development projects for which State aid might be sought);

(E) Veterans benefit appeals; and

(F) Personal bankruptcy—cases to be accepted on a limited basis only while the Pro Bono Committee assesses potential conflict problems.[3]

The office will sponsor training programs in these areas. In addition, reference materials in these areas are available in the library. The Committee will periodically review the categories of cases encompassed within the program and decide whether changes should be made.

This program has adopted a Retainer Agreement that should be signed by each client. A copy of this agreement will be sent to each volunteer attorney when a case is accepted. Each volunteer attorney will also be sent a proposed Motion and Order for Waiver of Court Costs that can be tailored to the particular client.

The Coordinating Committee also has sample pleadings available for use by volunteer attorneys.

V. *Lawyers' Time*

Volunteer attorneys shall carry out their pro bono responsibilities on their own time; however, as more fully described below, attorneys may use their currently unusable compensatory time for pro bono work. This does not mean that the lawyers may not do pro bono activities during normal working hours. Rather, lawyers must continue to account for at least 40 hours of professional services each week, plus whatever additional time is needed for the lawyer to provide the kind of lawyering that this office expects. Pro bono representation is to be undertaken in addition to, not in lieu of, these core responsibilities.

A lawyer must continue to certify that the required 40 hours per week were devoted to State activities. If the lawyer worked less than 40 hours in a week for the State as a result of pro bono representation, the lawyer is required to take leave to account for the 40 hour minimum. Although a lawyer need not take leave for small amounts of pro bono time during the work day, significant blocks of time, *i.e.*, in excess of one hour spent exclusively on a pro bono matter, should be recorded as leave. That leave can be of any type, including excess compensatory leave, *i.e.*, accumulated leave beyond that which is currently usable.[4]

VI. *Support Staff Time*

Support staff may assist volunteer attorneys within carefully observed limits. Ordinary agency tasks have priority, but limited typing of short letters or pleadings may be done. More extensive typing that poses the risk of material interference with agency activities should be done only with the express approval of the lawyer's division chief. If a volunteer attorney requires the assistance of additional support, he or she should contact the Committee members listed in Appendix A, #6 who will arrange for such assistance.

VII. *Identification*

Lawyers participating in the pro bono program should make clear to third parties that they are participating in this program and not acting in an official capacity. The attorney should in no way give the impression that the OAG is providing the representation. Volunteer attorneys should make every possible attempt to meet with opposing counsel and clients outside the office. A list of available locations is listed in Appendix B. If the volunteer attorney cannot locate available meeting space, he or she should contact the members of the Committee listed in Appendix A, #3 for assistance.

114   PRO BONO AND THE GOVERNMENT LAWYER

Volunteer attorneys should write all correspondence on the official pro bono program letterhead, which will be sent to all participating attorneys. Volunteer attorneys should use either their home address or the address listed in Appendix A. Attorneys may place and receive telephone calls from their State offices concerning *pro bono* activities.

VIII.   *Insurance*

All OAG attorneys participating in the OAG pro bono program will be covered by malpractice insurance carried by the Maryland Volunteer Lawyers Service or another referral source. You may contact the Committee member listed in Appendix A, #3 for additional information concerning insurance coverage.

IX.   *Expenses*

1. Financial Details

Expenses of the *pro bono* program will be paid through the Public Lawyers Legal Services Program, Inc., a §501(c)(3) corporation organized for that purpose. The Committee expects that expenses will be of two types, direct and indirect.

Direct expense would be such items as court costs, filing fees, transcripts and so forth. Participating attorneys should apply to the Fiscal Division of the Office of the Attorney General, (*see* Appendix A for address) for the necessary check, or may pay such amounts directly and then apply for reimbursement. Funding is limited, so please consult the member of the Coordinating Committee listed in Appendix A, #5 in advance before incurring expenses in excess of $150.

Indirect expense would include items that inherently must be supplied by the State, but which will be for the benefit of non-state private pro bono representation. This would include such items as paper, postage, photocopying and long-distance telephone usage.

There is no need (unless specifically requested by the agency) to account for minor amounts of these indirect costs on an immediate basis. It is expected that most files or cases will breed relatively little expense, and the reimbursement mechanism for such small items (3 to 4 letters—10 to 20 pages of copying) will be set after a review of ongoing operations. It is very possible that the agencies will forgo such minor reimbursements, because the cost to the agency may be less than the cost of processing the reimbursement. The final decision on whether reimbursement is required should be left to the agency whose resources are used; if reimbursement (or immediate reimbursement) is requested, the request should be honored.

Larger amounts (the rare 50-page enclosure to 10 people) should be reimbursed immediately at the attorney's own initiative; the attorney should send in the form and a check will be issued promptly. It should also be noted that an agency should never pay direct expenses such as court costs.

Mileage and parking are *not* reimbursable expenses at this juncture. Attorneys desiring a special exception to this rule should contact the Committee member listed in Appendix A, #4 to discuss the exigencies of their particular case.

Finally, attorneys should note that the form does not absolutely require a receipt for reimbursement to occur. Attorneys should make their best effort to procure and forward such receipts; their signature on the form constitutes their certification that the expense was actually incurred.

2. Trust Account Transactions

If an attorney needs to deposit client funds in a trust account, he or she should contact the Committee member listed in Appendix A.

3. Delivery

Checks will be sent to the attorney requesting same. If special arrangements are desired (pick-up, etc.) please call the Fiscal Division of the Office of the Attorney General in advance, and/or make a notation on the form.

X. *Closing A Case*

Once an attorney has completed his or her representation, a brief letter should be sent to the referring organization stating that the case has been completed and what was accomplished. A copy of this letter should also be sent to Kathleen Izdebski, Opinions and Advice.

The attorney should maintain the case file as long as he or she remains within the Office of the Attorney General. If the attorney leaves the office, the file should be sent to a member of the Pro Bono Coordinating Committee.

XI. *Computer Research*

Computer research (*i.e.*, Westlaw, Lexis) may only be done with the approval of a member of the Coordinating Committee.

XII. *Evaluation*

The program will be reviewed and modified as need be on a yearly basis.

Policy initially issued on: October 21, 1988
Policy revised on: November 29, 1994

Notes

1. No lawyer will be asked to handle more than one case or matter at a time.

2. If an unanticipated conflict of interest later arises that makes further representation or work impossible, the Committee will refer the case or matter back to the referring organization.

3. This list should not be construed as limiting activities previously permitted by an exception to the ban on private practice. *See* Policy on Private Practice of Law, §10.1.

4. Both for statistical purposes and OAG personnel requirements, the volunteer lawyer must record the type of leave taken for time devoted to pro bono activity.

APPENDIX ❦ 6C

Office of the Attorney General
Washington, D. C. 20590

March 6, 1996

DEPARTMENT OF JUSTICE POLICY STATEMENT ON PRO BONO LEGAL AND VOLUNTEER SERVICES

I. DEPARTMENT OF JUSTICE <u>PRO BONO</u> LEGAL AND VOLUNTEER POLICY

The Policy. Given the significant unmet need for legal and other community services in the nation, it is the policy of the Department of Justice to encourage and support efforts by Department employees to provide <u>pro bono</u> legal and volunteer services within their communities that are consistent with applicable federal statutes and regulations governing conflicts-of-interest and outside activities. While service in the Department of Justice is itself one of the highest forms of public service, the Department further strives to increase access to justice for all and to strengthen our communities. To this end, the Attorney General encourages Department employees to set a personal goal of at least 50 hours per year of <u>pro bono</u> legal and volunteer service.

> *COMMENT:*
>
> *<u>Scope of the Program</u>. The Department's Policy Statement on Pro Bono Legal and Volunteer Services (the "Policy Statement") will extend to all Department employees and encourage all volunteer work, legal or non-legal. This inclusive structure best reflects the Department's commitment to developing a sense of community responsibility, not only among lawyers but among all citizens.*
>
> *<u>The 50-hour goal</u>. The Department of Justice has adopted a 50-hour aspirational goal. In the context of pro bono legal services, the 50-hour aspirational goal is in accord with the American Bar Association's Model Rule 6.1, and falls within the range adopted by other state bar associations.*

II. DEFINITION OF <u>PRO BONO</u> LEGAL AND VOLUNTEER SERVICES

Definition. <u>Pro bono</u> legal work and volunteer services are broadly defined to include many different types of activities, performed without compensation.

A. <u>Pro bono</u> legal services. <u>Pro bono</u> legal services are those legal services performed without compensation and include, but are not limited to, the provision of legal services to:

117

1. persons of limited means or other disadvantaged persons;
2. charitable, religious, civic, community, governmental, health and educational organizations in matters which are designed primarily to address the needs of persons of limited means or other disadvantaged persons, or to further their organizational purpose;
3. individuals, groups or organizations seeking to secure or protect civil rights, civil liberties or public rights; or
4. activities for improving the law, the legal system, or the legal profession.

COMMENT: This definition is based on Rule 6.1 of the ABA Model Rules of Professional Conduct, with some modifications that, among other things, make clear that the legal services must be provided without fee. This definition of pro bono legal services includes a broad range of activities; the listed activities are intended as examples only. The Department recognizes, however, that statutory or regulatory restrictions may prohibit government lawyers from performing certain pro bono services. See Section III.

B. Volunteer services. Volunteer services are those activities, other than the practice of law, performed without compensation. They include, but are not limited to, the provision of services to:
1. persons of limited means or other disadvantaged persons; or
2. charitable, religious, civic, community, governmental, health and educational organizations in matters which are designed primarily to address the needs of persons of limited means or other disadvantaged persons.

COMMENT: The Department does not seek to restrict the type of volunteer activities in which employees may engage in their free time, provided that the activities do not violate any statutory or regulatory restrictions. See Section III.

The Attorney General encourages Department employees to participate in the Department-sponsored mentoring programs and volunteer activities that further the Department's program priorities. For example, the strong leadership skills of many Department employees could be put to good use helping at-risk youth in classrooms, youth clubs, shelters, and midnight basketball programs. The Volunteer Services Program Coordinator, see Section VI, will have information regarding such programs.

III. LIMITATIONS ON **PRO BONO** LEGAL AND VOLUNTEER SERVICES
A. Prior Approval.
1. Pro Bono Legal Services. An employee seeking to engage in any pro bono legal work must follow agency procedures for outside activities, and must consult with his or her Deputy-Designated Agency Ethics Official regarding prior approval requirements. See 5 C.F.R. § 2635.803 and note thereto.

Appendix 6C 119

Component heads are encouraged to designate some <u>pro bono</u> legal activities as preapproved such that the employee need only give advance notice to a designated supervisor before undertaking the outside activity.

    a. In general, approval of an employee's request to engage in <u>pro bono</u> legal work shall be granted if the work would not:

        (1) violate any federal statute, rule or regulation, including, for example, 18 U.S.C. § 201 <u>et seq</u>. and 5 C.F.R. Pt. 2635;

        (2) interfere with the proper and effective performance of the employee's official duties (including time and availability requirements of his or her position), <u>see</u> 5 C.F.R. § 2635.705;

        (3) create or appear to create a conflict of interest, <u>see</u> Section III.B. below; or

        (4) cause a reasonable person to question the integrity of the Department's programs or operations.

    b. Where an employee has been denied approval by the component head's designee to perform <u>pro bono</u> legal work, the decision will be appealed automatically to the component head.

2. <u>Volunteer Services</u>. An employee seeking to engage in volunteer activities must follow agency procedures for outside activities, and must consult with his or her Deputy-Designated Agency Ethics Official regarding prior approval requirements. <u>See</u> 5 C.F.R. § 2635.803 and note thereto.

The standards for granting approval for volunteer services are the same as those set forth above for volunteer legal services. <u>See</u> Section III.A.1.a.

<u>COMMENT</u>: *Offices may choose to institute their own <u>pro bono</u> or volunteer service programs in which certain activities are pre-approved. For example, the U.S. Attorney's Office in the Southern District of Florida has received permission from the Executive Office for U.S. Attorneys to run a <u>pro bono</u> program in conjunction with the Dade County Bar. Under this program, Assistant United States Attorneys in the Southern District have the opportunity and necessary approval to provide volunteer legal representation in select domestic violence, child advocacy, divorce, and small claims cases. The Attorney General urges all components to consult with the <u>Pro Bono</u> and Volunteer Services Committee, <u>see</u> Section VI.A., and the Department's Designated Ethics Official to determine which outside activities it may want to designate as preapproved.*

B. Conflicts of Interest.

    1. <u>General Standard</u>. Department employees may not engage in <u>pro bono</u> legal or volunteer services that create or appear to create a conflict of interest with their work for the Department. Under the Standards of Ethical Conduct for Employees of the Executive Branch, 5 C.F.R. § 2635, a conflict of interest generally exists where the services would:

120   PRO BONO AND THE GOVERNMENT LAWYER

    a. require the recusal of the employee from significant aspects of the employee's official duties, see 5 C.F.R. § 2635.802(b);

    b. create an appearance that the employee's official duties were performed in a biased or less than impartial manner, see 5 C.F.R. § 2635.502; or

    c. create an appearance of official sanction or endorsement, see 5 C.F.R. § 2635.702(b).

2. 18 U.S.C. § 205. With limited exceptions, outside activities may not include the representation of third parties before the federal government. See 18 U.S.C. § 205.

3. Criminal Representation. Department of Justice attorneys are prohibited by statute from providing pro bono legal assistance in any case in which the United States is a party or has a direct and substantial interest—which includes criminal defense representation in federal court, see 18 U.S.C. § 205. In the past, full-time Department employees have also been prohibited by regulation from providing outside professional services (including, for example, services as a lawyer, paralegal, investigator, secretary, economist or physician) in criminal or habeas corpus matters in any court. It is the Department's intention to continue that prohibition.

4. Responsibility for Conflicts Check

    a. The component head or the component head's designee will be responsible for completing the conflicts check for pro bono legal activities prior to approving such activities.

    b. The Department employee will be responsible for ensuring that his or her volunteer services do not present a conflict of interest, and do not otherwise violate any applicable statute or regulation.

COMMENT: The issue of conflicts should be determined by reference to the government-wide standards of conduct, 5 C.F.R. § 2635 (particularly §§ 2635.801–802), and any subsequently published Department of Justice supplemental regulations.

Application of these standards of conduct necessarily will involve the exercise of judgment. These judgments likely will differ from one component and situation to another. For this reason, each component will be asked to work with the Pro Bono and Volunteer Services Committee, see Section VI, and the Department's Designated Ethics Official in setting its own component-specific conflict standard. Deputy-Designated Agency Ethics Officials (DAEOs) in each component are available for consultation on conflicts questions, as is the Pro Bono Program Manager. See Section VI.B.

Hatch Act Policy: Outside activity by Department employees must comport with the regulations implementing the Hatch Act Reform Amendments of 1993, 5 C.F.R. Pt. 734, and with the February 27, 1996 Attorney General memorandum delineating the Department's policy concerning political activities by employees. Department policy holds all political appointees to the restrictions of 5 C.F.R. Pt. 734, subpt. D.

Non-Representational Assistance: Department employees may provide non-representational assistance without compensation, such as assistance in the filling out of forms for persons seeking government benefits, and may assist in the preparation of tax returns without compensation (e.g. through the Voluntary Income Tax Program), provided that the services satisfy the prior approval requirements of Section III.A of this Policy Statement, and do not present a conflict of interest as addressed in Section III.B.

C. Additional Considerations.

1. Retainer Agreement. The Pro Bono Program Manager, see Section VI.B., will have available a model retainer letter making explicit to a pro bono legal client that the attorney is acting in his or her own individual capacity and not on behalf of the Department. The client must countersign a retainer letter in acknowledgment of this fact.

2. Malpractice Coverage. Before agreeing to meet with or accept a pro bono legal client, a Department attorney should determine whether the referring pro bono program or organization has a malpractice insurance policy which covers volunteer attorneys. The Department of Justice does not provide malpractice coverage for pro bono work.

COMMENT: Generally, volunteer programs organized by the local bar or the more established referral programs do provide malpractice coverage. The Pro Bono Program Manager will have information regarding which programs provide malpractice insurance coverage for volunteer attorneys. Attorneys who choose to provide legal services without malpractice insurance coverage are acting at their own risk.

3. The District of Columbia Professional Licensing Fee. The D.C. Code has been amended to provide that members of the District of Columbia bar "engaged in the provision of legal services, on a pro bono basis solely or in combination with government service," an exemption from the requirement to pay the District of Columbia professional licensing fee of $250. D.C. Act 10-304.

4. Restrictions on the Unauthorized Practice of Law. Attorneys not licensed in the District of Columbia do not need to pay the District of Columbia licensing fee, but may only practice subject to the constraints of the District of Columbia's local rule regarding the unauthorized practice of law. D.C. Court of Appeals Rule 49.

COMMENT: D.C. Court of Appeals Rule 49 currently prohibits Department attorneys who are not members of the D.C. Bar from taking on pro bono representational work. The D.C. Bar is currently considering a revised Rule 49 which would exempt federal government attorneys who are members in good standing of another state bar and who accept pro bono cases under the supervision of a D.C. Bar member employed by or affiliated with a legal services or referral program, or other non-profit organization in D.C. The Pro Bono Program Manager will have information regarding the revision of Rule 49 for Department attorneys who are not members of the D.C. Bar but who wish to accept pro bono cases.

122   PRO BONO AND THE GOVERNMENT LAWYER

Department attorneys in other jurisdictions are advised to consult their local rules and regulations regarding any professional fees and practice restrictions that may exist.

IV.   USE OF OFFICIAL POSITION OR PUBLIC OFFICE

The Policy. Department of Justice employees who provide pro bono legal services or who participate in volunteer activities may not indicate or represent in any way that they are acting on behalf of the Department, or in their official capacity. The incidental identification of an employee's position or office— for example, when an office number and street address are not sufficient to ensure mail delivery or when receiving a telephone call—is not prohibited.

A.   A Department of Justice employee may not use office letterhead, agency or office business cards, or otherwise identify himself or herself as a Department employee in any communication, correspondence, or pleading connected with pro bono legal activities or other volunteer services.

B.   A Department of Justice attorney is responsible for making it clear to the client, any opposing parties, or others involved in a pro bono case, that the attorney is acting in his or her individual capacity as a volunteer, and is not acting as a representative of, or on behalf of, the Department.

V.   USE OF AGENCY RESOURCES

A.   Hours of Work. Department employees are encouraged to seek volunteer and pro bono legal opportunities that can be accomplished outside their scheduled working hours. However, pro bono legal or volunteer activities may sometimes occur during work hours. Supervisors are urged to be flexible and to accommodate, where feasible, the efforts of their employees to do pro bono legal or volunteer work. Employees seeking to participate in pro bono legal or volunteer activities during work hours may also be granted leave without pay, annual leave, or, in very limited circumstances, administrative leave, as explained in the comment.

When considering employee requests for leave to engage in pro bono legal or volunteer activities, supervisors should give due attention to the effect of the employee's absence on office operations.

The decision to grant an employee's request to engage in pro bono legal or volunteer activities during hours of work may not be affected by a supervisor's personal views regarding the substance of the pro bono activity.

COMMENT: The Attorney General recognizes the serious budgetary constraints and heavy workloads faced by each of the components. Therefore, while this Policy Statement asks supervisors to be flexible in dealing with employees seeking to engage in pro bono legal or volunteer activities, it also recognizes that supervisors must be able to judge whether such accommodations would interfere with the operation of the office.

Administrative Leave. As a general rule, it is inappropriate to pay an employee for time engaged in *pro bono* legal or volunteer services. However, in limited circumstances, it may be appropriate to excuse an employee from duty for brief periods of time without loss of pay or charge to leave to participate in volunteer activities. *See Federal Personnel Manual System, FPM Letter 992-1 (April 19, 1991).* Excused absence should be limited to those situations in which the employee's volunteer service meets one or more of the following criteria: Is directly related to the Department's mission; is officially sponsored or sanctioned by the Attorney General; or will enhance the professional development or skills of the employee in his or her current position. *Id.*

Prior Department of Justice ethics regulations have permitted supervisors to grant leave "for court appearances or other necessary incidents of representation." *See United States Attorneys' Manual 1-4.350.* Also, past Attorneys General and this Attorney General have authorized the granting of administrative leave to encourage participation in a project such as the mentoring program sponsored by the Department.

Administrative leave should not be granted for volunteer or *pro bono* legal activities that directly benefit an employee or those with whom an employee has a personal relationship.

B.   Use of Office Equipment. As a general rule, employees may use government property only for official business or as authorized by the government. See 5 C.F.R. § 2635.101(b)(9), .704(a). Department policy authorizes the following personal uses of government office and library equipment and facilities:
1. personal uses that involve only negligible expense (such as electricity, ink, small amounts of paper, and ordinary wear and tear); and
2. limited personal telephone/fax calls to locations within the office's commuting area, or that are charged to non-government accounts.

This Department policy permits personal use of equipment and facilities only if it involves negligible additional expense to the government—such as electricity, ink, small amounts of paper, and ordinary wear-and-tear. When office computers, printers and copiers are used in moderation, there is only negligible additional expense to the government for electricity, ink and wear-and-tear. Such use, therefore, is authorized as long as only small amounts of paper are involved and as long as the use does not interfere with official business. Employees wishing to use more than a small amount of paper must provide their own or pay for its cost. Employees should contact their supervisor if there is any question whether an intended use involves "negligible" expense or "small amounts" of paper.

This policy does not authorize the personal use of commercial electronic databases when there is an extra cost to the government. On the other hand, research using the library's books or microfiche would be authorized, as it involves only negligible additional expense to the United States.

124   PRO BONO AND THE GOVERNMENT LAWYER

The policy also authorizes limited personal telephone/fax calls to locations within the office's commuting area, or that are charged to non-government accounts (e.g., personal telephone credit cards). Again, such use must not interfere with official business, and supervisors should be consulted if there is any question over whether such use is in fact "limited."

The policy does not override statutes, rules or regulations governing the use of specific types of government property, such as electronic mail, and 41 C.F.R. (FPMR) § 201-21.601 (governing the ordinary use of long-distance telephone services). It may be revoked or limited at any time by any supervisor or component for any business reason. Any employee who has questions about the application of this section to any particular situation should consult his or her supervisor.

In using government property, employees must be mindful of their responsibility to protect and conserve such property and to use official time in an honest effort to perform official duties. See 5 C.F.R. § 2635.101(b)(9), .704(a), .705(a).

COMMENT: The above policy has been the Department's practice since 1989. It was codified as a section of the Justice Property Management Regulations, 41 C.F.R. (JPMR) § 128-1.5006-4, in April 1995.

C.   Clerical Support. Pro bono legal and volunteer work are not official duties, and may not be assigned to or otherwise required of support staff.

COMMENT: It may be coercive to ask subordinate employees if they will volunteer to help perform pro bono legal or volunteer services, i.e., the typing of briefs or documents. See 5 C.F.R. § 2635.705. On the other hand, support staff may wish to volunteer their services. The Pro Bono Program Manager and Volunteer Services Program Coordinator will develop a central pool of support staff who are willing to volunteer to support pro bono legal or volunteer projects. See Section VI.B.

VI.   ADMINISTRATION OF PRO BONO AND VOLUNTEER SERVICES PROGRAM

A.   Pro Bono and Volunteer Services Committee. A Pro Bono and Volunteer Services Committee will be established to oversee the implementation of the Department's Policy Statement. The Committee will be chaired by the Pro Bono Program Manager, see Section VI.B., and include representatives from law enforcement, the Attorney General's Advisory Committee, litigating and non-litigating components, and the Volunteer Services Program Coordinator, see VI.C.

COMMENT: The Department recognizes that further refinements of its Policy Statement will be necessary. Specifically, the implementation of the Policy Statement in law enforcement agencies and United States Attorney's Offices will need further examination. In addition, the approval process outlined in Section III.A. will need to be monitored closely.

B. <u>Pro Bono</u> Program Manager. The <u>Pro Bono</u> Program Manager will develop and publicize <u>pro bono</u> legal opportunities in order to facilitate an increase in such activities throughout the Department of Justice. The position will be located in the Office of Policy Development. The Program Manager will work with United States Attorney's Offices in the development of office-specific <u>pro bono</u> programs.

COMMENT: It is anticipated that each component and United States Attorney's Office will appoint an individual to publicize and coordinate <u>pro bono</u> activities within the component and office and to refer persons to the component's Deputy-Designated Agency Ethics Officer (DAEO) for conflict screening.

C. Volunteer Services Program Coordinator. The Volunteer Services Program Coordinator publicizes the volunteer services opportunities throughout the Department of Justice. The position is located in the Justice Management Division, Personnel Staff. The Coordinator refers employees to volunteer clearinghouses in their communities, assists employees in establishing and participating in Partners in Education programs, and organizes National Volunteer Week activities.

COMMENT: The position of Volunteer Services Program Coordinator already exists and works with contact persons in every component. This policy does not anticipate any change in the administration of the volunteer services program other than the involvement of the Coordinator in the <u>Pro Bono</u> and Volunteer Services Committee.

VII. DISCLAIMER

The Policy Statement is intended only to encourage increased <u>pro bono</u> legal and volunteer activities by Department employees, and is not intended to create any right or benefit, substantive or procedural, enforceable at law by a party against the United States, its agencies, its officers, or any person.

The United States and the Department of Justice will not be responsible in any manner or to any extent for any negligence or otherwise tortious acts or omissions on the part of any Department employee engaged in any <u>pro bono</u> or volunteer activity. While the Department encourages <u>pro bono</u> and volunteer activities by its employees, the Department exercises no control over the services and activities of employees engaged in <u>pro bono</u> or volunteer activities nor does it control the time or location of any <u>pro bono</u> or volunteer activity. Each employee is acting outside the scope of his or her employment whenever the employee participates, supports or joins in any <u>pro bono</u> or volunteer activity.

APPROVED: _____ DATE: 3/6/96

APPENDIX ❦ 6D

Contact People

American Bar Association
Center for Pro Bono
541 North Fairbanks Court
Chicago, IL 60611-3314
(312) 988-5770
[For information pack on
government lawyer pro bono
participation]

Linda Uliss Burke
Assistant City Attorney
City of Milwaukee
800 City Hall
200 East Wells Street
Milwaukee, WI 53202-3551
(414) 286-2601

Professor John Capowski
Widener University
School of Law
3800 Vartan Way
Harrisburg, PA 17110-9450
(717) 541-1992 or
    (717) 541-3986

Nancy G. Miller
Senior Counsel
Office of Policy Development
U.S. Department of Justice
Room 4236
10th & Constitution Avenue, N.W.
Washington, DC 20530
(202) 514-3116

Jack Schwartz
Chief Counsel for Opinions and
    Advice
Office of the Attorney General
State of Maryland
200 St. Paul Place
Baltimore, MD 21202
(410) 576-6327

Rodney T. Willett
Associate Counsel
International Municipal Lawyers
    Association
1110 Vermont Avenue, N.W., Suite
    200
Washington, DC 20005
(202) 466-5424
E-mail: imladc@aol.com

CHAPTER ❦ 7

Considering Ethics at the Local Government Level

*Mark Davies**

This chapter offers practical insights for municipal lawyers faced with drafting local ethics laws. A comprehensive discussion of over a dozen issues that may be appropriately addressed in an ethics law is provided, as well as references to how different jurisdictions have chosen to legislate guidance for their officers and employees.

Introduction

A local government ethics law is a municipal official's best friend and a private citizen's greatest ally.[1] It tells the official what the rules are and how to avoid breaking them. It protects the official against unjustified accusations of ethical impropriety. It promotes a more ethical government.[2]

The purpose of a municipal ethics law is thus threefold:

1. to provide ethics guidance to the municipality's officials;
2. to provide reassurance to the public that their public servants are acting in the best interests of the community; and
3. to encourage private citizens to participate in public service.

A municipal ethics law that does not meet these standards is worthless. Indeed, it is worse than worthless, because it gives officials a false sense of comfort and the public a false sense of confidence. Such a law will utterly fail to meet the expectations it raises and will consequently create only bitterness and disillusionment.

Underlying this three-fold purpose of a municipal ethics law are several assumptions. First and foremost, municipal ethics laws assume that the vast majority of municipal officials are honest and want to do the right thing. In

---

*The views expressed in this chapter do not necessarily reflect those of the New York City Conflicts of Interest Board.

128   CONSIDERING ETHICS AT THE LOCAL GOVERNMENT LEVEL

the experience of the author of this chapter, actual corruption at the local level is relatively rare. It happens, but far less often than people think.

Second, it is far better to prevent unethical conduct from occurring in the first place than to punish it after it occurs. Once tolled, the ethics bell can never be unsung. Once the ethics violation occurs, the damage is done; and the public loses just that much more confidence in the integrity of government. In the current political climate, where politicians and public servants rank somewhat below used car salesmen and carriers of loathsome diseases, even the slightest such loss hurts.

Third, local government differs in many respects from state government, and the locality's ethics law must reflect those differences. The geographic and subject matter jurisdiction of local government is far more restricted than that of state government. Thus, restrictions or disclosure requirements that appear wise at the state level may make no sense at the local level. So, too, municipal officials often have less access than their state counterparts to sophisticated legal counsel. Thus, a code of ethics written in lay terms becomes critical.

Most importantly, local government, unlike state government, depends heavily on volunteers. Zoning board members, planning board members, ethics board members, even many municipal legislators are unpaid, or only minimally paid. To subject these volunteers to onerous financial disclosure and ethics requirements would drive good people out of municipal government.

Fourth, "ethics laws" do not really regulate ethics. They regulate, primarily, financial conflicts of interest. A school superintendent who spends $10,000 to install a bathroom in his office while his students lack textbooks may have acted "unethically," but he has probably not, on those facts alone, violated any "ethics law." If, on the other hand, he spends the $10,000 to buy textbooks from his brother, he will have violated most municipal codes of ethics.

Fifth, ethics laws must be largely self-enforcing—by the official himself or herself, by peer pressure, by whistleblowers, by the media, and by the public. Ethics boards must view their enforcement actions largely as educational tools.

These purposes and assumptions dictate the content and structure of a good municipal ethics law. Specifically, such a law should be:

1. *Clear and concise.* A municipal officer or employee cannot obey an ethics law unless he or she can understand it. Therefore, it must be intelligible to the lay person without the need to consult lawyers or plain-language guides.
2. *Comprehensive.* An ethics law riddled with gaps provides a trap for the unwary official and a source of endless frustration for private citizens.
3. *Bright-line,* whenever possible. Officials need a beacon in the night, not a penlight in the fog. The work of a three-handed lawyer (on the one hand this, on the other hand that, on the third hand something else) may make a great law school exam, but it makes a lousy ethics law.

4. *Flexible.* Ethics laws regulate a rather vague area of human endeavor and will inevitably, albeit only occasionally, produce inequitable results. Some mechanism, such as waivers by a local ethics board, must exist to address those problems.
5. *Sensible.* Above all, a municipal ethics law must make sense—to the public official, to the media, and to the public. Officials may well refuse to obey, or obey only grudgingly, an ethics law that does not make sense to them.

A local ethics law should thus focus less on punishment than on prevention, less on prohibition than on disclosure and recusal. It must also be easy and inexpensive to administer and enforce. It must establish an independent ethics board that, while possessing the power to investigate and punish, views its primary mandate as giving quick advice and providing comprehensive ethics training and education.

Accordingly, a good ethics law contains three parts:

1. A code of ethics
2. Disclosure
3. Administration and enforcement

Unfortunately, few municipal ethics laws in this country meet these standards. Most are deficient—often seriously deficient—in one respect or another. Too often in developing municipal ethics laws, state or local governments appear simply to have thrown a bunch of provisions against the wall and kept what sticks. Knee-jerk reactions to public pressure generated by scandal have often prevailed over calm analyses of the necessity, purpose, and contents of an ethics scheme. Applying a corollary to Occam's razor, government should include in an ethics law the fewest and simplest provisions that achieve the law's goals. The enactors should thus first determine those goals and then measure every provision of the proposed ethics law against that yardstick. Provisions that further the law's goals should be included. Provisions that do not should be eliminated. If in doubt, leave it out.

This chapter seeks to facilitate that process and also to lay out, from the municipal perspective, in a rather general way the contents and workings of a good ethics law—to alert the private practitioner to the types of municipal ethics provisions he or she may encounter and to guide the municipal lawyer in drafting a new ethics law for his or her client. In other chapters in this book, the reader will find these topics discussed in greater detail.

Sources of Local Government Ethics Laws

Unfortunately for municipal officials and lawyers, ethics restrictions applicable to a municipality's officers and employees often lie scattered among a number of state and local laws. Such restrictions may be found not only in the municipality's own ethics law and interpretative opinions of the ethics board, but also in

1. The state constitution
2. State statutes
3. Local laws other than the municipality's ethics law
4. Agency regulations
5. Common law

Each of these possible sources is discussed below.

For example, to determine the permissibility of a gift to a Philadelphia official, one would need to consult the Pennsylvania State Ethics Act, the Standards of Conduct and Ethics in the Philadelphia Code, the Philadelphia Home Rule Charter, and Executive Order 16-92 on gifts. In addition, one should examine the rules and advisory opinions of the Pennsylvania State Ethics Commission and the Philadelphia Board of Ethics, as well as any applicable case law.

State Constitution

A few states provide municipal conflicts of interest restrictions in their state constitutions. For example, the Rhode Island Constitution pronounces that "[t]he people of Rhode Island believe that public officials and employees must adhere to the highest standards of ethical conduct, . . . avoid the appearance of impropriety and not use their position for private gain or advantage."[3] In addition, the Rhode Island Constitution requires the general assembly to "establish an independent non-partisan commission which shall adopt a code of ethics," provides that "[a]ll elected and appointed officials and employees of state and local government, of boards, commissions and agencies shall be subject to the code of ethics," and empowers the commission to remove them from office for unethical conduct, unless they are subject to impeachment.[4]

State constitutions may also contain restrictions aimed at specific types of unethical conduct. For example, the New York State Constitution prohibits municipalities from giving or loaning any money or property to or in aid of any individual or private corporation, association, or undertaking.[5]

State Statutes

A number of states regulate municipal ethics by state statute. In many instances these statutes include a conflict of interest code, a financial disclosure law, and an enforcement mechanism.[6] These state regulations may or may not contemplate supplementation by local ethics codes.[7] For example, the California Government Code requires that every agency, which includes local government agencies, adopt and promulgate a conflict of interest code.

At the same time, that state law imposes certain ethics requirements on municipal officers and employees.[8]

In addition, most, if not all, states have enacted statutes regulating certain specific types of ethics problems or providing specific remedies to address certain types of unethical conduct. For example, New York State prohibits certain hiring and retention decisions from being made on the basis of political associations and also permits a private citizen to sue to prevent an illegal official act by a municipal officer or employee.[9]

Local Laws Other Than Ethics Laws

To regulate unethical conduct, a municipality may enact local laws distinct from a code of ethics. For example, the New York City Charter, separate and apart from its ethics code, prohibits members, officers, and employees of the Department of Personnel and Civil Service Commission from holding certain political party positions.[10]

Agency Regulations

Individual agencies within a municipality may impose restrictions relating to the ethical conduct of the agency's employees. For example, the police chief of the City of Syracuse (New York) promulgated rules and regulations relating to off-duty employment of police officers, and the New York City Police Department has adopted guidelines regulating the acceptance of cash rewards and personal gifts. The City of Chicago's ethics law expressly authorizes city agencies to adopt rules that are more restrictive than that law.[11]

Common Law

Wholly apart from any statutory or administrative regulations, the common law has developed certain ethics restrictions on the conduct of local government officials.[12] For example, in some states the common law prohibits municipal officials from contracting with their own municipality. Thus in New York an employment contract between a town board member and the town has been held void because the common law does not recognize a contract between a municipality and its officers.[13] Similarly, "[p]ublic policy forbids the sustaining of municipal action founded upon the vote of a member of the municipal governing body in any matter before it which directly or immediately affects him individually."[14]

Courts may also sometimes use an ethics statute as a springboard for a common law ethics restriction. "It is not necessary . . . that a specific provision of the [statute] be violated before there can be an improper conflict of interest."[15] Lawyers should, therefore, carefully check the annotations to the applicable statutes for cases that expand upon the scope of the statutory law.

132   CONSIDERING ETHICS AT THE LOCAL GOVERNMENT LEVEL

Code of Ethics

Generally

As noted above, the first pillar of a good municipal ethics law is a comprehensive and comprehensible code of ethics. The contents of such codes may be grouped into over a dozen types of provisions. Each of these types is discussed below, with illustrations from various state and local ethics laws and from a proposed state ethics law for local governments and a model local ethics law.[16] However, one should note four preliminary matters.

INTERESTS VERSUS CONDUCT

Some ethics codes restrict interests. Most restrict conduct. Some restrict both. Restrictions on interests usually prohibit or limit a municipal official's interests in private firms that do business with the municipality or in contracts with the municipality. Restrictions on conduct prohibit the municipal officer or employee from engaging in certain specified conduct, such as using one's municipal position for private gain or accepting a gift from someone doing business with the municipality.

DEFINITIONS

In a good ethics law, the definitions narrow the scope of the code of ethics; they never expand it. So if a municipal employee reads and obeys the code of ethics but not the definitions, the official will not violate the law. In particular, substantive ethics provisions should not be buried in definitions. Indeed, definitions should be kept to a minimum.

Unfortunately, many ethics laws contain extensive and complex definitions that set a trap for unsuspecting officials. The lawyer must parse the definitions of an ethics law carefully. Words such as "appear" (any communication), "interest" (employment as well as ownership), and "position" (lawyers and consultants as well as officers, directors, and employees) present particular problems.[17]

In addition, definitions may, for example, deem a municipal official to have an interest in a contract if someone with whom the municipal employee is associated has an interest in the contract. "Associated" may include relatives, employers, business associates, or corporations in which the municipal official owns stock.[18] Such definitions can significantly expand the scope of the prohibition—to an extent that may in fact prove unacceptable in small municipalities. For example, the Anne Arundel County (Maryland) public ethics law includes not only biological and adopted children and stepchildren within the definition of "child" but also foster children and grandchildren.[19] Lawyers must, therefore, carefully review definitions for hidden ethics restrictions.

EXCLUSIONS

Virtually every ethics code contains exclusions from its provisions. The better codes contain narrowly drafted restrictions that require only a few exclusions, which are set forth in a separate section.[20] Some ethics laws, however, provide broad restrictions, often with exceptions and even exceptions to the exceptions within the ethics provision itself, supplemented by a separate section with more exclusions. For example, New York State's conflicts of interest law for municipalities—a model of how *not* to draft an ethics law—contains a broad prohibition on municipal officials having an interest in a contact with the municipality but then sets out an exception in that provision, another exception in the definition of "interest," and then fifteen further exceptions in a separate section.[21] One must question what kind of ethics law requires seventeen exceptions.

WAIVERS

As noted above, because ethics laws regulate a rather vague area of human endeavor, they inevitably, albeit only occasionally, produce inequitable or even irrational results. For example, a revolving door prohibition may prevent a city from placing one of its employees as the head of a nonprofit organization that provides services critical to the city. To address these types of problems, some ethics laws permit the local ethics board to grant waivers.

For example, the Rhode Island Ethics Commission may, in the case of hardship, waive the prohibition against a municipal official representing himself or herself before his or her own agency. So, too, Anne Arundel County permits the county ethics commission to waive that municipality's postemployment restrictions. New York City's ethics law grants broad waiver power to the city's conflicts of interest board.[22]

Waiver provisions present some danger to the integrity of the ethics law because they enable an ethics board to gut the law and may engender accusations of partiality. On the other hand, the lack of a waiver power can occasionally turn an ethics law into an unintended instrument of oppression that hurts not only the individual employee but the municipality itself. For example, the author of this chapter was once constrained to advise a town supervisor that his town would have to truck its bulk trash to another state, at considerable expense, because under the state ethics law the town could not contract to dump it in the local landfill owned by a town board member. Such results make the ethics law a joke. A waiver would have prevented this absurd outcome. However, waiver power should be vested only in an independent ethics board. Ethics laws that grant waiver authority to a legislative body are misguided, for they inevitably transform the waiver process into a political football.[23]

Prohibited Interests

A restriction on interests typically prohibits a municipal officer or employee from having an interest (a) in a firm or organization that does business with the officer's or employee's own municipality or municipal agency or (b) in a contract with the municipality. A prohibited interest in a firm or organization might arise from a position with the firm or organization or from an ownership interest in the firm or organization. A position interest would include officers, directors, employees, and perhaps even lawyers, brokers, and consultants. An ownership interest would include shareholders and partners. A municipal official might be deemed to have an interest in an entity or a municipal contract if someone with whom the official is associated has such an interest; and "associated" might include relatives, businesses, employers, and customers or clients of the municipal official.

For example, the Honolulu ethics code prohibits officers or employees of the city from acquiring a financial interest in business enterprises that the officer or employee has reason to believe may be directly involved in official action to be taken by the person. Chicago's Governmental Ethics Ordinance prohibits elected officials and employees from having a financial interest, inter alia, in any contract, work, or business of the city. Some ethics laws contain prohibitions on specific types of interests, such as a prohibition against municipal officials having an interest in legislation or in property before the appeals and equalization board or having a close relative serving on the same board or commission. Prohibited interest provisions are sometimes read to prohibit a municipal official from holding a second, incompatible public office, although some ethics laws specifically regulate compatibility of public offices.[24]

Interest restrictions essentially presume that merely having an interest in an entity doing business with the municipality, or in a contract with the municipality, constitutes a conflict of interest. Such restrictions place severe restraints upon the ability of municipal officers and employees to moonlight for a private company or to own private businesses. These restrictions may be unpalatable in smaller communities where such interests are virtually unavoidable. In such communities, disclosure and recusal (discussed later in this chapter) often offer the preferable alternative.

Use of Public Office for Private Gain

The rest of the ethics restrictions discussed in this section address not interests but conduct. Many ethics codes contain a general prohibition against municipal officers and employees using their official position for private gain—for themselves or for someone with whom they are associated. For example, the California conflicts of interest law provides:

> No public official at any level of the state or local government shall make, participate in making or in any way attempt to use his official position to influence a governmental decision in which he knows or has reason to know he has a financial interest.[25]

"Financial interest" is then defined to include, for example, a financial interest of the official's private business or employer.[26] Similarly, the Anne Arundel

County (Maryland) public ethics law provides that "[a]n employee may not use the prestige, title, or authority of the employee's office or position for the employee's private gain or the gain of another."[27]

Other ethics provisions prohibit the use of public resources for private purposes. For example, the ethics law of King County (Washington) states:

> No county employee shall request or permit the use of county-owned vehicles, equipment, materials or property or the expenditure of county funds for personal convenience or profit. Use or expenditure is to be restricted to such services as are available to the public generally or for such employee in the conduct of official business.

Similarly, Maui prohibits county officers or employees from using county property or personnel "for other than public activity or purpose."[28]

A number of codes contain a general prohibition against engaging in a business or transaction or having a financial interest in conflict with the proper discharge of one's official duties or using one's office to benefit a relative. Some ethics codes specifically restrict voting on a matter in which one has an interest.[29] Such provisions are not without difficulty. A general prohibition against acting in conflict with one's official duties provides, in the absence of interpretative rules, little guidance to the official and may be insufficiently specific to support criminal or even civil penalties. Restricting the voting rights of a legislative body raises thorny separation of powers and disenfranchisement issues, for unlike the executive branch, where another official almost always stands ready to step into the shoes of a recusing officer or employee, in the legislative branch no such alternates are permissible, with the result that the voters of that legislator's district receive no representation on that issue.

Such wrinkles aside, however, ethics codes that prohibit use of public office for private gain strike at the heart of ethical impropriety. Unfortunately, many codes contain no such prohibition.

Moonlighting

In addition to restrictions on having an interest in certain businesses or in using one's position for private gain, some ethics codes specifically regulate private employment by municipal officers and employees. Some of these provisions, such as those of Anne Arundel County (Maryland), are quite detailed, while others are far more general. For example, Westchester County (New York) merely provides that a county officer or employee "shall not engage in, solicit, negotiate for or promise to accept private employment or render services for private interests when such employment or service creates a conflict with or impairs the proper discharge of official County duties."[30] Such general prohibitions provide little guidance to officials and should either be eliminated or supplemented, if only by specific, narrowly tailored prohibited interest provisions, as discussed above. In addition, some ethics codes, such as that of King County (Washington), require the approval of a supervisor before an employee may undertake nonmunicipal employment.[31]

Appearances, Representation, and Contingent Compensation

Municipal ethics codes often prohibit the municipality's officers and employees from appearing or representing someone before an agency of the municipality or at least before the municipal official's own agency. For example, the Honolulu Charter provides that no elected or appointed officer or employee shall "[r]epresent private interests in any action or proceeding against the interests of the city or appear in behalf of private interests before any agency, except as otherwise provided by law."[32] That prohibition would apply even if the official does not attempt to use his or her municipal office for private gain.

Ethics codes also sometimes prohibit receipt of compensation from a private person where the compensation is contingent upon any action by the official's municipality, even if the official does not appear before the municipality.[33] Such contingent compensation agreements are thought to be fraught with potential for abuse of office.

These provisions ordinarily present little difficulty for municipal officials, at least if the provisions are narrowly drafted. But in a large municipality, for example, a ban on appearing before any agency of the municipality may make little sense for lower level employees who have little influence over the actions of another agency. In addition, waivers should be available in appropriate cases. For example, if a city's land use law requires the city to appoint an architect to its planning board, waivers will be necessary to permit the firm of an architect board member to appear occasionally before the board, with appropriate disclosures and recusal. Otherwise, the only architects likely to accept service on the board are those having no knowledge or involvement with architecture in the city. Finally, restrictions on a municipal official appearing before a municipal agency must permit the official to appear on his or her own behalf. For example, a zoning board member must be permitted to appear, with appropriate disclosures and recusal, before the zoning board to obtain a variance to build a deck on his or her own home. However, in such situations, the board member should, if possible, appear through someone else, such as a builder, architect, or lawyer, to avoid appearances of impropriety and allegations that "the fix is in."

Gifts

Even the most anemic ethics laws contain a restriction on the solicitation and receipt of gifts by municipal officials. Often the laws also regulate receipt of honoraria and travel expenses.[34] The better ethics laws provide reasonably bright-line rules. For example, the Anne Arundel County's ethics law prohibits the solicitation of gifts and further provides that

An employee may not knowingly accept any gift, directly or indirectly, from any person whom the employee knows or has reason to know:

(1) is doing or seeking to do business of any kind with the County;
(2) is engaged in activities that are regulated or controlled by the County;
(3) has financial interests that may be substantially and materially affected, in a manner distinguishable from the public generally, by the performance or nonperformance of any official duty of the employee; or
(4) is a lobbyist with respect to matters within the jurisdiction of the employee.[35]

Other ethics laws contain virtually unenforceable gifts provisions prohibiting, for example, the receipt of gifts "under circumstances in which it could reasonably be inferred that the gift was intended to influence [the official], or could reasonably be expected to influence him, in the performance of his official duties or was intended as a reward for any official action on his part."[36] In general whatever the ethics law requires, municipal officials are well advised to refuse any gift from someone with whom they deal or have recently dealt as a public official.

Some ethics laws treat political contributions as gifts. Some do not. Other ethics laws separately regulate political contributions. Indeed, to avoid preemption and First Amendment problems, municipalities may be well advised to exclude campaign contributions from the definition of gift but to prohibit inappropriate political activities by municipal officials, as discussed below.[37]

Compensation by Private Entities for Municipal Work

In addition to prohibiting use of public office for private advantage and restricting receipt of gifts, some ethics codes bar a municipal officer or employee from receiving compensation from any source other than the municipality for performing municipal services. For example, the Honolulu Charter provides:

No elected or appointed officer or employee shall . . . [r]eceive any compensation for such person's services as an officer or employee of the city from any source other than the city, except as otherwise provided by this chapter or by ordinance.[38]

Although ordinarily a wise provision, such a restriction may significantly undercut the ability of the municipality to enter into public-private partnerships. For example, the provision may prevent parks department employees from being paid in part by a private foundation. Such problems can be remedied either by the passage of a law permitting the private payments or by the private entity donating the money as a gift to the municipality, earmarked for parks department salaries. Most municipal ethics codes permit gifts to the municipality, and such block donations obviate, to some extent, the danger that individual employees will favor the donor. Nonetheless, municipalities

138   CONSIDERING ETHICS AT THE LOCAL GOVERNMENT LEVEL

and, if possible, their ethics boards should carefully consider the merits of each proposed public-private partnership, as such arrangements pose the danger that the donor's private interests may be placed above the public interest or that a donor-vendor may be favored over a competitor.

Confidential Information

Most ethics codes prohibit the release of confidential information or the use of confidential information for private gain. For example, Philadelphia's ethics law provides that no city officer or employee, including part-timers and unpaid officials, "shall directly or indirectly disclose or make available confidential information concerning the property, government or affairs of the City without proper legal authorization, for the purpose of advancing the financial purpose of himself or others."[39] Some statutes governing confidential information, like those of Philadelphia, the District of Columbia, and Los Angeles, prohibit release of information only if the release may result in a financial gain. Other confidential information provisions, such as those of Cook County (Illinois) and Seattle, prohibit release or use of the information even if it will result in no such gain. Many confidentiality provisions, such as Cook County's and New York City's, contain exceptions for certain types of disclosure, such as disclosure made in the course of official duties, disclosure required by law, or disclosure made within the scope of a whistleblower law or relating to waste, corruption, or conflicts of interest.

Restrictions on the release or use of confidential information protect the integrity of municipal records and the privacy of those who deal with the municipality and help prevent employee misuse of such information for personal advantage. However, lawyers should take care to determine the scope of the "confidentiality." In particular, some statutes, such as Chicago's, treat information as confidential unless its disclosure is *required* by the applicable freedom of information law. Other statutes, such as Los Angeles's, treat information as confidential only if its disclosure is *prohibited* by law.

Political Activities

Although partisan politics may play a smaller role at the local level, especially in small communities, than at the state or federal level, nonetheless many municipal governments rest upon a partisan political system. Restrictions on the political activities of municipal officials must, therefore, be approached with caution. In particular, one must avoid ethics restrictions that may cripple political parties, raise First Amendment problems, or so restrict the pool of volunteers that either the municipality or the local political parties will be unable to fill their vacant volunteer positions, such as zoning board members or ward leaders.

The purpose of political activity restrictions in ethics laws lies in the concern that mixing politics and municipal operations corrupts the public process, creates the appearance that political support will garner municipal favor, risks the displacement of the public good by partisan will, and generates pressure on nonpolitical municipal employees to provide political support to their elected superiors. Thus, for example, New York City prohibits its officers and employees from coercing other officers and employees to engage in political activities, requesting a subordinate to engage in a political campaign or make a political contribution, compelling or requesting anyone to make a political contribution under threat of prejudice or promise, or making a political contribution in consideration of becoming a city official or receiving a raise or promotion. In addition, New York City prohibits certain high-level officials from requesting that anyone make a political contribution to certain candidates for elective office or from serving as a political party leader (a so-called two hats provision).[40]

Superior-Subordinate Relationships

Restrictions on financial relationships between superiors and subordinates not only protect the subordinate but also prevent a municipal official from compelling a subordinate to take an action that benefits the superior, or his or her associate or business, to the detriment of the municipality or the public good. For example, the King County (Washington) Employee Code of Ethics prohibits a county employee from "[e]nter[ing] into a business relationship outside county government with any other employee for whom he or she has any supervisory responsibility." Similarly, the Alabama Code of Ethics prohibits a municipal officer or employee from soliciting a thing of value from a subordinate.[41]

While fulfilling a salutary purpose, such restrictions may occasionally work a hardship in an individual case. For example, the provisions could be read as preventing a superior and subordinate from entering into a personal relationship or sharing an apartment or, perhaps, from maintaining a business into which they had entered before they were superior and subordinate. In appropriate cases, waivers should be available.

Preemployment Restrictions

Although many ethics laws contain postemployment (revolving-door) restrictions, few address the preemployment situation. Yet when a municipal official takes an action that benefits his or her immediate past employer, a public outcry is almost certain. For that reason, even in the absence of preemployment restrictions, municipal officials would be well advised to disclose and recuse themselves in such instances. However, an actual statutory provision provides greater guidance. For example, the King County (Washington) Employee Code of Ethics prohibits a county employee, within one year of entering county employment, from awarding a county contract or participating in a county action "benefitting a person that formerly employed him or her,"

140   CONSIDERING ETHICS AT THE LOCAL GOVERNMENT LEVEL

absent disclosure and approval by the appointing authority. So, too, the Seattle Code of Ethics requires a city officer or employee to "disqualify himself or herself from acting on any transaction which involves the City and any person who is, or at any time within the preceding twelve (12) month period has been a private client of his or hers, or of his or her firm or partnership."[42]

Payment for a Municipal Position

Some ethics codes prohibit a person from paying to obtain a municipal position or from being paid to accept a municipal position. For example, the Pennsylvania ethics law provides that "[n]o person shall solicit or accept a severance payment or anything of monetary value contingent upon the assumption or acceptance of public office or employment." So, too, New York City's ethics law prohibits a public servant from giving or promising to give "any portion of the public servant's compensation, or any money, or valuable thing to any person in consideration of having been or being nominated, appointed, elected or employed as a public servant."[43]

Postemployment (Revolving Door)

Most ethics codes contain some kinds of restrictions on the activities of municipal officials after they leave municipal service.[44] Common restrictions include:

- A prohibition on an officer or employee negotiating for a job with an individual or company with whom or with which the officer or employee is dealing in an official capacity on behalf of the municipality
- A ban on nonministerial communications by a former official with the municipality or his or her former agency for some period, typically one or two years, after leaving municipal service (sometimes called an appearance ban)
- A lengthy or even permanent bar on the former official working on a particular matter on which he or she personally did substantial work while in municipal service (sometimes called a particular matter bar)
- A continuation after municipal service of the prohibition against the official disclosing confidential municipal information or using it for a private purpose

Postemployment restrictions seek to prevent former municipal officials from trading on their contacts with their former agency or municipal employer to the detriment of the municipality or the public (for example, sweetheart deals) and also seek to level the playing field between former municipal officials and their competitors in the private sector. However, overbroad postemployment restrictions may discourage qualified individuals from entering municipal service and may unfairly injure municipal officials who wish to return to the private sector. Accordingly, care must be taken to tailor such restrictions to the particular size and needs of the municipality and the particular position of the municipal official. For example, a small community may wish to impose only a one-year appearance ban but make it applicable to appearances before the entire municipality or, for example, to appearances before all departments and boards involved in land use issues. Alternatively, the municipality may wish to impose a municipality-wide appearance ban only on certain high-level officials whose influence on municipal government may extend beyond their former agency.

Few, if any, municipalities will find it necessary or advisable to prohibit a former official not only from appearing before the municipality for some period but also from working on matters involving the municipality for that period. That is, most municipalities will permit former officials during the appearance ban period to work for a company on a matter involving the municipality so long as they do not communicate with the municipality with respect to that matter or work on a particular matter they worked on in municipal service.

Postemployment restrictions can also work to the detriment of the municipality if they prevent the municipality from placing their employees in critical positions in the private sector (for example, as the executive director of a foster care agency upon which the municipality heavily depends), from hiring highly qualified former employees as consultants, from contracting with a former employee who happens to offer the best deal on goods or services, or from transferring municipal employees to a privatized agency. For that reason, a good ethics code will contain a provision authorizing the municipal ethics board to grant a waiver of the postemployment restrictions in appropriate circumstances. In addition, the code may exempt from those restrictions former employees who leave municipal service to work for another municipality or for the state or federal government (a so-called government-to-government exception).

Inducement of Violations

Few ethics codes prohibit a municipal official from ordering, aiding, or inducing another municipal official to violate the code. As a result, not infrequently a municipal officer or employee may with virtual impunity convince a colleague to commit an ethics violation. For example, if at the suggestion of the village administrator a secretary in village hall buys all village stationery supplies from the secretary's spouse, the secretary will almost certainly have violated the village's ethics law but the village administrator will not, unless that law includes a catch-all provision prohibiting a municipal official from taking any action incompatible with his or her official duties. To prevent such injustice, an inducement provision should be included in the ethics code. For example, the proposed bill of the New York State Temporary State Commission on Local Government Ethics prohibits a municipal officer or employee

142   CONSIDERING ETHICS AT THE LOCAL GOVERNMENT LEVEL

from "induc[ing] or aid[ing] another officer or employee of the municipality to violate any of the provisions of this code of ethics."[45]

Avoidance of Conflicts of Interest

Some ethics codes require that the municipal officials avoid conflicts of interest. For example, Westchester County's (New York) code of ethics provides that a county officer or employee "shall not invest . . . directly or indirectly in any financial, business, commercial or other private endeavor or entity, which creates a conflict with official County duties."[46] Although not a critical component of a code of ethics, such provisions encourage municipal officials to be on the alert for potential conflicts of interest.

Whistleblower Protection

The officers and employees of many municipalities enjoy protection against retaliation by other municipal officials for blowing the whistle on waste, fraud, corruption, or ethics violations. Occasionally this protection is set forth in the ethics law itself.[47] Without such protection, whether in the ethics code or elsewhere, municipal employees may well hesitate to report ethics violations or may resist cooperating in an investigation of an ethics violation.

Restrictions on Private Citizens and Companies

Generally

Municipal ethics laws, by their very nature, focus primarily upon the actions and interests of municipal officers and employees. Yet, private citizens and companies should have a stake in the integrity of municipal government. In particular, they should not be permitted to induce a municipal official to violate the ethics code. However, only a few ethics laws contain such inducement prohibitions, and even those ordinarily address only specified provisions of the code of ethics. Other ethics laws restrict certain actions by private citizens that might bring the municipal official into a violation of the ethics law. Examples of these various provisions are discussed below.

Inducement of Ethics Violations and Influencing Officials

If a bank, hoping to keep a town's financial business, gives a loan to the new town treasurer at a few percentage points below the bank's usual rate, the treasurer may well lose his or her job. Absent a quid pro quo, under most ethics laws nothing will happen to the bank. Thus to permit a private company, with virtual impunity, to corrupt a municipal official undercuts significantly the efficacy of the ethics law and constitutes gross unfairness to the official.

Restrictions on Private Citizens and Companies   143

Accordingly, such laws should prohibit private citizens and companies from inducing a municipal official to violate the code of ethics. For example, the Temporary State Commission's proposed bill provides:

> No person, whether or not a municipal officer or employee, shall induce or attempt to induce a municipal officer or employee to violate any of the provisions of section 800 [the code of ethics] of this article.[48]

Unfortunately, few ethics laws contain such a prohibition.

Alabama's code of ethics does prohibit any person from soliciting a municipal official or employee to "use or cause to be used equipment, facilities, time, materials, human labor, or other public property for such person's private benefit or business benefit, which would materially affect his or her financial interest, except as otherwise provided by law."[49] Since such actions by a municipal official or employee violate the code of ethics, this provision has the effect of punishing a private individual or company for inducing a public servant to violate the ethics law.

A number of ethics laws prohibit private persons from giving gifts—or additional compensation—to municipal officers and employees. For example, Ohio prohibits anyone from promising or giving to a municipal official or employee anything of value "that is of such a character as to manifest a substantial and improper influence upon him with respect to his duties." Massachusetts prohibits any person from "knowingly, otherwise than as provided by law for the proper discharge of official duties, directly or indirectly giv[ing], promis[ing] or offer[ing] such compensation [in relation to any particular matter in which the same city or town is a party or has a direct and substantial interest]." Cook County's Ethics Ordinance restricts contributions to candidates for county office or elected county officials by persons who are seeking to do business with the county or who have done business with the county during the previous four years.[50]

Appearances by Officials's Outside Employers

Appearances by a municipal official's outside employer or business before the official's municipal agency can create the impression that "the fix is in," even if the official recuses himself or herself from acting on the matter either as a public servant or as an officer or employee of the firm. However, a flat prohibition on appearances by an official's private firm may effectively prevent many good people from serving in municipal government. For that reason, these situations are probably best handled by restrictions on appearances coupled with the availability of ethics board waivers. The mere fact that the ethics board has reviewed the matter—and attached appropriate conditions to any waiver—goes far toward reassuring those who deal with the affected agency of its integrity.

Thus, for example, New York City's conflicts of interest law provides that no public servant shall have a position or an ownership interest in a firm that

144   CONSIDERING ETHICS AT THE LOCAL GOVERNMENT LEVEL

does business with that public servant's city agency. But the law further provides that the public servant may apply to the city's conflicts of interest board for a waiver of the prohibition. It should be noted that New York City's restriction falls on the public servant, not directly on his or her private employer or business. Other ethic laws, such as Massachusetts, directly restrict appearances by the private entity itself.[51]

Disclosure

The second pillar of a good municipal ethics law is disclosure. Three types of disclosure exist: transactional disclosure, applicant disclosure, and annual disclosure. Each of these types is considered below.

Transactional Disclosure

Of the three types of disclosure, transactional disclosure—that is, disclosure of a potential conflict of interest when it actually arises—is the most important and the least controversial. Recusal often, though not always, accompanies this type of pinpoint disclosure: "I would like to state for the record that the applicant for this zoning variance is my employer, and I therefore recuse myself from acting on this matter."

One should emphasize, however, that transactional disclosure and recusal do not provide a panacea for ethics problems. Sometimes this approach is inadequate or ill advised. For example, real estate brokers who do substantial business in a town should probably not be appointed to the town planning board since their frequent recusal will significantly undermine their ability to function effectively.[52] So, too, as discussed above, mandating recusal by legislators raises thorny issues of separation of powers and disenfranchisement of voters. In any event, in those states that require a public body to adopt a resolution by a majority of the body's total members, not just by a majority of those members present and voting, a recusal is indistinguishable from a negative vote.

Transactional disclosure ordinarily occurs on the record of a public body, if the disclosing official is a member of a public body, otherwise it occurs in a written statement to the official's superior. Recusal, if required, may merely prevent the official from acting on the matter or may in effect serve as a gag order, prohibiting the official from even discussing the matter with anyone. Whatever the scope of recusal contemplated by statute, lawyers should ordinarily advise their municipal clients to take the broadest possible view of recusal. Public perception of integrity in government suffers when municipal officials "recuse" themselves from voting on a matter in which they have a personal interest but then go on to discuss the matter at length "as a private citizen." In addition, recusal should ordinarily be accompanied by disclosure of the reason for the recusal, that is, of the nature and extent of the conflict of interest. Codes of ethics reflect these various permutations.[53]

Applicant Disclosure

Applicant disclosure represents the flip side of the transactional disclosure coin and thus provides a check on transactional disclosure. Applicant disclosure occurs when a person applying for a municipal permit or license, or a bidder for a municipal contract, discloses in the application or bid documents the name and office of any officers or employees of the municipality who have a financial interest in the applicant/bidder or in the application or bid. In fairness to the applicant or bidder, who may not know the identity of all such persons, the disclosure should be required only of those affected municipal officials actually known to the applicant or bidder or of whom the applicant or bidder should have knowledge. (Applicants should not be heard to claim that they were unaware one of their five shareholders worked for the municipality.) Some applicant disclosure laws may limit the scope of the disclosure to affected officials who might be expected to act on the matter; other laws may expand the scope of the disclosure to include officials whose relatives or private businesses have a financial interest in the applicant/bidder or in the application or bid. In the event that the application is oral, the disclosure could be made either on the records of the body to which the application is made or in a separate writing.

Although courts often require that litigants disclose the names of parent and subsidiary companies (for example, U.S. Supreme Court Rule 29.6), applicant disclosure is relatively uncommon. Nonetheless, some jurisdictions do require it, at least in certain contexts, such as land use.[54]

Annual Disclosure

Lengthy annual financial disclosure forms raise a firestorm among municipal officials. Yet properly structured and understood, annual disclosure plays a critical role in a municipal ethics scheme.

Unlike state government, most municipalities rely heavily upon volunteers or near-volunteers to staff many of their high-level positions, such as legislative bodies and planning and zoning boards. Overly intrusive financial disclosure poses a serious threat to municipalities' ability to attract and hold qualified volunteer board members and even elected officials.

It is often said in defense of lengthy financial disclosure forms that "sunlight is the best disinfectant." Maybe, but sunlight also causes cancer. Indeed, the imposition of blunderbuss financial disclosure reflects a serious misunderstanding of the purpose of municipal ethics laws. The purpose of such laws, including their annual disclosure component, lies not in catching crooks but in improving the reality and the perception of integrity in municipal government by preventing conflicts of interest *before* they occur.

Viewed in this light, the specific objective of annual disclosure is to reveal potential conflicts of interest before they arise and thus help to prevent them. Annual disclosure compels municipal officials, at least once each year, to focus on the requirements of the municipality's ethics provisions. It also serves as a check on transactional disclosure by alerting officials, their colleagues, the public, and the media to those areas where the official will probably have to transactionally disclose (and, if required, recuse); those colleagues, citizens, and media will almost certainly remind the official of that obligation should he or she forget.

Accordingly, an effective annual disclosure law

1. ties the disclosure to the code of ethics—for example, if under the ethics code stock ownership can become a conflict only where it exceeds a threshold value or percentage, the disclosure form should not require disclosure of stock interests falling below that threshold;
2. tailors the disclosure to the official's particular agency and position— for example, if no conceivable action of the official could affect the value of his or her private investments, disclosure of those investments makes little sense in the ethics context (agencies, such as a municipal department of investigation or office of internal affairs might wish such information to aid in the search for theft and corruption; but, fundamentally, ethics laws do not share those objectives);
3. requires that the disclosure forms be available to the public and the media since it is largely they who enforce the ethics laws (although some financial disclosure laws, such as those of Rhode Island and Chicago, expressly prohibit use of the forms for commercial purposes); and
4. provides for computerization of information contained on the forms to permit their comparison with other databases, such as lists of vendors to the municipality.

Annual disclosure laws differ widely throughout the country with respect to the type and extent of the information sought, its public availability, and the type of officials, or candidates for office, required to file. (New York State even sets forth in the law the text of the actual form, a singularly poor idea that prevents the ethics board from clarifying the shockingly imprecise language of the statutory questions.)

Disclosure of dollar amounts and of the finances of the filer's spouse have traditionally elicited the greatest objections from municipal officials. But one proposal requires disclosure only of (1) the location of that real property within the community in which the official or an immediate family member has an interest and (2) the source (not the amount) of the outside earned income of the official and his or her spouse.[55] Such disclosure would probably suffice in all but the largest municipalities.

Enforcement

Generally

Enforcement and administration form the third pillar upon which an effective ethics law rests. As discussed above, the primary purpose of such laws lies in prevention, not punishment. Enforcement, too, reflects that same purpose, for the primary goal of ethics enforcement is not punishment of the individual official but prevention of future ethics violations by all officials. Indeed, the seriousness and newsworthiness of an enforcement action makes it one of the most powerful teaching tools in an ethics board's work shed. For example, when the New York City Conflicts of Interest Board fined a former city employee $1,000 for sending his resume to a private company at the same time he was involved with that company in his city job, that enforcement action sent a powerful educational message to all city employees, alerting them to the existence and potency of the city's postemployment restrictions.

In addition, it has been shown time and again across the country that an ethics board without enforcement authority will not be taken seriously. Such a board instead becomes a toothless tiger, raising expectations it cannot meet and thus, paradoxically, increasing public cynicism. Historically, ethics laws that grant to an ethics board only advisory power simply do not work. No one listens. Enforcement therefore constitutes an indispensable part of an effective ethics scheme.

Ethics enforcement may be divided into four stages: investigation; pleadings and negotiation; adjudication, including imposition of penalties; and judicial review. This process is briefly summarized below. For a detailed discussion of enforcement and penalties, the reader is referred to chapter 11.

Stages of the Enforcement Process

Every respectable ethics board has the power to enforce the law it interprets.[56] Most boards may initiate investigations upon receipt of a complaint or upon their own initiative. (Virtually all boards have the prosecutorial discretion to dismiss a complaint at the outset if it appears that no possible violation of the ethics law has occurred. Some ethics laws, such as those of Pennsylvania and Rhode Island, provide penalties for frivolous complaints.[57]) Some boards act as their own investigators; other ethics boards use some other municipal agency, such as a department of investigation or inspectors general, as their investigators. Requiring the board to rely upon a separate investigatory agency has the advantage of reducing the board's costs and separating, to some extent, investigatory and adjudicatory functions but has the disadvantage of giving the board far less control over its investigations.

Following an investigation, the board's staff—or in some jurisdictions the board itself—will determine whether a possible violation of the ethics law may have occurred. At this point, in some jurisdictions, the board will serve a complaint or petition on the respondent official. In other jurisdictions, the board will first issue to the respondent a notice that the board has probable cause to believe that a violation may have occurred. The respondent will then have the opportunity to explain his or her actions. If the board accepts the explanation, it will dismiss the case. If the board sustains its previous finding of probable cause, a complaint or petition will be issued.

148   CONSIDERING ETHICS AT THE LOCAL GOVERNMENT LEVEL

Once the ethics board has formally notified the respondent of the proceeding, whether by a notice of probable cause or by a pleading, settlement negotiations may ensue. Avoiding the publicity attendant upon a hearing and final imposition of a penalty provides the greatest incentive for a municipal officer or employee, particularly an elected official, to settle a case early. Although many ethics boards have a strong policy against private settlements, even a public settlement gives the official some control over the content of the settlement document and thus some control over adverse publicity, particularly if the board agrees not to comment on the case beyond what the settlement papers state.

Indeed, ethics boards probably have their greatest leverage at the nonpublic stages of the proceeding. For example, if under the applicable ethics law a petition is public but a notice of probable cause is not, then the board will probably be best able to force a settlement in the period between the probable cause notice and the petition. For that reason, in view of their limited resources, ethics boards should carefully consider the issuance of a publicly available accusatory instrument.

If the case is not settled, after the issuance of the complaint or petition and the receipt of the respondent's answer, the parties may engage in limited discovery and motion practice, preparatory to trying the case at a hearing before either the board itself or a hearing officer.

Most ethics boards suffer from a sort of bipolar disorder engendered by the need both to prosecute and adjudicate the same claim. However, the inherent tension in that situation may be relieved by building a wall between those employees involved in the prosecution and those involved in the adjudication. For example, the ethics board members who will vote on whether a violation occurred and, if so, on the amount of the penalty should be insulated from the investigation and prosecution of the allegations.

After the hearing, the board will need to determine, based on the evidence, whether a violation of the ethics law has occurred. If it finds a violation, the board will need to determine the type and amount of the penalty. Penalties are discussed in the next section. If the respondent contests the board's determination, he or she may seek judicial review.

Penalties

Critical to the effective enforcement of an ethics law is the availability of a wide range of penalties, thereby permitting the ethics board to fit the punishment to the crime. In particular, the ethics board, either directly or though a court proceeding, must have the ability to impose penalties not only upon the municipal official who violated the ethics law but also upon any private individual or company that aided or abetted in that violation. Thus, the board should have the power, either directly or by the commencement of a civil court proceeding, to void any contract entered into in violation of the ethics law, such as a contract with a private vendor in which the official has a financial interest. So, too, the board should have the authority to commence a proceeding to debar from future municipal business any private individual or company that intentionally induced a violation of the ethics law. Other penalties against the nonmunicipal offender might include civil fines, criminal sanctions, restitution, damages, double or treble penalties, disgorgement of ill-gotten gains (even where the municipality suffered no loss as a result of the violation), civil forfeiture, and injunctive relief. Some jurisdictions, such as California, permit qui tam actions against violators of the ethics law. The cap on civil fines should be sufficiently high to discourage intentional violations and offset any possible gain received by the violator as a result of the violation.

Permissible penalties against municipal officers and employees should include, in addition to the foregoing, letters of warning, censure, or reprimand by the ethics board; recommendations of disciplinary action by the appointing authority, including suspension or removal from office (most ethics laws do not permit the ethics board itself to impose disciplinary action); and disqualification from holding office in the future.[58]

Administration

Ethics laws must be easy and inexpensive to administer and enforce. The last thing that any municipality needs in an ethics law is yet another complicated and expensive mandate. Moreover, the success of an ethics law depends above all else on the efficacy of its administration and on the independence of the body enforcing it. For that reason a good ethics law invests broad administrative responsibilities in an ethics board that is independent of the political process. So long as the reality and perception of that independence is maintained, the details of administration probably matter little. However, ethics boards should be lean and mean, a model of government efficiency.

The appointment and composition of ethics boards vary widely.[59] Some laws specify professions to be represented on the board, such as lawyers or clergy, and restrict the number of members who can be registered in the same political party. Many ethics laws restrict the political activity of board members and may prohibit them from holding any other public office or employment. To help preserve the board's independence, ethics laws often involve both the executive and legislative branches in the appointment process (either by giving each branch appointments or by establishing an advice and consent procedure), establish set terms of office for board members, stagger those terms, and make them overlap the term of the appointing authority. Board members should be removable only for cause and after a hearing. To ensure the continuous flow of new blood, some ethics laws establish a term limit for board members. Members usually either serve pro bono or receive only per diem compensation, with a cap.

The powers and duties of an ethics board may be grouped into six areas:

1. Training and educating municipal officers and employees about the ethics law, including writing and distributing educational materials

150   CONSIDERING ETHICS AT THE LOCAL GOVERNMENT LEVEL

and videotapes, conducting training sessions, and developing ethics compliance programs

2. Providing oral and written advice, including staff opinions and formal advisory opinions of the board, to municipal officials and their supervisors

3. Enforcing the ethics law, including referring, investigating, prosecuting, and conducting hearings on alleged violations and imposing penalties

4. Waiving conflicts of interest requirements, where appropriate

5. Collecting, reviewing, and maintaining disclosure forms and making them publicly available

6. Engaging in miscellaneous related activities, such as enacting rules and regulations, proposing legislative changes, and issuing annual reports.

If it is to be successful, an ethics board must undertake all of these duties.[60]

Confidentiality

The confidentiality of the records and proceedings of an ethics board presents one of the most controversial and contentious aspects of an ethics law. An unavoidable tension exists between the need to protect the privacy of the municipal officials, particularly those who have been unjustly accused of unethical conduct, and the need to educate officials, the media, and the public about the ethics law and to alert them to potential conflicts of interest in order to avoid such conflicts.[61] Too much openness deters officials and complainants from contacting the ethics board and discourages good people from serving in local government. Too much confidentiality creates the perception that the board is at best an irrelevancy and at worst a star-chamber.

In particular, a prohibition against disclosure of pleadings and hearings fosters the impression that the ethics board is a do-nothing agency, as months may go by between the first press reports of a potential ethics issue and its resolution by the board. Permitting the board to release its disposition of a complaint only if the board finds a violation substantially aggravates that problem. Moreover, excessive privacy in enforcement proceedings—based largely on the fear of politicians that for them an accusation is as good as a conviction— runs counter to the current trend toward greater openness in professional disciplinary proceedings.

Accordingly, as a general rule, the records and proceedings of ethics boards should be no less open than those of other agencies under the applicable open meetings and freedom of information laws. Such laws ordinarily protect investigatory, litigation, intraagency, interagency, and personnel matters. Enforcement proceedings should be public once the complaint or petition has been served. Criminal procedure laws provide a guide in that regard. Thus, discussions and documents relating to investigations would remain con-

Conclusion   151

fidential, as would the initial proceeding to determine whether there is probable cause to believe that an ethics violation occurred. Pleadings and all other postpleading litigation documents served on either side would be public, as would hearings and oral arguments. The deliberations of the board, like those of a court, would be confidential since, as the adjudicative body, the board is acting in a quasi-judicial capacity. Adopting this approach to confidentiality not only provides a fair balance between privacy and openness but also promotes integrity in government by focusing attention upon the ethics law and revealing how it plays out in practice.

Conclusion

In the words of Robert Service, "Now a promise made is a debt unpaid."[62] And municipal ethics laws typically scatter promises like grass seed across the political landscape. But unless those laws are prudently structured and effectively administered—and many, if not most, are not—their promise will remain largely an unpaid debt. Both municipal lawyers and private practitioners alike must ensure that the promise does not go unfilled, for so long as it does, their clients will inevitably suffer from the want of guidance and reassurance that only these laws can provide.

Notes

1. The meaning of the terms "official," "officer," and "employee" varies according to the particular ethics law. In this chapter, unless otherwise specified, the term "municipal official" includes all elected and appointed public servants of the municipality.

2. *See generally* Mark Davies, *Governmental Ethics Laws: Myths and Mythos,* 40 N.Y.L. SCH. L. REV. 177 (1995); Mark Davies, *The Public Administrative Law Context of Ethics Requirements for West German and American Public Officials: A Comparative Analysis,* 18 GA. J. INT'L & COMP. L. 319 (1988).

3. R.I. CONST. art. III, § 7.

4. *Id.* art. III, § 8.

5. N.Y. CONST. art. VIII, § 1.

6. *See, e.g.,* ALA. CODE §§ 36-25-1 through 36-25-30; CAL. GOV'T CODE §§ 82000-82054 (definitions), 83100-83123 (Fair Political Practices Commission), 87100-87500 (conflicts of interest), 89501-89503 (honoraria), 89506 (travel payments, advances, and reimbursements), 91000-91015 (enforcement); MASS. GEN. LAWS ch. 268A (conduct of public officials and employees) and ch. 268B (state ethics commission; financial disclosure); N.Y. GEN. MUN. LAW §§ 800-813; OHIO REV. CODE ANN. §§ 102.01-102.99; PA. STAT. ANN. §§ 401-413; R.I. GEN. LAWS §§ 36-14-2 through 36-14-21.

7. *See, e.g.,* CAL. GOV'T CODE §§ 82011 ("code reviewing body"), 82035 ("jurisdiction"), 82041 ("local government agency"), 87300-87312 (conflict of interest code); N.Y. GEN. MUN. LAW §§ 806 (local code of ethics), 808 (local ethics boards), 811 (financial disclosure forms); PA. STAT. ANN. § 411.

8. *See* CAL. GOV'T CODE §§ 82003, 87100, 87300.

9. N.Y. CIV. SERV. LAW § 107; N.Y. GEN. MUN. LAW § 51.

10. N.Y.C. Charter § 1126.

11. *See* Syracuse Police Benevolent Ass'n v. Young, 156 Misc. 2d 513, 593 N.Y.S.2d 718 (Sup. Ct., Onondaga County, 1992); NYC Police Department General Guidelines for Members

152   CONSIDERING ETHICS AT THE LOCAL GOVERNMENT LEVEL

of the Service concerning the Acceptance of Gifts and Other Compensation (Sept. 1992); Municipal Code of Chicago § 2-156-450.

12. For a collection of cases, *see* 63A AM. JUR. 2D *Public Officers and Employees* §§ 65, 322, 335-347 (1984); 62 C.J.S. *Municipal Corporations* § 545, at 1006 (1949), §§ 988-992 (1950).

13. Clarke v. Town of Russia, 283 N.Y. 272, 274, 28 N.E.2d 833, 835 (1940).

14. Pyatt v. Mayor and Council of Borough of Dunellen, 9 N.J. 548, 557, 89 A.2d 1, 5 (1952). *Accord:* Baker v. Marley, 8 N.Y.2d 365, 367, 170 N.E.2d 900, 901, 208 N.Y.S.2d 449, 450 (1960).

15. Zagoreos v. Conklin, 109 A.D.2d 281, 491 N.Y.S.2d 358, 363 (2d Dept. 1985). *See also* Tuxedo Conservation & Taxpayers Ass'n v. Town Board of Town of Tuxedo, 96 Misc. 2d 1, 408 N.Y.S.2d 668 (Sup. Ct., Orange County, 1978), aff'd, 69 A.D.2d 320, 418 N.Y.S.2d 638 (2d Dept. 1979).

16. *State laws:* ALA. CODE § 36-25-1 et seq. [hereinafter ALA.]; CAL. GOV'T CODE § 81000 et seq. [CAL.]; MASS. GEN. LAWS ch. 268A and ch. 268B [MASS.]; N.Y. GEN. MUN. LAW § 800 et seq. [N.Y.S.]; OHIO REV. CODE § 102.01 et seq. [OHIO]; PA. STAT. tit. 65, § 401 et seq. [PA.]; R.I. CONST. ART. III [R.I. CONST.]; R.I. GEN. LAWS § 36-14-1 et seq. [R.I.]. *Municipal laws:* Anne Arundel County Code art. 9 [Anne Arundel]; Chicago Mun. Code ch. 2-156 [Chicago]; Cook County (Ill.) Ethics Ordinance [Cook]; D.C. Code § 1-1457 et seq. [D.C.]; Rev. Charter of City and County of Honolulu art. XI [Honolulu Charter]; Honolulu Rev. Ordinances § 3-8.1 et seq. [Honolulu]; King County (Wash.) Code ch. 3.04 [King]; Los Angeles City Charter § 600 et seq. [L.A. Charter]; Los Angeles Mun. Code § 49.5.1 et seq. [L.A.]; Maui County (Haw.) Charter art. X [Maui]; N.Y.C. Charter § 2600 et seq. [N.Y.C.]; Philadelphia Home Rule Charter § 8-300 et seq. [Philadelphia Charter]; Philadelphia Code ch. 20–600 [Philadelphia]; Seattle Mun. Code ch. 4.16 [Seattle]; Westchester County Laws ch. 883 [Westchester]. *Proposed state law:* Proposed Bill of the New York State Temporary State Commission on Local Government Ethics, reproduced in Temporary State Commission on Local Government Ethics, *Final Report*, 21 FORD. URB. L. J. 1, 26 (1993) [hereinafter TSC bill]. *Model local law:* Model Local Ethics Law, reproduced in Mark Davies, *Keeping the Faith: A Model Local Ethics Law—Content and Commentary*, 21 FORD. URB. L. J. 61 (1993) [hereinafter Davies model law].

17. *See, e.g.,* PA. § 402; Anne Arundel § 1-101(k), (n); Chicago § 2-156-010(l); Cook § 1(i); Honolulu § 3-8.1; N.Y.C. §§ 2601(4), (12), (16), (18); Westchester § 883.11(f). Compare TSC bill § 803; Davies model law § 105.

18. *See, e.g.,* N.Y.S. § 800(3); R.I. § 36-14-2(8); D.C. § 1-1461(i)(3).

19. Anne Arundel § 1-101(c).

20. *See, e.g.,* TSC bill §§ 800, 801; Davies model law §§ 100, 102.

21. *See* N.Y.S. §§ 800(3), 801, 802.

22. *See* R.I. § 36-14-5(e); Anne Arundel § 3-109(b); N.Y.C. § 2604(e). *See also* TSC bill § 828; Davies model law § 211.

23. *See, e.g.,* Westchester § 883.21(1)(h).

24. *Position interests:* ALA. § 36-25-9(a); Anne Arundel §§ 1-01(k), (n), 3-105(b); Honolulu §§ 3-8.1, 3-8.2(b); King § 3.04.030(H), (M), (R); N.Y.C. §§ 2601(12), (16), (18), 2604(a); Seattle § 4.16.070(1)(b). *Contracts:* ALA. § 36-25-11; MASS. ch. 268A, §§ 14, 20; N.Y.S. §§ 800(3), 801; PA. § 403(f); R.I. § 35-14-5(h); Chicago §§ 2-156-010(I), 2-156-110; Cook §§ 1(i), 2.11; Honolulu § 3-8.2(e); King § 3.04.030(B), (R), (S); Seattle § 4.16.070(1)(d). *Legislation:* King § 3.04.030(N), (R), (S); Philadelphia § 20-607. *Property:* King § 3.04.030(O), (R). *Relatives:* King § 3.04.30(P). *Public offices:* MASS. ch. 268A, §§ 15A, 21A; Philadelphia Charter § 8-301.

25. Cal. § 87100.

26. Cal. §§ 87103, 87103.5.

27. Anne Arundel § 3-104(a). *See also* ALA. § 36-25-5(a); MASS. ch. 268A, §§ 13, 19, 23(b)(2), (3); OHIO § 102.03(D); PA. §§ 402 ("conflict of interest"), 403(a); R.I. § 36-14-5(d); Anne Arundel § 3-101; Chicago §§ 2-156-030, 2-156-080(a), (b); Cook §§ 2.2, 2.8(a); D.C. § 1-1461(b), (f); Honolulu Charter § 11-104; Honolulu § 3-8-2(a), (e); King § 3.04.030(A), (E), (R), (S); L.A. § 49.5.5; N.Y.C. § 2604(b)(1), (3); Seattle § 4.16.070(1)(b), (2)(a), (d); TSC bill § 800(1); Davies model law § 100(1).

Notes 153

28. King § 3.04.020(A); Maui § 10-4(1)(e). *See also* Ala. § 36-25-5(c), (d); Chicago § 2-156-060; Cook § 2.6; Seattle § 4.16.070(2)(b).

29. *Voting:* Ala. § 36-25-9(c); Anne Arundel § 3-102. *Relatives:* Chicago § 2-156-130; Cook § 2.12. *General:* R.I. §§ 36-14-5(a), 36-14-7; Honolulu Charter § 11-102(c); King 3.04.030(I); Maui § 10-4(1)(c); N.Y.C. § 2604(b)(2); Seattle § 4.16.070(1)(a), (2)(a); Westchester § 883.21(1)(f), (g).

30. Westchester § 883.21(1)(g). *See also* Mass. ch. 268A, § 23(b)(1); R.I. § 36-14-5(b); Anne Arundel § 3-105; Cook § 2.3; King § 3.04.030(I), (K), (R).

31. King § 3.04.030(I).

32. Honolulu Charter § 11-102(e). *See also* Ala. § 36-25-10 (notice to ethics commission but no prohibition); Mass. ch. 268A, §§ 11(a), (c), 17(a), (c); N.Y.S. § 805-a(1)(c); Ohio § 102.03(A)(1), 102.04(C), (D); R.I. § 36-14-5(e)(1)-(3); Anne Arundel § 3-105(c); Chicago § 2-156-090; Cook § 2.9; D.C. § 1-1461(h); Honolulu § 3-8.2(c); King § 3.04.030(L); Maui § 10-4(1)(d); N.Y.C. §2604(b)(6)-(8); Philadelphia § 20-602; Seattle § 4.16.070(2)(c); Westchester § 883.21(1)(c); TSC bill §§ 800(4), (5), 801(7); Davies model law §§ 100(4), (5), 102(7).

33. N.Y.S. § 805-a(1)(d); Honolulu § 3-8.2(d); King § 3.04.030(L); Westchester § 883.21(1)(d).

34. *Gifts:* Ala. §§ 36-25-5(e), 36-25-7; Cal. § 89503; Mass. ch. 268A, §§ 2, 3; N.Y.S. § 805-a(1)(a); Ohio § 102.03(E), (F); Pa. § 403(c); R.I. § 36-14-5(g); Anne Arundel § 3-106; Chicago § 2-156-040; Cook § 2.4; D.C. § 1-1461(c); Honolulu Charter § 11-102(a); Honolulu §§ 3-8.7, 3-8.8; King §§ 3.04.020(C), (D), 3.04.030(C), (D), (R); L.A. § 49.5.10(A); Maui § 10-4(1)(a); N.Y.C. § 2604(b)(5); Philadelphia § 20-604; Seattle § 4.16.070(3); Westchester § 883.21(1)(a); TSC bill § 800(3); Davies model law § 100(3). *Honoraria:* Cal. §§ 89501, 89502; Ohio § 102.03(H); Pa. § 403(d); Anne Arundel § 3-106(c)(8); Chicago § 2-156-040(g); Cook § 2.4(f). *Travel expenses:* Cal. § 89506; Ohio § 102.03(I); L.A. § 49.5.10(B).

35. Anne Arundel § 3-106.

36. N.Y.S. § 805-a(1)(a), held unconstitutionally vague in People v. Moore, 85 Misc. 2d 4, 377 N.Y.S.2d 1005 (Fulton County Ct. 1975).

37. *Gifts:* Ohio §§ 102.01(G), 102.03(G); R.I. § 36-14-5(g); D.C. § 1-1461(c). *Not gifts:* Cal. § 82028(b)(4); Pa. § 402 ("gift"); Anne Arundel § 1-101(I); Chicago § 2-156-040(d)(iii); Cook § 2.4(c)(iii); Honolulu Charter § 11-102(a); King §§ 3.04.017(G), 3.04.030(D); L.A. § 49.5.2(4) ("gift"); Philadelphia § 20-601(8); Seattle § 4.16.070(3); Westchester § 883.21(1)(a); TSC bill § 803(4); Davies model law § 105(4). *Separate regulation:* Cal. § 84100 et seq.; Pa. § 403(c); Cook § 2.15; Honolulu § 3-8.9; TSC bill § 800(1)(f); Davies model law § 100(1)(f).

38. Honolulu Charter § 11-102(d). *See also* Ala. § 36-25-7(d); Mass. ch. 268A, § 3(b); Chicago § 2-156-050; Cook § 2.5; D.C. § 1-1461(d); N.Y.C. § 2604(b)(13).

39. Philadelphia § 20-609. *See also* Ala. § 36-25-8; Mass. ch. 268A, § 23(c); N.Y.S. § 805-a(1)(b); Ohio § 102.03(B); Pa. §§ 402 ("conflict of interest"), 403(a); R.I. § 36-14-5(c), (d); Anne Arundel § 3-107; Chicago § 2-156-070; Cook County § 2.7; D.C. § 1-1461(e); Honolulu Charter § 11-102(b); King § 3.04.030(Q), (R); L.A. §§ 49.5.2 ("confidential information"), 49.5.3; Maui § 10-4(1)(b); N.Y.C. § 2604(b)(4); Seattle § 4.16.070(4); Westchester § 883.21(1)(b); TSC bill § 800(6); Davies model law § 100(6).

40. N.Y.C. § 2604(b)(9), (11), (12), (15). *See also* Chicago § 2-156-140; Cook § 2.13; Honolulu §§ 3-8.6, 3-8.9; King § 3.04.020(E); TSC bill §§ 800(7), 803(16); Davies model law §§ 100(7), 105(11).

41. King § 3.04.030(J), (R); Ala. § 36-25-5(e). *See also* N.Y.C. § 2604(b)(14).

42. King § 3.04.030(G), (R); Seattle § 4.16.070(1)(c). *See also* TSC bill §§ 800(1)(d), 803(3); Davies model law §§ 100(1)(d), 105(2).

43. Pa. § 403(e); N.Y.C. § 2604(b)(10).

44. *See, e.g.,* Ala. § 36-25-13; Mass. ch. 268A, §§ 12, 18, 21A; Ohio § 102.03(A), (B); Pa. § 403(g); R.I. § 36-14-5(e)(4); Anne Arundel § 3-109; Chicago § 2-156-100; Cook § 2.10; Honolulu Charter § 11-105; Honolulu § 3-8.3; King §§ 3.04.030(F), (R), 3.04.035; L.A. §§ 49.5.11, 49.5.12; Maui §§ 10-4(1)(g), 10-4(2); N.Y.C. § 2604(d), (e); Philadelphia § 20-603; Seattle § 4.16.075; Westchester § 883.21(1)(h); TSC bill §§ 800(8), 801(8); Davies model law §§ 100(8), 102(8).

45. TSC bill § 800(10). *See also* Cal. § 83116.5; Rules of the City of New York, title 53, § 1–13(d); Davies model law § 100(10). *Cf.* Honolulu § 3-8.2(f) (prohibiting city officers or

154   CONSIDERING ETHICS AT THE LOCAL GOVERNMENT LEVEL

employees from ordering any person to violate, or aiding or abetting any person in the violation of, certain charter provisions relating to the prohibition on political activities of persons in
civil service); King § 3.04.030(R) (prohibiting county officers and employees from acting "as an
accomplice in any act by an immediate family member which, if such act were performed by
the employee would be prohibited" by certain specified ethics provisions).

46. Westchester § 883.21(1)(f). *See also* L.A. § 49.5.8; TSC bill § 800(9); Davies model law
§ 100(9).

47. *See, e.g.,* ALA. § 36-25-24; MASS. ch. 268B, § 8; PA. § 408(j); R.I. § 36-14-5(m); Anne Arundel § 6-106; Cook § 2.14; King §§ 3.04.017(L), 3.04.060(D); L.A. § 49.5.4.

48. TSC bill § 802. *See also* Davies model law § 103.

49. ALA. § 36-25-5(d). California's Political Reform Act prohibits anyone from "purposely
or negligently caus[ing] any other person to violate any provision of [the Act], or . . . aid[ing]
or abet[ting] any other person in the violation of any provision of [the Act]," but then restricts
that prohibition to persons who have filing or reporting obligations under the act or who are
compensated for services involving the planning, organizing, or directing of any activity regulated or required by the act. CAL. § 83116.5.

50. OHIO § 102.03(F); MASS. ch. 268A, § 17(b); Cook § 2.15. *See also* MASS. ch. 268, §§ 3(a),
11(b); PA. § 403(b); R.I. § 36-14-5(i); Philadelphia § 20-604(2). *Cf.* R.I. § 36-14.1-2 (prohibiting
state vendors from providing goods and services for less than fair market value for personal use
of a procurement official of a state agency with which the vendor will be doing business in the
succeeding 24 months or has done business in the previous 24 months).

51. N.Y.C. § 2604(a), (e); MASS. ch. 268A, §§ 12(c), (d), 18(c), (d). *See also* R.I. § 36-14-5(f);
TSC bill § 804; Davies model law § 106.

52. *See* L.A. Charter § 600(P); L.A. § 49.5.8.

53. *See, e.g.,* MASS. ch. 268A, §§ 6A, 13(b), 19(b); N.Y.S. § 803; OHIO § 102.04(D), (E); PA.
403(j); R.I. §§ 36-14-5(e), 36-14-6; Chicago § 2-156-080(c); Cook § 2.8(b), (c); D.C. § 1-1461(g);
Honolulu Charter § 11-103; King § 3.04.037; Maui § 10-4(1)(f); N.Y.C. §§ 2604(a), (b)(1), 2605;
Philadelphia § 20-608; Seattle § 4.16.070(1); Westchester § 883.21(1)(e); TSC bill § 800(11);
Davies model law § 101.

54. *See, e.g.,* ALA. § 36-25-16; N.Y.S. § 809; R.I. § 36-14-5(f); King § 3.04.120; TSC bill § 806;
Davies model law §§ 108, 109.

55. TSC bill § 805(4). Accord: Davies model law § 107(4). *See also* ALA. §§ 36-25-14, 36-25-
15; CAL. §§ 87200-87210; MASS. ch. 268B; N.Y.S. §§ 810-813; OHIO § 102.02; PA. §§ 403(h), 404,
405; R.I. §§ 36-14-16 through 36-14-18; Anne Arundel § 4-101 et seq.; Chicago §§ 2-156-150
through 2-156-200; Cook §§ 3.1-3.3; D.C. § 1-1462; Honolulu § 3-8.4; King § 3.04.050; L.A.
§§ 49.5.6, 49.5.7, 49.5.20; Maui § 10-3; N.Y.C. § 2603(d); N.Y.C. Ad. Code § 12-110; Philadelphia
§ 20-610; San Francisco Ad. Code ch. 58; Seattle § 4.16.080; Westchester §§ 883.61-883.81; TSC
bill §§ 805, 812, 813, 824; Davies model law §§ 107, 201, 202, 208. *Commercial use of forms:* R.I. 36-
14-5(j); Chicago § 2-156-180(e). *Form set forth in law:* N.Y.S. § 812(5).

56. *See, e.g.,* ALA. §§ 36-25-4, 36-25-24, 36-25-27; CAL. §§ 83115-83121, 91000-91015; MASS. ch.
268A, §§ 9, 15, 21, ch. 268B, § 4; N.Y.S. §§ 811(1)(c)-(d), 812(6), 813(10)-(16); OHIO § 102.06;
PA. §§ 407(12)-(15), 408, 410.1; R.I. §§ 36-14-12 through 36-14-15; Anne Arundel §§ 6-101
through 6-204; Chicago §§ 2-156-380 through 2-156-400; Cook §§ 4.1(f)-(i), 4.2; Honolulu Charter § 11-107; King §§ 3.04.040, 3.04.055, 3.04.057; L.A. Charter § 600(O)-(S); L.A. §§ 49.5.19,
49.5.20; Maui § 10-2; N.Y.C. §§ 2603(d)-(h), 2606; Seattle § 4.16.090; TSC bill §§ 825-827; Davies
model law §§ 209, 210.

57. PA. § 410.1; R.I. § 36-14-5(k).

58. *See, e.g.,* ALA. § 36-25-27 (CF,F,M,R,T); CAL. §§ 83116, 91000 et seq. (CF,DA,DG,DQ,
I,M,Q,T,V); MASS. ch. 268A, §§ 2, 3, 9, 11–15, 17–21, 21B, 23, 25 (D,DA,DG,DQ,F,T,UF,V); N.Y.S.
§ 812(6), 813(13) (CF,M); OHIO § 102.99 (M); PA. § 409 (CF,DG,F,M,T); R.I. §§ 36-14-13(d), 36-
14-14, 36-14-19 (CF,DA,DG,I,M); Anne Arundel §§ 6-103, 6-201 through 6-204 (CF,DA,DG,I,
M,V,W); Chicago §§ 2-156-410 through 2-156-460 (D,DA,DG,UF,V); Cook §§ 5.1-5.3 (DA,UF,V);
D.C. § 1-1471 (F,M); Honolulu Charter § 11-106 (DA); Honolulu §§ 3-8.4(f), 3-8.5, 3-8.6(e), 3-

8.7(g), 3-8.8(f), 3-8.9(f) (CF,DA,DG,M,V); King § 3.04.060 (CF,DA,DR,M,V); L.A. Charter § 600(O) (CF,I); L.A. §§ 49.5.19, 49.5.20 (CF,DA,DR,I,M,Q,T); Maui § 10-5 (CF,DA); N.Y.C. § 2606 (CF,DA,DQ,M,V); Philadelphia Charter § 10-109 (DA,M); Philadelphia § 20-612 (DQ,M,V); Seattle §§ 4.16.90(H), 4.16.100 (DA,IN,V); Westchester §§ 883.71(2), 883.91 (CF,DA,M,UF); TSC bill §§ 807-810 (CF,D,DA,DG,DR,I,M,T,V); Davies model law §§ 110-113 (CF,D,DA,DG,DR, I,M,T,V). CF = civil fines; D = damages; DA = disciplinary action; DG = disgorgement of ill-gotten gains; DR = debarment; DQ = disqualification from future office; F = felony; I = injunctive relief; IN = criminal infraction (less than misdemeanor); M = misdemeanor; Q = qui tam action; R = restitution; T = double or treble penalties; UF = fine (not specified as civil or criminal); V = voiding contract; W = warning or reprimand.

59. *See, e.g.,* ALA. § 36-25-3; CAL. §§ 83100-83110; MASS. ch. 268B, § 2; N.Y.S. § 808; OHIO § 102.05; PA. § 406; R.I. § 36-14-8; Anne Arundel §§ 2-101; Chicago §§ 2-156-310 through 2-156-370; Cook § 4.1(a)-(e); Honolulu Charter § 11-107; King §§ 3.04.080, 3.04.090; L.A. Charter § 600(A)-(I); Maui § 10-2(1); N.Y.C. § 2602; Philadelphia § 20-606; Seattle § 3.70.010; TSC bill §§ 814-820, 822; Davies model law §§ 203-206.

60. *See, e.g.,* ALA. § 36-25-4; CAL. §§ 83111-83123, 87303, 87304, 87311, 87312, 91001; MASS. ch. 268A, §§ 6A, 10, ch. 268B, §§ 3-5; N.Y.S. §§ 808, 811(1)(d); OHIO §§ 102.02, 102.06, 102.08, 102.09; PA. §§ 405(d), 407, 408; R.I. Const. art. III, § 8; R.I. §§ 36-14-5(e), 36-14-9 through 36-14-15; Anne Arundel §§ 2-102, 2-103, 3-101(d), 3-108, 3-109(b), 4-102(c), (d), 4-106(b), 5-102(a), 5-103(a), 5-105(a), (e), 5-106, 5-107, 6-101 through 6-106, 6-201; Chicago §§ 2-156-150 through 2-156-190, 2-156-210 through 2-156-290, 2-156-380 through 2-156-400, 2-156-470; Cook §§ 3.1-3.3, 4.1(f)-(n), 4.2; D.C. § 1-1461(g), 1-1462; Honolulu Charter § 11-107; Honolulu §§ 3-8-4(d), (f), 3-8-5; King §§ 3.04.057, 3.04.100-3.04.130; L.A. Charter § 600(J)-(S); L.A. §§ 49.5.4, 49.5.6(E), (G), (H), 49.5.7, 49.5.9(B), 49.5.10(A)(8), 49.5.17-49.5.20; Maui § 10-2(2) through 10-2(6); N.Y.C. §§ 2603, 2604(e), 2606; Philadelphia §§ 20-606, 20-608(c), 20-610(1); Seattle §§ 3.70.100, 3.70.160, 4.16.080(A), (B), 4.16.090; Westchester §§ 883.71(2), 883.81(6)-(7); TSC bill §§ 821, 823-835; Davies model law §§ 207-215.

61. *See, e.g.,* CAL. §§ 81008, 83110; MASS. ch. 268B, §§ 4, 7; N.Y.S. § 813(18); OHIO §§ 102.06(B), (F), (G), 102.07; PA. §§ 404(e), 407(10), 407(11), 408(a), (c), (g), (h), (j), (k); R.I. §§ 36-14-12(c)(3), (6), 36-14-13(a)(5), (f); Anne Arundel §§ 2-102(a)(2), 3-102(f), 3-103(e), 6-105; Chicago §§ 2-156-180(d), 2-156-290, 2-156-400; Cook § 4.2; Honolulu Charter § 11-107; Honolulu § 3-8.4(e); King §§ 3.04.100(A), 3.04.110; L.A. Charter § 600(N), (O)(1)(a)(iii), (O)(1)(b), (O)(1)(c); L.A. § 49.5.4(C); N.Y.C. §§ 2603(c)(3), (f), (h)(4), (h)(5), (i), (k), 2604(e); Philadelphia §§ 20-606, 20-608, 20-610(4); TSC bill § 836; Davies model law § 216.

62. Robert Service, "The Cremation of Sam McGee," stanza viii.

CHAPTER ❦ 8

Whistleblower Law and Ethics

Robert T. Begg

This chapter is an overview of the law and ethics of whistleblowing. It begins with the reasons why whistleblowing is so controversial and then focuses on the conflict between competing public policies that has lead to a statutory erosion of the at-will employment doctrine. Next, federal and state whistleblower statutes and their underlying purposes are examined, as are statutory financial incentives meant to encourage whistleblowing. Common-law exceptions to the at-will doctrine are then explored as additional sources of remedies for whistleblowers. Finally, the chapter concludes by analyzing special issues encountered by in-house counsel and government lawyers who are placed in the role of whistleblower.

To whistle is "to utter a clear shrill sound, note, or song, as various birds . . . ; also formerly, to hiss, as a serpent."[1] As will be seen, this definition of the verb *whistle* rather nicely illustrates the role of a whistleblower in our society. A whistleblower is usually "an employee who refuses to engage in and/or reports illegal or wrongful activities of his employer or fellow employees."[2] As a legal doctrine, whistleblowing is modern enough to justify a home page on the Internet,[3] yet old enough to have been recognized by statute during the Civil War era,[4] and is now strongly entrenched in federal and most states' statutory or common law.

Whistleblowing is analyzed herein in its broadest sense, that in which individuals, virtually always employees, are encouraged to reveal wrongdoing for the public good and are protected from retaliation for doing so. At times there is a necessary overlap between two interrelated but distinct bodies of law. One is the law of retaliatory or wrongful discharge, which is concerned with a wide spectrum of causes for unjust dismissal, including dismissal for whistleblowing. The other is the law of whistleblowing, which is directed at many different forms of retaliation, including, but not limited to, discharge. Whistleblower law is also distinct in that it seeks to encourage employees to

156

come forward by providing protection against retaliation and also by providing financial incentives in some instances.

Distinctions will also be drawn between active whistleblowing, which entails voluntarily coming forward to report wrongdoing, and passive whistleblowing, in which the employee does nothing more than respond to a lawful request for information from a public entity or refuse to carry out an illegal instruction.[5]

The Controversial Nature of Whistleblowing

The act of whistleblowing has always tended to be controversial. Indeed, individual whistleblowers are frequently viewed in stark contrast as either heroes or villains or, as the definition quoted above suggests, as benevolent songbirds or venomous snakes. It all depends on one's perspective. This ambiguity exists because while the general public, and especially politicians and the media, may laud and wish to encourage corporate or governmental employees to come forward with information about threats to the public safety, gross waste, or illegal activities, those exposed by the disclosure will almost surely have an opposite reaction.[6] Managers of corporations or government agencies, coworkers, and even friends and neighbors often view whistleblowers as disloyal and treacherous spies, squealers, stool pigeons, or threats to their communities, rather than as heroes.

Although retaliation is not always the response to whistleblowing,[7] the instinctive reaction of some managers has been to retaliate against the whistleblower through dismissal, demotion, or other forms of harassment. Whistleblowers know that speaking out can be a threat to job security or can result in their being shunned as an outcast by coworkers, and even, in extreme cases, can be hazardous to their personal safety.[8] Whistleblowing often has a long-term impact on one's career, because bureaucracies supposedly never forget.[9] Therefore, it is not surprising that employees are reluctant to report improprieties either in-house or publicly, because they can anticipate both immediate and long-term negative consequences.

Normally, the decision to blow the whistle on improper activities is a voluntary and intensely personal one.[10] Except in very narrow circumstances, an employee is usually not required by law to report the improper or even illegal activities of an employer, although citizens are generally encouraged to do so.[11] Thus employees who blow the whistle are voluntarily placing what they perceive to be the public interest or a matter of conscience ahead of the interests of their employing business or institution.

The employer may respond by viewing the whistleblower's disclosure as a breach of one or more fundamental expectations inherent in their employment relationship. Both employers and employees have well-established expectations of the other's conduct and responsibilities. Employers have the right to expect their employees to perform their assigned work competently, to obey orders, to be loyal and avoid conflicts of interest, and to maintain appropriate confidences of the employer.[12] Employees in return expect compensation, a minimal degree of job security if they do their jobs well, and assurance that any job responsibilities or orders are not illegal or unethical.[13] Within these strictures employees still have rights and obligations as citizens and moral, religious, or political motivations that can have an impact on how they interpret or respond to the policies of their employer.[14] Thus a decision to expose improper conduct is a difficult one, which can be fraught with conflicting values, responsibilities, and loyalties.

Unfortunately, too often there is no bright-line rule that tells employees when they have a duty to blow the whistle or when that would be an inappropriate course of action. Do factors such as loyalty to one's employer, the need to avoid risk to the financial well-being of one's family, the desire "to play ball" within the work environment, or merely the wish just not to get involved, outweigh the desire of an ethical human being to prevent harm to the environment, nuclear catastrophe, or the waste of public resources? These choices create an ethical conundrum involving a confrontation between the whistleblower's self-interests and the consequences of remaining silent in an environment with few absolutely clear lines of demarcation.[15]

Views on how one should react in a given situation vary considerably. On one hand, virtually all will agree that an employee's refusal to obey an order to commit a criminal act is appropriate. Conversely, many might feel that it would be inappropriate to report this information to the news media or even to a law enforcement agency. In some instances an employee may have a fair degree of discretion as to an appropriate course of action, while in others the employee may have no option, such as when a code of professional responsibility mandates revelation of confidential employer information.[16] It is not unheard of for an employee to blow the whistle on relatively minor or trivial violations of law or regulations in order to use whistleblower protection provisions as a bar to legitimate negative personnel actions or to exact revenge on a coworker or supervisor.[17] So, while ethical issues and quandaries may exist for potential whistleblowers, difficulties also arise for employers who must at times deal with employees who are using the whistleblower protection mechanisms improperly to serve their own self-interests or political, moral, or religious agendas. Thus the employer's interest in being able "to manage his work force free from false or spurious claims of reprisal" is another factor to be included in the whistleblower protection calculus.[18]

Within this quagmire lawmakers have been required to determine the nature and scope of protection for whistleblowers by determining which employees are protected and which are not, and which types of activities are encouraged and which are not. As will be seen, public policies underlying protection for public and private sector employees can differ significantly. For example, the law may protect a public sector employee from reprisal for revealing gross mismanagement or waste of public funds, whereas a private sector employee is usually not protected for reporting an equivalent waste of corporate resources. Whistleblower protection for private sector employees is provided only when the public interest is directly affected.

The law in this area reflects a conflict between two public policies. The first public policy supports an employer's contractual right to hire, fire, and discipline employees, while a second, competing public policy encourages whistleblowers to come forward for the good of society to protect the public from harm, or to protect statutory rights. This second public policy is reflected in the common law and statutes that seek to prevent retaliation against whistleblowers in the first instance, or to provide a remedy when retaliation has taken place. Such antiretaliation policies, however, constitute an erosion of the long-standing doctrine of employment at will. An appreciation of the at-will employment doctrine is essential to an understanding of the law of unjust dismissal and specifically the law of retaliation for whistleblowing.

The At-Will Employment Doctrine

The at-will employment doctrine creates a presumption that applies when an employment contract fails to state a definite duration for the contract or specifically states that the employment is at will.[19] If no term or length of employment is stated or agreed to, the contract is presumed to be at will, and either the employer or the employee may terminate the employment agreement at any time, for any reason or for no reason.[20] The at-will doctrine, which assumes equal bargaining power between employer and employee, is premised on the freedom of contract and reflects the probusiness, laissez-faire economic attitudes of the late nineteenth and early twentieth centuries.[21]

The at-will doctrine is a uniquely American rule, having been articulated for the first time in an early treatise on master and servant law.[22] The rule represents a clear departure from the English common law that, when dealing with employment contracts for an indefinite term, assumes that the term is for one year.[23] Most other major industrialized economies have rules that provide greater protection for employees under contracts of indefinite duration[24] than does the American rule. The at-will doctrine developed during the late 1800s and was eventually adopted as a principle of common law by all American jurisdictions. Business and industry were strong supporters of the doctrine since it was easy to terminate workers in response to the business cycle or to dampen union activity. The impact on employees, however, was quite harsh.

Congress, state legislatures, and the courts attempted to mitigate the harshness of the rule by creating a number of exceptions premised on various public policy considerations. Public sector employees were the first to benefit from an exception to the at-will doctrine.[25] Most government employees at the state and federal levels are now protected from arbitrary dismissal by civil service statutes that require a "just cause" for firings. Public sector employees may also be protected from dismissal in certain circumstances by provisions of the United States Constitution. Freedoms of speech and association under the First Amendment have protected public employees from dismissal for public statements directly concerning matters of legitimate public concern.[26]

The first major exception to the at-will employment doctrine for private sector employees was the National Labor Relations Act, which guaranteed employees the right to organize and bargain collectively.[27] This allowed labor unions to negotiate for "just cause" provisions in their contracts, providing union members with far greater job security than nonunion employees, who are still subject to the at-will doctrine. A third wave of legislation limiting employers' right to fire at will consisted of federal and state civil rights initiatives prohibiting improper discrimination in the hiring and firing of employees. Discriminatory dismissals based on race, sex, color, religion, national origin, age, or disability are now prohibited.[28]

Parallelling the civil rights movement was an expansion of federal regulation of business conduct in the general areas of environmental protection, consumer protection, workplace safety, and public health.[29] While these business conduct statutes were aimed at protecting individuals, society, or the environment from specific enumerated harms,[30] it was also clear that the statutes must protect employees who were seeking to exercise their statutory rights in furtherance of the policy aims of Congress. Most of these statutes therefore contain provisions that protect employees from retaliation for exercising rights under the statute, for testifying in investigations, or for filing charges against an employer for violation of the statute.[31]

Despite this erosion of the common-law at-will employment doctrine, today forty-nine of the fifty states still retain either a common law or statutory version of the rule. The State of Montana has abrogated the rule with a just-cause statute,[32] and the statutory and court-made exceptions to the rule in many jurisdictions have greatly reduced management's unbridled discretion to fire employees for any or no reason.

Statutory Protection for Public Sector Whistleblowers—Why Is There a Need for Whistleblower Protection in the Public Sector?

Government in its many forms collects and spends vast amounts of money and employs millions of citizens in capacities ranging from garbage collectors to physicists to the president.[33] Corresponding to the magnitude of the enterprise of government is the opportunity for government employees to take advantage of their positions of public trust by making improper use of governmental resources, information, or authority. Taking note of this phenomenon in an earlier era, Benjamin Franklin said, "There is no kind of dishonesty into which otherwise good people more easily and frequently fall than that of defrauding the government."[34]

It is clearly in the public interest to prevent criminal acts by public employees, including theft, fraud, corruption, and self-dealing. But it is also important to prevent damage to the public weal from acts, such as waste of public resources, gross mismanagement, favoritism, or unethical conduct, that might not reach to the criminal level but are damaging nonetheless. To prevent improper activities by public employees, there are a panoply of institutional mechanisms and agencies charged with the formal responsibility of ferreting out governmental crime and corruption. These agencies conduct formal audits, inventories, and investigations in hopes of deterring, detecting, or remedying improper activities. One of the most important sources of information for these agencies is derived from public sector employees who become aware of improper activities.[35] Whistleblowers, in essence, are "an additional check and balance that insures government integrity and prevents government corruption."[36]

Information concerning improper acts comes to the attention of investigative agencies primarily in two ways. In the first instance an honest employee learns of an impropriety and voluntarily comes forward with information that results in the initiation of an investigation. This can be viewed as active whistleblowing and is often the only way in which a particular improper activity would ever be brought to light.[37] Unfortunately, it is still relatively rare for a public sector employee to come forward voluntarily to incriminate a supervisor or coworker because "squealing" continues to be frowned upon by many within our society.[38] Also, other factors, such as the wish not to stir up trouble, the desire to just do one's job and not get involved, and the fear of retaliation if an employee does come forward, militate against voluntarily speaking out. Most public employees know the costs and risks associated with whistleblowing and are not comforted by the formal legal protections that are in place to protect them. The enormous institutional hostility targeted at those who betray organizational norms cannot be eliminated by formal legislative language.[39]

The second way investigators learn of wrongdoing involves passive whistleblowing. Here, a public sector employee provides information concerning improper conduct when the employee is questioned during the course of an investigation. Although the employee may not have initiated the inquiry, he or she may have provided pertinent information that has incriminated or embarrassed a supervisor, coemployee, or other person with strong political connections. Such information could surface in a routine investigative interview or under oath pursuant to a subpoena. It is in the public interest for public sector employees to be encouraged to cooperate with investigating agencies and to testify fully and honestly under oath.[40]

Clearly society benefits when public employees are willing to come forward and to speak freely about inappropriate activities. It has long been recognized that it is in the public interest to provide protection from retaliation for public sector employees for doing so. Therefore, the federal government, many states, and even some local governments[41] have attempted to provide statutory protection for public employees to further this public interest.

Federal Statutory Protections for Whistleblowers

Although federal employees long enjoyed the protection of civil service statutes requiring "just cause" for dismissal, until 1978 there was no provision specifically applicable to federal employee whistleblowers. In that year Congress dramatically reformed the federal civil service laws. In addition to making retaliation for bona fide whistleblowing a "prohibited personnel practice," the 1978 Civil Service Reform Act (CSRA) created new government bodies to deal with employment issues relating to federal employees. These include the Office of Personnel Management, the Merit System Protection Board (MSPB), and the Office of Special Counsel (OSC).

Each of these bodies has specialized functions. The Office of Personnel Management executes, administers, and enforces rules for day-to-day personnel management and serves an advisory function to the agencies and the president.[42] The Merit System Protection Board is charged with ensuring adherence to merit system principles and with reviewing appealable agency actions affecting the merit system.[43] The Office of Special Counsel is required to protect employees from prohibited personnel practices, to file complaints for disciplinary action against those who commit prohibited personnel practices, and to protect whistleblowers.[44]

Despite the clearly expressed intent of Congress to protect whistleblowers, the promise of the CSRA was not fulfilled initially. Whistleblowers learned to their dismay that they were not adequately protected in those instances when they had come forward.[45] Congress had intended the OSC to play an activist role in protecting whistleblowers, but the reality was that the OSC's performance was uninspired and ineffectual, and at times it seemed even openly hostile to whistleblowers.[46]

Congress attempted to strengthen protection through the enactment of the Whistleblower Protection Act of 1989[47] (WPA), which significantly amended and expanded the CSRA. The WPA mandated that the OSC protect employees from prohibited personnel practices, especially whistleblowing, as its paramount function.[48]

Enactment of the WPA and its enhanced protections for whistleblowers led to a marked increase in the number of new complaints received by the OSC.[49] Surveys of federal employees who had requested assistance from the OSC suggested, however, that the OSC continued to be viewed as relatively ineffective in protecting whistleblowers from retaliation.[50] This led to significant amendments to the CSRA and WPA in 1994.[51]

Currently, basic protection for whistleblower activities for most federal employees is provided by provisions of the CSRA as amended and expanded by the WPA and 1994 amendments. Fundamental to the federal civil service is the concept of employment protection premised on a merit system in which employees are protected from eleven "prohibited personal practices." It is a merit system principle that federal employees be protected from reprisal for bona fide whistleblower activities and that retaliation for whistleblowing is a prohibited personnel practice.[52] Persons in a position to influence a personnel action shall not "take or fail to take, or threaten to take or fail to take, a personnel action with respect to any employee or applicant for employment" due to whistleblower activities.[53]

Whistleblower activities for purposes of these statutes are defined in section 2302(b)(8)(A)(B) as disclosures of information that the employee reasonably believes evidences "a violation of any law, rule or regulation, or gross mismanagement, a gross waste of funds, an abuse of authority, or a substantial and specific danger to public health or safety." Any such disclosures can be made to the special counsel, to the inspector general of an agency, or to other employees designated to receive such disclosures within an agency.[54] Such disclosures can be made to others, but only if doing so is not prohibited by law or by an executive order that requires disclosures to be kept secret in the interest of national defense or the conduct of foreign affairs.[55]

Upon receipt of an allegation of improper conduct by a whistleblower, the OSC must determine within fifteen days whether there is a substantial likelihood that the alleged agency misconduct actually occurred.[56] If there is a positive determination, the OSC informs the agency head, who must then conduct an investigation and submit a written report of findings to the special counsel, who must then take further action.[57] If there is no positive determination, the OSC may still pass on the information to the agency head with the consent of the whistleblower. If it is not transmitted to the agency head, the OSC shall return any documentation to the whistleblower, inform him or her why the disclosure is not being pursued, and also specify what other options are available should the individual wish to pursue the matter further.[58] The whistleblower's identity may not be disclosed by the special counsel without consent unless revealing it is necessary to prevent "imminent danger to public health or safety or imminent violation of any criminal law."[59]

If a whistleblower is retaliated against for a protected disclosure, the retaliation constitutes a prohibited personnel practice and the whistleblower may seek protection from the OSC. If permitted under law, rule, or regulations, the whistleblower may seek corrective action directly from the MSPB, rather than from the special counsel.[60] Since the OSC's paramount responsibility is the protection of federal employee whistleblowers, during an OSC investigation no disciplinary action can be taken against the employee for the activity under investigation without approval of the special counsel.[61] Protection is also provided by the OSC's ability to request a stay of a personnel action from any member of the MSPB for forty-five days if there "are reasonable grounds to believe that the personnel action was taken as a result of a prohibited personnel practice."[62] There are detailed OSC guidelines in place for keeping the whistleblower informed, for completing the investigation in a timely fashion, and for maintaining confidentiality. If the OSC is unable to achieve a correction of the prohibited personnel practice, or the employee's agency has not acted, the OSC may petition the MSPB for corrective action.[63] Judicial review is available in the case of an adverse order or decision of the MSPB.[64]

In order to prove a prima facie case for whistleblower retaliation, the OSC or the whistleblower must prove by a preponderance of the evidence four elements of the case.[65]

164   WHISTLEBLOWER LAW AND ETHICS

1. **"That the employee engaged in protected conduct."**
   This would be disclosure of information under section 2302(b)(8)(A) or (B) as noted above. The disclosure may be based on the employee's "reasonable belief" that there was improper activity or wrongdoing, even though the disclosures may ultimately be proven to be incorrect.[66]

2. **"That an official in an appropriate capacity knew about the whistleblower disclosures."**
   This may be either actual or constructive knowledge of the disclosure and can be proved by circumstantial evidence, such as if "the personnel action occurred within a period of time such that a reasonable person could conclude that the disclosure was a contributing factor in the personnel action."[67]

3. **"That a personnel action was taken or failed to be taken or that a threat was made to take or fail to take a personnel action in retaliation for disclosure."**
   Section 2302(a)(2)(A) defines personnel action in some detail including "(xi) any other significant change in duties, responsibilities, or working conditions." Thus both formal and informal forms of retaliation against a whistleblower are viewed as personnel actions.[68]

4. **"That there was a causal connection between the protected activity and the adverse personnel action."**
   The whistleblower must prove that the disclosure was "a contributing factor" in the decision to take the personnel action.[69] Thus the employee must demonstrate by a preponderance of evidence "that the fact of, or the content of, the protected disclosure was one of the factors that tended to affect in any way the personnel action."[70] The agency then has an affirmative defense if it can prove by "clear and convincing evidence" that it would have taken the same personnel action even without the disclosure, that is, there was a legitimate managerial reason for the agency action.[71] If the agency cannot meet the burden of proof on its affirmative defense, the MSPB shall order appropriate corrective action.[72]

Corrective action by the MSPB may include placing the whistleblowing employee, "as nearly as possible," in the position the employee would have been in had the retaliation for disclosure not occurred.[73] For example, a whistleblower may be granted reinstatement or a preference in receiving a transfer within the same or another agency to a position with comparable tenure and status to the employee's original position, assuming the employee is otherwise qualified.[74] Corrective actions may "include reimbursement for attorney's fees, back pay and related benefits, medical costs incurred, travel expenses, and any other reasonable and foreseeable consequential damages."[75]

In enacting the CSRA Congress intended "to channel grievances and disputes arising out of government employment into a single system of administrative procedures and remedies, subject to judicial review."[76] A line of judicial precedents emphasized that remedies under the CSRA were exclusive and that other remedies such as actions under the Federal Tort Claims Act,[77] constitutional claims,[78] and suits for back pay under the Tucker Act, 28 USC §1491 (1994),[79] were precluded by the CSRA.[80]

The Whistle Blower Protection Act of 1989 (WPA), by contrast, specifically provides at 5 U.S.C. § 1222 (1994), that except as provided in the individual right of action provisions of § 1221(i), nothing in chapters 12 (Office of Special Counsel) or 23 (Merit System Principles) "shall be construed to limit any right or remedy available under a provision of statute which is outside of both this chapter and chapter 23." The legislative history states the position, however, that "§ 1222 is not intended to create a cause of action where none now exists or to reverse any court decision. Rather § 1222 says it is not the intent of Congress that the procedures under these chapters of title 5, United States Code, are meant to be exclusive."[81] The courts, relying on the legislative history, have held, therefore, that remedies not available prior to the WPA are also not available under § 1222, and that the exclusivity of remedies under the CSRA as established by earlier precedents is still valid and controlling.[82] It was the intent of Congress to expand and enhance appeal rights available in other statutes rather than to create any new cause of action against the government.[83] Thus the preference for exclusivity of remedies under the CSRA remains, apparently, until Congress specifically creates new remedies outside the scope of the CSRA.

Federal Whistleblower and Antiretaliation Provisions outside the Merit System

The CSRA and WPA provide significant protections and remedies for most federal employee whistleblowers. But what of federal employees not covered by these enactments, or nonfederal employees in the public and private sectors, or employees who are retaliated against for activities that combine whistleblower and nonwhistleblower motivations?

The answer to some of these questions requires an examination of the broader federal regulatory structure. Over the past several decades, the federal government has expanded its role in regulating employment practices, workplace safety, consumer protection, financial institutions, transportation, and threats to the environment. Congressional intent in enacting legislation in these areas was primarily to protect the public against unfair or dangerous business or governmental practices or conditions. It soon became apparent that enforcement of these statutes and regulations was difficult if not impossible without the cooperation of employees of the businesses or governmental agencies who were aware of violations. Employees knew that, in an at-will employment environment, coming forward with incriminating information concerning their employers could result in retaliation. Congress responded by promulgating antiretaliation provisions in a large number of federal statutes. While many of these statutes protect active whistleblowers, others are meant to protect employees in the exercise of certain civic rights and responsibilities or in the enforcement of personal rights under a statute.

166 WHISTLEBLOWER LAW AND ETHICS

The following chart lists federal statutes that provide whistleblower and antiretaliation protection for public or private sector employees or both. Although it is recognized that not all these statutes are purely whistleblower in nature, an all-inclusive chart may be more useful than one that attempts to define too narrowly whistleblower protection. The chart lists the name of the provision, its citation, and whether targeted at public or private sector employees or both. The chart is divided into sections based on the nature of the subject matter dealt with in the statute.

Military		
Armed Forces Members' Communication with Congress and Inspector General	10 U.S.C. § 1034(b)	Public sector
Armed Services Contractor's Employees Protection	10 U.S.C. § 2409(a)	Private sector
Civilian Employees of the Armed Forces	10 U.S.C. § 1587(h)	Private sector
False Claims Act	31 U.S.C. §3730(b)	Both
Vietnam Era Veterans Readjustment Assistance Act	38 U.S.C. §§ 2021(b)(1)(A), (b)(3), and § 2024(c)	Both
Environment		
Asbestos Hazard Emergency Response Act	15 U.S.C. § 2651	Both
Asbestos School Hazard Detection and Control Act of 1980	20 U.S.C. § 3608	Public sector
Clean Air Act	42 U.S.C. § 7622(a)(1)(2)(3)	Both
Comprehensive Environment Response, Compensation and Liability Act of 1980	42 U.S.C. § 9610	Private sector
Federal Water Pollution Control Act	33 U.S.C. § 1367(a)	Private sector
Hazardous Substances Releases Act	42 U.S.C. § 9610	Both
Safe Drinking Water Amendments	42 U.S.C. § 300 j-9(i)(1)	Both
Solid Waste Disposal Act	42 U.S.C. § 6971(a)	Both
Toxic Substances Control Act	15 U.S.C. § 2622(a)	Private sector
Citizens' Rights and Responsibilities		
Bankruptcy Reform Act	11 U.S.C. § 525	Both
Civil Rights of Institutionalized Persons Act	42 U.S.C. § 1997d	Both
Employee Polygraph Protection Act	29 U.S.C. § 2002(3)(4)	Private sector
Family and Medical Leave Act of 1993	29 U.S.C. § 2615	Both
Jury Systems Improvement Act	28 U.S.C. § 1875(a)	Both
Public Health Service Act	42 U.S.C. § 300a-7	Private sector
Racketeering Influenced and Corrupt Organization Act (indirect application)	18 U.S.C. § 1964(c)	Private sector
Labor and Workplace Safety		
Fair Labor Standards Act	29 U.S.C. § 215(a)(3)	Both

Labor and Workplace Safety		
Federal Labor Relations—Unfair Labor Practices	5 U.S.C. § 7116(a)(4)	Public sector
Migrant Seasonal and Agricultural Protection Act	29 U.S.C. § 1855(a)	Private sector
National Labor Relations Act	29 U.S.C. § 158(a)(1)(3)(4)	Private sector
Occupational Safety and Health Act	29 U.S.C. § 660(c)(1)	Private sector
Transportation		
Federal Employers' Liability Act (Railroads)	45 U.S.C. § 60	Private sector
Federal Railroad Safety Act	45 U.S.C. § 441(a)(1)	Private sector
Longshore and Harbor Workers Compensation Act	33 U.S.C. § 948a	Private sector
Railway Labor Act	45 U.S.C. § 152	Private sector
Safe Containers for International Cargo Act	46 App. U.S.C. § 1506	Private sector
Surface Transportation Assistance Act	49 U.S.C. § 31105(a)	Private sector
Vessels and Seamen Laws	46 U.S.C. § 2114	Private sector
Hazardous Industries		
Energy Reorganization Act	42 U.S.C. § 5851(a)	Private sector
Federal Mine Safety and Health Act	30 U.S.C. § 815(c)	Private sector
Surface Mining Control and Reclamation Act of 1977	30 U.S.C. § 1293(a)	Private sector
Financial Institutions		
Federally Insured Credit Union Employees	12 U.S.C. § 1790b (a)	Private sector
Financial Institutions Reform, Recovery, and Enforcement Act of 1989	12 U.S.C. § 1831j	Private sector
Non-depository Financial Institutions Employee Protection	31 U.S.C. § 5328	Private sector
Resolution Trust Corporation Whistleblower Act	12 U.S.C. § 1441a (q)	Public sector
Consumer Protection		
Consumer Credit Protection Act	15 U.S.C. § 1674(a)	Both
Employee Retirement Income Security Act	29 U.S.C. § 1140	Private sector
Intergovernmental Communications		
Congressional Accountability Act of 1995	2 U.S.C.A. § 1317(a) (1996 supp.)	Public sector
Federal Employees' Right to Petition Congress	5 U.S.C. § 7211	Public sector
Miscellaneous		
Federal Acquisition Streamlining Act of 1994	41 U.S.C. § 265	Private sector

The impact of these federal whistleblower protection and antiretaliation statutes is significant. They encourage both public and private sector employees to come forward to protect their own personal interests in some cases, but more frequently to protect the public interest. The underlying public policies and justifications for whistleblower protection at the federal level have also been compelling at the state level. Many states have enacted whistleblower protection statutes in response to concerns of fraud and corruption in government and threats to the public health or safety by business enterprises and government.

Statutory Whistleblower Protection at the State Level

Generally

Currently forty-six states and the District of Columbia have adopted some form of statutory protection for whistleblowers. Arkansas, Mississippi, New Mexico, and Vermont have not adopted such statutes.

Although many state whistleblower statutes are modeled after the federal Civil Service Reform Act,[84] they vary considerably in the scope of who is covered under the statute and in the nature of the conduct protected or encouraged. Public policy in some states seeks to provide comprehensive coverage to a broad pool of potential whistleblowers, while other states have carefully refined and targeted their protections. Public sector employees are generally more likely to be protected by whistleblower statutes and to have a much broader range of protected conduct than are private sector employees or individuals.[85]

Making generalizations about these statutes can be useful for a broad understanding of state whistleblower protection, but is also dangerous relative to a specific state. A chart has therefore been prepared in Appendix 8A that lists citations to each state's whistleblower provisions and indicates the scope of coverage of the statute and the conduct that is sought to be protected, as well as remedies. It is important to consult the chart because definitions of generic terms, such as "state employee," often vary significantly from state to state. For example, some states exclude legislative or judicial employees from the definition of "state employee."[86] The chart does not include relatively common provisions that have been adopted by many states to prevent retaliation against employees for exercising rights under specific statutes such as workers' compensation, civil rights, or occupational safety and health, or for service on juries or in the National Guard. Also, general "just cause" civil service provisions have been excluded.[87]

State whistleblower statutes are premised on public policy concerns and public interests sufficient to override the at-will employment doctrine.[88] The purpose of these statutes is to encourage specified employees, and in some cases nonemployee individuals, to report or disclose certain types of information or to refrain from committing certain types of acts. This encouragement is provided in three distinct ways: (1) the statutes prohibit retaliation and provide remedies for whistleblowers who are retaliated against; (2) some statutes provide financial incentives either in the form of a remedy for retaliation (treble damages or punitive damages) or as pure financial rewards under false claims acts; (3) punishments, ranging from criminal sanction to dismissal from supervisory positions and fines, are established for those who retaliate against whistleblowers in many states.

Protected Conduct

The most common type of protected conduct is reporting, or threatening to report, a violation of a federal, state, or local law, rule, or regulation. Also frequently protected is disclosure of a substantial and specific threat or danger to the public health or safety. Such strong public policies support the enforcement of laws and the prevention of serious harm to the public that virtually all of the state whistleblower statutes provide protection to state and some other public sector employees for such disclosures, as do most of the statutes covering private sector employees.

Public policy also strongly favors ferreting out of "gross" mismanagement and "gross" waste or abuse of authority in governmental operations. Although public sector employees are usually protected for reporting such abuses in their employment, private sector employees are not, since the waste of private or corporate assets is not viewed as being on a par with the waste of public resources.[89]

Beyond the broad categories above, various states have identified other conduct that it is believed to be in the public interest specifically to protect. Examples include an employee's refusal to obey an illegal directive[90] or to expose oneself or others to a hazardous condition.[91] Many states have also adopted protections for workers in certain professions to encourage reporting, as in the case of health care providers[92] and those dealing with abused children.[93] Such workers may be required by law to report abuses, so corresponding whistleblower protections have been enacted. Some states have chosen to target public utilities workers[94] and those who report threats to the environment for special protection.[95]

In adopting whistleblower protection statutes, state legislatures felt compelled to distinguish between the types of information that should be disclosed in the public interest and types of information the revelation of which should be discouraged or prohibited. Thus many statutes specifically exclude from protection the reporting of information that is prohibited from disclosure by law.

Legislators were also very concerned about abuse by disgruntled, overzealous, or misinformed employees or by those seeking to use the statutes for their own personal interests rather than the public interest.[96] Concerns about false or unfounded reporting led to the requirement in many statutes that disclosures must be made "in good faith" or "truthfully" and be based on a reasonable belief that the disclosure evidences an improper activity.[97] It is also common for the statutes to discourage the reporting of merely technical or minimal violations of law or rules. Disclosures of waste, mismanagement,

170   WHISTLEBLOWER LAW AND ETHICS

or abuse of authority usually must be "gross" in nature before meriting protection in most states. Although some of these provisions are targeted at the
overzealous employee who reports minor rules violations or insignificant
amounts of waste, there is also a desire to prevent unscrupulous employees
from using technical or minor violations as a ruse to gain protection of the
whistleblower statutes as a shield to prevent discipline for legitimate reasons.[98]

Communications

Whistleblower statutes at their most basic level are concerned with communications from a person having knowledge of wrongdoing to a person in authority who can act upon that information. Just as state statutes vary in their coverage as to who may be a protected party in communicating information, they
also have variations as to the parties or institutions to whom disclosures may
or should be made and when.

Reflecting concerns about premature or misinformed reporting, some
statutes require a potential whistleblower first to exhaust internal remedies or
to seek internal corrections of wrongdoing or statutory violations before proceeding with a disclosure to outside authorities.[99] Giving notice to the appropriate supervisor about an employee's concerns provides an opportunity for
an agency or for the department of a business, acting in good faith, to attempt
to correct a violation or hazard. Potential complaints based on misinforma-
tion or false information can be nipped in the bud, while legitimate complaints can be addressed without external involvement that could prove harmful or embarrassing to an institution.[100] Most employers expect that an
employee's duty of loyalty mandates trying to resolve a matter internally to
avoid harming the employer by an inaccurate, inappropriate, or needless disclosure.[101] Even in states without the internal disclosure mandate, it would
seem wise for employees to exhaust internal remedies before going public to
prevent suspicions that they are motivated by a desire to intentionally inflict
harm on the institution or to serve their own personal interests, at the
expense of the institution.[102] Failure to exhaust internal remedies may be jus-
tified in circumstances where exhaustion of remedies is clearly futile or where
there is a hazardous condition posing an imminent risk of death or serious
injury and insufficient time to seek corrective action by the employer.[103]

After exhausting appropriate internal procedures, if required, an
employee may still reasonably believe it is necessary to disclose information
covered by the statute, but it must be reported to the appropriate body or
authority. In some instances this is the legislature, a legislative committee, or
an agency having oversight authority over particular public agencies or institutions. There is a strong public interest in the legislature being well
informed about what is occurring throughout state government, so persons
speaking to legislators or testifying before legislative committees often receive
special protection.[104] The legislature or executive bodies with oversight
responsibilities are particularly concerned about complaints or disclosures
relating to waste, abuse of authority, political abuse, or mismanagement.[105]

Although violations of law may usually be reported to *any* appropriate law enforcement authority, some statutes are very specific about reporting requirements, designating that disclosures be made to certain officials such as the attorney general[106] or the state auditor.[107] Other statutes are drafted very broadly, protecting all kinds of reports made to state or federal agencies or appropriate authorities, and in some cases, complaints made to "any persons."[108] Several states protect participation in investigations, hearings, or inquiries held by public bodies or court actions.[109] Communications with the news media are specifically protected only in Kentucky and Utah.[110]

To ensure that employees are aware of their rights under the whistleblower statutes, a number of state laws require that notices of employee rights be posted.[111] Some states have developed whistleblower hotlines to encourage whistleblowers to come forward,[112] and a number of states have adopted provisions in their statutes to protect confidentiality.[113]

Retaliation and Remedies

Forms of retaliation for whistleblower activity range over a wide spectrum. One extreme consists of mild harassment, as when coworkers give the whistleblower "the cold shoulder" or an anonymous note refers to him or her in derogatory terms. The other extreme is less subtle, such as being summarily discharged or finding the locks to one's office changed and a security guard posted at the door (which of course prevents access to personal files and any evidence carelessly left in the office).[114]

Some legislatures have attempted to define in detail the types of retaliatory actions or inactions that are prohibited.[115] This has the merit of specificity and also allows the statute to exclude trivial complaints of retaliation.[116] Other statutes do not define the term retaliation, which leaves the matter up to the courts or administrative apparatus to define.[117]

The most obvious and severe type of retaliatory action is dismissal. Being fired, when coupled with negative job references or no references, can literally drive a person out of a profession or occupation.[118] Dismissal of a perceived troublemaker can be disguised as a reduction in force or based on other seemingly legitimate job-ending rationales that the whistleblower has the burden of exposing. Equivalent to dismissal is the refusal to appoint a person to a position in the first instance because of whistleblower activities, so several jurisdictions provide whistleblower protection for job applicants as well as current employees.

Other formal retaliatory actions can include unwanted transfers or reassignments, reprimand, admonishment, or just the warning of a possible dismissal. Some retaliatory actions, such as salary reduction, failure to receive appropriate increases in wages and benefits, or failure to be considered for special financial awards or bonuses, hit the pocketbook. Financial and psychological damage can accompany negative or even neutral performance evaluations, which can eventually lead to demotions or to failure to receive an appropriate promotion or tenure. Subtle forms of harassment, such as informal lessening of job responsibilities, authority, or status, or even the withholding of work, can damage a career. Finding one's office moved to the basement, having all one's classes scheduled at what are perceived to be bad times, or being asked to undergo a psychiatric examination sends a strong message to a whistleblower.[119] Working conditions have been made so intolerable in some instances that the employee has resigned and has, in effect, been constructively discharged.[120]

Although whistleblowing is virtually always confined to the employment context, in certain circumstances nonemployees may be subject to retaliation also. Nonemployee whistleblowers may find themselves at a disadvantage when bidding for government contracts or privileges.[121] Whistleblowers who report problems in nursing homes, health care facilities, or other institutions may be concerned about retaliation against themselves or their relatives who may be housed there.[122]

Whistleblower protection statutes provide remedies for many of these forms of retaliation. In general the remedies seek to make the whistleblower whole in an economic sense or seek to punish the violator, which may provide psychological relief in that somehow justice has been served. Violators may be subject to criminal or administrative sanctions, or fines.

The statutes, while again varying widely, generally require the whistleblower first to exhaust administrative remedies before seeking judicial review. Usually, provision is made for a civil action that can provide appropriate injunctive relief or, in some states, actual damages or both. Typical remedies include reinstatement to the same or an equivalent position, back wages, reinstatement of fringe benefits and seniority rights, and costs of litigation including lawyers' fees and witness fees. It is important to note that some states specifically provide for exemplary or punitive damages[123] or triple damages,[124] while a small number of states place limitations on certain types of damages.[125]

Financial Incentives for Whistleblowing

Whistleblowers come forward for a variety of reasons. Some are motivated by altruism: the desire to do the right thing, to be a good citizen, or to prevent harm to others; while others come forward because there may be a chance to profit from blowing the whistle. As one commentator has noted: "Virtue may be its own reward, but for many, money is more gratifying."[126]

To this point the analysis of whistleblowing has focused on the most common approach to encouraging disclosures of wrongdoing, that is, extending remedies such as reinstatement, lost wages, or damages to whistleblowers who have suffered from retaliation. The federal government and a few states, in addition to the traditional approach of providing remedies, opt to entice whistleblowers to come forward by providing financial incentives as a form of encouragement.[127]

Preeminent among these statutes is the federal False Claims Act,[128] which was enacted in 1863 to deal with rampant fraud during the Civil War era. The original act allowed private persons, or "relators," who brought a qui tam action[129] against persons making false monetary claims against the federal government and prosecuted the case to final judgment, to receive one half of the damages and forfeitures recovered and collected, plus costs.[130] The current act is targeted at false or fraudulent claims, usually for goods or services that were not provided as claimed to the United States armed forces or government.[131] The qui tam plaintiff is usually an employee of a government contractor, who brings a civil action for violation of section 3729. The action is brought for both the person and the United States government, but in the name of the government.[132] The statute requires that the government be served with a copy of the complaint and a written disclosure of substantially all material evidence and information,[133] thus alerting the government to the action. If successful, a qui tam plaintiff receives a percentage of the recovery. The amount of the award may vary, depending on whether the government proceeded with the action[134] or not[135] and also based on the source of the disclosure of information.[136]

Awards can be significant and have successfully attracted the attention of whistleblowers and law firms alike.[137] In fact, it is not uncommon to have several law firms band together in a qui tam action to share resources and expertise and to spread the costs, especially when the case has been turned down by the government. While fraud against the Department of Defense has traditionally been the main subject of qui tam litigation under the False Claims Act, this has now been surpassed by fraud in the health care field, especially in the Medicare and Medicaid programs.[138] The False Claim Act is applicable to the entire array of federal programs, so the potential for uncovering wrongdoing is enormous, as is the potential for recovery by individuals and law firms in qui tam litigation in the future.

Ironically, financial incentives under the False Claims Act can create a conflict of interest for an employee who works for a company with internal whistleblower procedures. The employee may have a significant financial incentive to go outside the organization with information concerning a false claim, rather than to report the impropriety internally, which would be in the best interest of the organization.[139]

In addition to the financial incentives, whistleblowers are provided with specific protection against retaliation for involvement in an action under the False Claims Act. Remedies include any relief necessary to make the employee whole, plus two times back pay, interest, and compensation for any special damages.[140]

Several states have also adopted statutes that provide financial incentives for whistleblowers. Illinois, California, and Florida have enacted false claims statutes very similar to the federal False Claims Act, providing for qui tam actions by individuals with awards for success being similar to those provided by the federal statute.[141] Several other states have enacted false claims acts specifically relating to health care.[142] Also, several states' general whistleblower provisions provide cash incentives. For example, in South Carolina if a whistleblowing employee's report results in a savings of public money from

174 WHISTLEBLOWER LAW AND ETHICS

the elimination of abuses, the employee is awarded 25 percent of the estimated net savings but not in excess of $2,000.[143] In Oregon if damages are
awarded for whistleblower retaliation, the employee may receive actual damages or $250, whichever is greater.[144]

By contrast, some states are reluctant to provide whistleblower protection
to employees who might benefit financially from their disclosures.[145] Wisconsin seems a bit schizophrenic in that it does not allow employees to receive
anything of value for reporting, unless it is in pursuit of an award offered by a
governmental unit for information to improve government administration or
operations.[146]

Common-Law Protections for Whistleblowers

The statutory exceptions to the at-will employment doctrine, which have just
been examined, are premised on public policies that seek to mitigate the
harshness of a rule that allows for arbitrary or unreasonable dismissal of
employees. In the absence of specific statutory protections, or in furtherance
of public policies expressed in statutes not necessarily related to labor law, the
courts have encroached on the at-will doctrine by providing common-law
remedies for improper dismissals in certain circumstances, including whistleblowing.

Three major common-law exceptions to the at-will doctrine have evolved.
Remedies have been provided for dismissed employees based on implied-in-
fact contracts, implied-in-law or quasi-contracts, and the public policy exception to the at-will doctrine.

A majority of jurisdictions recognize wrongful dismissal claims premised
on an employer's breach of an implied-in-fact contract.[147] The employee must
show that the employer made representations orally or in writing that the
employee would not be discharged, except for good cause.[148] Written representations set forth in employee handbooks or other such policy guides or
manuals may imply that the parties intended to extend contractual rights,
such as job security, during periods of good job performance, even though
not expressly stated in the employment contract.[149] Such representations have
also been found in an employer's course of conduct concerning pensions,
sales commissions, or other benefits.[150] The doctrine of promissory estoppel
may also be applied to provide relief for persons who have resigned from
their employment in reliance on an offer of a new position with a second
employer, which offer is then withdrawn before the person has begun work.[151]

In a minority of jurisdictions, in circumstances where an employee cannot prove that a promise of job security was implied-in-fact, it may be possible
to show that the employer has breached an implied covenant of good faith
and fair dealing.[152] Implied-in-law contracts usually are brought as contract
actions but may be sounded in tort law or in both contract and tort. Generally,
it is not enough that an employee show an absence of just cause or good faith,

but rather the employee must prove bad faith or unfairness, and in some states, he or she must present evidence of a violation of public policy to prove a breach of the covenant.[153]

The public policy exception to the at-will doctrine is the primary vehicle for common-law remedies for whistleblowers. In some circumstances, courts have held that public policy allows an exception to the at-will rule. The common-law erosion of the at-will doctrine began in 1959 with the landmark California case, *Petermann v. Teamsters*,[154] where an employee was fired for refusing to commit perjury before a state legislative committee. The court of appeals, after taking note of the at-will rule, stated that the right to discharge an employee under an employment contract of indefinite duration "may be limited by statute . . . or by considerations of public policy."[155] While recognizing that "the term 'public policy' is inherently not subject to precise definition," the court noted that perjury is a crime and that false testimony interferes with the administration of justice.[156] "It would be obnoxious to the interest of the state and contrary to public policy and sound morality to allow an employer to discharge any employee . . . on the ground that the employee declined to commit perjury."[157] To effectuate fully the state's policy against perjury, the employer may be denied dismissal rights under the at-will rule and the employee may be entitled to civil relief.[158]

It was not until the mid 1970s that the public policy exception began to be adopted in other jurisdictions. Today a large majority of states have some form of public policy exception to the at-will rule for wrongful or retaliatory discharge.

While the exception originated as a contract action, the action now usually sounds in tort or in both contract and tort in some jurisdictions, which may allow for damages for emotional distress or punitive damages.

The fundamental problem relating to the public policy exception has always been the difficulty of defining public policy, or determining what activities are in the public interest to protect.[159] The wide variations in protected conduct that were seen in the state whistleblower protection statutes are also evident in the common law, as the judiciary struggled to provide remedies when appropriate but not to destroy completely the at-will employment rule. Some state courts have chosen to defer to the legislature for a determination of public policy, rather than to create a broad common-law public policy exception to the at-will doctrine.[160]

The public policy exceptions that have been recognized vary considerably in tone and content, but they have certain common characteristics. Normally, the underlying public policy must be one that enhances public interests, rather than merely private concerns; the public policy must be clearly expressed by a law, regulation, or constitutional provision; and the public policy exception is applied only when there is a dismissal from employment rather than lesser forms of retaliation.[161] The four categories in which employees are most frequently protected from discharge under the public policy exception concern refusal to commit an unlawful act, exercise of a

176   WHISTLEBLOWER LAW AND ETHICS

legal right or privilege, performance of a civic obligation, and active whistle-blower disclosures.[162]

The definition of whistleblower in the introduction to this chapter suggested that whistleblowing can be passive in nature, that is, a refusal to engage in wrongful activities of an employer; or active, in that the employee reports illegal or wrongful activities of the employer or coworkers to proper authorities. The first three categories noted above reflect passive whistleblowing in that the employee is discharged, not for actively communicating employer wrongdoing, but only for refusing to comply with an order to commit an improper or illegal act, for exercising a statutory right, or for performing a civic duty. The employer in effect has forced the employee to choose between his job and possibly going to jail, or forfeiting a worker's compensation claim, or failing to serve on a jury. Forcing these choices on the employee clearly defies the public policies in question. The public policy exception to the at-will doctrine thus seeks "to protect whistleblowers under either the rubric of one of these three general categories, or as an extension of these general categories."[163] While many jurisdictions seek to protect passive whistleblowers, in this sense, protection for active whistleblowers under the public policy exception has varied from state to state.[164]

Active whistleblowing entails reporting by an employee of information concerning improper activities occurring or threatening to occur within an organization. This reporting can be made either internally within the organization, or externally to appropriate public authorities. Since public sector employees generally have greater statutory whistleblower protection in such circumstances than private sector employees have, it is private sector employees who tend to be involved in most public policy exception whistleblower cases.[165]

Generally speaking, the courts have been willing to protect active whistleblowers under the public policy exception both for disclosures of criminal activities and for violations of noncriminal statutes.[166] Constitutional provisions may also provide a public policy basis for an action in some states; but whatever the source, the public policy must be clearly expressed before it can serve as a basis for the public policy exemption.[167] Since nothing is more basic than a state's enforcement of its criminal code, reporting of a violation of criminal law is a very compelling case for protecting a whistleblower.[168] Public policy clearly favors "citizen crime fighters,"[169] so whistleblower protection for refusal to commit or for reporting a criminal act is commonly provided by both statutes and the common law. Thus, public policy clearly favors resolving the employee's conflict between obeying an employer's illegal orders or ignoring criminal activity, and the loss of one's job, in favor of the whistleblower. Civil statutes may also provide the clear public policy mandate required for the exception, as for example, in the case of providing protection for health care professionals who may be required by statute to report certain types of patient abuse.

Once one gets past the public policies established by statute, finding a clearly mandated source of public policy to support the public policy exception becomes much more difficult, if not impossible, in some states. Several courts have ruled that without a violation of some specific law or regulation, complaints about product safety are usually not protected.[170] In addition, complaints about company mismanagement, policy disagreements with employers, or private concerns are not covered by the exception.[171] Also, judges, like legislators, are concerned about abuse of whistleblower protection provisions. Therefore, whistleblower disclosures that are made in bad faith, or where the employee does not have direct personal knowledge of the illegal activity, or where the whistleblower participated personally in the crime that is disclosed, or when the whistleblower has failed to exhaust internal channels before going public, may not be protected by the public policy exception.[172]

A retaliatory discharge for whistleblowing may give rise to overlapping statutory and common-law claims. It is quite possible that an employee who is a member of a union with a "just cause" contract could have potential remedies available under the contract, under a whistleblower protection statute, and under the common-law public policy exception in tort. Remedies could vary significantly, depending upon which claim is pursued. A whistleblower may not have an option as to which claim will prevail, however, due to the doctrine of preemption. Preemption "arises when a statutory remedy and a common law remedy exist for the same conduct, in circumstance implying a legislative intent to supplant common law."[173] Generally, there is a preference for a pervasive statutory scheme of regulation over a common-law remedy; therefore most state whistleblower statutes will preempt a common-law public policy exception.[174] Overlapping federal and state statutory claims can also lead to preemption. Federal statutes will preempt state law under the Supremacy Clause of the United States Constitution when they conflict.[175] Thus, for example, federal labor law will preempt state labor statutes when an employee asserts a state wrongful discharge claim that is also an unfair labor practice under federal law.[176]

Professional Ethics Codes as Sources of Public Policy

Remedies for whistleblowers are provided by statute or by some other clearly mandated source of public policy that will support the public policy exception in a tort or contract action for wrongful discharge. Frequently professionals will complain that they were wrongfully discharged because they insisted on adhering to a professional code of ethics that mandated their actions. They argue that violation of a code of ethics is equivalent in a public policy sense to violation of criminal statute, because such a violation can subject them to professional discipline. Here the professional is faced with the classic whistleblower conflict: the choice between violating one's ethical code, which can potentially result in sanctions, and losing one's job. Some states have recognized the problem and specifically provide protection in their whistleblower statutes for reporting of wrongdoing that is a violation of a code of conduct or code of ethics or for refusing an order to violate the ethics code.[177] Other jurisdictions provide statutory protection for reporting violations of a government employees' ethics code[178] or for reporting unethical practices in a state agency or department.[179]

Still, the vast majority of jurisdictions do not specifically deal with ethical codes in their whistleblower statutes. The courts have widely disparate views on whether professional codes of ethics are sufficiently clear examples of such strong public policy that they will warrant protection for wrongful discharge in defiance of the at-will doctrine.[180] As a source of public policy, ethical codes vary in status: some may be endorsed by the legislature,[181] others may have judicial involvement in their content,[182] while still other codes are merely the products of the professional organizations themselves,[183] and may not be infused with the public interest or have any form of official state imprimatur.

The cases that have dealt with retaliatory discharge for reporting ethical violations or for refusing to violate professional ethics codes fall into two categories.[184] The first category includes those cases that reject outright any non-legislative sources of public policy. These cases hold that only statutes or constitutions can evidence a clear public policy mandate sufficient to support the public policy exception in those jurisdictions.[185]

The second category of cases recognizes professional ethics codes as sources of public policy, but recognizes only those provisions of the code that clearly serve public interests, rather than just the interests of a particular profession, as sources of public policy. Usually the provision must also mandate that the professional act or not act in a designated way in a particular situation.[186] The public policy exception has been analyzed in these circumstances in wrongful discharge cases concerning ethical codes for accountants,[187] physicians,[188] pharmacists,[189] securities dealers,[190] and lawyers.[191] The courts find clearly mandated public interests in some ethical violations but not in others, and they have been very reluctant to protect professional employees when there are merely differences of professional opinion within an organization or where the employee has violated ethical obligations to a specific client or patient.[192]

Special Issues Encountered by Lawyers

Perhaps more so than any other professional group, lawyers gain information about improper or illegal client conduct whether employed in the public or private sector. Knowledge of client misconduct is usually gained after the fact, as when a lawyer is retained to represent a client who has been arrested for a crime, and the client then confides his guilt to the lawyer. Occasionally, a lawyer learns in advance of a client's intent to commit a criminal act. The lawyers' codes of ethics have long recognized that a lawyer can be placed in a position of knowing of client wrongdoing, and several rules attempt to provide guidance, especially the rules concerning confidentiality and those concerning entity representation.

Most information gained though the lawyer-client relationship is sacro-sanct, including revelations of past criminal acts.[193] There are, however, limits and exceptions to the confidentiality rules. Lawyers may in certain circum-stances reveal their client's intent to commit a future criminal act[194] and must, in some instances, reveal a client's perjury.[195] Also, the confidentiality rules do not protect a client who has sought out a lawyer for aid in perpetrating a crime or a fraudulent scheme.[196] Generally, lawyers may not actively partici-pate in or further the illegal acts of their clients, nor may the lawyer be forced to violate the rules of professional conduct.[197] Under these standards a lawyer must refuse to accept certain cases, or in other situations may or must with-draw from a representation.[198] When a lawyer is representing a specific per-sonal client under a retainer, as opposed to a corporate entity, the rules relat-ing to revelation of client wrongdoing are generally well understood and work reasonably well.

Also well understood is a lawyer's status vis-à-vis an individual personal client. Although lawyers in private practice usually do not view themselves as employees of their clients, the lawyer-client relationship is a contractual, fidu-ciary relationship that is nevertheless subject to the employment at-will doc-trine.[199] Except in certain limited circumstances, clients can fire their lawyers for any reason, or no reason, and the lawyer must withdraw, with the only recourse being a suit in quantum meruit for the fair value of services ren-dered.[200] Conversely, subject to certain exceptions, a lawyer is under no obli-gation to accept a person as a client initially and may withdraw from a repre-sentation if the withdrawal can be accomplished without material adverse affect on the client.[201] The employment relationship differs, however, for lawyers who are hired as in-house counsel or in other capacities within a cor-porate entity. Such lawyers are usually hired on a salaried basis with an expec-tation of continuing employment and clearly view themselves as employees of the organization. Despite the differences between retained lawyers and salaried in-house counsel, both are subject to the employment at-will doc-trine.

The In-House Counsel's Dilemma

In-house counsel, due to their role in the organization, often find themselves privy to confidential corporate information and may at times become aware of various types of wrongdoing by corporate officers or employees that could be detrimental to the organization. Such wrongdoing can range from waste of corporate assets to violations of law that could potentially result in legal actions being brought against the corporation.

In-house counsel who become aware of wrongdoing by corporate insid-ers may find themselves in a difficult position. The persons committing or threatening to commit improper or illegal acts may be corporate officers, directors, or others in positions of authority, potentially positions senior to that of corporate counsel. Thus in-house counsel will have to determine who is the appropriate person to whom he or she should report instances of misconduct and who has final say as to whether an action is improper or merely questionable business judgment. But after reporting wrongdoing internally, what must or should in-house counsel do when corporate officers continue to follow what counsel views as an illegal path, or one that will financially harm the corporation, or one that could harm innocent people? In-house counsel can thus easily be placed in the role of internal whistleblower, defending the interests of the corporation against insider wrongdoers; or potentially, in extreme cases, in-house counsel may have to determine whether it is proper to report information concerning illegal activities to public officials outside the organization. Lawyers' ethics codes attempt to aid in-house counsel in resolving some of these issues.

The Model Rules of Professional Conduct provide guidance for lawyers who discover wrongdoing in the corporate context by first making it clear that lawyers, whether employed or retained, represent the organization as a legal entity.[202] Since the legal entity is the client, lawyers are instructed that they must always act in the best interests of the entity, rather than in the interests of individuals who make up the constituent parts of the organization, although it is obvious that a lawyer must act through the organization's duly authorized representatives.[203] Difficulties can arise for counsel, however, when authorized corporate agents are involved in wrongdoing that can potentially harm the organization.

Model Rule 1.13(b) provides that when a lawyer gains knowledge "that an officer, employee or other person associated with the organization is engaged in action, intends to act or refuses to act in a matter related to the representation that is a violation of a legal obligation to the organization, or a violation of law which reasonably might be imputed to the organization, and is likely to result in substantial injury to the organization, the lawyer shall proceed as is reasonably necessary in the best interest of the organization." Among the factors that the lawyer must consider in determining the manner of response to the wrongdoing are the seriousness of the violation and its consequences, the role the lawyer plays in the representation and in the organization, the motivation of the persons involved, and organizational policies regarding such matters.[204]

The lawyer when determining the proper measures to take in dealing with a threat to the organization is cautioned by the rule to attempt to minimize disruption within the organization and to minimize the risk that information will be revealed to outsiders.[205] Among the options available to the lawyer when corporate agents are engaged in improper activities and refuse to heed counsel's advice are asking for reconsideration of the matter; advising that a separate legal opinion be sought for presentation to higher authorities; and referral of the matter to higher authority, even to the highest authority that can act on the matter if necessary.[206] If the lawyer is unsuccessful in preventing the organization from acting or failing to act in a matter that would be a clear violation of law and would be likely to cause substantial injury to the organization, the lawyer may resign in compliance with the withdrawal provisions of the model rules.[207]

Model Rule 1.13 expresses a clear preference for confidentiality over revelation of illegal conduct. In-house counsel may not reveal confidential knowledge of a clear violation of law even though the wrongdoing was condoned by the highest authority within the organization that could act on the matter. Rather than going to external public authorities with the information, counsel "may resign." The rule's tacit assumption is therefore that in those instances when internal remedies for unlawful insider conduct are unsuccessful, silence is *always* preferable to the alternative of allowing the company's lawyer to alert authorities outside the entity.[208]

The option to resign, although it does provide a solution, comes at a very high cost to the lawyer and in the final analysis does not resolve the lawyer's underlying concern about the wrongdoing. Depending on the circumstances, an in-house lawyer may not have the financial resources or other job opportunities necessary to make resignation a viable option. Fortunately, the resignation option decision is faced by the lawyer only when the wrongdoing is a clear violation of law and will likely cause substantial injury to the organization, which is a relatively high threshold of knowledge.[209]

The rule provides a degree of flexibility in that the lawyer is given the option to resign or not. The controlling term is "may" resign; but it seems likely that many, if not most, lawyers, after exhausting all available options to protect the best interests of the organization, will choose to keep silent and try to go on with their careers. Of course by this point the lawyer's accusations of wrongdoing have undoubtedly rocked the boat, important toes have been stepped on, and major embarrassment has been caused to numerous corporate officials. In all likelihood those who were the targets of the accusations will seek to rid the organization of this perceived troublemaker, and the lawyer will be fired. The at-will employment doctrine will have struck again. Of course, the same result would be likely to occur if in-house counsel had gone public with the information, but then counsel would be in an even less defensible position, since he or she would have violated the ethics rule.

A lawyer in such circumstances, of course, will be appropriately outraged at losing his or her job and will seek some form of recourse. Initially, however, it must be determined whether the information on which the in-house lawyer based his or her accusations is confidential. This creates a problem since this information will ultimately have to be revealed because it would form the basis for the lawyer's retaliatory discharge action. Confidentiality thus lies at the core of the dilemma courts face in dealing with in-house counsel who bring retaliatory discharge suits.

Any privilege relating to the information concerning corporate wrongdoing belongs to the organization as a legal entity, not to the in-house counsel.[210] It is highly unlikely that the organization's representatives would choose to waive the privilege since, in doing so, they would be revealing illegal conduct by corporate employees that could result in substantial injury to the organization. Also, it is unlikely that the organization would waive confidentiality since the highest authority in the organization has already refused to act. Although it is possible that the future criminal act exception to the confidentiality rule may allow in-house counsel to reveal the wrongdoing, this exception is quite limited and depends on the nature of the illegal act being contemplated by the corporate insiders.[211] Yet the prospect of the terminated in-house counsel disclosing the organizational client's confidential, probably incriminating communications during a lawsuit for damages may well seem abhorrent to some courts, striking as it would at such fundamental precepts of the profession as confidentiality and loyalty.[212] Surely a lawyer has a higher level of duty to a client, even if it is a corporate entity, than does a typical corporate employee and thus should not be allowed to breach a client's confidences or expectations of loyalty to recover in a wrongful discharge action.

The countervailing argument in favor of allowing a remedy for in-house counsel is premised on justice and fairness. If a nonlawyer employee would have a remedy under a whistleblower statute or a court-made exception to the at-will rule for a particular action, is it fair to deny the remedy to a lawyer for the same action?[213] If an in-house counsel follows the rules of the profession and is loyal to the employer in seeking to prevent harm to the organization, should public policy condone his or her being fired for doing so? Does public policy condone a lawyer's being fired for disclosing illegal activity to public authorities concerning a significant, clear threat or danger to the public health and safety when a nonlawyer would be protected?

The last decade has produced several cases dealing with the issues of retaliatory discharge and whistleblower protection for in-house counsel. The cases present contrary views as to whether lawyers, because of the fiduciary nature of their profession, enjoy the same degree of protection as do other private sector employees or whether such protections should be denied or limited in some fashion.

The first of these cases to reach a state's highest court, *Balla v. Gambro, Inc.*,[214] is a classic example of an in-house counsel being fired for whistleblowing. The plaintiff, the general counsel of an Illinois distributor of dialysis equipment, learned that defective machines had been shipped to his employer for distribution. He informed his superiors in the corporation that the machines posed a serious risk to health, were not in compliance with Food and Drug Administration regulations, and should be rejected. Upon learning that the company planned to sell the equipment anyway, he confronted the company president and told him that he would do anything necessary to stop the sale. Two weeks later the plaintiff was abruptly fired. In response, he brought a tort action for retaliatory discharge, alleging that he was discharged for reasons that contravened fundamental public policy.

The Illinois Supreme Court, while noting its adherence to the at-will employment doctrine, recognized that there was a limited and narrow tort-action exception for retaliatory discharge based on contravention of a clearly mandated public policy.[215] The court agreed that the plaintiff's discharge contravened the clearly mandated public policy of protecting the lives and property of the state's citizens, but it refused to allow him to maintain the retaliatory discharge action because of his role as general counsel for the defendant corporation.[216] The court had two reasons for rejecting his suit. First, the public policy to be protected, saving citizen's lives, was already adequately protected in this case. The plaintiff was obliged to reveal the information under the Illinois Rules of Professional Conduct, which require that a lawyer "shall reveal information about a client to the extent it appears necessary to prevent the client from committing an act that would result in death or serious bodily harm."[217] Unlike other nonlawyer corporate employees who have a choice as to their actions, in-house counsel under this rule do not have a choice of whether to follow their ethical obligations or to "follow the illegal and unethical demands of their clients."[218] Thus a tort remedy was redundant, since counsel's duty is mandated by the ethical rules and public policy is served.

The second reason asserted by the court for not extending the retaliatory discharge tort to in-house counsel was its undesirable effect on the lawyer-client relationship. Since the relationship is based on trust and confidentiality, granting the right to sue for retaliatory discharge might make employers "less willing to be forthright and candid with their in-house counsel," and less likely to turn to in-house counsel for advice regarding potentially questionable corporate conduct.[219] Thus lawyers were found to be different from other employees because of the fiduciary qualities that pervade the lawyer-client relationship.

The Illinois Supreme Court was not alone in declining to provide a tort remedy for in-house counsel in these circumstances. Until 1994, all other courts that considered the issue had refused to allow tort recovery for wrongful discharge of in-house counsel,[220] although some had allowed for damages under implied contract exceptions to the at-will doctrine.[221] For example, the Supreme Court of Minnesota in *Nordling v. Northern States Power Co.*,[222] held "that in-house counsel should not be precluded from maintaining an action for breach of a contractual provision in an employee handbook, provided, however, that the essentials of the attorney-client relationship are not compromised." The threat to the lawyer-client relationship was not viewed as significant in the case of a breach of an implied contract as it is in a tort action for retaliatory discharge.

At the opposite extreme from the *Balla* decision is the 1994 California Supreme Court's opinion in *General Dynamics Corporation v. Superior Court*.[223] There, in-house counsel Rose was fired because he investigated employee drug use, protested electronic bugging of the chief of security's office, and pointed out possible violations of federal law. He alleged in his complaint that General Dynamics "had by its conduct and other assurances impliedly represented to Rose over the years that he was subject to discharge only for 'good cause,'" which was not present in this firing, and that he was also fired for reasons "which violated fundamental public policies."[224] General Dynamics responded with the argument that they could fire their in-house lawyer "for any reason or for no reason."[225]

The court reaffirmed the rule that a client could unilaterally discharge his or her lawyer but noted that "there is a cost to be paid for such an action under the circumstances alleged in the complaint—either in lost wages and related damages in the case of the implied-in-fact contract claim, or as tort damages in the case of the public policy tort claim."[226] Thus in-house counsel may pursue a wrongful discharge claim for damages, even though reinstatement will never be available as a remedy.[227] The court held that an implied-in-fact contract action could lie for in-house counsel, since it would not be "likely to present issues implicating the distinctive values subserved by the attorney-client relationship."[228] These cases should therefore be treated the same as implied-in-fact actions brought by nonlawyer employees.

The court then examined the public policy wrongful discharge tort claim, noting that it arises out of duties implied in law. Such duties require employers to conduct their businesses in compliance with public policy. A tort action can therefore be viewed as a means to vindicate the public policy interest itself, while at the same time compensating the individual for the loss of employment.[229] After recognizing that some professional norms incorporate important public values, the court held that the case for protecting in-house lawyers from retaliation for insisting on adherence to mandatory ethical norms or for refusing to violate those ethical norms is clear, and in fact even more powerful than the claim of a similarly situated nonprofessional employee.[230]

After observing that the *Balla* decision had been criticized by commentators as a bizarre and anachronistic view of the lawyer's role, the court stated that it is precisely because of the unique role that lawyers play in our society that they should be accorded a retaliatory discharge remedy. When *"mandatory ethical norms . . . collide with illegitimate demands of the employer* and the attorney insists on *adhering to his or her clear professional duty,"*[231] the lawyer is entitled to a judicial remedy. Such a remedy will help to mitigate the economic and cultural pressures that can force an individual employee to conform with organizational misconduct without protest, particularly in view of the "illusory" remedy of the in-house lawyer's duty of withdrawal, "a course fraught with the possibility of economic catastrophe and professional banishment."[232]

This holding that in-house counsel may bring a tort action for wrongful discharge was limited in two ways. First the court distinguished between retaliatory discharge resulting from in-house counsel's following of an ethical obligation mandated by ethical rule or statute and where the lawyer's conduct "is merely ethically *permissible* but not *required* by statute or ethical code."[233] When merely permissible conduct is involved, two additional questions must be answered. First, would a nonlawyer employee have a retaliatory discharge cause of action for the same conduct, and second, does the statute or ethical rule "specifically permit the attorney to depart from the usual requirement of confidentiality with respect to the client-employer and engage in the 'non-fiduciary' conduct for which he was terminated?"[234]

The second limitation placed on the retaliatory discharge tort for in-house counsel reflects the concerns expressed in *Balla* relating to the fiduciary aspects of the lawyer-client relationship. The court expressed a desire to protect the fiduciary qualities of mutual trust and confidence that are inherent in the relationship. Therefore only in the instances where a disclosure is explicitly permitted or mandated by an ethics code or statute may an in-house counsel expose the client's secrets. If the elements of a wrongful discharge claim cannot be established without breaching the attorney-client privilege, the suit must be dismissed.[235] Thus there is a preference for confidentiality over the remedy for wrongful discharge, and an insistence that the statutory attorney-client privilege must continue to be strictly observed.[236] Finally, the court indicated that trial courts can and should apply ad hoc equitable remedies, such as sealing and protective orders, to allow in-house counsel to meet their burden of proof while still protecting privileged confidences.[237]

General Dynamic's significance lies in the fact that it is the first case to allow a public policy exception tort action to be brought for the retaliatory dismissal of an in-house counsel.[238] The court's opinion is tailored in a way that recognizes the current economic realities of practice as an in-house counsel, while attempting to preserve the employer/client's traditional rights of confidentiality and the right to fire one's lawyer. The court thus provides in-house counsel with meaningful potential tort and implied-in-fact contract remedies compared with the illusory nonremedy of withdrawal from employment that is contemplated in *Balla*.

The Law Firm Corollary to the In-House Counsel Dilemma

The California Supreme Court recognized the dilemma faced by in-house counsel who function in a one-client environment, which can lead to total economic dependence on that client/employer. Such dependency limits the number of realistic options available to in-house counsel upon learning of corporate wrongdoing, since, as was seen, a duty to withdraw from corporate employment can be no less than an order to commit economic suicide and, as such, hardly a satisfactory option.

A corollary to this dilemma is encountered by lawyer-employees of law firms, who may discover wrongdoing committed by other lawyers in the firm. Associates and even partners in law firms may have economic dependency on their firms equivalent to that which in-house counsel have on their corporate employers. They also have mandated ethical rules of conduct to which they must adhere or be subject to sanction. As members of a self-policing profession, individual lawyers have mandatory whistleblower responsibilities vis-à-vis other lawyers in certain circumstances. Thus Model Rule 8.3 requires that a lawyer who has knowledge of another lawyer's violation of an ethical rule that raises a substantial question as to that lawyer's honesty, trustworthiness, or fitness as a lawyer *shall* inform the appropriate professional authorities, unless the information is confidential.[239] Also, a law firm's senior managers and any other lawyers in a supervisory capacity have distinct obligations to ensure that lawyers within the firm conform to ethical standards.[240] As in the corporate environment, where Model Rule 1.13 suggests that a lawyer initially should try to resolve concerns about wrongdoing internally, it is also generally viewed as the best policy when an associate or partner in a law firm learns of unethical behavior within the firm.[241]

The first step in such cases is usually to confront the lawyer believed to be in violation of the rule. This allows the associate to determine the other lawyer's motivation and understanding of the ethical violation in an attempt to resolve the issue.[242] If this is not possible, or if confronting the rule violator is of no avail, it is next appropriate to consult others within the firm. Consultation with senior partners, department heads, or firm ethics committees, if available, may lead to peer pressure or to formal demands upon the rule violator to reform.[243] At this point the improper actions may be stopped before damage has been done or perhaps damages can be mitigated. There may be instances, however, where other lawyers in the firm do not believe a rule violation has occurred or where an ethical violation is merely arguable, in which case the associate may wish to reconsider his or her position on the potential rule violation.[244] Although it is viewed as highly unlikely that any firm would consciously allow a partner or associate to be in violation of the code of ethics, in the last analysis, an associate who is convinced that there is a substantial violation of the rules shall inform the appropriate authorities under Model Rule 8.3(a).[245] Note this outcome differs from that of in-house counsel under Model Rule 1.13. Model Rule 1.13 mandates silence and offers the option of resignation, while Model Rule 8.3 mandates reporting the ethical violation, unless knowledge of the violation was obtained as a confidence. The rules may be distinguishable in that, in the in-house counsel situation, the employer is also the client and thus there is a fiduciary relationship, while in the law firm setting, the employer is not a client of the employee and the rules would still protect any confidential matter that may be involved from being disclosed.

These rules can result in an associate being placed in the classic whistleblower dilemma.[246] If an associate learns of a substantial ethics rule violation by a firm lawyer, reports that violation internally within the firm, and the partners refuse to act, the associate must then blow the whistle externally. If the associate is then fired for insisting on a course of conduct mandated by the lawyer's code of ethics, is there any recourse available for the associate in a state that adheres to the at-will employment doctrine? Such recourse will lie only if there is specific protection provided by the state's whistleblower statute[247] or if the state's courts have adopted common-law exceptions to the at-will employment rule.

Just such a dilemma arose in the New York case of *Wieder v. Skala*.[248] In *Wieder*, an associate in a law firm became aware of conduct of another of the firm's lawyers that raised substantial questions about that lawyer's honesty and fitness as a lawyer. Wieder reported his concerns to two of the firm's partners, who conceded that the other lawyer was a pathological liar who had lied to other members of the firm regarding the status of legal matters. Wieder asked the partners to report the misconduct to the appropriate authorities under Disciplinary Rule 1-103, the New York equivalent to Model Rule 8.3, but they declined to act and in fact attempted to dissuade Wieder from reporting the matter himself, even to the extent of threatening him with dismissal. Eventually the firm did report the misconduct but thereafter continuously berated Wieder for forcing them to do so. Not long after, Wieder was fired. Wieder then brought a suit for wrongful discharge, alleging breach of contract and a violation of public policy sufficient to allow a tort action for compensatory and punitive damages.

Historically, the New York Court of Appeals has not been receptive to arguments that it adopt breach-of-implied contract or wrongful discharge tort exceptions to the at-will employment doctrine; rather, the court usually defers to the legislature for an appropriate statutory remedy.[249] In this case, after noting the lower court's holding that the state's whistleblower law was not applicable because there was no danger to the public health or welfare,[250] the court of appeals examined the breach of contract claim.

Since there were no allegations of express contractual limitations in this case,[251] the court had to determine if there were any implied duties that distinguished this case from earlier precedents. The court was able to find an implied-in-law obligation stating "that in any hiring of an attorney as an associate to practice law with a firm there is implied an understanding so fundamental to the relationship and essential to its purpose as to require no expression: that both the associate and the firm in conducting the practice will do so in accordance with the ethical standards of the profession."[252] The court stressed the importance of Disciplinary Rule 1-103 as being critical to the self-regulation of the legal profession and noted that a lawyer who fails to comply with the reporting requirement can be disciplined.[253] Thus by insisting that Wieder disregard the rule, the firm's partners were not only making it impossible for him to perform his ethical obligations, but also forcing him "to choose between continued employment and his own potential suspension and disbarment."[254] It is this unique characteristic of the profession, relating to this "core" disciplinary rule, that makes the relationship of an associate in a law firm to his employers intrinsically different from the nonlawyer employees of corporations whose claims for at-will exceptions were rejected in earlier New York cases.[255]

While the court held that Wieder had stated a claim for breach of an implied-in-law contractual obligation, the public policy tort claim was summarily dismissed, even though the court felt that the arguments were persuasive and the circumstances compelling. Although noting that the state's whistleblower statute had been criticized for failing to afford sufficient safeguards against retaliatory discharge, the court was determined to follow its pattern of leaving the problem to the legislature.[256]

Wieder is a significant departure from prior New York case law, but the opinion "is so replete with language of limitation and qualification" that its application will probably only encompass law firm associates in a situation precisely similar to *Wieder*.[257] One court has suggested that "*Wieder* goes to substantial lengths to confine its reach primarily and possibly exclusively to cases involving legal ethics."[258] Even then, one must ask which rules other than Disciplinary Rule 1-103 will qualify as "core" provisions of the Code of Professional Responsibility for purposes of the implied-at-law exception to the at-will doctrine. Surely, "core" provisions will be only those that are meant to safeguard the public or to protect the integrity and efficiency of the judicial process, compared with those rules having as their primary purpose the protection of "the exclusivity or economic welfare of the legal profession."[259]

The final section of this chapter examines special issues encountered by government employed lawyers relating to whistleblowing. Although many of these issues could potentially arise at any level of government, for purposes of analysis the focus will be on federal government lawyers.

Whistleblowing and the Federal Government Lawyer

Just as the "triangular relationship between a corporate lawyer, the client's agents, and the client itself accounts for many of the ethical complications in corporate representation,"[260] a comparable relationship exists between a governmental entity, its agents, and the lawyers employed by the entity, resulting in similar ethical complications. These complications are most likely to develop when differing or incompatible interests arise within the relationship,[261] as when a government lawyer learns of illegal conduct by other agency employees.

As in the corporate setting, the threshold question when representing a governmental entity is, who is the client? The response is the same as in the corporate setting: the lawyer represents the entity acting through its duly authorized agents. But government at all levels can be incredibly complex, and determining "who is the client" relative to a government lawyer's actions is not always immediately apparent and has been a source of controversy. One commentator has suggested that the appropriate response to, who is the client? should be: "[I]t depends" on why you are asking![262] For day-to-day purposes it may be most practical to view officials within the employing agency as the client of the government lawyer, but this may not resolve the issue in all circumstances and it may be necessary to view the "government as a whole" or other alternative officials as the client.[263]

Being a federal government lawyer differs from being a private sector lawyer in a number of significant ways. As a federal government employee, the lawyer faces a federal ethics regulatory structure (including statutes, regulations, executive orders, ethics codes, and general codes of conduct) that is highly detailed and complex.[264] This structure is in addition to the regulatory apparatus in place in the jurisdiction where the lawyer was admitted to the bar. With so much overlapping regulation it is not surprising that sometimes ethical mandates can conflict. Also, "[a] government lawyer serves the interests of many different entities: his supervisor in the department or agency, the agency itself, the statutory mission of the agency, the entire government of which that agency is part, and the public interest."[265] All of this regulation occurs in a governmental environment subject to a system of separation of powers with built-in checks and balances.[266] Furthermore, as will be seen, government employees may have affirmative duties to report crime in certain situations that may not be applicable to a private sector lawyer. Also because of the nature and vast scope of government operations, a government lawyer may have different obligations concerning certain types of client information than would a private sector lawyer.[267] For example, under the Freedom of Information Act, a government lawyer may be required by law to disclose documentary information that a private sector lawyer's client would deem confidential.[268] Congress, by statutorily consenting to disclosure, has in essence waived governmental confidentiality relative to such documents. On the other hand, contrary to open access laws, some federal statutes specifically prohibit the revelation of certain types of secret or confidential government information concerning individuals, military secrets, or trade secrets.[269] Such statutes subject a government lawyer who violates them to criminal liability above and beyond professional sanction for violating confidentiality.[270] In a more positive vein, federal government lawyers, who are covered by the Civil Service Reform Act, may have greater job security than private sector lawyers who are subject to the harshness of the at-will employment doctrine.[271]

At the most fundamental level a government lawyer remains a fiduciary who is required to be loyal, to avoid conflicts of interest, and to maintain the confidences of his client, usually viewed as the agency. These duties may be put to the test when the lawyer learns of wrongdoing within the agency. Under what circumstances must the government lawyer blow the whistle? What wrongdoing must be reported in light of the confidentiality and conflict of interest rules? Does the fiduciary duty of loyalty ever play a role?

Government lawyers are encouraged to come forward with information about criminal activities in certain circumstances. The federal government's Code of Ethics for Government Service states that "any person in government service should expose corruption whenever discovered."[272] By executive order, each federal agency is responsible for issuing regulations concerning standards of ethics and other conduct for agency employees.[273] For example, the standards promulgated by the Department of Justice state that "Department employees *shall* [emphasis added] report to their U.S. Attorney or Assistant Attorney General, or other appropriate supervisor, any evidence or nonfrivolous allegation of misconduct that may be in violation of any law, rule, regulation, order, or applicable professional standards."[274] Federal agency lawyers would seem to have an implied duty under 28 U.S.C. § 535(b) (1994) to report any information, allegations, or complaints of criminal misconduct received within their departments or agencies involving government officers and employees to the agency head or, if the agency head is involved, to the attorney general.[275] Public policy, as reflected in federal whistleblower protection statutes, also strongly encourages agency lawyers to come forward with information concerning violations of law, rule, regulation, or gross mismanagement,

190   WHISTLEBLOWER LAW AND ETHICS

gross waste of funds, abuse of authority, or a substantial and specific danger to public health or safety.[276]

These reporting requirements can place federal lawyers in a dilemma due to their professional responsibilities concerning confidentiality, loyalty, and conflict of interest. Confidentiality, however, appears to be the preeminent issue that arises when a government lawyer learns of wrongdoing by other government employees. Model Rule 1.6 states that a "lawyer shall not reveal information relating to representation of a client unless the client consents," and Model Rule 1.13(a) makes it clear that the confidentiality duty is owed to the governmental entity. But in reality the government lawyer is dealing with people, the agents of the government, and it is to those people with whom the lawyer works that the lawyer's duty and loyalty normally flow, unless and until the lawyer learns of illegality or other wrongdoing. It is at this point where ethical problems may arise because "obligations to report wrongdoing within and without the agency may override normal duties of confidentiality owed to the agency and its responsible official."[277]

Upon encountering information concerning wrongdoing by another federal employee, what factors should a government lawyer consider before proceeding? Given the complex regulatory environment within government and the typical adverse reaction to whistleblowing by supervisors and coworkers, it may be advisable to proceed with caution. First, the lawyer should examine the nature of the wrongdoing that is involved. Distinctions must be drawn between significant violations of law, rules, and regulations and mere technical violations. While forms of corruption such as bribery or misappropriation of funds that rise to the level of a violation of law will merit disclosure, a coworker's habit of taking home pencils, or a lobbyist's buying a drink for the agency head, may better be ignored. There are "a maze of demeaning and nitpicking restrictions" that have been imposed "to prevent malingering and misappropriation of government property,"[278] the violation of which in the usual course of business does not merit the government lawyer's serious attention as a whistleblower. The whistleblower protection statutes were drafted to encourage reporting, but only the reporting of acts of gross mismanagement, waste, or abuse of authority, not trivial transgressions.

Another potential area of ethical concern arises when a lawyer confronts changes in policy within the larger administration or within his or her agency. A government lawyer may totally disagree with a change of policy, rule, or position for a number of perfectly sound reasons. While the lawyer may believe that a new policy is wrong or wrongheaded, unless the proposed action is clearly illegal, or unless the lawyer is placed in the position of bringing a frivolous claim or defense and there is no good faith basis for a modification or extension of existing law, the lawyer must follow an order of his supervisors to proceed.[279] Lawyers who substitute their "individual moral judgement for that of a political process which is generally accepted as legitimate" are acting unethically.[280]

A lawyer who strongly opposes a policy change may face both conflict of interest and confidentiality problems. If the lawyer so vehemently objects to the client's lawful objectives that he or she cannot advance them, then withdrawal from the representation is required. For a government employee this may entail requesting a transfer, attempting to withdraw from the matter and requesting reassignment to another project, or ultimately resignation. This parallels in-house counsel's options under Model Rule 1.13(c). Confidentiality becomes an issue if the lawyer is so opposed to a lawful change in policy or position that he or she seeks to go public with sensitive information in an effort to sway public opinion against the change. Leaking of such information to the press or public interest groups would appear to be a violation of the agency's expectation of confidentiality under Model Rule 1.6 because the rule applies to all information relating to the representation no matter what its source. The comment to this rule states that "[t]he requirement of maintaining confidentiality of information relating to representation applies to government lawyers who may disagree with the policy goals that their representation is designed to advance."[281] Also, if the policy change is clearly illegal it would be appropriate for the agency lawyer to report first to authorities within the government.[282]

A second factor to consider before proceeding to divulge information relates to the basis of the lawyer's knowledge concerning the wrongdoing. Is the knowledge based on rumor or innuendo or on documents or credible witnesses? The federal whistleblower statute requires a "reasonable belief" that evidences wrongdoing.[283] Considering the potential consequences of a false charge, one would be well advised to base accusations on a solid factual and legal foundation. Federal agencies have ethics officers with whom a lawyer could consult, and lawyers can always seek ethics opinions from bar associations, including the Federal Bar Association. Model Rule 1.13(b), which was discussed relating to in-house counsel, provides some guidance for resolving issues internally within an organization, and agency rules also may provide for informal methods of dealing with ethical concerns.[284]

As was seen, a government lawyer who reasonably believes that another government officer or employee has violated the criminal law, or other rule, law, regulation, or ethics code may be required by statute or agency rule to report the wrongdoing to the appropriate authorities, unless such disclosure would be unlawful. Some information is made confidential by law or may have been ordered to be kept secret by executive order in the interest of national defense or in the conduct of foreign affairs.[285]

Government lawyers can learn of illegal activities in a number of ways, some of which do not raise issues of confidentiality, but when an employee of the agency personally provides self-incriminating information to the lawyer concerning an illegal act, that employee may have an unjustified expectation of confidentiality.[286] Normally, in the private sector, when a client informs his or her lawyer of past criminal acts, that information is privileged. In the corporate setting, when employees of the corporation inform in-house counsel of illegal acts performed within the scope of their employment, the privilege belongs to the corporation and corporate officers ultimately determine whether the information will remain confidential. The lawyer must ultimately abide by the corporate officer's decision. If in-house counsel objects to the decision, he or she must remain silent and "may resign," as mandated by Model Rule 1.13(c).

The result in a government setting would be somewhat different. As in the corporate setting, employees who incriminate themselves to a government lawyer have no personal claim to confidentiality. The privilege is held by the entity. But unlike the duty of in-house counsel in the corporate setting, the government lawyer cannot remain silent and allow the illegal act to be ignored. The lawyer must report the act to the appropriate authorities within the agency, who are then required to inform the attorney general.[287] If the head of the agency is involved in the illegal activities, the lawyer would have to directly inform the attorney general.[288] "The duty of disclosure inside the organization does not stop at the boundaries of the agency,"[289] as it does in the corporate setting. Model Rule 1.13(c)'s preference for confidentiality is not applicable in the public sector, because it is virtually never in the public interest to allow a significant illegal act by government employees to remain undisclosed.

As was noted earlier in the discussion of the federal Civil Service Reform Act, all federal employees are protected from retaliation for disclosing information that the employee "reasonably believes evidences a violation of any law, rule, or regulation or gross mismanagement, a gross waste of funds, an abuse of authority, or a substantial and specific danger to the public health or safety," if reported to the special counsel, or to the inspector general of an agency or other appropriately designated agency employees.[290] Federal employees can report this same information to anyone inside or outside government including the media, Congress, or advocacy groups, unless the disclosure is specifically prohibited by law or required to be kept secret in the interests of national defense or in the conduct of foreign affairs.[291]

Federal government lawyers who are covered by these provisions may have a conflict between the statutory encouragement to disclose wrongdoing and their professional duty to maintain confidentiality. Confidentiality may not necessarily be an obstacle to a government lawyer's disclosure of a clear violation of law, but knowledge of other types of wrongdoing are more problematical. Reasonable people can disagree over what constitutes gross waste, gross mismanagement, abuse of authority, or a threat to public safety in particular circumstances. Personal opinion and political orientation can color one's perception of what constitutes gross behavior or a "reasonable belief." An agency lawyer can be placed in numerous situations where the line between appropriate whistleblowing and inappropriate revelation of confidential agency information is murky at best.[292] Any time an agency takes a position based on "questionable" legal authority, or plans a novel expansion of regulatory authority, or fails to act in the public safety area, and an agency lawyer who disagrees goes public, what are the consequences?[293]

Agency officials are likely to view disclosure of confidential positions, plans, and strategies as a disloyal act, one that breaches the lawyer's duty of confidentiality to the agency. The lawyer could then be disciplined by the agency for violation of an agency ethics rule or by the jurisdiction in which the lawyer was admitted for violation of that jurisdiction's ethical standards. The agency lawyer would, on the other hand, view such discipline as retaliation for legitimate whistleblowing and thus contrary to the statute.

Assuming that the lawyer's disclosures are based on a reasonable belief of wrongdoing and are not in and of themselves unlawful disclosures, it appears that agency regulations or state ethics rules requiring confidentiality do not override the whistleblower protection provisions.[294] The public policies reflected in the whistleblower protection statutes would override any federal agency regulations and preclude state disciplinary action.[295] "The supremacy clause assures that the federal policy of disclosure prevails over the inconsistent state policy of confidentiality."[296] Thus, while seemingly at odds with the legal profession's traditional view that confidentiality is fundamental to the lawyer-client relationship, the whistleblower protection provisions encourage whistleblowing by government lawyers at the expense of the traditional role of confidentiality. As one commentator has suggested, perhaps the American Bar Association, which generally supported enactment of the whistleblower protection provisions, "never considered the possibility that a lawyer might act as a whistleblower and that such conduct would be inconsistent with normal professional duties of confidentiality."[297]

Conclusion

Some things never change. Corruption and abuse of power in government service and profiteering by businesses have long been with us and seem likely to continue as major societal concerns. In order to combat these ills, government encourages individuals to come forward and blow the whistle concerning illegal acts and other forms of wrongful conduct. This encouragement has taken two forms. One form provides remedies for whistleblowers against whom retaliatory acts have been committed, while the second provides financial incentives to encourage whistleblowing.

The public policies that seek to protect whistleblowers directly clash with the long-standing doctrine of employment at will, which is premised on public policies supporting the freedom of contract. While the at-will doctrine has been eroded significantly by statute and common law, it remains in force in forty-nine states. State legislatures and courts, in general, remain leery of limiting employers' rights to fire or discipline employees unless fundamental public interests are implicated. Whistleblower protection laws and judicial exceptions also clash with traditional notions concerning the lawyer-client relationship, especially in situations involving lawyer employees of corporate and governmental entities. Issues concerning loyalty, confidentiality, conflict of interest, and the right to fire one's lawyer at will, arise when in-house counsel for corporate entities learn of insider wrongdoing. Lawyers for government agencies face similar confidentiality and loyalty issues but may have different responsibilities than their private sector brethren.

Another thing that never seems to change is the animosity shown toward whistleblowers by supervisors and coworkers. Whistleblowing remains controversial, and the cultural taboo against informing on coworkers remains strong. Despite whistleblower protection statutes and judicial remedies, employees remain hesitant to come forward out of fear of formal and informal reprisals, or just because they do not want to get involved. Financial incentives in false claims acts seem to be successful at overcoming this reticence.

A large, complex body of law, judicial precedent, and commentary has evolved concerning whistleblowing. Since some things never change, it is sure to continue growing, at least until such time as corruption and wrongdoing are eliminated from government and the business community.

Notes

1. 20 OXFORD ENGLISH DICTIONARY, 258–59 (2d ed. 1989).

2. BLACK'S LAW DICTIONARY 1596 (6th ed. 1990). *See also* MARCIA P. MICELI & JANET P. NEAR, BLOWING THE WHISTLE: THE ORGANIZATIONAL AND LEGAL IMPLICATIONS FOR COMPANIES AND EMPLOYEES 15–21 (1992) [hereinafter MICELI & NEAR], for a detailed discussion of the definition of whistleblowing.

3. The Government Accountability Project's Home Page, <http://www.halcyon.com/tomcgap/> has information about whistleblowing with links to a number of sites. The Department of Labor, Office of Administrative Law Judges, Law Library, Whistleblower Collection is at <http://www.oalj.dol.gov/libwhist.htm>.

4. The False Claims Act, 31 U.S.C. §§3729–3733 (1994), was originally enacted in 1863 (R.S. §3492) to deal with profiteering during the Civil War.

5. DANIEL P. WESTMAN, WHISTLEBLOWING: THE LAW OF RETALIATORY DISCHARGE 19–20 (1991) [hereinafter Westman].

6. Tom Devine, *A Whistleblower's Checklist*, Government Accountability Project, <http://www.accessone.com/gap/www/checklist.htm> at 1 [hereinafter Devine].

7. MICELI & NEAR, *supra* note 2, at 180, 232. Organizational responses to whistleblowing range from doing nothing, to retaliation, to reward.

8. "Since the establishment of the OSC, [Office of Special Counsel] one Special Counsel has taught a course for Federal managers on how to fire whistleblowers. Another has expressed disdain for whistleblowers by referring to them as malcontents and informants and likening them to bag ladies and mental health patients. One Special Counsel even warned would-be whistleblowers to keep quiet or they would get their heads blown off." H.R. REP. No. 99-859, at 17. "A recent study of eighty-four whistleblowers revealed that 82% experienced harassment after blowing the whistle, 60% were fired, 17% lost their homes, and 10% admitted to attempted suicide." David Culp, *Whistleblowers: Corporate Anarchists or Heroes? Towards a Judicial Perspective,* 13 HOFSTRA LAB. L.J. 109, 113 (1995) [hereinafter Culp].

9. Admiral Hyman Rickover is quoted as saying: "If you are going to sin, sin against God, but not against the bureaucracy—God will forgive you, the bureaucracy never will." Bruce D. Fisher, *The Whistleblower Protection Act of 1989: A False Hope for Whistleblowers,* 43 RUTGERS L. REV. 355, 355 (1991). *See* MICELI & NEAR, *supra* note 2, at 224–30 for discussion of the long-term consequences for the whistleblower and the organization.

10. *See* Devine, *supra* note 6; MICELI & NEAR, *supra* note 2, at 103–38, for an examination of personal variables that may affect whistleblowing.

Notes 195

11. Lois A. Lofgren, *Whistleblower Protection: Should Legislatures and the Courts Provide a Shelter to Public and Private Sector Employees Who Disclose the Wrongdoing of Employers?*, 38 S.D. L. Rev. 316 (1993) [hereinafter Lofgren]; WESTMAN *supra* note 5, at 24–27, 105. Examples of exceptions to the rule are health care workers who may be required by law to report certain types of abuse and certain government employees required by law to report illegal acts.

12. WESTMAN, *supra* note 5, at 23–24; An argument can be made that "the concept of loyalty to a corporation is a red herring because loyalty requires a mutual bond tying people to each other—reciprocity which a corporation is incapable of giving. Nevertheless, the concept of loyalty to employer is deeply rooted in American industrial relations." Martin H. Malin, *Protecting the Whistleblower from Retaliatory Discharge*, 16 U. MICH. J. L. REFORM 277, 307 (1983) [hereinafter Malin].

13. WESTMAN, *supra* note 5, at 22.

14. John L. Howard, *Current Developments in Whistleblower Protection*, 39 LAB. L.J. 67, 71 (1988) [hereinafter Howard].

15. See Devine, *supra* note 6.

16. For example, in Balla v. Gambro, Inc., 145 Ill. 2d 492, 584 N.E.2d 104 (1991), an in-house counsel was not protected from the consequences of whistleblowing because he was required under the Model Rules of Professional Conduct to report his employer's intention to sell defective dialysis equipment.

17. Howard, *supra* note 14, at 71; ALAN F. WESTIN, WHISTLE BLOWING! LOYALTY AND DISSENT IN THE CORPORATION 134 (1981)[hereinafter WESTIN].

18. Howard, *supra* note 14, at 71.

19. *Protecting At-Will Employees against Wrongful Discharge: The Duty to Terminate Only in Good Faith*, 93 HARV. L. REV. 1816, 1818 (1980) [hereinafter Protecting At-Will Employees]; HENRY H. PERRITT, JR., 1 EMPLOYEE DISMISSAL LAW AND PRACTICE §1.65 at 70 (3d ed. 1992) [hereinafter PERRITT].

20. ANDREW D. HILL, "WRONGFUL DISCHARGE" AND THE DEROGATION OF THE AT-WILL EMPLOYMENT DOCTRINE 5 (1987) [hereinafter HILL].

21. *Id.,* at 4.

22. H.G. WOOD, A TREATISE ON THE LAW OF MASTER AND SERVANT, §134, at 272–73 (2d ed. 1886); *see* STUART H. BOMPEY ET AL. Wrongful Termination Claims: A Preventive Approach 2–4 (2d ed. 1991) [hereinafter BOMPEY ET AL.].

23. Jay M. Feinman, *The Development of the Employment at Will Rule*, 20 AM. J. LEGAL HIST. 118, 119–122 (1976); HILL, *supra* note 20, at 1; 1 WILLIAM BLACKSTONE, COMMENTARIES *425.

24. *See* HILL *supra* note 20, at 11–12; Committee on Labor and Employment Law of the Assn. of the Bar of City of N.Y., *At-Will Employment and the Problem of Unjust Dismissal*, 36 THE RECORD 170, 175–80 (1981).

25. The first federal civil service statute was the Pendleton Act, 22 STAT. 403 (1883), which was enacted to eliminate abuses arising out of the patronage system. *See* Bush v. Lucas, 462 U.S. 367, 381–84 (1982), for a brief history of federal civil service reform.

26. Pickering v. Board of Educ., 391 U.S. 563 (1968); Connick v. Myers, 461 U.S. 138 (1983); Waters v. Churchill, 114 S. Ct. 1878 (1994).

27. 49 Stat. 449, §7 at 452 (1935).

28. Title VII of the Civil Rights Act of 1964, 42 U.S.C. §§ 2000e et seq. (1994); Age Discrimination in Employment Act of 1967, 29 U.S.C. §§621 et seq (1994); Rehabilitation Act of 1973, 29 U.S.C. §§701 et. seq. (1994); Americans with Disabilities Act, 42 U.S.C. §§12101 et seq. (1994).

29. Cass R. Sunstein, *Interpreting Statutes in the Regulatory State*, 103 HARV. L. REV. 405, 409 (1989); Protecting at Will Employees, *supra* note 19, at 1827.

30. PERRITT, *supra* note 19, at 211.

31. Many of the federal statutes with such provisions are listed in the chart of federal statutes *infra*.

32. "Wrongful Discharge From Employment Act," MONT. CODE ANN. §§39-2-901 to 39-2-915 (1995).

196   WHISTLEBLOWER LAW AND ETHICS

33. U.S. Dept. of Commerce, *Statistical Abstract of the United States* 322 (1995), Chart No. 507 shows that in 1992 there were a total of 18,745,000 governmental employees, of which 3,047,000 were federal civilian employees, 4,595,000 were state employees, and 11,103,000 were employed by local governments. Total payrolls were $43,120,000,000. Chart No. 517 at 333 shows federal government outlays exceed $1.5 trillion dollars.

34. JAMES B. HELMER, JR. ET AL, FALSE CLAIMS ACT: WHISTLEBLOWER LITIGATION xiii (1994).

35. N.Y. STATE COMMISSION ON GOVERNMENT INTEGRITY, GOVERNMENT ETHICS REFORM FOR THE 1990S: THE COLLECTED REPORTS OF THE NEW YORK STATE COMMISSION ON GOVERNMENT INTEGRITY 688 (1991) [hereinafter COMMISSION ON GOVERNMENT INTEGRITY].

36. John D. Feerick, *Toward a Model Whistleblowing Law,* 19 FORDHAM URB. L.J. 585, 587 (1992) [hereinafter Feerick].

37. COMMISSION ON GOVERNMENT INTEGRITY, *supra* note 35, at 688; Feerick, *supra* note 36, at 587.

38. COMMISSION ON GOVERNMENT INTEGRITY, *supra* note 35, at 688.

39. "We have found that despite the existence of the whistleblowers statute, many public employees continue to have a deeply held fear of reprisals." *Id.,* at 689; Roger C. Cramton, *The Lawyer as Whistleblower: Confidentiality and the Government Lawyer,* 5 GEO. J. LEGAL ETHICS 291, 315 (1991) [hereinafter Cramton].

40. COMMISSION ON GOVERNMENT INTEGRITY, *supra* note 35, at 693.

41. *See, e.g.,* New York, N.Y., Admin. Code § 12-113 (1986).

42. 5 U.S.C. §1103 (1994).

43. 5 U.S.C. §1204 (1994).

44. 5 U.S.C. §1212 (1994).

45. S. REP. No. 103-358, at 2, *reprinted in* 1994 U.S.C.C.A.N. 3550. "At that time, OSC had not brought a single corrective action case since 1979 to the Merit Systems Protection Board on behalf of a whistleblower."

46. *Id.* "Whistleblowers told the Governmental Affairs Committee that they thought of the OSC as an adversary, rather than an ally, and urged the Committee to abolish the office altogether."

47. Pub. L. No. 101-12, 103 Stat. 16.

48. *Id.* at §2(b)(2)(A). See the note following 5 U.S.C. §1201 (1994) for the congressional purpose of the act.

49. S. REP. No. 103-358, at 2, *reprinted in* 1994 U.S.C.C.A.N. 3550.

50. *Id.* at 2–3, and 3551.

51. Pub. L. 103-424, 108 Stat. 4361 (1994).

52. Merit system principles are enumerated at 5 U.S.C. §2301 (1994). Subsection (9) provides protection from reprisal for whistleblower's disclosures.

53. 5 U.S.C. §2302(b)(8) (1994).

54. *Id.* §2302 (b)(8)(B).

55. *Id.* §2302(b)(8)(A).

56. *Id.* §1213(h).

57. *Id.* §§1213(c) through (f).

58. *Id.* §1213(g)(2)(3).

59. *Id.* §1213(h).

60. *Id.* §1221(a).

61. *Id.* §1214(f).

62. *Id.* §1214(b)(1)(A)(1); for practices and procedures for appeals and stay requests of personnel actions allegedly based on whistleblowing *see* 5 C.F.R. §§1209.1–1209.12 (1996).

63. 5 U.S.C. §1214(b)(2)(C) (1994).

64. *Id.* §1221(h)(1).

65. *Federal Civil Service Law and Procedures: A Basic Guide* 126–27 (Ellen M. Bussey, ed., 2d ed. 1990), sets forth the four elements of the prima facie case but does not include changes resulting from the 1994 amendments; the text above does.

66. *Id.* at 126, n.41. *See* Ellison v. Merit Sys. Protection Bd., 7 F.3d 1031, 1034–35 (Fed. Cir. 1993).

67. 5 U.S.C. §1221(e)(1)(A)(B) (1994); *see* S. Rep. No. 103-358, at 8, reprinted in 1994 U.S.C.C.A.N. 3556.

68. *See* S. Rep. No. 103-358, at 9–10, *reprinted in* 1994 U.S.C.C.A.N. 3557–3558.

69. 5 U.S.C. §1221(e)(1) (1994).

70. Marano v. Dept. of Justice, 2 F.3d 1137, 1143 (Fed. Cir. 1993).

71. 5 U.S.C. §§1214(b)(4)(B)(ii) and 1221(e)(2) (1994).

72. *Id.* §1214(b)(4)(B)(i).

73. *Id.* §1214(g)(1).

74. *Id.* §3352(a).

75. *Id.* §1214(g)(2).

76. Rivera v. United States, 924 F.2d 948, 951 (9th Cir. 1991).

77. Premachandra v. United States, 739 F.2d 392 (8th Cir. 1984); Rivera v. United States, 924 F.2d 948 (9th Cir. 1991).

78. Bush v. Lucas, 462 U.S. 367, 388 (1983), holding that the CSRA precluded a First Amendment Bivens claim, describing the CSRA as "an elaborate remedial system that has been constructed step by step with careful attention to conflicting policy considerations."

79. United States v. Fausto, 484 U.S. 439 (1988).

80. Rivera v. United States, 924 F.2d 948, 951-52 (9th Cir. 1991).

81. 135 Cong. Rec. H750 (daily ed. Mar. 21, 1989), cited in Massimino v. Department of Veterans Affairs, 58 M.S.P.R. 318, 324 (1993).

82. Gergick v. Austin, 997 F.2d 1237, 1239 (8th Cir. 1993); Rivera v. United States, 924 F.2d 948 (9th Cir. 1991).

83. *See* Massimino v. Department of Veterans Affairs, 58 M.S.P.R. 318, 324 (1993).

84. Lofgren, *supra* note 11, at 326.

85. Westman, *supra* note 5, at 113. "Virtually any mismanagement in government affects the public interest because public monies may be squandered."

86. Georgia, Nebraska, New York, North Dakota, South Carolina, Wisconsin.

87. Westman, *supra* note 5, at 59, notes that civil service protections are much less satisfactory than specific whistleblower laws because (1) they may not provide an affirmative right of action including damages, but merely a defense to retaliation; and (2) the "just cause" standard gives civil service commissioners great latitude in specific whistleblower situations.

88. Lofgren *supra* note 11, at 322; Alfred G. Fileu, Primer on Individual Employee Rights 188 (1992).

89. Compare for example the difference in coverage between public and private sector employees in Florida (Appendix 8A).

90. Arizona, Florida, District of Columbia, Idaho, Maine, Massachusetts, Minnesota, Nebraska, New Hampshire, New Jersey, New York, North Dakota, Tennessee, Utah, and Wyoming.

91. Three states specifically mention hazardous conditions: Connecticut, Maine, and Ohio.

92. Delaware, Indiana, Michigan, North Dakota, Oregon, Rhode Island, Tennessee, Virginia, Washington, Wisconsin, and Wyoming.

93. Alabama, North Dakota, Tennessee, and Virginia.

94. Connecticut, Maine, and Pennsylvania.

95. Louisiana, Illinois, Massachusetts, New Jersey, Ohio, and Pennsylvania.

96. Valerie P. Kirk and Ann Clarke Snell, *The Texas Whistleblower Act: Time for a Change,* 26 Texas Tech L. Rev. 75, 102 (1994) (hereinafter Kirk and Snell); Howard, *supra* note 14, at 71.

97. Kirk and Snell, *supra* note 96, at 103; Lofgren, *supra* note 11, at 326, 334.

98. Kirk and Snell, *supra* note 96, at 102-103; Howard, *supra* note 14, at 71.

99. Internal reporting is required in Colorado, Florida, Indiana, Maine, New Hampshire, New Jersey, and New York. Washington and Alaska allow employees to adopt internal reporting

198 WHISTLEBLOWER LAW AND ETHICS

requirements in the employer's personnel policies. Several states, on the other hand, expressly prohibit employers from requiring whistleblowers to exhaust internal procedures before external disclosure (such as Kansas and Missouri).

100. Malin, *supra* note 12, at 308.

101. *Id.* at 310.

102. *Id.* at 313.

103. *Id.* at 313; Kirk and Snell, *supra* note 96, at 90–91.

104. Iowa, Maine, Missouri, and Nevada.

105. WESTMAN, *supra* note 5, at 53–54.

106. Connecticut and Florida.

107. California, Delaware, Washington, and Missouri.

108. WESTMAN, *supra* note 5, at 55.

109. Hawaii, Maine, Michigan, New Hampshire, Rhode Island, and Utah.

110. WESTMAN, *supra* note 5, at 55.

111. Alaska, Hawaii, Iowa, Maine, Michigan, Minnesota, New Hampshire, New Jersey, Pennsylvania, Rhode Island, Tennessee, Texas, Washington, and West Virginia.

112. Florida, Iowa, and North Carolina. The federal government has a whistleblower hotline also: D.C.: (202) 633-9125; Continental U.S.: (800) 572-2249. The U.S. Office of Special Counsel home page has a Whistleblower Disclosure Hotline at <http://www.access.gpo.gov/osc/#14>.

113. Florida, Georgia, Illinois, Minnesota, and Washington.

114. WESTIN, *supra* note 17, at 34.

115. See, for example, Oklahoma and Florida.

116. Kirk and Snell, *supra* note 96, at 85.

117. *Id.*

118. *See* WESTIN, *supra* note 17, at 40, 50, for the story of a General Electric engineer who was blackballed from corporate employment after his disclosures concerning the risks of a nuclear accident.

119. *See* WESTIN, *supra* note 17, at 48. Federal civil service law views a decision to order psychiatric testing or examination as a personnel action at 5 U.S.C. §2301 (a)(2)(A)(x) (1994).

120. ISIDOR SILVER, 1 PUBLIC EMPLOYEE DISCHARGE AND DISCIPLINE 8 (2d ed. 1995) [hereinafter SILVER]; Mourad v. Automobile Club Ins. Ass'n., 186 Mich. App. 715, 465 N.W.2d 395 (1991).

121. Prohibited in Alaska.

122. Prohibited in Indiana, Michigan, North Dakota, Tennessee, Virginia, Washington, Wisconsin, and Wyoming.

123. Alaska, California, Illinois, Kentucky, Montana, New Jersey, North Carolina, and Tennessee.

124. Louisiana, Massachusetts, and North Carolina.

125. South Carolina, and Texas.

126. Elletta Sangrey Callahan and Terry Morehead Dworkin, *Do Good and Get Rich: Financial Incentives for Whistleblowing and the False Claims Act,* 37 VILLANOVA L. REV. 273, 336 (1992) [hereinafter Callahan and Dworkin].

127. *Id.* at 273, 278-83. In addition to the False Claims Acts discussed *infra,* the federal government provides rewards to tax informers, 26 U.S.C. §7623(1994) and also for customs informers, 19 U.S.C. §1619 (1994). *See also* Major Fraud Act, 18 U.S.C. §1031(g) (1994).

128. 31 U.S.C. §§3729-3733 (1994).

129. "It is an action brought by an informer, under a statute which establishes a penalty for the commission or omission of a certain act, and provides that the same shall be recoverable in a civil action, part of the penalty to go to any person who will bring such action and the remainder to the state or some other institution." BLACK'S LAW DICTIONARY 1251 (6th ed. 1990).

130. *See generally,* ABA Section of Public Contract Law, *Qui Tam Litigation Under the False Claims Act* (1994).

131. 31 U.S.C. §3729(a) (1994). The act generally applies to two classes of misconduct. "The first is the presentation of a claim knowing it to be false. The second is the use of false

documentation in support of a claim." John Cosgrove McBride & Thomas J. Touhey, 2 Government Contracts §14.30 at 14-11 (1996).

132. 31 U.S.C. §3730(b) (1994).

133. *Id.* §3730(b)(2).

134. *Id.* §3730(d)(1). If the government proceeds with the action, and the person bringing the action is the primary source of information rather than governmental sources or the media, the qui tam plaintiff shall receive at least 15 percent but not more than 25 percent of the proceeds of the action or settlement of the claim, depending on the contribution to the prosecution of the action, plus expenses, lawyer's fees and costs. *See* note 136 *infra.*

135. *Id.* §3730(d)(2). If the government does not proceed, the person bringing the action or settling the claim shall receive an amount the court believes is reasonable but not less than 25 percent nor more than 30 percent of the proceeds plus expenses, lawyer's fees and costs.

136. *Id.* §3730(d)(1). "Where the action is one which the court finds to be based primarily on disclosures of specific information (other than information provided by the person bringing the action) relating to allegations or transactions in a criminal, civil, or administrative hearing, in a congressional, administrative, or Government Accounting Office report, hearing, audit or investigation, or from the news media, the court may award such sum as it considers appropriate, but in no case more than 10% of the proceeds. . . ."

137. *See* Callahan and Dworkin, *supra* note 126, at 323–24, discussing how large rewards may be a way to offset the significant personal and financial risks faced by whistleblowers. *See* also Devine, *supra* note 6, at 6, who describes how some firms are encouraged by the prospect of "pot of gold" victories in whistleblower cases, especially where punitive damages are available. There is also the *Qui Tam* Information Center on the Internet at <http://www.quitam.com/>, which helps potential whistleblowers with lawyer selection. The Taxpayers against Fraud also maintain an informative home page relating to the False Claims Act at <http://www.taf.org/>.

138. Priscilla R. Budeiri, *The Return of Qui Tam,* 11 The Wash. Law. 24, 27 (Sept./Oct. 1996).

139. Callahan and Dworkin, *supra* note 126, at 334–35.

140. 31 U.S.C. §3730(h)(1994); *see* Timothy P. Olson, *Taking the Fear out of Being a Tattletale: Whistle Blower Protection under the False Claims Act* and Neal v. Honeywell, Inc., 44 DePaul L. Rev. 1363 (1995).

141. Whistleblower Reward and Protection Act, 740 Ill. Comp. Stat. Ann. 175/1–175/7 (1996 Supp.); Florida False Claims Act, Fla. Stat. Ann. §§68.081–68.092 (1996 Supp.); Cal. Gov't Code §§ 12650 et seq. (Deering 1996 Supp.); all three statutes provide antiretaliation provisions: Fla. Stat. Ann. §68.088 (1996 Supp.) 740 Ill. Comp. Stat. Ann. 175/4(g) (1996 Supp.); Cal. Gov't Code §12653 (Deering 1996 Supp.).

142. Arkansas Medicaid Fraud False Claims Act, Ark. Code Ann. §§ 20-77-901 et seq. (Michie 1995 Supp.); Connecticut Health Insurance Fraud Act, Conn. Gen. Stat. Ann. §§53-440 et seq. (West 1996 Supp.); Tennessee Medicaid False Claims Act, Tenn. Code Ann. §§ 71-5-181 et seq. (1995); Tennessee Health Care False Claims Act, Tenn. Code Ann. §§ 56-26-401 (1994); Utah has a "False Claims Act" relating to medical benefits that does *not* provide for a qui tam action, Utah Code Ann. §§ 26-20-1 et seq. (1995).

143. S.C. Code Ann. §8-27-20(B) (1995 Supp.).

144. Or. Rev. Stat. §659.530 (1995).

145. 43 Pa. Cons. Stat. §§1422, 1423 (West 1991); W. Va. Code §6C-1-2(d) (1988); *see* Callahan and Dworkin, *supra* note 126, at 279.

146. Wisc. Stat. Ann. §230.83(2) (West 1984).

147. Lionel J. Postic, Wrongful Termination: A State by State Survey xx (1994) [hereinafter Postic]; this text is a compilation of information on wrongful termination for each state plus very useful charts. A similar compilation is available in Lex K. Larson, 2 Unjust Dismissal §§10.01–10.52 (1996).

148. *See, e.g.,* Bompay et al., *supra* note 22, at 19–21; James N. Dertouzos et al., *The Legal and Economic Consequences of Wrongful Termination* 5–7 (The Institute for Civil Justice—Rand 1988) [hereinafter Dertouzos et al.]; Silver, *supra* note 120, at 390.

149. *Id.*

150. Lex K. Larson, 1 Unjust Dismissal §304[3](a–d)(1996) [hereinafter Larson].

151. *See* Restatement of the Law of Contracts §90 (1932); Bompay et al., *supra* note 22, at 35–36; Larson, *supra* note 150, at §304[1].

152. *See* Postic, *supra* note 147, at xx; Perritt, *supra* note 19, at 315–316; Restatement (Second) of Contracts §205(1979).

153. *See* Silver, *supra* note 120, at 390–91; Perritt, *supra* note 19, at 390.

154. 174 Cal. App. 2d 184, 344 P.2d 25 (1959).

155. *Id.* at 188, 344 P.2d at 27.

156. *Id.*

157. *Id.*

158. *Id.* at 188–89, 344 P.2d at 27–28.

159. Larson *supra* note 150, at §6.02.

160. New York is a prime example, *see* Murphy v. American Home Prod. Corp., 58 N.Y.2d 293, 448 N.E.2d 86, 461 N.Y.S.2d 232 (1983).

161. Larson, *supra* note 150, at §6.02; Stephen M. Kohn & Michael D. Kohn, The Labor Lawyer's Guide to the Rights and Responsibilities of Employee Whistleblowers 40 (1988).

162. Larson, *supra* note 150, at §6.02.

163. Westman, *supra* note 5, at 81.

164. *Id.* at 102.

165. *Id.* at 113.

166. *Id.* at 108.

167. *See* Harney v. Meadowbrook Nursing Ctr., 784 S.W.2d 921, 922 (Tenn. 1990); Gantt v. Sentry Ins., 1 Cal. 4th 1083, 824 P.2d 680, 4 Cal. Rptr. 2d 874 (1992).

168. Palmateer v. International Harvester Co., 85 Ill.2d 124, 132; 421 N.E.2d 876, 879 (1981).

169. *Id.* at 132, 421 N.E.2d at 880.

170. Geary v. U.S. Steel Corp., 456 Pa. 171, 319 A.2d 174 (1974); Campbell v. Eli Lilly & Co., 413 N.E.2d 1054 (Ind. App. 1980).

171. Westman, *supra* note 5, at 112; Wagner v. City of Globe, 150 Ariz. 82, 89; 722 P.2d 250, 257 (1986).

172. Westman, *supra* note 5, at 105–107, 113–55.

173. Perritt, *supra* note 19, §2.40 at 175.

174. *See* Silver, *supra* note 120, at 428; Perritt, *supra* note 19, at §2.40.

175. U.S. Const. art. VI.

176. Perritt, *supra* note 19, at §§2.40, 2.41; Silver, *supra* note 120, at §20.18.

177. Pennsylvania, South Carolina, and West Virginia.

178. Louisiana.

179. Connecticut.

180. *See* Silver, *supra* note 120, at §20.5 at 403; Seymour Moskovitz, *Employment-At-Will & Codes of Ethics: The Professional's Dilemma,* 23 Val. U.L. Rev. 33, 56–66 (1988).

181. *See,* for example, Rocky Mount. Hosp. & Med. Serv. v. Mariam, 916 P.2d 519, 526 (Colo. 1996), where the court examines the legislative endorsement of the Colorado State Board of Accountancy rules.

182. For example the New York Lawyer's Code of Professional Responsibility Disciplinary Rules have been adopted as court rules.

183. *See* Wright v. Shriners Hosp., 412 Mass. 469, 589 N.E.2d 1241, 1244 (1992); Schodolski v. Michigan Consolidated Gas Co., 412 Mich. 692, 316 N.W.2d 710, 712 (1982); Sullivan v. Mass. Mutual Life Ins., 802 F. Supp. 716, 727 (D. Conn. 1992); McGrane v. Reader's Digest Ass'n., Inc., 863 F. Supp. 183, 185 (S.D. N.Y. 1994).

184. *See* Rocky Mount. Hosp. & Med. Serv. v. Mariani, 916 P. 2d 519, 524–525 (Colo. 1996).

185. Gantt v. Sentry, Ins., 1 Cal. 4th 1083, 4 Cal. Rptr. 2d 874, 881, 824 P.2d 680, 687 (1992); Firestone Textile Co. Div. v. Meadows, 666 S.W.2d 730, 733 (Ky. 1983); Brockmeyer v. Dunn & Bradstreet, 113 Wisc. 2d 561, 335 N.W.2d 834, 840 (1983).

Notes   201

186. Rocky Mount. Hosp. & Med. Serv. v. Mariani, 916 P.2d 519, 524–525 (Colo. 1996).

187. *Id.* at 528, holding the Colorado State Board of Accountancy Rules of Professional Conduct to be a source of public policy for purposes of a claim of wrongful discharge.

188. Pierce v. Ortho Pharmaceutical Corp., 84 N.J. 58, 417 A.2d 505, 512 (1980). "In certain instances a professional code of ethics may contain an expression of public policy," but under the circumstances of this case the Hippocratic oath did not contain a clear mandate of public policy that prevented the doctor's research.

189. Kalman v. Grand Union Co., 183 N.J. Super. 153, 443 A.2d 728 (1982).

190. Sullivan v. Mass. Mutual Life Ins. Co., 802 F. Supp. 716, 727 (D. Conn. 1992), stating that because ethical codes in the securities industry are promulgated by private groups they do not have the force of law and cannot establish public policy.

191. Wieder v. Skala, 80 N.Y.2d 628, 593 N.Y.S.2d 752, 609 N.E.2d 105 (1992), limiting its holding to a specific "core" disciplinary rule; McGonagle v. Union Fidelity Corp., 383 Pa. Super. 223, 556 A.2d 878, 885 (1989); General Dynamics v. Superior Court, 7 Cal. 4th 1164, 876 P.2d 487, 32 Cal. Rptr. 2d 1 (1994).

192. WESTMAN, *supra* note 5, at 91.

193. M.R. 1.6(a); D.R. 4-101(B). References to M.R.s are to the ABA Model Rules of Professional Conduct (1983). References to D.R.s or E.C.s are to the ABA Model Code of Professional Responsibility (1998).

194. M.R. 1.6(b)(1), "A lawyer may reveal such information to the extent the lawyer reasonably believes necessary to prevent the client from committing a criminal act that the lawyer believes is likely to result in imminent death or substantial bodily harm." *Compare* D.R. 4-101(c)(3) "A lawyer may reveal: the intention of his client to commit a crime and the information necessary to prevent the crime."

195. M.R. 3.3(a)(2)(4),(b)(c); D.R. 7-102(A)(4), (B)(1).

196. M.R. 1.2(d); D.R. 7-102(A)(7)(8), D.R. 1-102(A)(3)(4).

197. M.R. 8.4(a),(b),(c); D.R. 1-102(A)(1); RESTATEMENT, THE LAW GOVERNING LAWYERS §34 (1996).

198. M.R. 1.16; D.R. 2-109 and D.R. 2-110.

199. *See, e.g.,* Fracasse v. Brent, 6 Cal. 3d 784, 100 Cal. Rpt. 385, 494 P.2d 9 (1972).

200. *See* M.R. 1.16 (a)(3) and cmt. 4; D.R. 2-110(B)(4); RESTATEMENT, THE LAW GOVERNING LAWYERS §44 and cmt. b and §52 (1996).

201. *Compare* M.R. 1.16(b) and D.R. 2-110(c).

202. M.R. 1.13(a).

203. M.R. 1.13(a), cmts. 1 and 2.

204. M.R. 1.13(b); E.C. 5-18 does not provide the detailed guidance of M.R. 1.13, but state versions such as the N.Y. Lawyers' Code of Professional Conduct have adopted the content of the model rule in their versions of E.C. 5-18.

205. M.R. 1.13(b).

206. M.R. 1.13(b)(1)(2)(3).

207. M.R. 1.13(c); GEOFFREY C. HAZARD, JR. & W. WILLIAM HODES, 1 THE LAW OF LAWYERING § 1.13:111, at 403 (1996), "The strongest action a lawyer may take *under this rule* with respect to the outside world is to resign, and perhaps to 'give notice of the fact of withdrawal' to third parties."

208. Stephen Gillers, *Model Rule 1.13(c) Gives the Wrong Answer to the Question of Corporate Counsel Disclosure,* 1 GEO. J. LEGAL ETHICS 289, 299 (1987). The future crime exception under M.R. 1.6(b)(1) may be available to allow in-house counsel to inform authorities of prospective criminal acts, but it is limited to those criminal acts likely to result in "imminent death or substantial bodily harm." *Id.* at 302.

209. M.R. 1.13(c).

210. *See* CHARLES W. WOLFRAM, MODERN LEGAL ETHICS §§6.5.1 to 6.5.4 (1986) [hereinafter WOLFRAM].

211. *See* note 194.

212. *See* LARSON, *supra* note 150, at Appendix XXI-1.

202   WHISTLEBLOWER LAW AND ETHICS

213. *See* notes 187–91 *supra* for cases recognizing professional ethics rules as a source for the public policy exception to the at-will doctrine.

214. 145 Ill.2d 492, 584 N.E.2d 104 (1991); the court relied heavily on the earlier Illinois case of Herbster v. North American Co. 150 Ill. App. 3d 21, 501 N.E.2d 343 (1986).

215. *Balla,* 584 N.E.2d at 107.

216. *Id.* at 107–108.

217. The Illinois version of Rule 1.6(b) states that a lawyer "shall reveal" as compared to the M.R. version of Rule 1.6(b), which states that a lawyer "may" reveal such information.

218. *Balla,* 584 N.E.2d at 109.

219. *Id.*

220. *See* Damian Edward Okasinski, Annotation, *In House Counsel's Right to Maintain Action for Wrongful Discharge,* 16 A.L.R. 5th 239 (1993), collecting cases; RESTATEMENT, THE LAW GOVERNING LAWYERS, Rptr's Note to §44 cmt. b (1996), citing cases on the availability of retaliatory discharge claims for lawyer employees.

221. Mourad v. Automobile Club Ins. Assn., 186 Mich App. 715, 465 N.W.2d 395 (1991); General Dynamics v. Superior Court, 7 Cal. 4th 1164, 876 P.2d 487, 32 Cal. Rptr. 2d 1 (1994).

222. 478 N.W.2d 498, 502 (Minn. 1991).

223. 7 Cal. 4th 1164, 876 P.2d 487, 32 Cal. Rptr. 2d 1 (1994).

224. *Id.,* 876 P.2d at 490.

225. *Id.* at 491.

226. *Id.* at 495.

227. *Id.*

228. *Id.* at 496.

229. *Id.* at 497.

230. *Id.* at 498.

231. *Id.* 501 (emphasis in original).

232. *Id.* at 501–502.

233. *Id.* at 502–503 (emphasis in original).

234. *Id.* at 503.

235. *Id.* at 503–504.

236. *Id.* at 504.

237. *Id.*

238. Rodd B. Lape, General Dynamics Corp. v. Superior Court: Striking a Blow for Corporate Counsel, 56 OHIO ST. L.J. 1303, 1320 (1995).

239. M.R. 8.3(a)(c). Note that information gained through participation as a member of a lawyer assistance program is viewed as confidential. *Compare* D.R. 1-103(A), "A lawyer possessing unprivileged knowledge of a violation of D.R. 1-102 [Misconduct] shall report such knowledge to a tribunal or other authority empowered to investigate or act upon such violation."

240. *See* M.R. 5.1. There was no corresponding provision in the model code *but see* N.Y. C.P.R. D.R. 1-104.

241. ABA Inf. Op. 1203 (1972); N.Y. City Op. 1982-79.

242. N.Y. City Op. 1982-79.

243. *Id.*

244. *Id.*; ABA Inf. Op. 1203 (1972).

245. N.Y. City Op. 1982-79.

246. Law firm partners can also become involved in whistleblower incidents. *See* Amy Boardman, *Whistleblower Seeks One More Hearing,* LEGAL TIMES at 2 (Sept. 16, 1996).

247. *See* Parker v. M&T Chemicals, Inc., 236 N.J. Super. 451, 566 A.2d 215 (1989), for an example of a state whistleblower protection statute being applied to allow damages for wrongful discharge of in-house counsel.

248. 80 N.Y.2d 628, 609 N.E.2d 105, 593 N.Y.S.2d 752 (1992).

249. *Wieder,* 80 N.Y.2d at 633, 639; Sabetay v. Sterling Drug, 69 N.Y.2d 329, 506 N.E.2d 919, 514 N.Y.S.2d 209 (1987); Murphy v. American Home Products Corp., 58 N.Y.2d 293, 301, 448

N.E.2d 86, 461 N.Y.S.2d 232 (1983); Robert LaBerge et al., *Employment Law,* 44 SYRACUSE L.REV. 243, 262–69 (1993).

250. N.Y. LAB. LAW §740 (McKinney 1988); *Wieder,* 80 N.Y.2d at 633.

251. Weiner v. McGraw-Hill Inc., 57 N.Y.2d 458, 443 N.E.2d 441, 457 N.Y.S.2d 193 (1982), provided for an exception to the at-will rule premised on an express limitation found in the language of the employer's personnel handbook.

252. *Wieder,* 80 N.Y. 2d at 635–36.

253. *Id.* at 636.

254. *Id.* at 636–37.

255. *Id.* at 637.

256. *Id.* at 638–39.

257. Sandra J. Mullings, Wieder v. Skala: *A Chink in the Armor of the At-Will Doctrine or a Lance for Law Firm Associates?* 45 SYRACUSE L. REV. 963, 964 (1995) [hereinafter Mullings]. See Rojas v. Debevoise & Plimpton, 167 Misc. 2d 451, 634 N.Y.S.2d 358 (N.Y. Sup. Ct. 1995), for an example of when a lawyer did not have an implied-in-fact contract action, because she was not required to subvert the core purpose of the employment. Her actions in speaking to the F.B.I. about the actions of a partner were extrinsic to the purpose of her employment and the firm did not insist that she act unethically.

258. McGrane v. Reader's Digest Ass'n., Inc., 822 F. Supp. 1044, 1049 (S.D. N.Y. 1993).

259. *Id.* at 1049; *see* Mullings, *supra* note 257, at 994.

260. Stephen Gillers, *Model Rule 1.13(c) Gives the Wrong Answer to the Question of Corporate Counsel Disclosure,* 1 GEO. J. LEGAL ETHICS 289, 294 (1987).

261. *Id.* at 294–95.

262. WOLFRAM, *supra* note 210, at §13.9.2 at 757.

263. *See* chapter 2 of this text for a detailed discussion of the issue of who is the client for the government lawyer. *See also* M.R. 1.13 cmt. [7].

264. *See* Kathleen Clark, *Do We Have Enough Ethics in Government Yet? An Answer from Fiduciary Theory,* 1996 U. ILL. L.REV. 57, 66. A number of federal agencies have adopted the American Bar Association's Model Rules or Model Code of Professional Responsibility by regulation. See, for example, 28 C.F.R. §45.735(1)(b)(1996), where the Department of Justice adopts the code of professional responsibility. ABA Committee on Government Standards (Cynthia Farina, reporter) *Keeping Faith: Government Ethics & Government Ethics Regulation,* 45 ADMIN. L. REV. 287, 290, 334 (1993) [hereinafter *Keeping Faith*].

265. *Conflicts of Interest in the Legal Profession,* 94 HARV. L. REV. 1244, 1414 (1981).

266. *See* Geoffrey P. Miller, *Government Lawyers' Ethics in a System of Checks and Balances,* 54 U. CHI. L. REV. 1293 (1987) [hereinafter Miller].

267. Cramton, *supra* note 39, at 294.

268. 5 U.S.C. §552 (1994); *see* WOLFRAM, *supra* note 210, at §6.5.6; RESTATEMENT, THE LAW GOVERNING LAWYERS §124, cmt. b (1996), for a discussion of the application of the privilege for the government under open-meeting, open-file, and whistleblower statutes.

269. Cramton, *supra* note 39, at 295.

270. 18 U.S.C. §1905 (1994), providing for fines, imprisonment, and removal from office for improper disclosure of confidential information.

271. "The 'civil service' consists of all appointive positions in the executive, judicial, and legislative branches of the Government of the United States, except positions in the uniformed services." 5 U.S.C. §2101 (1994).

272. H. R. Con. Res. 175, 85th Cong., reprinted as an appendix to part 45 of 28 C.F.R. following §45.735-27 (1996).

273. Exec. Order No. 11222.

274. *The Department of Justice Manual,* vol. 2 at 1-193 (1995-1 Supp.).

275. Cramton, *supra* note 39, at 303.

276. 5 U.S.C. §2302(b)(8) (1994).

277. Cramton, *supra* note 39, at 301; *see* WOLFRAM *supra* note 210, at §13.9.2.

204   WHISTLEBLOWER LAW AND ETHICS

278. *Keeping Faith, supra* note 264, at 334.

279. Cramton, *supra* note 39, at 303–304; M.R. 3.1.

280. Miller, *supra* note 266, at 1294.

281. M.R. 1.6, cmt. [6]; *See also* RESTATEMENT, THE LAW GOVERNING LAWYERING §206 cmt. e. (1996).

282. Cramton, *supra* note 39 at 305–306; *see* M.R. 1.6, cmt. 16; "Where the client is an organization, the lawyer may be in doubt whether contemplated conduct will actually be carried out . . . the lawyer may make inquiry within the organization as indicated in rule 1.13(b)."

283. 5 U.S.C. §2302(b)(8)(1994).

284. *See* 28 C.F.R. §45.735-2(b)(1996).

285. 5 U.S.C. §2302(b)(8)(1994).

286. See M.R. 1.13(d) and cmt. 8, discussing the situation where the organization's interests become adverse to interests of its constituents.

287. Cramton, *supra* note 39, at 303.

288. *Id.*

289. *Id.*

290. 5 U.S.C. §2302(b)(8)(B) (1994).

291. *Id.* §2302(b)(8)(A); Cramton, *supra* note 39, at 308.

292. Cramton, *supra* note 39, at 309.

293. *Id.*

294. *Id.* at 312.

295. *Id.*

296. *Id.*

297. *Id.* at 314.

APPENDIX ❦ 8A
State Whistleblower Provisions

State	Citation	Coverage	Protected Conduct	Remedy
ALABAMA				
The State Employees Protection Act	Ala. Code § 36-26A-1 to 7 (Michie 1997).	State employees.	Reporting under oath or by affidavit a violation of state law, regulation, or rule to a public body.	Civil action for wages, compensatory damages, or combination of remedies.
Whistleblower protection relating to child labor laws	Ala. Code § 25-8-57 (Michie 1997).	Any person, including employees, applicants, and former employees.	Opposing illegal conduct under child labor laws, making a charge, testifying, assisting, or participating in an investigation, proceeding, or hearing. Disclosing information, refusing to obey an illegal order, challenging or revealing violations of child labor laws.	Violators are subject to fine.
ALASKA				
Alaska Whistleblower Act	Alaska Stat. § 39.90.120 to .150 (Michie 1997).	Public employees both state and local, including public or quasi-public corporations or authorities. Public employees *or other persons* who may wish to bid on public contracts, receive land under state law or ordinance, or receive another right, privilege, or benefit.	Good faith reporting to a public body on a matter of public concern, or participating in a court action, investigation, hearing, or inquiry held by a public body on a matter of public concern. This means violation of a state, federal or municipal law, regulation, or ordinance; a danger to the public health or safety; gross mismanagement, substantial waste of funds, or a clear abuse of authority; or a matter for investigation by the ombudsman.	May bring a civil action and the court may grant appropriate relief, including punitive damages. Also civil fines of not more than $10,000.

State	Citation	Coverage	Protected Conduct	Remedy
ARIZONA				
Public employee whistle-blower protection	Ariz. Rev. Stat. Ann. §§ 38-532 to 534 (1998).	State officers or employees, employees of community college districts, school districts, and counties.	Disclosing information of a matter of public concern to a public body that the employee reasonably believes evidences a violation of any law or mismanagement, gross waste of monies, or abuse of authority.	Rescission of the personnel action and recovery of lost pay and benefits. Also may seek injunctive relief in a civil action. Violator subject to civil penalty up to $5,000.
Employment Protection Act	Ariz. Rev. Stat. Ann. § 23-1502 (1998).	Any employee.	An employee cannot be terminated in violation of a state statute nor may an employer terminate an employee in retaliation for: (1) The refusal by the employee to commit an act or omission that would violate the Constitution of Arizona or any state statute. (2) The disclosure by the employee in a reasonable manner that the employee has information or a reasonable belief that the employer, or an employee of the employer, has violated, is violating, or will violate the Constitution of Arizona or the statutes of this state to either the employer or a representative of the employer who the employee reasonably believes is in a managerial or supervisory position and has the authority to investigate the information provided by the employee and to take action to prevent	Any remedy specifically provided by statute, or if there is no statutory remedy, the employee may bring a tort claim for wrongful termination in violation of public policy.

ARIZONA Employment Protection Act *(continued)*		further violations of the Constitution of Arizona or statutes of this state or an employee of a public body or political subdivision. The statute also prohibits termination for exercise of a variety of listed statutory rights.	
ARKANSAS No general whistleblower protection provisions			
CALIFORNIA Reporting of Improper Governmental Activities Act	Cal. Gov't Code §§ 8547.1 to .12 (Deering 1997 Supp.)	State employees or job applicants and any individual, corporation, trust, association, any state or local government, or any agency or instrumentality of the foregoing. University of California employees have separate provisions.	Right to disclose information to the state auditor of improper governmental activities that are violations of federal or state laws or regulations, including corruption, malfeasance, bribery, theft, or misuse of government property, fraudulent claims, fraud, coercion, conversion, malicious prosecution, or willful omission to perform duty, or is economically wasteful or involves gross misconduct, incompetency, or inefficiency.	Civil damages. Violators may receive a fine not to exceed $10,000 and imprisonment for up to one year. Punitive damages may be awarded for malicious acts.
Disclosure of Information: Local Government	Cal. Gov't Code §§ 53296 to 53299 (Deering 1997 Supp.).	Employees or job applicants of local agencies defined as any county, city, city and county, and any district, school district, community college district, municipal or public corporation, political subdivision, or public agency of the state or any instrumentality of these agencies.	Disclosing information regarding gross mismanagement or a significant waste of funds, an abuse of authority, or a substantial and specific danger to public health or safety.	Violators are subject to a fine not to exceed $10,000 and imprisonment for up to one year. Injured employee may bring civil action if the supervisor acted with malicious intent, and punitive damages may be awarded where the party acted with malice.

State	Citation	Coverage	Protected Conduct	Remedy
Employee's right to disclose information to government or law enforcement agencies does *not* apply to confidential communications.	Cal. Lab. Code §§ 1102.5 to 1106 (Deering 1997).	Applies to public and private sector employees.	Prevents public or private employers from adopting rules, regulations, or policies to prevent employees from disclosing or for retaliating due to a violation of federal or state statute or noncompliance with a state or federal regulation, except for rules prohibiting employees from violating confidentiality of the attorney-client privilege, the physician-patient privilege, or trade secret information.	Violators can be imprisoned for up to one year or may receive a fine not to exceed $1,000 or both. Corporations can be fined up to $5,000. Employees can seek civil damages.
COLORADO				
Public Employees Whistle-blowing Protection Act	Colo. Rev. Stat. §§ 24-50.5-101 to 107 (1997).	Employees of the State of Colorado, including any person employed by a state agency, which is any board, commission, department, division, section or other agency of the executive, legislative, or judicial branches of government.	Truthful disclosures of non-confidential information, including written provision of evidence to any person, or the testimony before any committee of the general assembly, regarding any action, policy, regulation, practice, or procedure, including but not limited to, the waste of public funds, abuse of authority, or mismanagement of any state agency.	Any employee not in the state personnel system, or any employee in the state personnel system who has filed a complaint but no reasonable basis was found for the charges, may bring a civil action. Prevailing employees may recover damages, court costs, and such other relief as the court deems appropriate.
Private Enterprise Employee Protection	Colo. Rev. Stat. §§ 24-114-101 to 103 (1998).	Any person employed by a private enterprise under contact with a state agency.	Truthful disclosures of non-confidential information concerning a private enterprise under contract with a state agency that, if not disclosed, could result in the waste of public funds, endanger the public health, safety, or welfare, or adversely affect the interests of the state.	Employee may bring a civil action to recover damages, costs, and other relief as the court deems appropriate.

CONNECTICUT

General whistleblower protection provision	Conn. Gen. Stat. Ann. § 31-51m (West 1997 Supp. Pamph.).	Both public and private sector employees.	Truthful reporting of a violation or suspected violation of any state or federal law or regulation or any municipal ordinance or regulation to a public body or participating in an investigation, hearing, or inquiry held by a public body or court action.	After exhausting all available administrative remedies, may bring a civil action for the reinstatement of the previous job, payment of back wages, and reestablishment of employee benefits. Court may allow costs and lawyer's fees.
			Municipal employees are protected for reporting to a public body concerning unethical practices, mismanagement, or abuse of authority.	
Right to act in case of hazardous conditions	Conn. Gen. Stat. § 31-40t (West 1997 Supp. Pamph.).	Both public and private sector employees.	Informing another employee that the other employee is working in or exposed to a hazardous condition or refusing to expose oneself to a hazardous workplace condition under certain circumstances.	Administrative resolution by the labor commissioner of all issues relating to any dispute.
Disclosure to auditors of public accounts	Conn. Gen. Stat. § 4I.61dd. (Lexsee 1997 et. ALS 55).	State employees (and quasi-public agencies).	Disclosing information to the auditor of public accounts or the attorney general of any matter involving corruption, unethical practices, violation of state laws or regulations, mismanagement, gross waste of funds, abuse of authority, or danger to the public safety occurring in any state department or agency (and quasi-public agencies).	File claim with Employees' Review Board or in accordance with collective bargaining agreement.

State	Citation	Coverage	Protected Conduct	Remedy
Disclosure by employees and contractors of information of wrongdoing by public service companies, contractors, and Nuclear Regulatory Commission licensees	Conn. Gen. Stat. § 16-8a (West 1997 Supp.).	Any employee of a public service company, holding company, or Nuclear Regulatory Commission licensee operating a nuclear power facility in the state or those directly or indirectly providing goods and services to those companies.	Disclosing information involving substantial misfeasance, malfeasance or nonfeasance, or of the discharge, discipline, or other penalizing of a person for reporting misfeasance, malfeasance, or nonfeasance, in the management of the company or facility to the department of public utility control.	Department of public utility control may issue orders, including cease and desist orders, and impose penalties.
Code of ethics for public officials	Conn. Gen. Stat. § 1-82(e) (West 1997 Supp.).	Any individual.	Disclosing information to the State Ethics Commission of violations of the Ethics Code for Public Officials.	Not stated.
DELAWARE				
Public employee whistle-blower protection	Del. Code Ann. tit. 29, § 5115 (1997 Supp.).	Any full or part-time state employee or employee of a school district, county, or municipality.	Truthful reporting to an elected official of a violation or suspected violation of a law or regulation of the federal or state governments or of a school district, county, or municipality.	Employee may bring a civil suit for appropriate injunctive relief, actual damages, or both.
Nursing homes providing care to Medicaid recipients	Del. Code Ann. tit. 16, § 1154 (1997).	Any person or agency.	Participating in an investigation by the ombudsperson into long-term health care facilities	Not stated.
DISTRICT OF COLUMBIA				
Public employee whistle-blower protection	D.C. Code Ann. §§ 1-616.1 to 1-616.3 (1998). (1992).	District employees.	Disclosing or threatening to disclose an activity, policy, or practice that the employee reasonably believes is a violation of law or rule or misuse of government resources or funds. Providing information or testimony before a public body. Objecting to or refusing	May institute a civil action for a restraining injunction, rescission of the retaliatory action, reinstatement of a position or its equivalent, reinstatement of benefits and seniority, compensation for lost wages and benefits, and payment of costs and lawyer's fees.

DISTRICT OF COLUMBIA Public employee whistle-blower protection *(continued)*			to participate in an activity or practice that the employee reasonably believes is a violation of law or rule or is fraudulent or criminal.	
FLORIDA Whistleblower's Act	Fla. Stat. Ann. §§ 112.3187 to 112.31895 (1998).	Employees of state agencies and independent contractors or any person who discloses information to an appropriate agency.	Disclosing information concerning any violation or suspected violation of any federal, state, or local law, rule, or regulation committed by an employee or agent of an agency or independent contractor that creates and presents a substantial and specific danger to the public's health, safety, or welfare or any act or suspected act of gross mismanagement, malfeasance, misfeasance, nonfeasance, gross waste of public funds, or neglect of duty by an employee or agent of an agency or independent contractor.	After exhausting administrative remedies, can bring civil suit. Remedies include stays, temporary reinstatement, reinstatement to the same or equivalent position, reinstatement of full fringe benefits and seniority, compensation for lost wages, benefits, or remuneration, costs, and lawyer's fees.
Private sector whistle-blower protection	Fla. Stat. Ann. §§ 448.101 to 448.105 (1998).	Employees of private individuals or of a firm, partnership, institution, corporation, or association that employs ten or more employees.	Disclosing or threatening to disclosure to any appropriate government agency an activity, policy, or practice that is a violation of law, rule, or regulation. Providing information or testimony to government investigative agencies. Objecting to or refusal to participate in illegal acts or those violating rule or regulation. Must first in writing, notify supervisor or employer and afford a reasonable opportunity to correct the activity, policy, or practice.	Civil action. Court may issue a restraining injunction, order reinstatement to the same or equivalent position, reinstatement of fringe benefits and seniority rights, compensation for lost wages, benefits, or remuneration, or any other compensatory damages allowable at law.

211

State	Citation	Coverage	Protected Conduct	Remedy
GEORGIA				
Public employees whistle-blower protection	Ga. Code Ann. § 45-1-4 (1998).	Any employee of the executive branch of the state or of any other department, board, bureau, commission, authority, or other agency *but not the* office of the governor, the judicial branch, or the legislative branch.	Making a complaint or disclosing information concerning the possible existence of any activity constituting fraud, waste, and abuse in or relating to any state programs and operations.	Court proceeding to set aside the retaliation.
HAWAII				
Whistleblowers' Protection Act	Haw. Rev. Stat. §§ 378-61 to 378-69 (1997).	Both public and private sector employees.	Truthful reporting to a public body of a violation or suspected violation of federal, state, or local law or rule. Participation or request to participate in an investigation hearing or inquiry held by a public body or a court action.	May bring a civil action for appropriate injunctive relief, or actual damages, or both. The court may order appropriate reinstatement, back wages, full reinstatement of fringe benefits and seniority rights, plus costs and lawyer's and witness fees. Violators may be fined up to $500.
IDAHO				
Idaho Protection of Public Employees Act	Idaho Code §§ 6-2101 to 6-2109 (1997).	State employees plus employees of any political subdivision or governmental entity eligible to participate in the public employees' retirement system.	Communicating in good faith the existence of any waste of public funds, property, or manpower, or a violation or suspected violation of a law, rule, or regulation of the state, a political subdivision, or the United States. The employer must be given a reasonable opportunity to correct the waste or violation. Participates or gives information in an investigation, hearing, court proceeding, legislative or	Civil action for appropriate injunctive relief or actual damages, or both, plus reasonable court costs and lawyer's fees. A court may issue a restraining injunction, order reinstatement to the same or an equivalent position, reinstate full fringe benefits and seniority rights, compensate for lost wages, benefits, and other remuneration. Violators may be fined not more than $500.

IDAHO

Idaho Protection of Public Employees Act *(continued)*			other inquiry or form of administrative review. Objecting to or refusing to carry out a directive that the employee reasonably believes violates a federal, state, or local law, rule, or regulation.	

ILLINOIS

Whistleblower protection under the state personnel code	20 Ill. Comp. Stat. Ann. 415/19c.1 (1998).	State employees.	Disclosing information that the employee reasonably believes evidences a violation of any law, rule, or regulation; or mismanagement, a gross waste of funds, an abuse of authority, or a substantial and specific danger to public health or safety if the disclosure is not specifically prohibited by law.	Administrative remedies such as reinstatement and back pay are available under the personnel code. Final administrative decisions are subject to judicial review.
Whistle Blower Protection Act	5 Ill. Comp. Stat. Ann. 395/0.01 (1998).	Employees of constitutional officers of the state.	Disclosing information that the employee reasonably believes evidences a violation of any law, rule, or regulation or mismanagement, a gross waste of funds, abuse of authority, or a substantial and specific danger to public health or safety if the disclosure is not specifically prohibited by law.	Not specified.
Whistleblower protection for school employees	105 Ill. Comp. Stat. Ann. 5/34-2.4c (West 1998 Supp.).	Employees of the board of education or a local school council member.	Disclosing a violation of law, rule, regulation, or policy, or waste, fraud, mismanagement, abuse of authority, or a danger to the health or safety of students or the public.	Violation is a Class A misdemeanor.

State	Citation	Coverage	Protected Conduct	Remedy
Immunity under the Guardianship and Advocacy Act	20 Ill. Comp. Stat. Ann. 3955/34 (1998).	Private citizens and employees of service providers.	A person who in good faith files a complaint or provides information to the commission or any of its divisions.	Not specified.
Toxic Substances Disclosure to Employees Act	820 Ill. Comp. Stat. Ann. 255/14(b) (1998).	Employees of businesses that have twenty or more employees or five or more full-time employees in Illinois and employees of the state and its political subdivisions. Also includes prospective employees and employee representatives.	Exercising rights under the act, or making a claim, or filing any complaint or action, or testifying in any proceeding related to the act.	Violators may be ordered to cease and desist, reinstate the employee, provide back pay, plus lawyer's fees and hearing costs. Violators are also subject to fines and punitive damages.
INDIANA				
State Employees Bill of Rights	Ind. Code Ann. § 4-15-10-4 (Burns 1998).	Employees of state agencies (does not include state colleges or universities or elected officials).	Reporting in writing a violation of federal law or regulation, or a state law or rule or an ordinance of a political subdivision; or the misuse of public resources.	Violators commit a Class A infraction. The reporting employee may not be dismissed, have salary increases or benefits withheld, be transferred or reassigned, be denied a promotion, or be demoted. Employees may pursue other legal remedies under section 4-15-10-6.
Private sector whistleblower protection for public contractors	Ind. Code Ann. § 22-5-3-3 (Burns 1998).	Employees of a private employer that is under public contract.	Same as above.	Civil action. Violator commits a Class A infraction.
Whistleblower protection for local government employees	Ind. Code Ann. § 36-1-8-8 (Burns 1998).	Employees of a political subdivision.	Same as above.	May process an appeal under personnel policy or collective bargaining agreement. Violator commits a Class A infraction.

Whistleblower protection for employees of state educational institutions	Ind. Code Ann. § 20-12-8 (Burns 1998).	Employees of any university, college, or other educational institution for the purpose of providing programs of collegiate or university education or other postsecondary education that is supported in whole or in part by state funding.	Same as above.	Same as above.
Interference with health facilities investigation	Ind. Code Ann. § 16-28-9-3 (Burns 1998).	Residents or employees of health care facilities.	Contacting or providing information to any state official; or initiating, participating in, or testifying concerning a health facilities investigation.	Violator commits a Class C misdemeanor and/or civil penalty not to exceed $25,000.

IOWA

State employees' disclosure of information	Iowa Code Ann. § 70A.28 (1997).	State employees of the executive and legislative branches of government, including employees of the general assembly; and the state board of regents.	Disclosing information that evidences a violation of law or rule, mismanagement, a gross abuse of funds, an abuse of authority, or a substantial and specific danger to the public health or safety. A person in a supervisory capacity may not require an employee to inform the supervisor that the employee made a disclosure of information permitted by this section, unless the employee represented that the disclosure was the official position of the employee's immediate supervisor or employer.	May be enforced through a civil action. Violators commit a simple misdemeanor. Relief includes reinstatement, with or without back pay, or any other equitable relief the court may deem appropriate, including lawyer's fees and costs. Appropriate injunctive relief is also available.
Employees of political subdivisions protection	Iowa Code Ann. § 70A.29 (1997).	Employees of political subdivisions of the state.	Disclosing information that evidences a violation of law or rule, mismanagement, a gross abuse of funds, an abuse of authority, or a substantial and specific danger to public health or safety.	Same as above.

State	Citation	Coverage	Protected Conduct	Remedy
KANSAS				
Whistleblower protections for state employees	Kan. Stat. Ann. § 75-2973 (1997).	State agency employees.	State agency employees' communications concerning operations of the agency with members of the legislature. Reporting by agency employees of violations of state or federal law or rules and regulations. Employees are not required to give notice to supervisors or appointing authority prior to reporting, with some exceptions.	Officers or employees in the classified civil service have administrative remedies under the act, including modification or reversal of the agency action or other appropriate relief. Violators may be suspended or dismissed. Right to appeal is preserved. Officers or employees in the unclassified service may bring a civil action for appropriate injunctive relief or actual damages. The court can order reinstatement, back wages, reinstatement of fringe benefits and seniority rights, actual damages, or a combination of remedies. Also costs of litigation, including lawyer's and witness fees may be awarded.
KENTUCKY				
Public employee whistleblower protection	Ky. Rev. Stat. Ann. §§ 61.101 to 61.103 (Michie 1996).	Employees of the Commonwealth of Kentucky or any of its political subdivisions.	Good faith communicating of facts or information relative to an actual or suspected violation of any law, executive order, regulation, mandate, rule, or ordinance of the United States, the Commonwealth of Kentucky, or any of its political subdivisions, or relative to mismanagement, waste, fraud, abuse of authority, or a substantial and specific danger to public health or safety. No	Notwithstanding other administrative remedies, employees may bring a civil action for appropriate injunctive relief or punitive damages, or both.

KENTUCKY Public employee whistle-blower protection (*continued*)			prior notice can be required of such report, disclosure, or divulgence. The statute also protects any person who aids or substantiates any employee who makes public the above listed wrongdoing.	
Interference with long-term care ombudsman	Ky. Rev. Stat. Ann. § 216.541 (Michie 1996).	Employees or residents of long-term care facilities	Filing a complaint or providing information to the long-term care ombudsman.	Violators shall be fined from $100 to $500.
LOUISIANA Freedom from reprisal for disclosure of improper acts	La. Rev. Stat. Ann. § 42:1169 (West 1998 supp.).	Public employees in section A. State employees in section B.	A. Any public employees reporting a violation of the Code of Governmental Ethics or of any order, rule, or regulation issued thereunder or any other alleged acts of impropriety within any governmental entity shall be free from discipline or reprisal. B. Public employees in state government reporting information reasonably believed to be a violation of any law or any order, rule, or regulation or any other alleged acts of impropriety related to the scope and/or duties of public employment or public office within any branch of state government shall be free from discipline or reprisal.	Reinstatement of employment and lost income and benefits.

State	Citation	Coverage	Protected Conduct	Remedy
Prohibition against reprisal for reporting environmental violations	La. Rev. Stat. Ann. § 30:2027 (West 1998 supp.).	Employees of any firm, business, private or public corporation, partnership, individual employer or federal, state, or local government agency.	Disclosing or threatening to disclose an activity, policy, or practice of the employer, or another employer with whom there is a business relationship, that the employee reasonably believes is a violation of any state, federal, or local environmental statute, ordinance, or regulation or testifies or provides information to any investigation, hearing, or inquiry into a violation.	Civil action and shall recover triple damages from the employer, plus costs including lawyer's fees. The employee is also entitled to all other civil and criminal remedies available under state, federal, or local law. Damages shall include, but not be limited to, lost wages, lost anticipated wage increase, or wages from lost promotion, any property lost as a result of lost wages, lost benefits, and any physical and emotional damages resulting therefrom.
MAINE				
Whistleblowers' Protection Act	Me. Rev. Stat. Ann. tit. 26, §§ 831 to 840 (Michie 1997).	Public and private sector employees.	Good faith reporting of what the employee has reasonable cause to believe is a violation of law or rule of Maine, or its political subdivisions or the United States, or of a condition or practice that would put at risk the health or safety of that employee or any other individual. The employee is requested to participate in an investigation, hearing, or inquiry held by a public body or in a court action. Good faith refusal to carry out a directive that could expose the employee or any individual to a condition that would result in serious injury or death, after having sought and been unable to obtain a correction of the dangerous condition.	Employee may bring a complaint before the Maine Human Rights Commission for action under title 5, § 4612.

Testimony by state employees to legislative committees	Me. Rev. Stat. Ann. tit. 5, §§ 21 to 33 (1997).	State employees, meaning any employee of an agency, independent agency, or parts of agencies that receive support from the general fund or that are established, created, or incorporated by reference to the laws, except nonpartisan staff of the legislature.	Right to represent himself or herself and testify before or provide information to a legislative committee on his or her own time or to respond to a legislative inquiry.	Civil action including an action for injunctive relief. The court may order reinstatement, back wages, reinstatement of fringe benefits and seniority rights, plus costs of litigation and lawyer's and witness fees.
Public utilities employees' testimony	Me. Rev. Stat. Ann. tit. 35-A, § 1316 (1997).	Employees of public utilities licensed to do business in Maine.	Testifying or providing information in good faith to a legislative committee or the public utilities commission regarding the operation of a public utility or because the employee brought the matter to the attention of a supervisor.	Same as above.

MARYLAND

Maryland Whistleblower Law	Md. Code Ann. State Pers. & Pens. §§ 3-302 (1997).	Classified and unclassified service employees in the executive branch of state government and applicants for employment in the classified service of the executive branch of state government.	Disclosing information that the employee or applicant reasonably believes evidences an abuse of authority, gross mismanagement, or gross waste of money; a substantial and specific danger to public health or safety; or a violation of law; or seeks a remedy provided by the whistleblower law, unless disclosure is prohibited by law.	Remedial actions include removal of detrimental information from employee's personnel record; hiring, promoting, reinstating, or ending a suspension; back pay; granting leave or seniority; and action against the violator. If a hearing is held, the prevailing complaint may be awarded appropriate relief, including those listed above as well as costs and lawyer's fees.

State	Citation	Coverage	Protected Conduct	Remedy
MASSACHUSETTS				
Retaliatory action against employees	Mass. Gen. Laws Ann. Ch. 149, § 185 (1998).	Public and private sector employees.	Disclosing or threatening to disclose a policy or practice of the employer, or of another employer with whom the employee's employer has a business relationship, that the employee reasonably believes is a violation of a law, rule, or regulation or that poses a risk to public health, safety, or the environment. Providing information or testifying in relation to, or objecting to, or refusing to participate in an activity policy or practice that the employee reasonably believes is a violation of law, rule, or regulation or poses a risk to the public health, safety, or the environment.	Civil action in which all remedies available in common law tort actions shall be available, plus in addition to any legal or equitable relief the court may issue temporary restraining orders or injunctions, reinstate to the same or equivalent position, reinstate fringe benefits and seniority rights, compensate for three times the lost wages, benefits, and other remuneration and interest thereon and order costs and lawyer's fees.
MICHIGAN				
Whistleblowers Protection Act	Mich. Comp. Laws. Ann. §§ 17.428 (1) (1998).	Public and private sector employees. Employee includes a person employed by the state or a political subdivision except state classified civil service.	Truthful reporting or being about to report, a violation or suspected violation of a law, regulation, or rule of Michigan or its political subdivisions or the United States to a public body; or because the employee is requested by a public body to participate in an investigation, hearing, or inquiry held by that public body, or a court action.	Civil action for appropriate injunctive relief, or actual damages, or both, including costs, reasonable lawyer's and witness fees. Court may order reinstatement, back wages, reinstatement of fringe benefits and seniority rights. Violators are subject to a civil fine of no more than $500.

Health facility reporting	Mich. Comp. Laws. Ann. § 333.20180 (M.S.A. 14.15 [20180] (1998).	An employee or person under contract to a health facility or agency or any other person acting in good faith.	Making a report or a complaint, including but not limited to a violation of the health facility article or its regulations, or who assists in originating, investigating, or preparing a report or complaint or who assists the department in carrying out its duties.	Immunity from civil or criminal liability and is protected by the Whistleblower Protection Act, above, including its remedies.

MINNESOTA

Whistleblower statute	Minn. Stat. Ann. §§ 181.931 to .935 (West 1997).	Both public and private sector employees.	Good faith reporting of a violation or suspected violation of any federal or state law or rule to an employer or to any governmental body or law enforcement official, or the employee is requested to participate in an investigation, hearing, or inquiry, or refusal to perform an action that the employee has an objective basis in fact to believe violates any state or federal law, rule, or regulation and the employee informs the employer that the order is being refused for that reason.	Any remedies provided by law, plus a civil action to recover any and all damages recoverable at law, together with costs, disbursements, and lawyer's fees, and such injunctive and equitable relief as determined by the court.

MISSISSIPPI

No statutory whistleblower protection

State	Citation	Coverage	Protected Conduct	Remedy
MISSOURI				
An act relating to certain rights of employees	Mo. Ann. Stat. § 105.055 (West 1997).	Employees of state agencies.	Agency employees may discuss the operations of the agency with any member of the legislature or the state auditor.	Administrative remedies include modification or reversal and such relief as the board considers appropriate. Board action may be appealed pursuant to law.
			Disclosing of any alleged prohibited activity under investigation or any related activity, or information the employee reasonably believes evidences a violation of any law, rule, or regulation; or mismanagement, a gross waste of funds, or abuse of authority; or a substantial and specific danger to the public health or safety; unless disclosure is specifically prohibited by law; nor may an employee be required to give advance notice of the report with some exceptions.	
MONTANA				
Wrongful Discharge From Employment Act	Mont. Code Ann. §§ 39-2-901 to 915 (1997).	A person who works for another for hire.	Refusing to violate public policy or reporting a violation of public policy.	Lost wages and fringe benefits, not to exceed four years, with interest.
				Punitive damages otherwise allowed by law if it is established by clear and convincing evidence that the employer engaged in actual fraud or actual malice in the discharge of the employee.

NEBRASKA

State Government Effectiveness Act	Neb. Rev. Stat. §§ 81-2701 to 2710 (1997).	Employees of state agencies, departments, boards, commissions, or other governmental units but does *not* include, any court; members or employees of the legislature or legislative council; governor or staff; political subdivisions, instrumentalities formed under interstate compacts; or entities of the federal government.	Disclosing information alleging wrongdoing by an agency or employee that is a violation of any law, results in gross mismanagement or gross waste of funds; or creates a substantial and specific danger to public health or safety. Providing information or testimony pursuant to an investigation under the State Government Effectiveness Act.	The State Personnel Board may stay or reverse the action or grant back pay or other appropriate relief. Appeal is available under the Administrative Procedure Act for damages, reinstatement, back pay, and such other relief as the court may deem appropriate, and shall receive reasonable lawyer's fees.
Opposition to unlawful practice under Fair Employment Practice Act	Neb. Rev. Stat. § 48-1114 (1998).	Private sector employees.	Goes beyond protection under the employment discrimination laws as in many states, to include opposing any practice or refusing to carry out any action unlawful under federal or state law.	It is an unlawful employment practice under the Nebraska Fair Employment Practice Act, thus making available that act's remedies.

NEVADA

Disclosure of improper governmental action	Nev. Rev. Stat. Ann. §§ 281.611 to .671 (Michie 1997 Supp.).	State officer or employee.	Disclosing information concerning improper governmental action by a state officer or employee that is in violation of any state law or regulation; an abuse of authority; or a substantial and specific danger to the public health or safety; or a gross waste of public money.	A hearing officer may under Nev. Rev. Stat. Ann. § 284.390(6) set aside the action and reinstate the employee with full pay. Judicial review is available.
Protection for peace officers	Nev. Rev. Stat. Ann. §§ 289.110 to 289.120 (Michie 1997).	Peace officers but not those employed by the state.	Disclosing improper governmental action, which means any action taken by an officer or employee of a law enforcement agency, while in the performance of his official duties that is a violation of any state law or regulation.	After exhausting internal grievance procedures and administrative remedies, a court may provide appropriate injunctive or other extraordinary relief.

State	Citation	Coverage	Protected Conduct	Remedy
Testimony before legislature or committees	Nev. Rev. Stat. Ann. § 218.5343 (Michie 1997).	State agency employees, except employees in the classified service who have not completed their probationary period.	Testifying before a house or committee of the legislature on one's own behalf or retaliation in an attempt to affect the behavior of another employee who is testifying.	The statute states that such retaliatory actions are unlawful but does not specify a remedy.
Protection of communications	Nev. Rev. Stat. Ann. §§ 41.640 to 41.670 (Michie 1997).	Any person.	Good faith communication of a complaint or information to a legislator, officer, or employee of the state or a political subdivision, or to a legislator, officer, or employee of the federal government, regarding a matter reasonably of concern to the governmental entity is immune from civil liability on claims based on the communication.	Immunity. Government may provide defense to the action.
NEW HAMPSHIRE				
Whistleblowers' Protection Act	N.H. Rev. Stat. Ann. §§ 275-E:1 to 275-E:7 (Michie 1997).	Both public and private sector employees.	Good faith reporting of what the employee has reasonable cause to believe is a violation of any law or rule of this state, or a political subdivision of this state, or the United States; or participating in an investigation, hearing, or inquiry conducted by a governmental entity, including a court action, that concerns allegations that the employer has violated any law or rule of the state, political subdivision or United States. Also refusing to execute a directive that in fact violates any law or rule.	Remedies include reinstatement, back pay, fringe benefits and seniority rights, appropriate injunctive relief, or any combination of remedies.

NEW JERSEY

Conscientious Employee Protection Act	N.J. Stat. Ann. §§ 34:19-1 to 8 (West 1998 supp.).	Both public and private sector employees.	Disclosing or threatening to disclose an activity, policy, or practice of the employer, or another employer with whom there is a business relationship, that the employee reasonably believes is a violation of law, rule, or regulation. Providing information to, or testifying before, any public body conducting an investigation, hearing, or inquiry into any violation of law, rule, or regulation by the employer, or another employer with whom there is a business relationship. Objecting to, or refusing to participate in any activity, policy, or practice that the employee reasonably believes is a violation of law, rule, or regulation; is fraudulent or criminal; or is incompatible with a clear mandate of public policy concerning the public health, safety, or welfare or protection of the environment.	Civil action—all remedies available in common law tort actions, plus any legal or equitable relief provided by statute. The court may also order: a restraining injunction; reinstatement to the same or an equivalent position; reinstatement of full fringe benefits and seniority rights; compensation for lost benefits, wages, and other remuneration; reasonable costs and lawyer's fees; punitive damages; a civil fine against the violator.

NEW MEXICO

Does not provide statutory protection for whistle-blowers

State	Citation	Coverage	Protected Conduct	Remedy
NEW YORK				
Retaliatory action by public employers	N.Y. Civ. Serv. Law § 75-b (McKinney 1998 supp.).	Public employees, except judges or justices and members of the legislature.	Disclosing to a governmental body information regarding a violation of law, rule, or regulation that presents a substantial and specific danger to the public health or safety; or which the employee reasonably believes to be true and reasonably believes constitutes an improper governmental action, which means any action that is undertaken in the performance of official duties, whether or not within the scope of employment, that is a violation of state, local, or federal law, rule, or regulation.	Dismissal of the disciplinary proceeding, reinstatement with back pay, and if an arbitration procedure, other appropriate action as is permitted in the agreement. Employees not subject to arbitration or collective bargaining agreements may commence a court action under the terms and conditions of section 740 of the labor law (see below).
Retaliatory personnel action by employers; prohibition	N.Y. CLS Labor Prac. § 740 (1998).	Private sector employees.	Disclosing or threatening to disclose to a supervisor or to a public body an activity, policy, or practice of the employer that is in violation of law, rule, or regulation which violation creates and presents a substantial and specific danger to the public health or welfare. Providing information to or testifying before, any public body conducting an investigation, hearing, or inquiry into any such violation of law, rule, or regulation by the employer. Objecting to, or refusing to participate in any such activity, policy, or practice in violation of a law, rule, or regulation.	Civil action in which the court may order: a restraining injunction; reinstatement to the same or an equivalent position; reinstatement of full fringe benefits and seniority rights; lost wages, benefits, and other remuneration; and reasonable costs disbursements, and lawyer's fees. Nothing diminishes rights privileges or remedies under any other law or regulation or under a collective bargaining agreement or employment contract; except instituting an action under section 740 is deemed a waiver of rights and remedies available under any other contract, collective bargaining agreement, law, rule, or regulation, or under the common law.

NORTH CAROLINA

Whistleblower protection for state employees	N.C. Gen. Stat. §§ 126-84 to 88 (1997).	State employees.	Reporting evidence of activity by a state agency or employee constituting a violation of state or federal law, rule, or regulation; fraud; misappropriation of state resources; or substantial and specific danger to the public health and safety.	Court action for damages, an injunction, reinstatement, back wages, full reinstatement of fringe benefits and seniority rights, costs, reasonable lawyer's fees, or any combination of remedies. If the court finds the employee was injured by a willful violation, the court shall award triple actual damages plus costs and lawyer's fees.

NORTH DAKOTA

Public Employees Relations Act	N.D. Cent. Code §§ 34-11.1-01, 34-11.1-04, and 34-11.1-05 to .1-08 (1997).	Public employees but *not* persons elected to public office, members of the legislative council staff, persons holding appointive statutory office, one deputy or principal assistant and secretary for each elected or appointive statutory official, and all members of the governor's staff.	Reporting the existence of a job-related violation of state or federal law or agency rules or job-related misuse of public resources. After working hours statements, pronouncements, or other activities not otherwise prohibited by law that pertain to matters of public concern if the employee does not purport to speak or act in an official capacity.	Not specified but does not limit any other legal right or remedy.

State	Citation	Coverage	Protected Conduct	Remedy
Whistleblower protection generally	N.D. Cent. Code § 34-01-20 (1997 supp.).	Private sector employees.	Good faith reporting of a violation or suspected violation of federal or state law or rule to an employer, governmental body, or law enforcement official.	Commissioner of Labor is to use authority under sections 34-06 to 34-14 to assure compliance.
			Being requested by a public body or official to participate in an investigation, hearing, or inquiry.	
			Refusing an employer's order to perform an action that is believed to violate state or federal law, rule or regulation.	
Prohibition of retaliation for certain acts	N.D. Cent. Code § 25-01.3-05 (1997).	Employees of facilities for persons with mental disabilities or mental illness.	Reporting abuse, neglect, or exploitation of a person with developmental disabilities or mental illness.	Violator is guilty of a Class B misdemeanor.
	N.D. Cent. Code § 50-25.1-09.1 (1997 supp.).	Employees involved in child protection services or required by law to report.	Reporting child abuse or neglect.	Civil action for all damages, including exemplary damages, costs, and lawyer's fees.
	N.D. Cent. Code § 50-25.2-11 (1997).	Employees of adult protective services.	Reporting abuse or neglect of a vulnerable adult.	Civil action for all damages.
	N.D. Cent. Code § 50-10.1-05 (1997).	Employees of long-term care facilities, as well as residents or any other person.	Filing of a complaint or providing information to a long-term care ombudsman.	Not specified.
OHIO				
Whistleblower's Protection	Ohio Rev. Code Ann. §§ 4113.51 to .53 (Anderson 1996).	Both public and private sector employees.	Reporting to proper authority of a violation of state or federal law or any ordinance or regulation of a political subdivision that the employer has authority to correct, that is either a criminal offense likely to cause an imminent risk of	Civil action for appropriate injunctive relief, or the court may order reinstatement to the same or a comparable position, back wages, full reinstatement of fringe benefits and seniority rights, or any combination of these remedies. Costs, lawyer's

OHIO

Whistleblower's Protection
(continued)

physical harm to persons or a hazard to public health or safety or is a felony, that the employer does not correct within 24 hours.

Reporting criminal violations of the air pollution control, solid and hazardous wastes, safe drinking water, and water pollution control statutes to proper authorities.

Notifying the employer of a violation by a fellow employee of any state or federal statute, or ordinance or regulation of a political subdivision, or any work rule or company policy and the employee believes the violation is a criminal offense, likely to cause an imminent risk of physical harm to persons, or a hazard to public health or safety or is a felony.

fees, witness and expert fees may be awarded. Interest may be included in back pay award for a deliberate violation.

OKLAHOMA

Whistleblower protection

Okla. Stat. Ann. tit. 74, § 840-2.5 (1997 supp.).

State government employees.

Disclosing public information; reporting any violation of state or federal law, rule, or policy; mismanagement; a gross waste of public funds; an abuse of authority; or a substantial and specific danger to public health or safety. Reporting such information without giving prior notice to the employee's supervisor or anyone in the employee's chain of command. Discussing the operations and functions of the agency with the governor, members of the legislature, or others.

May appeal to the Oklahoma Merit Protection Commission for corrective action under section 840-6.6.

State	Citation	Coverage	Protected Conduct	Remedy
OREGON				
Whistleblower Law	Or. Rev. Stat. §§ 659.505 to 545; and 240.316 and 659.035(1)(b) (1997).	Employees employed by or under contract with the state, but not employees of a contractor under contract to construct a public improvement.	Discussing, in response to an official request, with the legislature the activities of the state, any agency, or political subdivision; or any person authorized to act on behalf of the state, any agency, or political subdivision. Disclosing information evidencing a violation of any federal or state law, rule, or regulation by the state, agency, or political subdivision; mismanagement, gross waste of funds or abuse of authority or substantial and specific danger to public health and safety resulting from the action of the state, agency, or political subdivision.	In addition to administrative remedies an employee may bring a civil action for appropriate injunctive relief or damages or both. If damages are awarded, the court shall award actual damages or $250, whichever is greater.
Prohibition against retaliation in health care facilities	Or. Rev. Stat. § 659.035(1)(a), (2) and (3) (1997).	Certain employees providing services or working in health care facilities.	Good faith reporting of possible violations of chapter 441 (Health Care Facilities) or ORS 443.400 to 443.455 (Residential Facilities and Homes).	Treated the same as civil rights violations under 659.121, allowing for injunctive relief and damages in a civil action. Remedies include reinstatement, back pay, costs, and lawyer's fees.
Retaliation for initiating or aiding criminal or civil proceedings	Or. Rev. Stat. § 659.550 (1997).	Any employee, both public and private sector.	In good faith: reporting criminal activity; causing a complaint's information or complaint to be filed; cooperating with any law enforcement agency conducting a criminal investigation; bringing a civil proceeding against an employer; or testifying at a civil proceeding or criminal trial.	Same as above.

Legislative testimony	Or. Rev. Stat. § 659.270 (1997).	Same as above.	Testifying before the legislative assembly or any of its interim or statutory committees, including advisory committees or subcommittee or task forces.	Same as above.
Retaliation in drug abuse and alcohol treatment	Or. Rev. Stat. § 430.755 (1997).	Any person.	Reporting suspected abuse or neglect by an alcohol or drug abuse treatment facility, community program, or person.	Private action for actual damages, and a penalty up to $1,000, notwithstanding any other remedy provided by law.
PENNSYLVANIA Whistleblower Law	43 Pa. Cons. Stat. §§ 1421 to 1428 (West 1998).	Public employees.	Making a good faith report, or being about to report to the employer or appropriate authority an instance of wrongdoing or waste. Wrongdoing is the violation of a federal or state statute or regulation, of a political subdivision ordinance or regulation, or of a code of conduct or ethics designed to protect the interests of the public or the employer. Waste is employer's conduct or omission that results in substantial abuse, misuse, destruction, or loss of funds or resources from commonwealth or political subdivision sources. An employee being requested to participate in an investigation, hearing, or inquiry by appropriate authority or in a court action.	Civil action for appropriate injunctive relief or damages or both. As deemed appropriate, the court shall order reinstatement, back wages, full reinstatement of fringe benefits and seniority rights, actual damages, or a combination of remedies. Court may award costs, lawyer's fees and witness fees.

State	Citation	Coverage	Protected Conduct	Remedy
State ethics commission protection	65 Pa. Cons. Stat. § 408(j) (1998 supp.).	Public officials and employees including employees of the state ethics commission.	Filing a complaint with or providing information to the state ethics commission or testifying in any commission proceeding. Employees of the commission providing nonsecret information about the internal operations of the commission to legislators or their staff or testifying in a legislative proceeding.	Not specified.
Public utilities employees protection	66 Pa. Cons. Stat. § 3316 (1998).	Employees of public utilities.	Employees who make or are about to make a good faith report to the employer or proper authorities on an instance of wrongdoing or waste. An employee requested to participate in an investigation hearing or inquiry by appropriate authority or in a court action relating to the public utility.	Civil action for injunctive relief or damages or both, including reinstatement, back wages, reinstatement of fringe benefits and seniority rights, actual damages, or a combination of these remedies. Costs, lawyer's fees and witness fees may be awarded.
Hazardous sites cleanups	35 Pa. Cons. Stat. § 6020.1112 (West 1998).	Both public and private sector employees.	Making or being about to make a good faith report to the employer or appropriate authority of an instance of wrongdoing under the Hazardous Sites Cleanup Act.	Same as under the Whistleblower Law.
Radioactive waste disposal	35 Pa. Cons. Stat. § 7130.509 (West 1998).	Employees of operators of low-level waste facilities, a contractor developing such a facility or developing procedures or regulations associated with the Appalachian Compact low-level nuclear waste facility.	Making a good faith report or about to report to the employer or appropriate authority an instance of wrongdoing.	Same as above.

Municipal waste	53 Pa. Cons. Stat. § 4000.1712 (West 1998).	Employees of municipal and quasi-municipal corporations.	Same as above.	Same as above.

RHODE ISLAND

Rhode Island Whistle-blowers' Protection Act	R.I. Gen. Laws §§ 28-50-1 to 28-50-9 (1997).	Both public and private sector employees.	Reporting or being about to report to a public body a violation that has occurred or is about to occur of a law, regulation, or rule of the state, a political subdivision, or the United States. Being requested to participate by a public body in an investigation, hearing, or inquiry held by that public body or in a court action.	Civil action for appropriate injunctive relief, actual damages, or both. The court shall order reinstatement, back wages, full reinstatement of fringe benefits and seniority rights, actual damages or any combination of remedies. Costs may be awarded.
Long-term care	R.I. Gen. Laws § 42-66.7-8 (1997 Supp.).	Officer or employee of a long-term care facility; guardians, family members, and residents of such facilities; and volunteers.	Communicating with the long-term care ombudsman or for information given or disclosed in good faith.	Not specified.

SOUTH CAROLINA

Whistleblower protection	S.C. Code Ann. § 8-27-10 to 8-27-50 (Law Co-op 1997 supp.).	Public employees with the exception of those listed at section 8-17-370, which excludes *among others* members and employees of the general assembly, certain employees of the office of the governor, and elected public officials, and judicial officials.	Filing a report with the appropriate authority of wrongdoing, which means action by a public body that results in substantial abuse, misuse, destruction, or loss of substantial public funds or resources. It also includes an allegation that a public employee has intentionally violated federal or state law or regulations or political subdivision ordinances or regulations or a code of ethics, not of a technical or minimal nature.	A nonjury civil action for reinstatement, lost wages, actual damages not to exceed $15,000, and reasonable lawyer's fees not to exceed $10,000 for a trial or $5,000 for an appeal. The employee must first have exhausted all grievance and administrative remedies.

State	Citation	Coverage	Protected Conduct	Remedy
SOUTH DAKOTA				
Grievance for retaliation against whistleblower	S.D. Codified Laws § 3-6A-52 (Michie 1998).	State employees or persons paid by state funds with exceptions enumerated at § 3-6A-13.	Reporting a violation of state law through the chain of command of the department or to the attorney general's office or filing a suggestion pursuant to this section.	May file a grievance with the career service commission.
TENNESSEE				
Education Truth in Reporting and Employee Protection Act of 1989	Tenn. Code Ann. §§ 49-50-1401 to 1411 (1996).	Public education employees.	Reporting or disclosing falsification of statistical data reports or information relating to operation of a local education agency or the waste or mismanagement of public education funds to the department of education or committee of the general assembly or their individual members, officials, or employees.	Civil action for appropriate injunctive relief or damages. Court shall order as appropriate: reinstatement, back wages, full reinstatement of fringe benefits and seniority rights, actual damages, or any combination of remedies, also costs of litigation and lawyer's fees.
Refusal to participate in illegal activities	Tenn. Code Ann. § 50-1-304 (1998).	Employees covered by title 50.	Refusing to participate in, or refusing to remain silent about, illegal activities, which means violation of the criminal or civil code of this state or the United States or any regulation intended to protect the public health, safety, or welfare.	Cause of action for retaliatory discharge and any other damages to which the employer may be entitled.
Mental health, mental retardation, or alcohol and drug services facilities	Tenn. Code Ann. § 33-2-512 (1998).	Any person making a report or investigation.	Making a report of abuse, dereliction, or deficiency in the operation of a licensed facility.	Immunity for liability. Civil action for appropriate compensatory and punitive damages.
Juvenile abuse report	Tenn. Code Ann. § 37-1-410 (1996).	Any person reporting under section 37-1-403.	Reporting of brutality, abuse, neglect, or sexual abuse of children.	Same as above.

Tennessee Adult Protection Act	Tenn. Code Ann. § 71-6-105 (1998).	Any person making a report or investigation.	Reporting abuse, neglect, or exploitation of certain vulnerable adults.	Same as above.
TEXAS				
Protection for reporting violations of law	Tex. Gov't Code Ann. §§ 554.001 to 554.009 (West 1998 supp.).	Public employees.	Good faith reporting of a violation of a state or federal statute, an ordinance of a local governmental entity, or a rule adopted under statute or ordinance by the employing governmental entity or another public employee to an appropriate law enforcement authority.	May sue for: injunctive relief, actual damages, court costs, and reasonable lawyer's fees. Employee is also entitled to reinstatement to the former or an equivalent position; lost wages; and reinstatement of fringe benefits and seniority rights. Monetary limits are placed on certain types of damages by § 554.003(c). Violator is subject to a civil penalty not to exceed $15,000.
UTAH				
Utah Protection of Public Employees Act	Utah Code Ann. §§ 67-21-1 to 67-21-9 (1998).	Public employees.	Communicating in good faith the existence of any waste of public funds, property, or manpower, or a violation or suspected violation of a law, rule, or regulation of the state, a political subdivision of the state, or any recognized entity of the United States. Participation or giving information in an investigation, hearing, court proceeding, legislative or other inquiry, or other form of administrative review held by a public body. Objecting to or refusing to carry out a directive that is reasonably believed to violate a law or regulation of the state, a political subdivision of the state, or the United States.	Civil action for injunctive relief or actual damages, or both, including court costs and lawyer's fees. Court may order reinstatement at the same level, back wages, full reinstatement of fringe benefits and seniority rights, actual damages, or a combination of remedies. Witness fees may also be available.

State	Citation	Coverage	Protected Conduct	Remedy
VERMONT Does *not* provide specific statutory protection for whistleblowers				
VIRGINIA While Virginia does *not* have a general whistleblower protection statute, it does provide protection in two specific areas.				
Child abuse or neglect	Va. Code Ann. § 63.1-198.03:1 (Michie 1998 supp.).	Any person.	Good faith reporting of child abuse or neglect pursuant to requirements of section 63.1-248.2 et seq., which mandates reporting by certain professionals and staff persons and also provides for a child abuse hotline.	Immunity is provided by section 63.1-248.5.
Nursing facilities	Va. Code Ann. §§ 32.1-138.4 and .5 (Michie 1998 supp.).	Any person.	Good faith complaint or providing information or cooperating with agencies responsible for protecting the rights of patients of nursing home facilities or for asserting any right protected by state or federal law.	Not specified.
WASHINGTON Disclosure of improper governmental action	Wash. Rev. Code Ann. §§ 42.40.010 to 42.40.050 (1996 supp.) and § 49.60.210(2) (Michie 1997).	State employees.	Disclosing to the auditor information concerning improper governmental action, or for identifying rules warranting review or providing information to the rules review committee. Improper governmen-	Remedies are provided under chapter 49.60, which deals with discrimination and the Human Rights Commission.

WASHINGTON

Disclosure of improper governmental action (*continued*)

			tal action is that which is undertaken in the performance of the employee's official duties, whether or not the action is within the scope of the employee's employment, and is a violation of any state law or rule, is an abuse of authority, is a substantial and specific danger to the public health or safety, or is a gross waste of public funds.	
Local government whistle-blower protection	Wash. Rev. Code Ann. §§ 42.41.010 to 42.41.902 (Michie 1997).	Local government employees, specifically including cities, counties, school districts, and special purpose districts.	Reporting information concerning improper governmental action (see above).	Administrative law judge may grant reinstatement, with or without back pay; injunctive relief to return the employee to the position held before the retaliatory action and to prevent reoccurrence, also costs and lawyer's fees. Final decisions are subject to judicial review.
Health care providers	Wash. Rev. Code Ann. § 43.70.075 (Michie 1997).	Whistleblowers—a consumer, employee, or health care professional.	Protects identity of a whistleblower who complains, in good faith, to the Department of Health about improper quality of care by a health care provider or in a health care facility.	Chapter 49.60 remedies of an employee.

State	Citation	Coverage	Protected Conduct	Remedy
WEST VIRGINIA				
Whistle-Blower Law	W. Va. Code §§ 6C-1-1 to 6C-1-8 (1998).	Public employees.	Making a good faith report to the employer or appropriate authority of an instance of wrongdoing or waste. Being requested or subpoenaed by an appropriate authority to participate in an investigation, hearing, or inquiry held by an appropriate authority or in a court action. Wrongdoing is a violation of a federal or state statute or regulation, of a political subdivision ordinance or regulation, or of a code of conduct or ethics designed to protect the interest of the public or the employer.	Civil action for injunctive relief or damages or both. Court shall order as appropriate reinstatement, back wages, full reinstatement of fringe and seniority rights, actual damages, or any combination of remedies, plus costs and lawyer's and witness fees.
WISCONSIN				
Employee Protection	Wis. Stat. Ann. §§ 230.80 to 230.89 (1997).	Public employees except persons employed by the office of the governor, the courts, the legislature, service agencies under subchapter IV of chapter 13, and certain persons and their immediate supervisors assigned to an executive salary group.	Disclosing information that the employee reasonably believes demonstrates a violation of any state or federal law, rule, or regulation or mismanagement or abuse of authority in state or local government, a substantial waste of public funds, or a danger to public health and safety.	The commission may order reinstatement with or without back pay; transfer to an available position; expungement of adverse material from the personnel file; and reasonable lawyer's fees. The commission may also make interlocutory orders. Judicial review is available.

Patients' rights	Wis. Stat. Ann. § 51.61(5)(b)9 and (d) (1997).	Any person, patient or employee.	Contacting or providing information to any official or an employee of any state protection and advocacy agency, or for initiating, participating in, or testifying in a grievance procedure or in an action for a remedy.	Action to recover damages as well as exemplary damages of not less than $500 but not more than $1,000, plus costs and lawyer's fees.

WYOMING

State Government Fraud Reduction Act	Wyo. Stat. Ann. §§ 9-11-101 to 9-11-104 (1997).	State employees, excluding independent contractors and some part-time employees.	Acting in good faith within the scope of employment reports: a demonstration of fraud, waste, or gross mismanagement in state government office; a violation of law, regulation, code, or rule of this state or the United States; a condition or practice that would put at risk the health or safety of that employee or any other individual; or participates or is requested to participate in any investigation, hearing, or inquiry concerning the above; or refuses to carry out a directive beyond the scope of employment that would expose anyone to a condition likely to result in serious injury or death after having sought and been unable to obtain a correction of the condition from the employer.	After exhausting all administrative remedies, may bring a civil action. Recovery is limited to reinstatement of the previous job, back wages, and reestablishment of employee benefits, plus costs and lawyer's fees.
Health care facilities and services	Wyo. Stat. Ann. § 35-2-910(b) (Michie 1997).	Residents, patients or employees of health care facilities.	Reporting a violation of any state or federal law, rule, or regulation.	Not specified.

CHAPTER ❦ 9

Gift Giving in the Public Sector*

Richard Rifkin

When, if at all, is it appropriate for public officials to accept anything of any value from someone who may be seeking access to the official? This chapter offers some practical advice on how to analyze gift giving in the public sector.

What Is the Right Rule?

There is a temptation to begin and end a discussion of gifts to public employees by saying that those in the private sector should never offer or give any gift to any public employee, nor should public employees, on their part, ever solicit or accept any gift. This "not even a cup of coffee" rule is, in fact, imposed by some governmental agencies, often those engaged in law enforcement. It has the advantage of being clear, and it is uncompromising in terms of maintaining government integrity.

However, for most public employees, the rule is not, and generally cannot, be this simple. Such an absolute rule has the significant disadvantage of being utterly impractical in our society and, in large part, unenforceable. As a result, the standards for differentiating between acceptable and unacceptable gifts have become quite complex. Unfortunately, simple solutions do not work when they are applied to day-to-day affairs.

To analyze gift giving in the public context, it is critical that we understand why gifts are harmful in terms of government ethics. Without doubt, public employees should be prohibited from accepting a gift in return for a favor to the donor, but we do not need our modern ethics laws to bar gifts of this nature. They have long been prohibited by criminal bribery statutes.

Today's ethics laws generally restrict the giving or accepting of gifts even where there is no clearly defined quid pro quo. This often leads to a misun-

---

* Nothing in this chapter is meant to reflect the view of the New York State Ethics Commission or the New York State Department of Law.

derstanding of why it is wrong for a public employee to accept a gift. An often-heard phrase is that a public employee cannot be bought by a drink or a dinner. A Connecticut legislator was recently quoted as saying that when lobbyists take him to dinner, they "don't even talk that much about business."

Yet, the entertaining of public officials and employees is extensive, especially on the part of vendors and lobbyists.[1] Those on the public payroll are often invited to dinners, receptions, golf outings, sporting events, theater, and conventions held in glamorous locations. Clearly, those entities in the private sector that spend money in this manner must expect a return on their investment.

Developing a Relationship through Gifts

For the vendor, lobbyist, or other person doing business with a government official, these gifts offer the opportunity to spend time in a social setting with the official. Developing a relationship is part of the art of a lobbyist or salesperson, even when there is no pending business. Gift-giving, usually in the form of entertainment, is an effective means of carrying out this important function. When it comes time for the official to act, whether it involves legislation, rulemaking, a contract award, or any other decision-making function, the private sector representative will be calling on "an old friend." Even if the government official acts "on the merits," there is an uneraseable public perception that he or she was influenced by the earlier gift. The integrity of the official's action becomes open to question. Thus, the gift and the later official action become intertwined.

In addition to the problem of public perception, there is a real advantage gained by the private sector individual who has previously entertained or given a gift to a public official. He or she has gained access that may not be available to other interested private parties. Human nature comes into play. It is difficult, if not impossible, for a public official, including one of complete honesty and integrity, to deny a request for a meeting or to refuse to take a telephone call from someone with whom he or she has spent time on a social basis or from whom a gift was received. Thus, the gift giver has an opportunity to argue his or her case where others may not have a similar chance.

Why Not a Total Bar?

The reader may ask, if gift-giving and entertaining so distort governmental decision making, why should they not be totally prohibited? An example illustrates the difficulty. As often occurs, a government official may be invited to participate in a conference concerning a subject in which he or she is considered an expert. Many such conferences are sponsored by private sector organizations. If an all-day conference includes lunch for all participants, is the government official expected to leave the room when it is served and eat alone in the nearest coffee shop? Such a mandate seems absurd. Yet, an absolute prohibition on all gifts would appear to require such a result. It would similarly require an officer or employee to reject any award where a plaque is given or to refuse to accept even token gifts or coffee set out for attendees at a meeting in the offices of a private sector entity.

If absurdities are to be avoided, absolutes must be avoided. However, if all gifts are not prohibited, the complex question necessarily arises of which gifts should be permitted and which should be barred. While states and many localities have specific laws in an attempt to define where the line should be drawn, they are all based on the same approach.

On the assumption that every gift, no matter how insignificant, has some potential to influence public employees, the challenge for legislators and ethics bodies is to distinguish those where the potential is sufficiently significant so as to prohibit them. This is where judgment is demanding and difficult.

How to Distinguish among Gifts

Monetary value has the distinction of offering the clearest division between valid and invalid gifts. On the fair assumption that gifts of a lesser amount are less corrupting than gifts of a larger amount, many states and localities have prohibited gifts over a certain amount. Other states impose conditions on larger gifts or require the reporting of such gifts.[2] The logic of this approach is easily understood by the public, it is easy to administer, and it is clear to potential givers and recipients. These are all important in terms of ethics laws. However, monetary value alone does not offer protection against abuses. All too often, the circumstances under which a gift is given are crucial, and here the distinctions are not so simple.

In some situations, gifts of even small amounts are problematical from an ethics perspective. For example, even if all gifts over $100 were prohibited, it would be hard to argue that it is acceptable for the representative of a potential contractor to treat an agency decision maker to a $35 lunch while the agency is in the process of letting a contract for a project. Similarly, it would be inappropriate for one of the parties to an administrative hearing that lasts all day to take the hearing officer to lunch, even if it were just a hamburger and coffee at the nearest fast-food establishment. Numerous other examples could be cited. They demonstrate that monetary strictures alone do not guarantee the maintenance of appropriate ethical standards.

From this analysis, the difficulties facing governmental ethics bodies can be understood. If the appropriateness of a gift depends upon the circumstances at the time it is given, such bodies are faced with attempting to define each of those circumstances, which is an impossible task. The best that can be accomplished is to offer general guidance and then to apply the guidelines on a case-by-case basis. For those in the private sector wishing to offer a gift and those in the public sector who are recipients of any offer, seeking advice becomes critical to avoid running afoul of the law. For ethics bodies, this means trying to develop guidelines that will, as well as possible, aid members of the public in understanding their obligations.

Guidelines

In general, guidelines should be based on the risk of undue influence that may arise as a result of a gift. Certainly, a gift from a private entity that does business or has contracts with an official's agency, or is regulated by the agency or regularly lobbies the agency, is of far greater concern than a gift from an entity that has little or no relationship with the agency. In recognition of this concept, many states and localities treat gifts from entities with connections to an official's agency, or to the government for which the official works, differently from gifts from other entities. Here, the "source" of the gift is critical, and gifts from a source dealing with the official's agency or government are sometimes barred or more restricted than gifts from other sources.[3]

Guidelines on gifts may also look beyond the source to the setting. There is a significant difference between a one-on-one meal with a government official, where there is the opportunity for shared, lengthy, private time between two individuals, and the meal mentioned earlier where an official participating in a conference accepts a lunch received by all participants in a large setting. While the latter clearly does not raise the problems presented by the former, that could change if the conference sponsor also pays for the official's transportation and lodging, and the conference is held in the setting of a first-class resort.

Another factor often relevant to the validity of a gift is its motive. Although this is obviously subjective, it must be determined in any specific situation by objective facts. Where two individuals, one of whom is a government official, have both a personal and a business relationship, the question that will arise is whether a gift is given for personal or business reasons. A government ethics body will look at what motivated the gift. Was there an occasion, such as a wedding, when gifts are customary? Did the individual offering the gift pay for it with his or her own funds, or was it paid for by the firm or company for which the individual works? Even if personal, was it charged as a business expense or deducted as such an expense?[4] These factors, taken together, determine motive.

Conclusion

All of this brings us back to where we began—the issues surrounding the ethical aspects of gifts to government officials are complex and not easily resolved. That is why most states and many localities have established entities to guide those affected. However, the risk to government employees, and especially to private sector individuals, is that they will not recognize when advice is needed. This is not because of any lack of integrity on the part of either, or their blindness to principles of ethical behavior; rather, it because of the nature of gift giving in our society. In the private sector, travel and entertainment is, in many cases, an important part of life. Salespersons are expected to entertain customers and potential customers. Professional firms often entertain clients. Golf outings, as well as attendance at major sporting events and theater, are everyday occurrences. It is part of our culture.

When dealing with government and government officials, much of this way of life leads to ethical problems. It is sometimes difficult for individuals to understand how significantly different are the considerations with regard to gift-giving and entertainment in public sector situations. But these considerations must be understood! In short, the rules are different, and the consequences of not understanding the rules may be serious.

It is the responsibility of government to define the rules as well as it can and to make advice as available as possible. It is the responsibility of individuals in the private sector who deal with government, as well as government officials, to make every effort to understand the rules. All of this may seem obvious, but experience has shown that there remains a serious lack of understanding of the restrictions on gift-giving in the public sector.

Notes

1. A review of the restrictions among the states on gift giving demonstrates that there is special concern with respect to vendors and lobbyists. Some states specifically prohibit gift giving entirely by those seeking state contracts or lobbying state agencies, while others place tight restrictions on such gifts. Gifts from vendors are addressed in Arkansas (Policy Memo #4, Department of Finance and Administration, Office of State Purchasing); Florida (FLA. STAT. §§112.3148(2)(e), 112.3148(4)); Idaho (IDAHO CODE §18-1356(2)); Nebraska (NEB. REV. STAT. §81-161.05); North Carolina (N. C. GEN. STAT. §133-32(a)); Tennessee (TENN. CODE ANN. §12-3-106); Texas (TEX. CODE ANN. §36-01(5)); Utah (UTAH CODE ANN. §§63-56-72,73); Virginia (VA. CODE ANN. §7.11-75); Washington (WASH. REV. CODE §43.19.1937). Gifts from lobbyists are specifically addressed in California (CAL. GOV'T CODE §86203); Massachusetts (Acts of 1994, Ch. 43, 292); Nebraska (NEB. REV. STAT. §§49-149-1(1) and (2)).

2. States with laws based on monetary standards include Alaska (ALASKA STAT. §36.52.130(b)); California (CAL. GOV'T CODE §89505(a)); Colorado (Col. Administration Procurement Code of Ethics #6); Connecticut (State Ethics Comm., Regs. 1-81-20(b) and (c)); Delaware (DEL. CODE ANN. §§5812)(a), 5813)(a)(4)(e)); Florida (FLA. STAT. §§112.3148(4) and (5); Hawaii (Haw. Rev. Stat. §84-11.5); Illinois (5ILCS 420/4A101, 102); Indiana (40 IND. ADMIN. CODE 2-1-6(9a), (b), 2-1-4(K); Kansas (KAN. STAT. ANN. §46-237(a) and (b)); Maine (ME. REV. STAT. ANN., tit 2 § 6); Massachusetts (4 MASS. APP. 584, interpreting "substantial value" of Mass. Gen. L. 268A: 3 (a), (b) to mean $50); New York (N.Y. PUB. OFF. LAW §73(5)); Oregon (OR. REV. STAT. §§244-040(2) and (5)); Pennsylvania (65 P.S. §405 (b)).

3. Such a source is sometimes called a disqualified service. States that bar or restrict gifts from such a source include Alabama (ALA. CODE §36-25-12) Connecticut (State Ethics Commission Reg. 1-81-20 (b) and (c); Indiana (40 IND. ADMIN. CODE 21-1-4(K)); Iowa (IOWA CODE ANN. 68B.22); Kansas (KAN. STAT. ANN. §46-237(c)); Louisiana (R.S. 1950 Tit 42, Ch. 15 §1115); Maryland (MD. CODE ANN. Art 40A §3-106(a)); New York (State Ethics Commission Advisory Opinion No. 94-16); Oklahoma (Rules of the Ethics Commission §257:20-1-9(b)); Oregon (OR. REV. STAT. §§244.040(2) and (5)); West Virginia (W. VA. CODE §6B-2-5(6)(1)).

4. See, for example, New York State Ethics Commission Advisory Opinion 94-16.

CHAPTER ❦ 10

Conflicts of Interest

Hugh B. Weinberg*

This chapter highlights the issue of outside activities that may cause a conflict of interest for government lawyers. For purposes of discussion, the author has chosen to focus on provisions in the law affecting New York City, as an example of how one jurisdiction addresses these issues.

Introduction

Lawyers who work in the public sector, like anyone else, sometimes find themselves considering or looking for a second job in the private sector. Such outside employment might involve going to work part-time for a private law firm or company, or it might involve engaging, on a part-time basis, in the private practice of law as a solo practitioner. The motivation for pursuing outside employment might be economic, or it might be caused by a desire to pursue other areas of interest. Whatever the motivation, government lawyers may, in most cases, pursue outside legal work, though they are of course required to act in accordance with the relevant provisions of the applicable government ethics laws.[1]

Ethics laws are not intended to restrict the lives of government lawyers to such an extent that government employment becomes an onerous or undesireable experience. Rather, those laws are essentially codes of conduct that, if followed, are designed to "preserve the trust placed in the public servants of the [government], to promote public confidence in government, to protect the integrity of government decision–making and to enhance government."[2] This principle is particularly important for government lawyers, who have fiduciary relationships with the officials and agencies that are their clients.[3]

Some people might feel that government ethics laws are either unnecessary or unenforceable and, at the very least, make public sector employees'

---

* The views in this chapter do not necessarily reflect those of the author's current or previous employers.

245

246   CONFLICTS OF INTEREST

lives difficult. However, these rules are not hard to understand or obey. The purpose of this chapter is to discuss in general the kind of ethics laws that apply to government lawyers' outside activities. In order to provide a point of reference for this discussion, this chapter will focus primarily on chapter 68 ("Conflicts of Interest") of the New York City Charter, section 2600 et seq., and on various opinions issued by the New York City Conflicts of Interest Board pursuant to that law. Other chapters in this book refer to ethics laws of various other municipalities and states, which contain provisions that are analogous to those discussed here.

The scope of chapter 68 encompasses and is intended to address a broad range of government employees' outside activities. In the case of government lawyers, these would include having part-time positions with law firms or private companies, working for certain clients, and representing private clients before the government or on matters involving the government. Also, while chapter 68 does not specifically deal with lobbying activities, government lawyers who seek to act as lobbyists on behalf of nongovernmental entities are subject to these provisions.

Prohibited Interests

In New York City, government lawyers who are considering working for particular firms or taking on particular clients must first ascertain whether these firms or clients engage in business dealings with the city. In other cities or states, the relevant inquiry might be limited to whether the prospective firms or clients have business dealings with the government agency served by the government employee who seeks to work for them. "Business dealings with the city" are defined broadly in chapter 68 to include any transaction with the city involving the sale, purchase, rental, disposition, or exchange of any goods, services, or property, any license, permit, grant, or benefit, and any performance of or *litigation with respect to any of the foregoing*.[4] Note that only certain kinds of litigation on behalf of or against the city would fall under this definition and be considered "business dealings" with the city. Other jurisdictions' laws might classify a broader range of litigation activities involving the government as "business dealings."

Thus, in addition to the more conventional meanings of "business dealings," many ethics laws also incorporate litigation against or otherwise involving the government or a particular governmental body as "business dealings." For example, a lawyer who represents a contractor in his lawsuit against the city to obtain payment for services rendered would be deemed to have business dealings with the city. If, however, the lawyer is suing the city for a personal injury that was sustained on city-owned property, such litigation would probably not be considered a business dealing.

Specifically excluded from the definition of business dealings in New York City are transactions involving a city employee's residence or any ministerial matter.[5] As to the first exception, this would mean that a government lawyer could own a cooperative or condominium apartment, and sometimes serve on its board of directors, notwithstanding that it might be engaged in various business dealings with the government (for example, obtaining building permits or dealing with housing violations). Also excluded are ministerial matters, which are administratie acts, including the issuance of licenses, permits, or other permission by the city, which are carried out in a prescribed manner and which do not involve substantial personal discretion.[6]

In New York City, whether an outside employer or client has business dealings with the city is often *the* threshold question in looking at the propriety of such outside employment.[7] In other jurisdictions, the relevant question might be more limited and only ask whether the private employer or client has business dealings with the government agency served by the government lawyer, as opposed to *any* agency of the government. This information is important because in New York City employees are prohibited from having positions with or ownership interests in firms that are engaged in business dealings with *any* city agency.[8] Likewise, city employees, including part-time city employees (such as members of boards or commissions), may not work for or have ownership interests in firms that have business dealings with their own agencies.[9] Because these prohibitions are so broad, city employees may, under some circumstances, obtain waivers or orders from the Conflicts of Interest Board, which would allow them to hold these otherwise prohibited positions or ownership interests. Waivers and orders are discussed below.

Prohibited Conduct Generally

Generally, if a New York City government lawyer's outside employer or client does not engage in business dealings with the city (or, as mentioned above, with his or her own city agency), then most of the time that employment is permissible under the city's ethics laws, provided that this employee follows some simple rules. Some of these rules are so self-evident that they are essentially axiomatic to most public servants. For example, city employees may not work for any private employers or on any noncity business at times when they are required to perform services for the city.[10] While this is a basic principle contained in most ethics laws, there would appear to be a basic incompatibility between engaging in most aspects of a private law practice and pursuing a full-time public service job. This is particularly true where a lawyer's private activities involve, for example, appearing in court or conducting a real estate closing, both of which activities occur during conventional work hours; however, other activities, such as doing legal research and writing briefs, can be done anytime. The Conflicts of Interest Board has not taken a strict position on the hours a city lawyer may spend on his outside law practice, though common sense should, of course, be used when considering how many hours to spend on outside employment.[11]

New York City employees and officials (and most other government employees) are also prohibited from using or attempting to use their official

248   CONFLICTS OF INTEREST

positions to obtain any financial gain, contract, license, privilege, or other private or personal advantage, direct or indirect, for the city employee or for any person or firm associated with the city employee.[12] This means, among other things, that city employees may not use their city positions or titles to obtain private advantages, including business advantages for themselves or their firms. Furthermore, they may not use office equipment such as computers and copiers, or other city resources, to conduct private business or for other noncity purposes. Pursuant to the relevant charter sections, the Conflicts of Interest Board has conducted investigations or enforcement proceedings against individuals who have, for example, used city computers or other city equipment to conduct their private businesses. Moreover, under these provisions, the Conflicts of Interest Board has charged individuals with violations of chapter 68 for having used stationery bearing the official city letterhead for anything other than a city purpose.

An example of how the Conflicts of Interest Board has applied the "use of position for private advantage" provisions is contained in the board's Advisory Opinion No. 92-33, in which a city employee who was charged with the enforcement of certain criminal laws was advised that he could not, in the course of his private law practice, represent defendants who had been charged with criminal offenses in the criminal court system within the city because, among other things, the city employee, as an investigator, arresting officer, or witness, "would become known to judges and prosecutors, and would be in a position to use his contacts and knowledge of the criminal justice system, obtained through public service, in order to secure more favorable treatment for the defendants that he represents. At the very least, the degree of familiarity with court and law enforcement personnel, along with the practices of police and public prosecutors, creates the perception of capitalizing on an official position in order to secure more favorable treatment for clients. Such a perception would be unacceptable under New York City Charter section 2604(b)(3)."

A variation on the above scenario might involve a government lawyer's intentional, and thus more blatant, attempt to help his or her firm or client. For example, a government lawyer could, on behalf of a private client, attempt to persuade a government colleague that a case involving the client should be settled at terms favorable to the client (and therefore at terms less favorable to the government).

The situation from the advisory opinion presented a problem under New York City Charter section 2604(b)(3) because it created an appearance that the government lawyer was in a position to use his status as a public servant in a law enforcement–related job to help his private clients; however, in the second situation, a government employee would be seen as deliberately attempting to help an individual with whom the employee had a financial relationship. Both situations are typical of the kind of cases that arise under New York City Charter Section 2604(b)(3) and similar ethics provisions contained in other laws.[13]

The "appearance of impropriety" can sometimes be problematic for government ethics agencies that are trying to preserve the integrity of government functions and the decision-making process while simultaneously attempting to provide clear and comprehensible guidance for those employees who are affected by government ethics rules. That is, an "appearance" can be a nebulous or highly subjective thing, sometimes existing only as the result of public perception (and in some cases, misperception). One hypothetical situation that could give rise to appearance problems would be where a government lawyer who regularly defends the government in civil rights lawsuits also serves as a member of the local bar association's civil rights committee, which occasionally submits amicus curiae briefs in support of plaintiffs in civil rights actions against the government. In such cases, under New York City's ethics law, it might be permissible for the government employee to continue serving on the committee, but he or she would probably be required to completely recuse himself or herself, both as a government employee and as a committee member, from any involvement whatsoever in the civil rights action and related matters.[14] However, recusal does not always suffice as a means to prevent the possible appearance problem. For example, if the government lawyer served as the head of the unit that defended all civil rights actions against the government, and he or she had final sign-off authority on all major litigation decisions, then recusal might not be feasible. In such a situation, the government lawyer might have to resign altogether from the committee.[15]

Another rule that is part of New York City's conflicts of interest law and that is as basic as those discussed above provides that no city official or employee shall disclose any confidential information concerning the property, affairs, or government of the city that has been obtained as the result of his or her official duties and that was not otherwise available to the public, or use any such information to advance any direct or indirect financial or other private interest of the city official or employee or of any person or firm with which he or she is associated.[16] New York City's law provides, however, that this confidentiality rule does not prohibit any city official or employee from disclosing any information that he or she knows or reasonably believes to involve waste, inefficiency, corruption, criminal activity, or conflict of interest. Such "whistleblower" exceptions are not uncommon in government ethics laws. Such provisions ensure, among other things, that a government employee is free to disclose government wrongdoing, when he or she becomes aware of it. At the same time, however, government lawyers have to be careful not to betray the attorney-client privilege.

The foregoing principles should be obvious to anyone who has ever worked in government. Any government employee is expected to abide by these kinds of rules concerning outside employment. Government lawyers are held to a higher standard of care, because, while the government bodies that they serve are their putative clients, these lawyers also have a fiduciary duty to the public, whom they ultimately serve. Government lawyers are, after all,

250   CONFLICTS OF INTEREST

public servants. Thus, the principles discussed above, and the rules discussed below concerning *who* a government lawyer may work for or represent are necessarily broad in order to assure that government lawyers act in the best interests of their government employers *and* the public.

Waivers and Orders Allowing Otherwise-Prohibited Interests

In addition to the basic restrictions that apply to *all* nongovernment activities engaged in by government employees, there is the additional condition, discussed above, that a private employer or client may not have business dealings with the government. Again, in some jurisdictions, that restriction might be limited to the government employee's own agency, rather than being a government-wide ban.[17] The purpose of such a restriction is to protect against the possibility that a government employee's private judgment could affect the performance of his or her official duties.

The kind of government-wide ban described above might, at first blush, seem overbroad, particularly in New York City, which has dozens of separate agencies, many of which never interact. However, the kinds of concerns implicated by these provisions can arise in particular factual situations. If, for example, a government lawyer works for the central law department of a state or city government, working primarily on environmental matters, and he or she also works part-time for a private firm that is involved in nonenvironmental commercial matters concerning the government, the lawyer could still be in a position to obtain special treatment for his or her private clients. Because of circumstances such as these, it is better to have certain broad-based prohibitions; however, at the same time, precisely because the prohibition is so broad, it is important for any government body charged with the enforcement of ethics rules to have the power to waive certain prohibitions.

Such a waiver power is essential for an ethics board to be able to permit certain conduct that, while ordinarily prohibited by the law, should be permitted because it does not create any actual conflicts or, more importantly, because the conduct actually furthers the purposes and interests of the government.

The New York City Conflicts of Interest Board has the power to grant orders and waivers allowing city employees to retain ownership interests in or positions with firms that do business with the city. For example, a newly appointed government lawyer who is an equity partner in a private law firm that does business with the city would be required to either divest the interest or disclose this interest to the Conflicts of Interest Board and comply with its order. When such an interest is disclosed, the board issues an order as to whether or not such interest, if retained, would conflict with the proper discharge of the city employee's duties. In making such a determination, the board takes into account, among other things, the nature of the government employee's official duties, the manner in which the private interests may be affected by any action of the city, and the appearance of conflict to the public.

If the board determines that a conflict exists, the board's order may require divestiture or such other action as it deems appropriate, such as recusal from certain matters that may mitigate such a conflict, taking into account the financial impact of any decision on the government employee.[18] Thus, for example, if a government lawyer's official duties involve the prosecution of criminal cases, and his or her private firm handles a large volume of criminal cases in the same jurisdiction, then an order requiring divestiture would probably be issued, both because of the nature of the individual's official duties and because of the likelihood of the appearance of a conflict to the public.[19] Under the New York City rule, a government lawyer who handles his or her agency's disciplinary cases would probably not be allowed to start up a new firm to represent other government employees before the city, even if the lawyer's agency was not involved in those matters. Again, there would be an appearance of a conflict because a reasonable person could assume that this individual was using his or her government position to, among other things, drum up business or gain access to confidential information.

Under New York City law, the ownership interest of a government employee's spouse or unemancipated child is imputed to the government employee.[20] Thus, if a government employee's spouse has an equity interest in a law firm, it would be a conflict of interest for the government employee if the law firm engages in business dealings with the city, unless the government employee has obtained an order from the Conflicts of Interest Board, as described above.

The Conflicts of Interest Board examines city employees' requests for guidance in matters affecting their spouses' interests, as it examines all requests for advice, on a case-by-case basis, in light of the particular facts of each case. Thus, in one advisory opinion, the board addressed two requests that asked whether it would violate the conflicts of interest law if a city agency were to award a contract to perform services to a law firm with which their spouses were associated.[21] In one case, the board concluded that the city employee's spouse could not be awarded the contract because the city employee was in a managerial position and in regular contact with those city employees who would be involved in both the contractor selection process and, later, the ongoing supervision of the contract. Thus, the city employee in the first case could not be sufficiently isolated, through recusal or other means, from either the award of the contract or the performance of the contract. In the second case, however, the city employee was separated from both the award of the contract and its ongoing supervision, because the division of the agency where the city employee worked was not involved in the administration of contracts.[22]

New York City's conflicts of interest law distinguishes between prohibited ownership interests in and prohibited positions with firms that do business with the city.[23] To allow the retention of otherwise prohibited ownership interests, the Conflicts of Interest Board issues orders, which are described above. To allow a city employee to hold an otherwise prohibited position, the board issues waivers. Such waivers are granted by the board when it determines that

252   CONFLICTS OF INTEREST

the holding of the proposed position would not conflict with the purposes and interests of the city. As a prerequisite to obtaining a waiver, a city employee must obtain the written approval of the head of his or her city agency (not merely his or her supervisor) and submit it to the board, which usually, though not always, defers to the agency head's judgment, provided that the approval is something more than a rubber stamp approval.[24]

In determining whether to grant a waiver, the Conflicts of Interest Board considers, among other things, the hours and compensation involved in performing outside work and whether there is any possible relationship between a city employee's official duties and his or her outside activities. For example, if a government lawyer wanted to work part-time for a private law firm that contracted with the city, the board would look at this situation to determine whether, in the course of performing his or her official duties, the employee had any dealings with the firm, and whether, in his or her work for the firm, the employee would be expected to have any personal dealings with the city. If there were business dealings between the city employee's firm and his or her own agency, the board would scrutinize this situation more carefully and might still grant a waiver, but only on the condition that the city employee recuse himself or herself, both as a city employee and as an employee of the firm, from any such dealings.

Sometimes the board, in granting a waiver, imposes certain conditions. For example, as mentioned above, the board might require the city employee to refrain from working on any of the private firm's matters that involve the city and, at the same time, agree to not work on any matter affecting the private firm that might come before the city employee in his or her official capacity. Again, the purpose of many of the restrictions contained in ethics laws is not to prevent government employees from engaging in outside employment and earning additional income; rather these rules are intended to protect against the abuse of government and its trappings and to help the public employee avoid the appearance of divided loyalties.

In one of its advisory opinions, the Conflicts of Interest Board denied a request for waiver where the city employee had sought to work for a private law firm that had a significant number of cases involving the city.[25] Also, the city employee's official duties as a legislative aide had involved working in some of the same substantive areas of the law in which the private firm was active. This was one of the occasions when it was determined that recusal would be insufficient to prevent possible conflicts.

Working for Not-for-Profit Organizations and Other Volunteer Activities

The question of possible conflicts can even arise where the government lawyer's outside activities involve pro bono or volunteer work, or are conducted in connection with a not-for-profit enterprise that essentially operates in furtherance of the public interest. For example, if a government lawyer wants to serve pro bono as a lawyer for a social services organization that deals with the government body that the lawyer serves, he or she runs the risk of having to take a position, in court or in negotiations, that is against the interests of that body. The lawyer also risks being perceived as using his or her position to obtain a special advantage for the lawyer's client organization, possibly at the expense of other similarly situated social services organizations that might be in competition with his or her client for government funding or other forms of government support.

With respect to acting as a lawyer for not-for-profit organizations, even when they are engaged in business dealings with the city, New York City's conflicts of interest law provides that a government lawyer may pursue such an activity, but only if he or she takes no direct or indirect part in the business dealings between the organization and the city; the organization has no direct or indirect interest in any business dealings with the city agency in which he or she is employed and is not subject to supervision, control, or regulation by such agency; the activity is performed only at times during which the government lawyer is not required to perform services for the city; and he or she receives no salary or other compensation in connection with such activity. If the organization does have any interest in business dealings with the city agency in which the government lawyer is employed, then the government lawyer may still pursue this noncity activity, but the head of the agency must first determine that such activity is in furtherance of the purposes and interests of the city.[26]

Representing Private Interests before the Government

The foregoing discussion applies to the outside conduct of all government employees and not only government lawyers. There are only a limited number of jurisdictions that, within their conflicts of interest or ethics laws, have provisions that specifically address the outside activities of government lawyers.[27] New York City, however, has two provisions that deal directly with the representation of private clients.

The first of these two provisions is more general and also applies to other professionals, such as architects and engineers, whose work often involves representing private clients. This rule provides that no city employee shall, for compensation, represent private interests before any city agency or appear directly or indirectly on behalf of private interests in matters involving the city.[28] The city's conflicts of interest law states that "appear" means to make any communication, for compensation, other than those involving ministerial or routine matters.[29] Such communications would include personal appearances, letters, and telephone calls. In some situations, an appearance before the city by the city employee's private employer could be considered an indirect appearance by the employee. For example, if the firm sends correspondence to a city agency on letterhead that prominently displays the city employee's name (as a member or employee of the firm), this could be considered an appearance by the city employee. Further, if a member of the firm

254 CONFLICTS OF INTEREST

appears for a hearing before the city and makes explicit reference to the city employee or actually appears on behalf of the city employee (in his or her role as a member or employee of the firm), this too would probably be deemed an appearance. The Conflicts of Interest Board has determined that, without a waiver, an appearance before the city by a private law firm in which a city employee is a partner would be a conflict of interest, as an indirect appearance before the city, by the city employee.[30] In contrast, the board has allowed the private law firm of a newly appointed city employee to continue, on a limited basis, representing clients before the city employee's own agency on already pending matters, because immediate divestiture of such matters could have created substantial hardships for the clients.[31]

In addition to prohibiting the presentation of private interests before the city, this section of the New York City law also bars city employees from representing private clients anywhere on matters involving the city. Thus, someone who works as a lawyer for the city could not, as part of his or her private law practice, work on a personal injury lawsuit against the city even if it involved neither the city lawyer's agency nor the kind of case on which the lawyer worked for the city.

This provision of New York City's conflicts of interest law thus continues the emphasis on separating public duties from private interests and on assuring that positions of public trust are not used—intentionally or inadvertently—to obtain a private advantage. Again, this kind of provision appears to be broad in scope, but if the agency charged with enforcing it has available at its disposal a waiver mechanism or some other means that allows it to act in an equitable manner, then it can go a long way toward preventing abuses of office and, equally important, enhancing public confidence in government.

Provisions that deal with representing private interests before the government generally do not, however, prevent government employees from contacting government agencies on behalf of their own interests. For example, if someone has a problem with real estate tax assessments on his or her home, this individual would be allowed to contact and deal with the city's tax commission.[32] Similarly, these provisions were probably not intended to prohibit government lawyers from occasionally making phone calls on behalf of their mothers or other close relatives, provided such actions were taken in accordance with other relevant parts of the ethics law.[33] Generally, city employees, including lawyers, may also represent cooperative and condominium boards (of buildings where they reside) or community groups before the city without compensation. Again, this might depend on the facts of an individual's situation, including the nature of that person's official duties.

The single provision in New York City's conflicts of interest law that applies explicitly to government lawyers states that no city employee shall appear a lawyer or counsel against the interests of the city in any litigation to which the city is a party, or in any action or proceeding in which the city, or any city employee, acting in the course of official duties, is a complainant.[34] This provision does not apply to city lawyers who are employed by elected officials and who appear as lawyer or counsel for those officials in any litigation, action, or proceeding in which the officials have standing and authority to participate by virtue of their capacities as officials. Also, this section of New York City's law is not intended to expand or limit the standing or authority of any elected official to participate in any litigation, action, or proceeding or to affect in any way the powers and duties of the city's corporation counsel.[35]

This section of the New York City law, dealing primarily if not exclusively with the outside activities of government lawyers, is intended to ensure, among other things, that the city's interests in adjudicative proceedings are considered in a fair and impartial manner and are not compromised by the knowledge, experience, or contacts of a city employee appearing on behalf of a party whose interests are adverse to the city, and who may attempt to use such knowledge, experience, or contacts to secure a private advantage.

As a result of the concerns giving rise to this kind of provision, the New York City Conflicts of Interest Board has, for example, issued an advisory opinion, discussed earlier in this chapter, in which it found that it would create a conflict of interest for a city employee who was a law enforcement officer with extensive official involvement with the city's criminal court system to, in the course of a private law practice, represent criminal defendants.[36] In that opinion, the board noted that in many criminal cases, the complaining witness is a city law enforcement officer acting in the course of his or her official duties, and if this city employee were to have represented criminal defendants, this could have created the appearance of the complaining witness's testimony being influenced by the presence of a professional colleague. Furthermore, if the city employee's official duties were to become known or had been known to the judge or jury, they might be inclined to give greater deference to the arguments presented by the defense, in light of the defense counsel's status as a law enforcement officer. In either case, the city's interests in convicting and punishing offenders and in deterring future criminal conduct could be compromised, in contravention of the city's conflicts of interest law. The rationale supporting the board's decision could also apply to government lawyers who attempt to pursue a private civil practice. Of paramount concern is, or course, whether the proposed law practice (or individual case) is not consistent with the best interests of the city, which is, in turn, determined by considering the proposed activity in light of the various provisions of the conflicts of interest law, as discussed throughout this chapter.

General Practice of Law

Notwithstanding what must seem like a plethora of regulations concerning government lawyers' outside activities, most jurisdictions do not prohibit the private practice of law, with the exception of some individual agencies that might have specific reasons for completely barring outside activities. Again, as was emphasized above, one of the functions of government ethics laws is to protect the integrity of the decision-making and other governmental processes. By providing flexible but clear standards of conduct, those who draft these laws are able to provide guidance to individuals who seek to augment their government salaries or to broaden their horizons, so that these goals may be accomplished in such a way as to protect against real or apparent conflicts of interest.

The New York City Conflicts of Interest Board, in recognizing that lawyers who work for the city need guidance as to the rules affecting their private law practices, has issued an advisory opinion that provides general guidance for government lawyers.[37] In that opinion the board noted that several government lawyers had come forward seeking advice about their law practices, which involved handling, among other things, real estate closings, general legal counseling, uncontested divorces, trusts and estates, and name changes.

The board's discussion started by acknowledging that many government agencies had traditionally barred or at least limited the practice of law by their employees. The opinion then focused on decisions of its predecessor agency, the New York City Board of Ethics and various New York State courts.[38] In one opinion, the Board of Ethics had cautioned one city employee about the difficulties that confront a lawyer who is restrained from practicing his or her profession during normal business hours.[39] The board noted that New York courts had affirmed the validity and rationale of government agencies having regulations that prohibit the lawyers whom they employed from having private practices. For example, in one case, the court had upheld a regulation that prohibited lawyers employed in the corporation counsel's office from engaging in the private practice of law, except in unusual circumstances and then only with agency permission. The court noted that this regulation was promulgated to achieve the highest level of professionalism, to eliminate the appearance of impropriety, and to assure that the lawyers in the office would devote their full time to their city jobs, thus eliminating what was considered the inevitable infringement on their official responsibilities caused by private practice.[40]

The board, after discussing the historic tradition (in New York at least) of government lawyers being prohibited from having private law practices, held in its advisory opinion that city employees who were lawyers could engage in the private practice of law during their off-duty hours, provided that they do not use city office space or equipment and that their practices were otherwise conducted in compliance with the city's conflicts of interest law. The board then proceeded to give a condensed presentation of the provisions discussed in this chapter.

In conclusion, the board expressed concern that a government lawyer's private practice of law, even outside of normal business hours and not on city premises, might nevertheless conflict with the proper discharge of his or her official duties. A mere appearance of conflict could have such an impact. It was therefore the board's opinion that the city's conflicts of interest law required city employees who were lawyers to obtain written agency approval to engage in the private practice of law.[41]

Conclusion

While many conflicts of interest laws and related rules dealing with government lawyers' outside employment might seem obvious and others might seem harsh or inexplicable, such laws and rules all have rational bases. Ultimately, conflicts of interest laws protect both public servants, including government lawyers, and the general public, in that they assure that our government employees will not be affected by their private interests when they are called upon to make official decisions. At the same time, such assurances inspire the public's trust in those employees.

Notes

1. Chapter 68 ("Conflicts of Interest"), New York City Charter, § 2600 et seq., the ethics law which applies to all New York City officials and employees, and which is fairly typical of many government ethics laws, has been used as a framework for the discussion in this chapter. Where appropriate, relevant sections of the law and advisory opinions issued pursuant to the law will be discussed below.

2. New York City Charter § 2600.

3. Of course, every state has, in addition, codes of professional responsibility that contain provisions designed to assure, among other things, that all lawyers—public and private—act in the best interests of their clients. Similarly, government ethics laws are intended to, among other things, assure that all government employees, including lawyers, do not have interests that conflict with their official duties.

4. New York City Charter § 2601(8).

5. New York City Charter § 2601(8).

6. New York City Charter § 2601(15).

7. Employees who work for the city on a part-time basis, such as members of boards and commissions, are required to determine whether their prospective employers or clients have business dealings with their own city agencies.

8. New York City Charter § 2604(a)(1)(b). "Position" means a position in a firm, such as an officer, director, trustee, employee, or any management position, or as a lawyer, agent, broker, or consultant to the firm. New York City Charter § 2601(18). "Ownership interest" means an interest in a firm held by a city employee, the city employee's spouse or unemancipated child, which exceeds $5000 in cash or other form of commitment, whichever is less, or 5 percent or $29,000 of the firm's indebtedness, whichever is less, and any lesser interest in a firm when the city employee or the employee's spouse or unemancipated child exercises managerial control or responsibility regarding any such firm. New York City Charter § 2601(16), as modified by Board Rules, § 1-11. The definition of "firm" encompasses sole proprietorships, joint ventures, partnerships, corporations, and any other form of enterprise. New York City Charter § 2601(11).

9. New York City Charter § 2604 (a)(1)(a).

10. *See* New York City Charter § 2604(b)(2), which provides that no city employee shall engage in any business, transaction, or other private employment, or have any financial or other private interest, direct or indirect, which conflicts with the proper discharge of his or her official duties. This provision is, potentially, very broad in scope and, as such, it is considered a "catch-all" provision. Thus, this section has been cited by the Conflicts of Interest Board in advisory opinions where the nature or subject matter of the noncity work presented potential conflicts with the employee's official duties (member of city commission who was also a law assistant to a state court judge was advised to recuse herself if any matter involving the commission were to come before the court (Advisory Opinion No. 91-11); aide to city council member was not permitted to work for a private firm because the areas of law practiced by the firm were too

258   CONFLICTS OF INTEREST

closely related to the aide's city council duties (Advisory Opinion No. 95-17); law firm of city commission member could not be retained by a private industry group in connection with possible litigation concerning the commission's own rules (Advisory Opinion No. 96-5).

11. Chapter 68 sets forth only the minimum standards of conduct for New York City employees. Any city agency may adopt stricter rules and, if so desired, may prohibit its employees from engaging in any outside employment.

12. New York City Charter § 2604(b)(3). A person or firm "associated" with a city employee includes a spouse, child, parent, or sibling; a person with whom the city employee has a business or other financial relationship; and each firm in which the city employee has a present or potential interest. New York City Charter § 2601(5).

13. Because the first situation, contained in the advisory opinion, utilizes the somewhat amorphous standard, "appearance of impropriety," this kind of case most often arises in New York City when the Conflicts of Interest Board is exercising its advisory function. That is, the board might advise a city employee that, because a certain course of prospective conduct could conceivably result in an appearance of impropriety, the employee should not engage in that conduct or seek to be recused from a particular situation. On the other hand, in cases involving affirmative attempts to use city jobs to advance private interests (i.e., involving past conduct), the board has and continues to conduct enforcement proceedings in which violations of chapter 68 are alleged. *See* New York City Charter § 2603.

14. Note that the discussion of this hypothetical does not take into account the possible effect, if any, lawyers' codes of professional responsibility would have on the government lawyer's conduct.

15. It is worth noting that ethics laws, unlike other laws, have some gray areas that encompass concepts such as the "appearance of impropriety." As indicated above, appearance problems can arise through unintentional or inadvertant conduct, where there is no actual corruption or wrongdoing per se. Thus, referring to these kinds of laws as ethics laws can sometimes be misleading because that phrase suggests a clear dichotomy between good and bad or, more to the point, between what is ethical and what is unethical.

16. New York City Charter § 2604(b)(4).

17. In New York City, regular employees of the city (those who are regularly scheduled to work 20 hours or more per week) may not hold positions with private firms or represent private clients that do business with the city. Part-time city employees are prohibited from having positions with private firms or representing private clients that do business with the city agencies that they serve. *See* New York City Charter §§ 2604(a)(1)(b) and (a)(1)(a), respectively.

18. New York City Charter § 2604(a)(4).

19. Many government agencies have their own rules about their employees' outside activities, sometimes directed specifically at their lawyers. It would not be surprising, therefore, if the agency for which this government lawyer worked had its own rule prohibiting its lawyers from engaging in the private practice of law. In New York City, agencies may promulgate their own rules of conduct, which must be as stringent or more stringent than those found in the city's conflicts of interest law. There will always be certain agencies, or certain classes of government employees, who will need specialized rules because of their job descriptions.

20. New York City Charter § 2601(16).

21. Advisory Opinion No. 91-2.

22. This advisory opinion demonstrates both the kind of analysis used by ethics agencies in dealing with government employees' outside interests and, in addition, provides an example of the significant impact this kind of rule can have not only on the government employee, but on his or her family as well.

23. Under New York City law a *position* of a city employee's spouse in a private firm is not imputed to the city employee in the way that a spouse's *ownership interest* is imputed to the city employee; however, as indicated above, a city employee is not permitted to take official action to benefit his or her spouses's employer. *See* New York City Charter § 2604(b)(3).

24. New York City Charter § 2604(e).

Notes 259

25. Advisory Opinion No. 95-17.

26. New York City Charter § 2604(c)(6). The Conflicts of Interest Board has also granted waivers pursuant to Charter § 2604(e), discussed above, when the city employee who was seeking permission to work for a particular not-for-profit organization would not be able to meet one of the other conditions contained in § 2604(c)(6).

27. Some of the jurisdictions that do not have provisions that specifically address the outside activities of government lawyers might include such coverage in their respective codes of professional responsibility.

28. New York City Charter § 2604(b)(6). For part-time city employees, this prohibition applies only to the city agency for which they work. This kind of rule is fairly common and appears in some form in many ethics codes.

29. New York City Charter § 2601(4).

30. *See* Advisory Opinion No. 96-5.

31. Advisory Opinion No. 94-24.

32. *See also,* New York City Charter § 2601(8), which excludes from the definition of prohibited business dealings with the city any transactions which involve city employees' residences.

33. For example, the government employee would still be prohibited from invoking his or her status as a government employee or from using his or her position in any other improper way to obtain a private advantage for anyone. *See* Charter § 2604(b)(3).

34. New York City Charter § 2604(b)(7). For part-time employees, this prohibition is limited to the employees' own city agency. While very few ethics codes contain rules which explicitly concern lawyers' activities, the more general "representing private interests" provisions, which *are* contained in many such codes, would of course cover the same kinds of activities.

35. These exceptions are intended to make clear that under certain circumstances, it is appropriate for government lawyers to be involved in the types of activities generally proscribed in New York City Charter § 2604(b)(7), which is cited and discussed above. For example, one elected official who is not part of the executive branch of government could, on behalf of his or her constituents, sue a particular agency of the executive branch. The provision concerning the city's corporation counsel merely states what should be obvious; that is, a government lawyer in that position is required, by the very nature of the duties of the job, to act in certain matters involving the city.

36. Advisory Opinion No. 93-23.

37. Advisory Opinion No. 91-7.

38. The New York City Charter was amended, effective January 1, 1990. Among other amendments the New York City Conflicts of Interest Board replaced the New York City Board of Ethics. Also, the substantive conflicts of interest provisions were revised, and the Board was given a broader range of powers, including enforcement powers, than that enjoyed by its predecessor agency.

39. New York City Board of Ethics Opinion No. 578 (1980). In that opinion the board cited with approval the case of Goldstein v. Bartlett, 401 NYS 2d 706 (Sup.Ct., Albany Co., 1978), *affirmed on the opinion below,* 408 NYS2d 1020 (1978).

40. Civil Service Bar v. Schwartz, 452 NYS 2d 478 (Sup.Ct., NY Co., 1982), *aff'd,* 468 N.Y.S.2d 998 (1982). The Board of Ethics also cited Matter of Lazarus v. Steingut, 494 N.Y.S.2d 930 (Sup.Ct., NY Co., 1985), in which the court concluded, among other things, that the private practice of law by attorneys who worked for the Workmen's Compensation Board poses a potential conflict between private interests and public service.

41. As noted above, in New York City, agencies may promulgate rules that are stricter than those required by the city's conflicts of interest law. Thus, any city agency may, when warranted, completley bar the private practice of law by its employees.

CHAPTER ❦ 11

Enforcement of Local Ethics Law

Joan R. Salzman*

This chapter is a guide to procedures and penalties in enforcement litigation, using New York City as a model and comparing it with several other jurisdictions. Local boards such as the New York City Conflicts of Interest Board have civil power to enforce the conflicts of interest law and financial disclosure requirements. It is important for public servants to become familiar with their local ethics laws and essential for private parties (such as vendors of goods and services) engaged in local government business and their counsel to understand the consequences of a violation of an applicable local ethics law.

Elected and appointed officers and employees shall demonstrate by their example the highest standards of ethical conduct, to the end that the public may justifiably have trust and confidence in the integrity of government. They, as agents of public purpose, shall hold their offices or positions for the benefit of the public, shall recognize that the public interest is their primary concern, and shall faithfully discharge the duties of their offices regardless of personal considerations.

—Revised Charter of the City and County of Honolulu 1973 (1994 ed.) § 11-101.

Local ethics laws share a common theme: that public officials must not violate the public trust by attempting to realize personal gain through abuse of office.[1] If public officials breach that trust, they face severe penalties, both civil and criminal, and, in addition, may lose their jobs or be subjected to other disciplinary sanctions. Enforcement of local ethics laws should be viewed as an aspect of an ethics commission's education function. Enforcement of the law teaches by example. When a prominent local official is pub-

---

* The views expressed in this chapter do not necessarily reflect those of the New York City Conflicts of Interest Board.

licly reprimanded and fined a substantial amount by a local ethics board, other public officials pay attention and conscientious agencies use such an example as part of their training of their employees.

The New York City Conflicts of Interest Board (the NYC Board) has many features in common with other local ethics boards. Its five members are appointed by the mayor with the advice and consent of the city council to staggered six-year terms.[2] Members of the NYC Board can hold no other public office and must meet at least once a month.[3] Many local ethics boards have formal procedures for imposing stiff penalties on local officials and employees for unethical conduct and for violation of related financial disclosure laws. Such boards have the power and the duty to bring formal charges against local officials, to conduct trial-like hearings, and to impose penalties on those found to have violated the law.

It is important for government employees to become familiar with local ethics laws. Knowledge of the enforcement provisions of such laws is also important to private lawyers who represent private, corporate, or other clients (that is, vendors of goods or services) doing business with a local government. Such vendors must know that certain local ethics boards have the power, as the NYC Board does, in consultation with the head of the relevant agency, to void a transaction that derives from a violation of a conflicts of interest code. In this way, ethics laws thought to apply only to government employees may have real and serious consequences for private business as well.

Moreover, private lawyers may need to know local ethics laws to counsel their corporate clients about ethical issues arising in connection with the hiring of local officials as they leave public service and enter the private sector. Lawyers for local governmental agencies will want to counsel these agencies' personnel so that they understand the law and avoid costly and potentially devastating violations.

Many lawyers who work for a locality are constrained by specific ethics rules, including, for example, rules concerning the private practice of law before government agencies, the solicitation of employment from entities involved in government business on which such lawyers currently work on behalf of the government, and the appearance before one's former local government agency after leaving government service.

Typical local financial disclosure laws[4] require local officials and employees to file detailed forms annually disclosing their income, assets and liabilities, and other personal financial information about themselves and their spouses. The very preparation of these forms causes public officials to think twice about their proposed conduct, and the completed forms provide an invaluable source of information about possible conflicts of interest.

Advice versus Enforcement

Ethics commissions typically have multiple functions: (1) to provide advice to conscientious public servants who want to conduct themselves according to law and who seek advice to prevent trouble; (2) to educate government employees about the local ethics law; (3) to publish rules of conduct and hearing rules consistent with principles of due process of law; (4) to require public employees to file financial disclosure reports; and (5) to enforce the ethics and financial disclosure laws against public employees whose past conduct has contravened the code of ethics. Enforcement should be seen as part of the mandate that the local ethics commission educate the public about the conflicts of interest law. Enforcement lawyers may work closely with education staff in efforts to train government workers by teaching about the results of particular cases, publishing articles, issuing press releases, lecturing, and helping create educational videotapes.

An ethics board's advisory function ordinarily applies to future conduct, while its enforcement function applies to past conduct. This temporal distinction can have very serious consequences for officials who seek ethics advice too late. Thus, for example, under New York City's Charter, an official whose past conduct has been the subject of criticism in the media may be ineligible for board advice once the conduct at issue is completed; the request for advice will be deemed a complaint about oneself, and, therefore, an enforcement problem for the NYC Board.[5] This occurred in the case of *David Begel*, NYC Board Case No. 96-40. In April of 1996, the NYC Board issued an enforcement disposition letter—made public with the express consent of the respondent, the former communications director for the New York City (NYC) Board of Education. Begel admitted that for one month, in November of 1995, he was both a consultant to the Efficacy Institute and a full-time employee of the board of education while he was aware that Efficacy held contracts with local NYC school districts. The NYC Board found that Begel had violated the provisions of the NYC charter that prohibit the holding of certain interests or positions in firms engaged in business dealings with the city. However, due to mitigating factors, including the facts that Begel had come forward promptly, that he had returned his $1,500 consulting fee to Efficacy, and that the relevant time period was short (only one month), the board imposed no monetary fine.

Many jurisdictions empower local ethics boards to render advisory opinions when the boards receive a request in writing. For example, under the Chicago Governmental Ethics Ordinance (Chicago Ord.) § 2-156-380(k), Chicago's ethics board has the power and duty to render advisory opinions upon real or hypothetical circumstances when requested in writing by an official or employee or by a person who is personally and directly involved. The opinions are available to the public, but the identities of the person requesting the advice and of any person whose conduct is involved are kept confidential. In New York City, the NYC Board has a similar requirement of a signed, written request, but also requires facts to be presented, as opposed to hypothetical questions.[6]

It is common practice to allow as a defense to an ethics enforcement action reasonable reliance upon an ethics board's advisory opinion. New York City provides for this defense,[7] as do New York State[8] and Maui County, Hawaii.[9] Reliance upon board advice, however, is unreasonable if the party seeking the advice of the board misrepresented the facts to the board precisely to avoid prosecution and to misuse the board advice as a shield.[10]

In an attempt to prevent abuse of the advice-giving process, and in recognition of the complications that may arise in subsequent criminal prosecutions from informal staff advisory letters approving of proposed conduct where the facts were misrepresented to the board, the NYC Board has in recent years added the following cautionary language to written advice by its staff and other forms of advice:

> The views expressed in this letter are conditioned on the correctness and completeness of the facts supplied to us. If such facts are in any respect incorrect or incomplete, the advice we have given to you may not apply. If at any time you would like further advice based on a change of circumstances or additional information, please contact us.

This language allows for investigation into the facts surrounding the representations by a public servant to the board in a few, appropriate cases without being so draconian as to deter honest public servants from seeking board advice as needed.

Complaints

Ethics boards receive complaints from the public and from other agencies, and many boards can generate their own investigations because of reports in the press. Many jurisdictions require that the complaint be in writing, sometimes on a prescribed form, and some require that the allegations be signed and sworn to.[11] In New York City, the NYC Board may, but is not obliged to, respond to oral complaints.[12]

Some jurisdictions impose time limits on themselves for responding to complaints. In the City of Los Angeles, the Los Angeles City Ethics Commission reviews complaints and makes an initial determination as to whether there is sufficient cause to conduct an investigation of alleged violations of the conflicts of interest ordinances and city charter.[13] Los Angeles requires that within fourteen days after receipt of a complaint, the commission must notify in writing the person who made the complaint of any action the commission has taken or plans to take on the complaint with a statement of reasons for its action or nonaction. If no decision has been made within fourteen days, the person who made the complaint must be notified of the reasons for the delay and must receive notification of the actions of the commission.[14] Not all local boards provide such close reporting to the complainant.

In King County, Washington, complaints are filed with an ombudsman (the director of the office of citizen complaints).[15] The complaint must be in writing, verified, and signed by the complainant, who may state in writing whether he or she wants his or her name to be kept confidential. The complaint must describe the basis for the complainant's belief that one or more of the ethics code's provisions have been violated.[16] The ombudsman must then serve a copy of the complaint, within twenty days after the filing of the complaint, by certified mail, return receipt requested, upon the person alleged to have committed one or more violations of the ethics code and "promptly" make an investigation of the complaint.[17]

In Seattle, the administrator (the executive director of the Seattle Ethics and Elections Commission) must conduct a preliminary investigation within thirty days of receipt of a complaint to determine whether the complaint, on its face, alleges facts that, if true, would constitute a violation of the ethics code.[18] At the request of the Administrator, the Seattle Ethics and Elections Commission may, for good cause shown, extend the time for completion of the preliminary investigation, or the Board may order the administrator to shorten the time. The test for requiring an investigation shorter than 30 days is the avoidance of prejudice or irreparable harm to the person alleged to have violated the ethics code.[19]

Some localities, such as King County and Seattle, require that the complaint be specific and provide the facts underlying the allegations. Under the Seattle Code of Ethics § 4.16.090(B), the written, signed complaint must state the nature of the alleged violations, the dates, time, and place of each occurrence, and the name of the person alleged to have violated the ethics code. The complainant must provide the administrator with all available documentation or other evidence to demonstrate a reason for believing that a violation has occurred.[20] If a member of the Ethics and Elections Commission files the complaint, that member is then disqualified from participating in any proceedings that may arise from the complaint.[21]

Who Investigates?

In the case of New York City, a separate agency, the NYC Department of Investigation, conducts investigations into conflicts of interest and reports to the board.[22] The investigative agency typically has the power to subpoena witnesses and documents[23] and can go to court to enforce its subpoenas as necessary. The NYC Board itself has the power to subpoena witnesses to trial.[24]

Local government ethics agencies may not have the statutory mandate or adequate funding to perform investigations in-house, although great efficiencies can be realized by having investigators and trial lawyers working closely together in the same office on a daily basis. The way that investigations are conducted and the amount of independence granted to ethics agencies vary widely with the statutory mandates of local ethics agencies.[25]

Many local ethics agencies have the power and the duty to conduct investigations, inquiries, and hearings concerning any matter covered by their conflicts of interest law.[26] In extremely small ethics agencies, such as that of Anne Arundel County, Maryland, the executive director performs all initial investigations at the direction of the ethics commission and reports the findings to the commission.[27] The executive director of the Cook County Ethics Board similarly conducts investigations and presents the findings to the board for appropriate action.[28] The executive director has some power to compel the

Who Investigates? 265

production of evidence, although the Cook County Ethics Ordinance requires that information necessary to any investigation be made available to the executive director upon "written request" (not subpoena).[29] The Cook County Ethics Board has the authority to issue a subpoena for the appearance of witnesses, the production of evidence, or both, in the course of both investigations and hearings.[30]

Some statutes place limits on a local ethics commission's powers with respect to legislators. For example, in Chicago, the board of ethics has the power and duty to investigate and act upon complaints but has no authority to investigate any complaint alleging a violation of the ethics law by an alderman or employee of the city council.[31] If the Chicago Board of Ethics receives a complaint about an alderman or employee of the city council, it must transmit the complaint within two days of receipt to the standing committee of the city council having jurisdiction over such complaints.[32] In the process of investigating complaints of ethics law violations, the Chicago Board of Ethics may, by a majority vote, request the issuance of a subpoena by the city council under Illinois law.[33]

All ethics agencies with enforcement powers must allow for the exercise of prosecutorial discretion so that only appropriate cases will be pursued—for example those that state a violation of law if all the allegations are deemed to be true such that they would survive a motion to dismiss. Chicago's law articulates this basic, commonsense approach to managing ethics enforcement cases: "The Board may exercise appropriate discretion in determining whether to investigate and whether to act upon any particular complaint or conduct."[34] Similarly, the Los Angeles Ethics Commission investigates only if the complaint identifies the specific alleged violation that forms the basis for the complaint and contains sufficient facts to warrant an investigation.[35]

The subject of an investigation eventually receives notice of the charges against him or her. In Chicago, prior to the conclusion of the investigation, the ethics board must provide notice to the person under investigation of the substance of the complaint and an opportunity to present such written information as the person may wish, including the names of any witnesses he or she may want to have interviewed by the board.[36] King County, Washington, has a similar provision that requires the King County ombudsman, during the investigation, to consider any statement of position or evidence with respect to the allegations of the complaint that the complainant or the respondent wishes to submit.[37]

An important aspect of an ethics investigation is the written, investigative report. Thus, in New York City, the NYC Department of Investigation, "within a reasonable time," investigates the complaint referred by the NYC Board and submits a confidential written report of factual findings to the board.[38] In New York City, this report is only a point of departure. The board uses it to decide whether there is probable cause to believe that a violation of law occurred. In Chicago, by contrast, the board of ethics must prepare its own written report at the conclusion of its investigation.[39] The report must include

266   ENFORCEMENT OF LOCAL ETHICS LAW

a summary of the investigation, a complete transcript of any proceeding, including any testimony heard by the board and recommendations for appropriate legal action.[40] If the Chicago board determines that the complaint is not sustained, it must so state in its report and must notify the person investigated and any other person whom the board has informed of the investigation.[41] If the Chicago board finds that corrective action should be taken, it must send its report to the head of the department or agency in which the employee works, or to the mayor if the person investigated is an agency head, appointed official, or elected official other than an alderman, or to the Chair of the relevant city council committee or alderman for whom the employee works.[42] The board also sends its report to the city's corporation counsel.[43]

Any person to whom the Chicago board has sent its report with a recommendation for action must report back to the board, in writing, all actions taken on the board's recommendations, within thirty days of receipt of the report.[44] To the extent the recipient of the report declines to follow the board's recommendations, he or she must provide a statement of reasons for his or her decisions.[45] Nothing precludes the board from notifying the subject of the investigation, prior to or during an investigation, that a complaint against him or her is pending, and, where appropriate, recommending corrective action. Any such early notice must be in writing and must also be transmitted simultaneously to the corporation counsel.[46]

In jurisdictions where the investigative report provides a launching point for a full administrative trial on the merits, the enforcement lawyer must examine the evidence (documents, witness statements), meet with investigators, ask follow-up questions, interview witnesses, and transform the report into a complete trial preparation. It is good practice, where appropriate and possible, for an ethics board to notify the alleged violator when a complaint is not sustained, particularly where that person knows he was investigated and has been pilloried in the press, and there will otherwise be no formal name clearing. Not all enforcement news from an ethics agency is bad, and clearing an accused employee who did nothing wrong is an important public function.

Jurisdiction over Former Government Employees

It is very important for a local government ethics agency to have jurisdiction over former government employees. This is so for very practical reasons. By the time an investigation is completed, an employee who is having difficulties related to abuse of office may be fired or leave on his or her own (particularly in cases that involve using one's government position to solicit more lucrative jobs in the private sector) before an enforcement action can be completed. Local government employees who have violated an ethics code should not escape government service with impunity merely because they resign voluntarily and go quietly.

New York City's charter very clearly provides in several sections that the NYC Board retains power over former employees.[47] Jurisdictions whose statutes do not address the problem of retaining jurisdiction over former employees may find that their power is successfully challenged in court, as was the case in New York State.

In *Flynn v. State Ethics Commission*, 87 N.Y.2d 199, 638 N.Y.S.2d 418, 661 N.E.2d 991 (1995),[48] New York's highest state court held that the New York State Ethics Commission's investigative and adjudicatory authority over the adjutant general of the state Division of Military Affairs ended when he retired from state service. The court found that "the governing statute does not confer . . . extended jurisdiction over a former employee expressly or by necessary implication . . . ." 87 N.Y.2d at 200–201, 638 N.Y.S.2d at 419, 661 N.E.2d at 992. The case involved allegations that Flynn had accepted free tickets worth $500 to an antique show sponsored by a private organization and held at the Park Avenue Armory in New York City. The armory was under Flynn's state military authority. The court based its decision on the principle that the State Ethics Commission is a "creature of statute" and, therefore, lacks powers not granted to it expressly or by necessary implication. 87 N.Y.2d at 202, 638 N.Y.S.2d at 420, 661 N.E.2d at 993.

The *Flynn* court reasoned that even a resignation from office without an admission of guilt served an important goal of the ethics law—to restore public trust and confidence in government:

> Thus, giving the pertinent provisions their ordinary meaning, we discern no express or implied jurisdictional reach beyond the actual tenure and service of an employee. Rather, the precise and core grant of statutory authorization to investigate and punish unethical conduct allows the Commission to accomplish the salutary purpose of exposing corrupt or unethical employees in the ranks of State government. If the employees are rooted out by adjudication or by inducing a voluntary departure, a major objective is served. As the Appellate Division observed, the petitioner in this case essentially fulfilled a principal goal of the statute by resigning, albeit without expressly acknowledged or adjudicated guilt, but without the necessity either of a largely academic trumpeting of power by the Commission.

87 N.Y.2d at 203, 638 N.Y.S.2d at 420–21, 661 N.E.2d at 993–94.

The *Flynn* court refused to base an implied grant of jurisdiction on the statutory $10,000 civil penalty provision but left open the possibility of legislative change:

> We decline to rest such a significant and unlimited interpretation of the Commission's jurisdictional charter on such a strained and slim reed, which is substantively different from the lifetime bans expressly prescribed by statute and constitutional mandate in other areas expressly imposing a future disqualification. Had the Legislature wished to add a similar extended power to the mission of this specially charged Commission, it could have and should have explicitly so prescribed. Open-ended jurisdiction is too important and fundamental to leave to indefinite interpretive molding.

87 N.Y.2d at 203–204, 638 N.Y.S.2d at 421, 661 N.E.2d at 994.

The *Flynn* court also found that the "revolving door" provisions of the New York statutes, which by definition apply to former state officers and employees to prohibit appearances before their former agencies within two years of leaving state service, could not be extended to all ethics provisions:

> If the Commission wishes to exert timeless, across-the-board jurisdiction, it should seek that extraordinary power and delegation explicitly from the Legislature, the source of its existence and special, limited charter.

87 N.Y.2d at 205, 638 N.Y.S.2d at 422, 661 N.E.2d at 995.

In response to the *Flynn* case, the New York State Ethics Commission has proposed legislation to eliminate the former official loophole. See 1997 NYS Ethics Commission Legislative Proposal No. 10. The commission has proposed a bill that would give it clear authority to pursue former state officers and employees, former candidates for statewide elective office, and former political party Chairs and hold them responsible for actions they took while in state service or party office or as candidates. The postemployment jurisdiction would not be unlimited; rather, the commission would be authorized to issue a notice of delinquency or a notice of reasonable cause within five years after the termination of service or candidacy, but in no event more than seven years after the commission of the alleged violation or the failure to file a financial disclosure statement or the filing of a false statement. This proposed statute of limitations is the same one applicable to prosecution of misdemeanors involving misconduct in public office.[49]

Confidentiality

When do an ethics board's proceedings become public? Some agencies open their proceedings only after full due process is afforded and a violation is found, and then only to publish the final findings and order. Other jurisdictions open their proceedings with the publication of a petition. All ethics enforcement agencies recognize the tension between protection of the reputation of the target of an investigation prior to full hearing and the complainant's and the public's right to know the progress of cases concerning alleged misconduct in office.

In New York City, the "records, reports, memoranda and files of the board" are "confidential and . . . not subject to public scrutiny."[50] However, the NYC Board's rules provide for release of materials relating to complaints upon a waiver of confidentiality by the respondent and a board determination that confidentiality is not otherwise required; the board's rules also provide for publication of the board's final findings, conclusions, and orders issued upon a violation:

> *Confidentiality.* All matters relating to complaints submitted to or inquired into by the Board, or any action taken by the Board in connection therewith or hearings conducted by the Board or OATH [NYC's administrative

tribunal, the Office of Administrative Trials and Hearings], shall be kept confidential unless the public servant waives confidentiality and the Board determines that confidentiality is not otherwise required. Hearings conducted by the Board or by OATH shall be public if requested by the public servant. Final findings, conclusions, and orders issued upon a violation of Chapter 68 shall be made public.[51]

Because all proceedings are confidential unless the NYC Board finds a violation of the conflicts of interest law, the NYC board also provides that if the board dismisses a petition after a hearing and finds that the public servant accused has not engaged in unlawful acts, the dismissal order and findings of fact and conclusions of law are not made public.[52] In this way, a confidential complaint that cannot be substantiated never enters the public record and the public servant's reputation remains intact, unless the public servant accused (perhaps in response to media attacks) wants to waive confidentiality and the board makes a determination that confidentiality is not otherwise required.

Most jurisdictions provide for some variant of these confidentiality requirements.[53]

Probable Cause, Petition, and Answer

Many jurisdictions provide a pre-petition notice to respondents, called a probable cause or reasonable cause notice, that the ethics board has cause to believe that the ethics law has been violated. The probable cause stage affords the respondent ample process and an early opportunity to convince a local board that the complaint cannot be substantiated before the commencement of more formal proceedings. The respondent typically has an opportunity to respond in writing or orally and to be represented by counsel or any other person.

The NYC Board may make an "initial determination," based on a complaint, investigation, or other information available to it, that there is "probable cause to believe that [a] public servant has violated" the relevant provisions of the city charter.[54] The NYC Board must then notify the public servant of its determination in writing.[55] The notice must contain a statement of the facts upon which the board relied for its determination of probable cause and a statement of the provisions of law allegedly violated.[56] The notice must also inform the respondent of his or her right to be represented by counsel or any other person and include the board's procedural rules.[57] The public servant has fifteen days (twenty if service was by mail) to answer the notice, either orally or in writing, and may respond to, explain, rebut, or provide information concerning the allegations in the notice.[58] The NYC board recently eliminated the initial determination of probable cause requirement in financial disclosure cases and generally eliminated the requirement that the probable cause notice be served by both first class and certified mail, return receipt requested.[59] Enforcement cases that involve the failure to file financial disclosure reports or to pay a fine for filing a report late tend to involve routine, identical issues and can be brought against scores of respondents at the same time. The probable cause notices in these cases placed an undue burden on the board's staff and resources. Service of the probable cause notice, still required in conflict of interest cases, may now be effected by first class mail alone.[60]

The NYC Board reviews the response to the notice of initial determination of probable cause and will either dismiss on written notice to the respondent[61] or sustain its initial finding.[62] If the board finds that there is still probable cause following a response to the probable cause notice, the board's enforcement lawyer will serve a more formal, written petition, triggering formal enforcement proceedings and a trial on the merits.[63] The petition reflects the board's determination of probable cause.[64]

Service of the petition upon the respondent in NYC commences formal proceedings.[65] The petition must set forth the facts that, if proved, would constitute a violation of the conflicts of interest law or the financial disclosure law.[66] And the petition must advise the respondent of his or her rights to file an answer, to a hearing, to be represented at such hearing by counsel or any other person, and to cross-examine witnesses and present evidence.[67] The respondent must serve an answer, personally or by certified or registered mail, return receipt requested, within eight days after service of the petition (thirteen if the service was by mail).[68] Failure to answer means that all the allegations of the petition are deemed admitted, but the board's enforcement lawyer must still submit for the record an offer of proof establishing the factual basis on which the board may issue an order.[69] The answer must be in writing and must contain specific responses, by admission, denial, or otherwise, to each allegation of the petition and must assert any affirmative defenses. The respondent may also include in the answer any mitigating facts. The answer must be signed (either by the respondent or his or her representative) and show the full name, address, and telephone number of the respondent. If the respondent is represented, the answer must show the representative's name, address, and telephone number.[70]

Pleadings may be amended as of right within twenty-five days prior to a hearing. If the amendment is presented later, there must be either consent of the parties or leave of the board or the administrative law judge conducting the hearing.[71]

A respondent can admit the facts alleged and elect to forego a hearing. If this occurs, and this provision is rarely invoked, the board may, after consulting with the head of the relevant agency served by the respondent, or with the mayor if the case involves an agency head, issue an order finding a violation and imposing appropriate penalties.[72]

There is a very important provision—important because so many NYC employees are members of unions—that circumscribes the NYC Board proceedings at this early stage: it provides for referral of cases back to the agency served by the respondent for possible disciplinary action if he or she is subject to the jurisdiction of any state law or collective bargaining agreement that provides for the conduct of disciplinary proceedings. The agency to which the case is referred must consult with the board before issuing any final decision.[73] At the early stages of any case involving a minor violation or where related disciplinary charges are pending, the board may also refer the matter to the agency served by the respondent.[74] In these cases also, the agency must consult with the board before issuing a final decision.[75]

Some agencies can demand corrective action at the early, probable cause stage. For example, in Cook County, Illinois, the board of ethics, upon a determination that there is reason to believe that a violation of the ethics ordinance has occurred, may notify the subject of the complaint and request corrective action, and recommend disciplinary or other action to the president of the Cook County Board of Commissioners or to the appropriate elected official. All recommendations must be in writing and must include a specific statement of reasons in support of the recommendations.[76] Similarly, King County, Washington's employee code of ethics provides that if the board of ethics finds reasonable cause to believe that the ethics code was violated, the ombudsman must prepare an order to that effect and deliver copies of the order to the complainant, the respondent, the highest ranking supervisor of the respondent, the office of the prosecuting lawyer, and the board of ethics, and the original order must be filed with the divisions of records and elections. The "reasonable cause order" must include a finding that one or more violations of the ethics code has occurred and the factual basis for the finding.[77]

Discovery

In New York City, prehearing matters, such as conferences, discovery, and motion practice are handled either by a designated board member or by an administrative law judge (ALJ) in a case heard by the city's central administrative tribunal, the Office of Administrative Trials and Hearings (OATH).[78] Some truncated form of pretrial discovery may be allowed prior to an administrative ethics trial. For example, in New York City, the parties can serve document requests upon each other and must respond within fifteen days of receipt of the request.[79] However, other discovery devices, such as depositions and interrogatories, are not permitted except upon motion for good cause shown.[80] Sanctions (including preclusion of evidence and declaration of default) are available against a disobedient party or lawyer or representative who refuses to comply with discovery requirements.[81]

Trial

The trial may be held either by an ethics board itself or one of its members,[82] or may be delegated to an ALJ.[83] In many administrative hearings, usual rules of evidence are not binding, and hearsay may be presented if it has probative

272   ENFORCEMENT OF LOCAL ETHICS LAW

value and relevance.[84] In a typical ethics board proceeding, each party has the right to call and examine witnesses on any matter relevant to the pleadings; to introduce documentary and physical evidence; to cross-examine opposing witnesses on any matter relevant to the issues of the complaint; to impeach any witness; to rebut evidence against him or her; and to represent himself or herself or to be represented by any other person permitted to serve as a representative, whether the representative is a lawyer or not.[85] Some agencies face time limits within which they must commence a hearing.[86]

In New York City, OATH will usually conduct the hearings, although the board or a board member may do so. In a case where an OATH ALJ conducts the hearing, a copy of the petition must be sent to OATH at the time the petition is served upon the respondent, and OATH's rules supplement the board's procedural rules.[87] Subpoenas requiring the attendance of witnesses and production of documents may be issued only by an ALJ in an OATH case or by a board member where the hearing is conducted by the board or by a member of the board, upon the application of a party, or on the ALJ's or the board member's own motion.[88] After the hearing in an OATH case, the ALJ issues a report and recommendation to the board.[89] This model is analogous to the federal system of referrals to U.S. magistrate judges.

The order of proceedings in a New York City hearing is that the Board's prosecuting counsel, who has the burden of proof by a preponderance of the evidence, must initiate the presentation of evidence and may present rebuttal evidence.[90] The civil standard of proof by a preponderance of the evidence figures significantly in decisions on whether the board will proceed with a civil enforcement case or defer to a separate, criminal prosecutor's office. A criminal prosecution brought by a district attorney will require a higher standard of proof—beyond a reasonable doubt—than the board's civil standard. As noted below in the section on cooperation with other law enforcement agencies, ethics boards and criminal law enforcement agencies must be in close contact so that the most sensible approach to a case, given the strength of the evidence, can be taken and the case brought by the proper agency. The respondent may introduce evidence after the board prosecuting counsel has completed his or her case. Any opening statements are made first by the board's prosecuting counsel; closing statements are made first by the respondent. The order of proceedings may be modified at the direction of the ALJ, the board, or a board member.[91]

In New York City, the NYC Board has a very specific posthearing procedure under which the ALJ sends a confidential report of recommended findings of fact and conclusions of law, along with the original transcript of the proceeding and all trial exhibits, to the parties and to the board for review and final action. The board must review the nonbinding written report and recommendation of the ALJ. The parties have ten days from service of the ALJ's report and recommendation to submit comments to the board.[92] The board then considers all the evidence in the record of the hearing, as well as any comments, and states its final findings of fact and conclusions of law and issues an order imposing any penalties it deems appropriate under the conflicts of interest law or the financial disclosure law.[93] The order must include notice of the respondent's right to appeal to the New York State Supreme Court.[94] If there is a recommendation of discipline, the board may recommend penalties to the appropriate agency head, who must report back to the board the action taken.[95] The board will publish the final findings, conclusions, and order if a violation is found, but a finding of no violation is not published. In jurisdictions where petitions are public, the publication practices will differ.

Settlement

At any time a case can settle. Settlements may typically require a monetary fine and a public admission of a violation of the ethics law. An example of a stipulated disposition of a New York City case, *COIB v. Sergio Matos*, No. 94-368, is included in Appendix 11A. In New York City, any disposition that contains an acknowledgment that the respondent violated the city charter (conflicts of interest law) or the administrative code (the financial disclosure law) must be made public.[96] Some agencies refer to their settlements as consent orders for corrective action.[97] Others suspend hearings while a settlement recommendation is pending before an ethics board.[98]

In many cases, a public servant may desire to have a quick resolution of charges against him or her, endure the momentary press coverage, and resume his or her public career. Any calculation by the public servant about whether to settle before trial depends in large part upon the strength of the evidence. An adjudicated finding based on a full opportunity to litigate may be more detailed and more damaging than an early, stipulated disposition.

"Commingling" of Adjudicative and Prosecutorial Functions

Ethics agencies have had varied experience with the issue of commingling of adjudicative and prosecutorial functions. The question is whether a particular agency's rules provide sufficient separation of powers (insulating the ultimate decision maker from the prosecution) to afford the respondent due process of law. Due to budget constraints, many of these agencies are small yet have to fulfill broad mandates, including enforcement of local ethics codes. Courts like those of Massachusetts recognize that it is safe to assume that ethics commissioners are honorable and will issue fair judgments and do not require absolute separation of functions. Some codes, such as those of New York City and Massachusetts, have a limited separation of powers, while others, such as Pennsylvania, due to some protracted and difficult litigation, impose extraordinarily strict separations of the ethics agency's functions.

Under New York City's procedural rules, ex parte communications are prohibited, once the petition is issued, between the enforcement lawyer and

274   ENFORCEMENT OF LOCAL ETHICS LAW

the board members concerning the merits of the case, except with respect to ministerial matters involving the case or on consent of the respondent or his or her counsel, or in an emergency.[99] This rule takes into account the need for the board's enforcement lawyer to effectuate settlements and allows ex parte communications on consent. Massachusetts has a similar rule that prohibits any ex parte communication between the prosecuting staff and the commission once a case has gone into "adjudication" with the order to show cause.[100] Violation of the Massachusetts ex parte rule must be placed on the confidential record and is grounds for dismissal.[101] Massachusetts allows its ethics commission to see investigative materials,[102] and the Massachusetts Supreme Judicial Court has rejected particular challenges to combined investigative and adjudicative functions.[103]

Pennsylvania, by contrast, had so much litigation on this subject that its state ethics commission completely revamped its rules and practices to effect a near-complete separation of functions. See *Lyness v. Commonwealth of Pennsylvania State Board of Medicine*, 529 Pa. 535, 605 A.2d 1204, 1209–10 (1992) (for purposes of Pennsylvania constitutional due process requirement, "if more than one function is reposed in a single administrative entity, walls of division [must] be constructed which eliminate the threat of appearance of bias. . . . [W]here the very entity or individuals involved in the decision to prosecute are 'significantly involved' in the adjudicatory phase of the proceedings, a violation of due process occurs."). *Lyness* held that the need for separation of functions was particularly compelling where the administrative board had carte blanche in reviewing the hearing examiner's finding and replacing it with its own adjudication, with limited appellate review in court. *Id.*, 605 A.2d at 1210. Actual bias was not required. *Id.*, 605 A.2d at 1211. See also *Stone and Edwards Ins. Agency, Inc. v. Department of Insurance*, 538 Pa. 276, 648 A.2d 304 (1994), *aff'g* 161 Pa. Commwlth. 177, 636 A.2d 293 (1994) ("walls of division" satisfied where no interaction occurred between enforcement deputy and commissioner who had no prosecution functions, even though the statute vested the commissioner with prosecutorial and adjudicative authority); *George Clay Steam Fire Engine and Hose Company v. Pennsylvania Human Relations Commission*, 162 Pa. Commwlth 468, 639 A.2d 893, 901–903 (1994), *allocatur denied*, 540 Pa. 614, 656 A.2d 120 (1995) (*Lyness* does not require a complete separation of powers within state agencies; adequate separation of prosecutorial and adjudicative functions in fact where staff finds probable cause and commissioners adjudicate, and thus, regulations placed all prosecution functions in staff).

Ex parte settlement communications are strictly prohibited in Pennsylvania. Under its revamped rules, the Pennsylvania Ethics Commission does not even see investigative materials and does not make probable cause determinations. Those are made by the executive director. The chief counsel to the Pennsylvania Ethics Commission has nothing to do with prosecuting cases, except to transmit settlement agreements from the executive director to the commission.[104]

Some ethics agencies have only a one-lawyer staff (as in Anne Arundel County, Maryland). In this age of "downsizing" and severe budget constraints on government ethics agencies, a reasonably limited separation of powers, as in New York City or Massachusetts, should suffice. Agencies should not be put to the burden of total separation of powers for civil enforcement proceedings, and, in the absence of any actual prejudice in a particular case, the respondent will receive a fair hearing.

Penalties

A typical ethics board can impose a variety of civil penalties, and its enabling statute may also make a violation of the law a misdemeanor. The civil penalties typically include a monetary fine, removal or suspension from office, and nullification of contracts.

In NYC, the penalties the board is empowered to impose include:

1. Civil monetary fine up to $10,000[105]
2. Recommending suspension or removal from office after consultation with an agency head[106]
3. Voiding a contract or transaction after consultation with an agency head, if doing so would be in the interest of the City[107]

Set forth on pages 278–281 is a table comparing some of the penalties that can be imposed under various ethics commissions' codes.

In New York City, a criminal law enforcement authority may charge a city employee with a misdemeanor. Upon conviction in a separate criminal proceeding conducted by a local district attorney, the public servant must forfeit public office automatically. The relevant provision reads:

> Any person who violates [the operative provisions of the NYC Charter] shall be guilty of a misdemeanor and, on conviction thereof, shall forfeit his or her public office or employment.[108]

This provision has resulted in at least one NYC case in the withdrawal of a guilty plea where the defendant did not understand the consequences of her plea. The case raises issues relating to certificates of relief from civil disabilities that arise from criminal convictions.[109] Appendix 11B is a proposed allocution for guilty pleas to inform defendants of the severe consequences (automatic job loss) of a criminal conviction. Criminal conviction of buying one's public office leads to a lifetime disqualification from being elected, appointed, or employed in city service in New York City.

Certain localities, such as Los Angeles, may provide private rights of action to sue for injunctive relief to enjoin violations of a local ethics code.[110] Local ethics boards typically provide for judicial review of board actions.[111]

Some ethics boards have very specific statutes of limitations.[112] For example, Los Angeles requires actions to be filed within four years after the date the violation occurred. The District of Columbia mandates that all actions of its board of elections and ethics or the United States attorney to enforce the D.C. law be initiated within three years of the actual occurrence of the alleged violation. By contrast, the NYC board's charter and rules specify no time limit for commencement of board actions.

Many localities provide some type of "whistleblower" protection for people who complain and fear reprisals for giving evidence against powerful officials.[113] These statutes generally impose civil or criminal liability on government employees who retaliate against others for complaining about violations of the local conflicts of interest code.

Cooperation with Other Law Enforcement Agencies

It is essential that local ethics boards and other law enforcement agencies cooperate. In many cases, more than one agency may have jurisdiction over the same violations. For example, every bribe is also a conflict of interest, but it may be more sensible for criminal charges to be brought than civil administrative charges. The ethics agency must coordinate with the investigators, the district attorney, and the agency employing the respondent and decide which agency will proceed first. If the district attorney will seek criminal sanctions, the ethics board may defer action and its staff can assist the district attorney with legal expertise on local laws. If the district attorney chooses not to indict, the ethics board may decide to proceed because it has a lower burden of proof ("preponderance of the evidence" versus "beyond a reasonable doubt"). Decisions on which agency will proceed first involve consideration of the relative resources of the various agencies as well as the potential preclusive effects of a ruling in one forum upon a later proceeding in another forum.

Some ethics boards specifically provide in their statutes for particular types of cooperation between government agencies. For example, in Chicago, the board of ethics must request the assistance of other appropriate agencies when it determines that assistance is needed in conducting investigations, or when required by law.[114] And the Chicago board has the power and duty to consult with city agencies, officials, and employees on matters involving ethical conduct.[115] Chicago's law provides in addition that the procedures and penalties in the ethics code do not limit the power of the city council to discipline its own members or the power of other city agencies otherwise to discipline officials or employees or to adopt more restrictive rules.[116] Similarly, Cook County's ethics ordinance requires county agencies, employees, and officials to cooperate with the ethics board and its executive director.[117]

The interaction between law enforcement agencies is shown by a financial disclosure enforcement case from New York City, *COIB v. Indravadan Desai*.[118] There, the New York State Supreme Court rejected a challenge by a former city employee to a $10,000 fine imposed by the NYC Board for his failure to file a 1992 financial disclosure report. The former employee had sought to stay the administrative case because there was then a criminal case pending against him, and he did not want any information he might disclose to the board used against him in the criminal case. The court ruled that the ALJ had properly exercised his discretion in denying the application to stay the board's enforcement proceeding during the pendency of the criminal case, where the employee had deliberately defaulted on the board hearing, had received a number of adjournments, was required as a city employee to file the report, and had failed to demonstrate that permitting the hearing to go forward would jeopardize him in the criminal matter.

Some local ethics agencies are required by law to refer cases for criminal prosecution. For example, in King County, Washington, the ombudsman must investigate and report apparent criminal violations to the "appropriate law enforcement authorities."[119]

Ethics agencies may have information that will be useful in a criminal prosecution, particularly where a government official has made representations to the ethics agency to elicit advice. If those representations turn out to have been false, they may be at the core of a criminal conflict of interest or more serious crime. The ethics board's enforcement staff must be prepared to respond to grand jury subpoenas in a way that is consistent with the board's particular confidentiality rules.

Conclusion

Local ethics agencies can and do contribute significantly to setting and enforcing standards of excellence in government. Even in a large city, a small, well-run ethics board enforcement unit of only three or four able lawyers, with a small cadre of veteran investigators, can form a self-sufficient litigation team and complete a number of important cases each year. The publication of enforcement results heightens public awareness of conflicts of interest issues and increases the number of legitimate complaints filed with the local board, as the public realizes that complaints will be taken seriously. And effective enforcement has a deterrent effect on improper conduct. Enforcement litigation is complex and challenging, in part because it requires particular sensitivity during the legal process to confidentiality and to the interests and reputations of alleged violators of conflicts of interest laws.

Through their various enforcement mechanisms, local ethics boards promote the universal purposes of conflicts of interest laws: government integrity and the highest standards of ethical conduct by government officials. With adequate funding and staff, such agencies can continue to educate the public through enforcement cases and create a new atmosphere of public confidence in local officials.

Notes

1. *See, e.g.,* District of Columbia (D.C.) Law § 1-1461(a): "The Congress declares that elective and public office is a public trust, and any effort to realize personal gain through official

278   ENFORCEMENT OF LOCAL ETHICS LAW

conduct is a violation of that trust[;]" New York City Charter (NYC Charter) § 2600 (Preamble): "Public service is a public trust. These prohibitions on the conduct of public servants are enacted to preserve the trust placed in the public servants of the city, to promote public confidence in government, to protect the integrity of government decision-making and to enhance government efficiency."

2. *See* NYC Charter § 2602(a)–(c).

3. NYC Charter § 2602(h). The NYC Board has the support of a full-time staff headed by its executive director and counsel.

4. *See, e.g.,* NYC Administrative Code (NYC Ad. Code) § 12-110.

5. "Advisory opinions shall be issued only with respect to proposed future conduct or action by a public servant." NYC Charter § 2603(c)(2).

"A public servant or supervisory official of such public servant may request the board to review and make a determination regarding a past or ongoing action of such public servant. Such request shall be reviewed and acted upon by the board in the same manner as a complaint received by the board under [the complaint provisions] of this section." NYC Charter § 2603(g)(1).

6. NYC Charter § 2603(c). *See also* Anne Arundel County, Maryland Public Ethics Law (Anne Arun. Co. Code) § 3-108; and Cook County, Illinois Ethics Ordinance (Cook Co. Ethics Ord.) § 4.1(j).

7. "A public servant whose conduct or action is the subject of an advisory opinion shall not be subject to penalties or sanctions by virtue of acting or failing to act due to a reasonable reliance on the opinion, unless material facts were omitted or misstated in the request for an opinion." NYC Charter § 2603(c)(2).

8. *See* New York State (NYS) Executive Law § 94(15), which provides that someone who, in good faith, acted in reliance on an advisory opinion of the New York State Ethics Commission, may introduce the opinion and use it as a defense in any criminal or civil action, unless he or she omitted or misstated material facts in the request for the opinion.

9. Maui County Code of Ethics (Maui Co. Code) § 10-2(5).

10. NYC Charter § 2603(c)(2); NYS Executive Law § 94(15).

11. *See, e.g.,* Anne Arun. Co. Code § 6-101, which provides that any person may file a signed, written complaint with the ethics commission on the commission's form, or the ethics commission may commence a case sua sponte. The ethics commission may dismiss the complaint at any time if the evidence does not support further action. *Id.* The Chicago Board of Ethics has the power and duty to initiate and to receive complaints about violation of its ethics law. *See* Chicago Ordinance (Chicago Ord.) § 2-156-380(a). Cook County, Illinois, has a similar provision. *See* (Cook Co. Ethics Ord.) § 4.1(f) (board shall initiate and receive complaints of violations of ethics law and shall investigate and act upon such complaints as are presented by the agency's executive director). In Los Angeles (L.A.), the complaint must be sworn and may be submitted by any person. L.A. City Charter § 600(O)(1)(a)(i). In New York State, complaints must be sworn. *See* NYS Executive Law § 94(12).

12. *See* Vol. II, Report of the NYC Charter Revision Commission, Dec. 1986–Nov. 1988, at 162.

13. L.A. City Charter § 600(O)(1)(a)(i).

14. L.A. City Charter § 600(O)(1)(a)(ii).

15. King County, Washington, Employee Code of Ethics (King Co. Code) §§ 3.04.017(H)(1), 3.04.055.

16. King Co. Code § 3.04.055(B).

17. King Co. Code § 3.04.055(C).

18. Seattle Code of Ethics (Seattle Code) §§ 4.16.030(A), 4.16.090(C).

19. Seattle Code § 4.16.090(C).

20. Seattle Code § 4.16.090(B).

21. Seattle Code § 4.16.090(A).

22. NYC Charter § 2603(e), (f).

23. *See* L.A. City Charter § 600(R)(1) (commission and any special prosecutor may subpoena witnesses, compel their attendance and testimony, administer oaths and affirmations,

take evidence and require by subpoena the production of any books, papers, records, or other items material to the performance of the commission's duties or exercise of its powers); NYS Executive Law § 94(16)(d) (commission has power and duty to conduct any investigation necessary to carry out the provisions of the executive law; pursuant to this power and duty, the commission may administer oaths or affirmations, subpoena witnesses, compel their attendance, and require production of any books or records that it may deem relevant or material); Revised Charter of the City and County of Honolulu 1973 (1994 ed.)(Honolulu Charter) § 11-107 (seven-member ethics commission is authorized to hold hearings and to conduct investigations concerning the application of the charter); King Co. Code § 3.04.055(D) (ombudsman is directed to ascertain the facts concerning the violation of the ethics code and must conduct the investigation in an objective and impartial manner; ombudsman is authorized to use subpoena power to compel sworn testimony and require the production of any records relevant or material to the investigation except information that is legally privileged or otherwise required by law not to be disclosed); Maui Co. Code § 10-2(3) (in the course of investigations, the nine-member Maui Board of Ethics has the power to administer oaths and subpoena witnesses and to compel the production of books and papers pertinent to the investigation).

24. NYC Charter § 2602(g).

25. Maui's code of ethics requires that the county council and the mayor cooperate and provide financing and personnel reasonably required by the board of ethics in the performance of its duties. Maui Co. Code § 10-2(6).

26. *See, e.g.,* Chicago Code § 2-156-380(b); Maui Co. Code § 10-2(a) (board of ethics appointed by the mayor with the approval of the county council has the power to initiate, receive, hear, and investigate complaints of violations of the ethics code). The Maui board can initiate impeachment proceedings against elected officers and officers appointed to elective office who are found by the board after investigation to have violated the Maui ethics code. Such proceedings are brought in the name of the board, which must be represented by special counsel of the board's choosing. Maui Co. Code § 10-2(b).

27. Anne Arun. Co. Code § 6-102(a).

28. Cook Co. Ethics Ord. § 4.1(f).

29. Cook Co. Ethics Ord. § 4.1(g).

30. Cook Co. Ethics Ord. § 4.1(h).

31. Chicago Ord. § 2-156-380(a).

32. *Id.* Similarly, in New York City, the NYC Board is not empowered to impose penalties against members of the city council or its employees but may recommend to the council such penalties as it deems appropriate, and the council must report to the board what action was taken. NYC Charter § 2603(h)(3).

33. Chicago Ord. § 2-156-380(b).

34. *Id.*

35. L.A. City Charter § 600(O)(1)(a)(i).

36. Chicago Ord. § 2-156-390(a).

37. King Co. Code § 3.04.055(E).

38. NYC Charter § 2603(f)(1). In addition to reporting to the NYC Board its findings in cases referred to it by the board, the Department of Investigation must also report to the board concerning the results of all investigations that involve or may involve violations of the NYC Charter conflicts of interest provisions, whether or not such investigations were made at the request of the board. NYC Charter § 2603(f)(2).

39. Chicago Ord. § 2-156-390(b).

40. *Id.*

41. *Id.*

42. *Id.*

43. *Id.*

44. *Id.*

45. *Id.*

46. *Id.*

280   ENFORCEMENT OF LOCAL ETHICS LAW

47. NYC Charter §§ 2603(c)(5), (e)(3), (g)(3), and (h)(7).

48. The cases reported below are: Flynn v. State Ethics Comm'n, 208 A.D.2d 91, 622 N.Y.S.2d 997 (3d Dep't 1995), *aff'g* Index No. 7124-93, slip op. (Sup. Ct. Albany Co. Dec. 23, 1993)(Kahn, J.).

49. NYS Criminal Procedure Law § 30.10(3)(b).

50. NYC Charter § 2603(k).

51. 12 Rules of the City of New York (RCNY), tit. 53, chap. 2, § 2-05(f).

52. 12 RCNY, tit. 53, chap. 2, §§ 2-04(d), 2-05(f).

53. Anne Arun. Co. Code § 6-105(a), (b) (complaints confidential unless a finding of a violation has been made or the matter has been referred for prosecution or the respondent has agreed in writing to the release of information; respondent has the right to know the identity of the complainant if the complaint goes to a hearing or a civil or criminal action begins); NYS Executive Law § 94(17)(b) (no meeting or proceeding of the NYS Ethics Commission shall be open to the public, except if expressly provided otherwise by the commission); NYS Executive Law § 94(11), (12), (14)(initial notice of alleged violations and written responses are confidential; a commission determination of no violation at any stage is sent to the respondent and to the complainant but is otherwise confidential, but a copy of any notice of delinquency or notice of reasonable cause sent under financial disclosure or conflict of interest provisions shall be sent to the reporting person, the complainant, the temporary president of the senate and the speaker of the assembly in the case of an elected official, or to the appointing authority; such notice is also included in the reporting person's file and is available for public inspection); Cook Co. Ethics Ord. § 4.2 (investigations conducted confidentially, and final determination of the board must be made available to the public with deletions as necessary to comply with Illinois freedom of information law); Chicago Ord. § 2-156-400 (complaints, investigations, and recommendations confidential except as necessary to carry out the powers and duties of the board or to enable another agency or person to consider and act upon the notices and recommendations of the board; without identifying the person complained against or the specific transaction, the board may comment publicly on the disposition of its requests and recommendations, and publish summary opinions to inform city personnel and the public about the interpretation of the provisions of the Chicago ethics ordinance); L.A. City Charter § 600(O)(1)(a)(iii) (investigation shall be conducted confidentially and members or employees of the commission who, prior to a probable cause determination, disclose information about a preliminary investigation, except as necessary to conduct the investigation, are liable for monetary penalties, and unauthorized release of confidential information is sufficient grounds for termination of the employee or commissioner responsible); L.A. City Charter § 600(O)(1)(b), (O)(1)(c)(i)(c) (probable cause hearings are private unless the alleged violator files with the commission a written request that the proceeding be public; and the commission's finding that no violation has occurred shall be published in a declaration).

54. NYC Charter § 2603(h)(1).

55. *Id.* Unlike New York City, New York State sends its "reasonable cause" notice not only to the respondent but also to the complainant, if any, and, in the case of a statewide elected official, to the temporary president of the senate and the speaker of the assembly, and, in the case of a state officer or employee, to the appointing authority for the respondent. NYS Executive Law § 94(12)(b).

56. NYC Charter § 2603(h)(1). *Compare* L.A. City Charter § 600(O)(1)(b) (no finding of probable cause to believe that a provision of the charter or city ordinances relating to, inter alia, conflicts of interest or government ethics, shall be made by the commission unless, at least twenty-one days prior to the commission's consideration of the alleged violation, the person alleged to have committed the violation is notified of the allegations, is provided with a summary of the evidence, and is informed of his or her right to be present in person or represented by counsel at any proceeding of the commission held to consider whether probable cause exists).

57. NYC Charter § 2603(h)(1); 12 RCNY, tit. 53, ch. 2, § 2-01(a).

58. NYC Charter § 2603(h)(1); 12 RCNY, tit. 53, ch. 2, §§ 2-01(a), 2-05(e).

Notes 281

59. 12 RCNY, tit. 53, ch. 2, §§ 2-01(a), 2-05(c)-(d). *Compare* L.A. City Charter § 600(O)(1)(b) (notification by registered mail with return receipt requested).

60. 12 RCNY, tit. 53, ch. 2, §§ 2-05(c)-(d). Petitions, however, must be served by both first class mail and certified mail, return receipt requested, or by other specified methods, including personal service or by a method agreed upon by counsel. *Id.*

61. NYC Charter § 2603(h)(2); 12 RCNY, tit. 53, ch. 2, § 2-01(d). *Compare* King Co. Code § 3.04.055(F), (G) (results of the investigation shall be reduced to written findings of fact, and the finding shall be made that there is or is not reasonable cause to believe that the respondent violated the ethics code; a finding of no reasonable cause must be served on both the complainant and the respondent); *see also* Seattle Code § 4.16.090(D)(where the administrator determines that the violation was inadvertent or minor, or there are no reasonable grounds to believe that a violation has occurred, administrator must dismiss the complaint, in writing, setting forth the facts and provisions of law on which the dismissal is based, and must provide a copy of the written dismissal to the complainant, to the person named in the complaint as the alleged violator, and to the board).

62. The Seattle administrator issues to the alleged violator a charging document that includes the provisions of the law that allegedly were violated and the conduct that constitutes the violation, with a copy to the board and then schedules a hearing before the board. Seattle Code § 4.16.090(E).

63. NYC Charter § 2603(h)(2); 12 RCNY, tit. 53, ch. 2, § 2-02(a), (b).

64. 12 RCNY, tit. 53, ch. 2 § 2-02(a), (b).

65. *Id.* § 2-02(b).

66. *Id.*

67. *Id.*

68. *Id.* §§ 2-02(c), 2-05(e).

69. *Id.* § 2-02(c)(3).

70. *Id.* § 2-02(c)(2).

71. *Id.* § 2-02(d).

72. *Id.* § 2-01(c).

73. NYC Charter § 2603(h)(2); 12 RCNY, tit. 53, ch. 2, §§ 2-02(a), 2-04(c).

74. NYC Charter § 2603(e)(2)(d); 12 RCNY, tit. 53, ch. 2, § 2-02(a).

75. 12 RCNY, tit. 53, ch. 2, § 2-04(c).

76. Cook Co. Ethics Ord. § 4.1(i).

77. King Co. Code § 3.04.055(H).

78. *See* 12 RCNY, tit. 53, ch. 2, § 2-03(d)(1); OATH Rules of Practice, 12 RCNY, tit. 48 (OATH Rules).

79. OATH Rules § 1-33.

80. *Id.* § 1-33(b).

81. *Id.* § 1-33(e).

82. 12 RCNY, tit. 53, ch. 2, § 2-03(a). *See also* Chicago Ord. § 2-156-380(b); L.A. City Charter § 600(O)(1)(c)(i) (public hearing); King Co. Code § 3.04.057(A)–(E)(ombudsman's order may be appealed to the board of ethics upon a written request containing a brief statement of the reasons for seeking an appeal hearing; a verbatim record is made; burden of proof is on the ombudsman; hearing must be held within a reasonable time after receipt of the request for appeal).

83. 12 RCNY, tit. 53, ch. 2, § 2-03(a).

84. Anne Arun. Co. Code § 6-102(e); OATH Rules § 1-46.

85. King Co. Code § 3.04.057(D); Anne Arun. Co. Code § 6-102(d); 12 RCNY, tit. 53, ch. 2, § 2-01(a).

86. Seattle Code § 4.16.090(F). The Seattle Ethics Board must commence its hearings within 30 days from the date that the administrator schedules the hearing.

87. 12 RCNY, tit. 53, ch. 2, § 2-03(a), (c).

88. *Id.* § 2-03(b).

89. *Id.* § 2-04(a).

282 ENFORCEMENT OF LOCAL ETHICS LAW

90. *Id.* § 2-03(d)(3).

91. *Id.* § 2-03(d)(3); OATH Rules § 1-46.

92. 12 RCNY, tit. 53, ch. 2, § 2-04(a).

93. *Id.* § 2-04(h).

94. In April 1996, after a full trial on the merits, the NYC Board fined former city comp-troller Elizabeth Holtzman $7,500 for violating the City Charter with respect to her participa-tion in the selection of a Fleet Bank affiliate as a comanager on a city bond issue and a loan by Fleet Bank to her United States Senate campaign. *In re Holtzman,* No. 93-121. After two appel-late reviews of the case, the Court of Appeals of New York State affirmed the board's findings at 91 N.Y.2d 488 (1998), holding that "[a] City official is chargeable with knowledge of those busi-ness dealings that create a conflict of interest about which the official 'should have known.'" 91 N.Y.2d at 497 (citation omitted).

95. 12 RCNY, tit. 53, ch. 2, § 2-04(b). *See also* King Co. Code § 3.04.057(E) (following review of the evidence, board must enter written findings and conclusions within a reasonable time); Seattle Code § 4.16.090(F) (board must issue a written determination stating whether the law has been violated and setting forth the facts and law upon which the determination is based); Maui Co. Code § 10-2(4) (after due deliberation on issues before it, board shall make findings of fact and conclusions of law and transmit them to the appropriate appointing authority and to the prosecuting authority for disposition).

96. 12 RCNY, tit. 53, ch. 2, § 2-05(h). *See* COIB v. Matos, No. 94-368 (1996) (admission with $1,000 fine for sending resume to city contractor while directly concerned with that con-tractor's particular matter with the city); COIB v. Rubin, No. 94-242 (1995) (admission of viola-tion of official duties by adjudication of father-in-law's parking tickets but no fine because of the absence at the time of a board rule implementing the "catch-all" section of the charter gen-erally prohibiting conflicts with the proper discharge of one's official duties). The NYC Board imposed a $5,000 fine in 1995 on a former high-level city official who interviewed for a job with a city bidder and accepted meals worth more than $50 per year from that bidder while working on that bidder's city matter. *See also In re Begel,* No. 96-40 (prohibited interest in a firm engaged in business dealings with the city but no penalty imposed because of mitigating circumstances). The board now has a "catch-all" rule pursuant to NYC Charter § 2604(b)(3) and can now issue fines for specified conduct that conflicts with official duties *and* is not captured by other provi-sions of the charter and board rules. *See* 12 RCNY, tit. 53, ch. 2, §§ 1–13.

97. Anne Arun. Co. Code § 6-103(b).

98. Seattle Code § 4.16.090(E).

99. 12 RCNY, tit. 53, ch. 2, § 2-05(g).

100. Commonwealth of Massachusetts State Ethics Commission Enforcement Procedures §§ 9, 11(A), (B).

101. *Id.* § 11(B), (C).

102. *Id.* § 4(C).

103. *See* Craven v. State Ethics Comm'n, 390 Mass. 191, 454 N.E.2d 471 (1983) (no actual improper combination of investigative and adjudicatory functions where staff investigated and Chair did not participate in decisions to investigate and issue order to show cause, and, even if he did so participate, this did not deprive plaintiff of due process); Raymond v. Board of Regis-tration in Med., 387 Mass. 708, 715–17, 443 N.E.2d 391, 395-397 (1982) (actual prejudice must be shown).

104. Pennsylvania State Ethics Commission Rules and Regulations.

105. NYC Charter § 2606(b); NYC Administrative Code (NYC Ad. Code) § 12-110(h).

106. NYC Charter § 2606(b).

107. NYC Charter § 2606(a).

108. NYC Charter § 2606(c).

109. *See* NYS Correction Law § 701(2) (granting to a first offender a certificate of relief from civil disabilities may avoid city charter's automatic job forfeiture provision, NYC Charter § 2606(c)). In exercising discretion as to whether to grant such a certificate, courts consider, first and foremost, whether granting the certificate is in the "public interest." Correction Law

§ 702(2)(c). Granting such relief may not be in the public interest depending upon the conduct admitted and the purposes of the conflicts of interest law (general and specific deterrence, symbolic and educational value of job forfeiture, and communication to the public of the great importance of honest government). In New York, a certificate of relief from disabilities "may be limited to one or more enumerated forfeitures, disabilities or bars, or may relieve the first offender of all forfeitures, disabilities and bars." Correction Law § 701(1). Thus, the courts have discretion in deciding to limit the relief sought. *See* Matter of Dark v. New York City Hous. Auth., N.Y.L.J., p. 28, col. 1 (Sup. Ct. N.Y. Co.)(Jan. 12, 1996); Op. Atty. Gen. 91-F10 at 332.

110. L.A. Ord. § 49.5.19(C) (any person residing within the City of Los Angeles may sue for injunctive relief to enjoin violations of, or to compel compliance with, the provisions of the City of L.A. Governmental Ethics Ordinance).

111. *E.g.,* L.A. City Charter § 600(S) (any interested person may seek judicial review of any action of the Commission); 12 RCNY, tit. 53, ch. 2, § 2-04(b) (an order finding a violation shall include notice of the public servant's right to appeal to the NYS Supreme Court).

112. *See* L.A. Ord. § 49.5.19(B)(5), (E); D.C. Law § 1-1471(f).

113. Cook Co. Ord. § 2.14; Anne Arun. Co. Code § 6-106; L.A. Ord. § 49.5.4; King Co. Code § 3.04.060(D).

114. Chicago Ord. § 2-156-380(b).

115. Chicago Ord. § 2-156-380(d).

116. Chicago Ord. § 2-156-450.

117. Cook Co. Ethics Ord. § 4.1(g).

118. Index No. 403858/95, slip op. (N.Y. Co. Mar. 15, 1996) (Sklar, J.).

119. King Co. Code § 3.04.055(A).

Penalties for Violations

Board	Monetary Penalty	Removal/Other Discipline	Voiding a Contract	Criminal Penalty
Anne Arun Co. Code §§ 6-103; 6-104; 6-201; 6-202, 6-203, 6-204	$1,000 per day by court order. Withhold salary until respondent complies with court order. Forfeit and return anything of value.	Censure, removal, reprimand; board or judicial cease and desist order.	Court may void an official action involving conflict of interest but may not void a public obligation. Action must be brought within ninety days of the occurrence of official action.	Criminal referral to prosecuting authority if there are reasonable grounds to believe respondent committed a criminal offense. Commission to make all evidence under its control available to prosecuting authority. Knowing/willful violation subjects one on conviction to a fine up to $1,000 or imprisonment not more than six months or both. Remedies are cumulative, not mutually exclusive. Withhold salary until respondent complies with court order. If defendant is a business entity, each officer or partner is criminally liable for knowing/willful authorization or participation in violation.
Chicago Ord. §§ 2-156-410(a), (b), 2-156-420, 2-156-430, 2-156-440.	$500 per offense upon conviction (knowing violation or false, misleading or incomplete information). Actions for an accounting for any pecuniary benefit received in violation of code, and for damages.	Employment sanctions including discharge/removal; removal of appointed officials for code violation or furnishing false/misleading information to board and failure to provide information requested by board.	Any contracts entered in violation of conflicts code voidable. All contracts must include provision for compliance with ethics code.	Any person found by a court to be guilty of knowingly violating code or furnishing false, misleading, or incomplete information to board with intent to mislead, upon conviction, shall be punished by a fine up to $500 per offense.
Cook Co. Ord. §§ 3.3, 5.1, 5.2, 5.3.	$500 per offense for knowing violation of code or knowingly furnishing false/misleading information to board. Same for financial disclosure violations.	Employment sanctions including discharge for violation of ordinance or knowingly furnishing false or misleading information in any board inquiry.	Any contract negotiated, entered into, or performed in violation of code voidable.	Upon conviction, $500 fine per offense (knowing violation of code or knowingly furnishing false/misleading information).

Board	Monetary Penalty	Removal/Other Discipline	Voiding a Contract	Criminal Penalty
D.C. Law § 1-1471(a), (b), (d). Prosecutions are by U.S. attorney in the name of the United States.	$5,000 for violation of code; $10,000 for knowingly false or misleading statement to board.	—	—	Any person or political committee in violation fined up to $5,000 or imprisoned up to six months, or both. For knowingly false or misleading statement, report, voucher, or other paper or statement, up to $10,000 fine or imprisonment up to five years, or both.
Honolulu Rev. Charter §§ 11-106, 11-107; Honolulu Rev. Ordinances §§ 3-8.4(f), 3-8.5(a)-(c).	City, by corporation counsel, may recover any fee, compensation, gift, or profit received by any person as a result of violation of codes by an officer or employee or former officer or employee. Action to be brought within two years of violation. For late filing of financial disclosure reports, $100 for the first late filing; $200 for the second late filing, and an additional $200 for each subsequent late filing.	Impeachment; removal, reprimand, probation, demotion, suspension, discharge. Appointing authority to notify commission promptly of action taken.	Any contract entered into in violation of codes is voidable on behalf of city, and interests of third parties who may be damaged by voiding shall be taken into account. Action to void official act must be brought within ninety days after matter is referred to commission.	For failure to file financial disclosure statement, the conflicts of interest penalties, and a criminal penalty up to $2,000 or imprisonment not more than one year, or both.
King County, Washington, Employee Code of Ethics § 3.04.060.	Loss of pay not more than one month's salary. Civil liability imposed on any person who either directly or as an accomplice commits a violation of code.	If found guilty, disciplinary action, including termination from employment. Members of boards and commissions found guilty of a negligent violation of code subject to immediate removal from appointment.	Any person who willfully attempts to secure preferential treatment in his or her dealings with the county by offering valuable consideration, thing of value, or gift, whether in the form of services, loan, thing, or promise to any county official or employee, shall have current contracts with the county cancelled and shall be unable to bid on any other county contract for two years.	Any negligent or willful violation of code is a misdemeanor, punishable upon conviction by a fine not to exceed $1,000 or imprisonment in county jail not more than ninety days or both. Criminal liability imposed on any person who either directly or as an accomplice commits a violation of code. Those who act as accomplice or who retaliate against complaining employee are subject to criminal and civil penalties of code.

Board	Monetary Penalty	Removal/Other Discipline	Voiding a Contract	Criminal Penalty
L.A. Ord. §§ 49.5.19, 49.5.20; L.A. City Charter § 600(O)(1)(c)(i), (d).	$5,000 per intentional or negligent violation or triple the amount the person failed to report properly or illegally expended, gave/received, whichever is greater. Private plaintiff retains 50 percent of recovery; balance to city's general fund. 100 percent to general fund in action by city attorney or commission. Prevailing party (other than an agency) gets costs of litigation, including attorney's fees. For late filing of financial disclosure reports, $25 per day after the deadline until report is filed. Commission can waive this fine if lateness was not willful, but after thirty days, no waivers granted.	Administrative discipline by appointing authority. Cease and desist order by commission; order to file reports, documents, information; order to pay up to $5,000 per violation or treble damages. If convicted of a misdemeanor under code, person is disqualified as a lobbyist or city contractor for four years following date of conviction unless the court at the time of sentencing specifically determines not to apply this penalty. Any person can sue for injunctive relief to compel compliance with code.	Any person who causes another to violate code or who aids and abets violation is liable personally.	Knowing/willful violation is a misdemeanor. One aiding and abetting another in the violation of code is also liable. Prosecution to be commenced within four years after date of violation.
Maui County Code of Ethics § 10-5.	Fine to be provided by ordinance adopted by county council.	Nonelected officers or employees may be suspended or removed from office by the appropriate appointing authority. Elected officers may be impeached.	—	—
NYC Charter § 2606; NYC Administrative Code § 12-110(h).	$10,000 for conflict of interest, or intentional failure to file financial disclosure report or false or misleading report.	Board can recommend suspension or removal from office after consultation with agency head. Conviction for buying public office leads to lifetime disqualification from being elected, appointed, or employed in city service.	Void a contract or transaction after consultation with agency head.	Violation of conflicts of interest or financial disclosure code is a misdemeanor. Automatic forfeiture of public office upon conviction in a criminal proceeding brought by district attorneys. Actual knowledge of a business dealing with the city

Board	Monetary Penalty	Removal/Other Discipline	Voiding a Contract	Criminal Penalty
NYC Charter § 2606; NYC Administrative Code § 12-110(h). (*cont'd*)				is required for a criminal conviction based upon holding a prohibited interest in a firm doing business with the city. Violation of financial disclosure law is punishable by imprisonment up to one year or $1,000 fine or both.
NYS Exec. Law § 94(13).	$10,000 for knowing violation of public officers law and willful failure to file financial disclosure report or false statement.	Disciplinary action by appointing authority.	—	Class A misdemeanor if referred to appropriate prosecutor.
Philadelphia Code § 20-612(1)-(2).	$300.	Except for financial disclosure violations, lifetime disqualification from holding any appointed office or employment with the city, its agencies, authorities, boards, or commissions, in addition to other penalties provided by law.	City council has right to repeal legislation enacted in violation of code. Mayor, with concurrence of a majority of all the members of the city council, may void any award, contract, lease, case, claim, decision, decree, or judgment made in violation of code, provided that officer or employee acted in official capacity.	$300 and imprisonment not more than ninety days.
Seattle Code of Ethics § 4.16.090(H), 4.16.100.	$500.	Board may recommend disciplinary action, including suspension, discharge, removal from office, or other action as appropriate city authority deems necessary and proper. Board makes written report to the appropriate city authority, which must report back within fourteen calendar days the disciplinary action taken, except that this provision must not derogate from employee's rights under any collective bargaining agreement or city personnel ordinance.	If violation involves conduct of a former officer or employee, board may recommend to the administering city authority that no contract be entered into or that a contract be terminated and proceedings begun anew to prevent injury to the city or to avoid unfair advantage to a competitor.	Infraction, $500 maximum.

APPENDIX ❦ I I A

THE CITY OF NEW YORK
CONFLICTS OF INTEREST BOARD
————————————————————————————————————X

In the Matter of   :   <u>DISPOSITION</u>
                                                                        COIB Case No. 94-368
     SERGIO MATOS,   :   OATH Index No. ___

Respondent.   :
————————————————————————————————————X

Respondent Sergio Matos states the following:

1. I was employed by the City of New York Department of Environmental Protection ("DEP") from approximately October 1988 through February 10, 1995. As of May 1990, my title was Associate Staff Analyst. During my employment at DEP, I also served as Director of Site Assessment for the Division of Hazardous Materials. I was a public servant during my employment at DEP.

2. While I was employed at DEP, I participated in writing the technical aspects of the scope of the work included in a Request for Proposals for a contract involving remediation of lead contaminated soils at the New York City Police Department Firing Range at Rodman's Neck in the Bronx ("Rodman's Neck"). Virtually from its inception, I served as the project manager on this project. In addition, I served on a DEP technical advisory committee ("TAC"), which was considering whether to recommend awarding the contract to Marcor Environmental Corp. ("Marcor").

3. On January 20, 1994, the TAC recommended that Marcor be awarded the contract. This recommendation was accepted by DEP and the TAC was thereupon disbanded.

4. On March 22, 1994, I sent an unsolicited letter to Michael Wyatt, Senior Vice President of Marcor. A copy of that letter is annexed hereto and incorporated herein by reference. In the letter, I wrote to Mr. Wyatt that I was interested in a challenging management position in environmental science. I enclosed a copy of my resume with the letter for Mr. Wyatt's consideration. I understand that this letter could be interpreted as a request for employment. Mr. Wyatt received that letter and I discussed it with him. Marcor never interviewed me for a job and never hired me.

5. On June 22, 1994, DEP, with approval from the Mayor's Office, formally awarded the contract to Marcor. The contract was worth approximately $10,000,000.

6. Although the TAC completed its work when it made its recommendation in January, 1994, I was never removed from responsibility for the Rodman's Neck project, and I never recused myself from the project. In the period between the TAC recommendation in January 1994 and the award of the contract to Marcor in June 1994, I actively participated in deciding which fixative should be used by Marcor in the lead remediation process. I attended a public hearing on April 7, 1994 concerning the contract. Upon the award of the contract to Marcor in June 1994, I assumed the task of supervising the project in the field.

7. I admit that this conduct constituted a conflict of interest in violation of Section 2604(d)(1) of the City Charter in that I was directly concerned with or personally participating in the Rodman's Neck project at the time I sent the attached letter. I wrote the letter to Marcor at a time after the TAC was disbanded and the Marcor recommendation had been accepted and approved (January 20, 1994) and before the contract had been formally awarded to Marcor on June 22, 1994. Section 2604(d)(1) provides:

> No public servant shall solicit, negotiate for or accept any position *** (ii) with any person or firm who or which is involved in a particular matter with the city, while such public servant is actively considering or is directly concerned or personally participating in such particular matter on behalf of the city.

I understand that my sending the attached letter to Marcor was improper, and that I should have recused myself completely, in writing, from the Rodman's Neck Project if I wanted to send my resume to Marcor. I also understand that my sending the attached letter to Marcor created the appearance of a conflict of interest in violation of Sections 2604(b)(2) and (b)(3) of the City Charter, which provide:

> No public servant shall engage in any business, transaction or private employment, or have any financial or other private interest, direct or indirect, which is in conflict with the proper discharge of his or her official duties. [Section 2604(b)(2).]

> No public servant shall use or attempt to use his or her position as a public servant to obtain any financial gain, contract, license, privilege or other private or personal advantage, direct or indirect, for the public servant, or any person or firm associated with the public servant. [Section 2604(b)(3).]

8. In addition, I agree to file a financial disclosure report for 1995 with the Conflicts of Interest Board upon execution of this Disposition. This report was due on or about April 10, 1995, within 60 days of my separation from City service, and was overdue. (I have now filed that report with the Board as of December 6, 1995.)

9. In acknowledgment of the foregoing, I agree to pay a fine of $1,000 to the Board, on the following terms and conditions. I have submitted to the Board a sworn Affidavit with documentary proof of financial hardship. The

circumstances of my financial hardship include that, as a result of the incidents recited above, I resigned my City job in the face of departmental charges at DEP; I have been unemployed for nearly a year; I have exhausted all my funds and savings on basic living expenses since I left City service, and that I am in debt. Based upon my Affidavit of hardship, I submit $250 herewith. I agree that I shall submit to the Board, by December 15, 1996, a sworn Affidavit wherein I shall set forth my financial circumstances as of December 15, 1996, and specifically include the facts concerning whether or not I am then gainfully employed, and, if so, the name and address of my employer and the amount of my annual salary, attaching documentation of any such salary. It is further agreed that if I have secured gainful employment by December 15, 1996, paying as much as my last annual City salary or more, I shall pay the balance of the fine ($750) according to a payment schedule to be agreed upon mutually by the Board and by me. In the event, however, that I have not secured gainful employment paying as much as my last annual City salary or more, by December 15, 1996, then the Petition herein shall be dismissed, this matter shall be closed, and my fine shall be deemed paid in full upon the acceptance by the Board of my claim of failure to secure gainful employment at least equal to my last annual City salary by December 15, 1996.

10. I agree that this statement is a public and final resolution of the charges against me. Furthermore, I agree to provide a copy of this Disposition to any City agency where I might apply for employment upon the request of such agency or in response to any inquiry calling for such information, and, in any event, prior to accepting employment with the City.

Sergio Matos

The New York City Conflicts of Interest Board accepts this Disposition and the terms contained therein as a final disposition of the charges against Sergio Matos in the above-captioned case, and accordingly, shall dismiss the Petition herein against Mr. Matos upon full performance by Mr. Matos of this Disposition.

The Conflicts of Interest Board
By: Sheldon Oliensis, Chair

Dated: March 8, 1996

Appendix 11A   291

Brooklyn, New York
March 22, 1994

Michael Wyatt
Senior Vice President
Marcor Environmental
P.O. Box 1043
Hunt Valley, Maryland 21030

Dear Michael:

Enclosed please find a copy of my resume for your consideration. I am interested in a challenging management position in environmental science.

For the past four years I have directed personnel involved in both the emergency response to hazardous materials spills and in the long-term assessment and remediation of contaminated sites. The emergency response experience involved the identification and immediate amelioration of imminently hazardous conditions which might occur as the result of spills, accidents, explosions or abandoned chemicals. Those efforts are geared towards the protection of human health and the environment.

For the past two years I have directed a site assessment and remediation program for the City of New York. This program manages the design and implementation of site assessments, including the interpretation of analytical data and the design of remedial strategies. This program was also charged with remediating NYSDEC-listed hazardous waste sites by designing and conducting Remedial Investigations and Feasibility Studies. Environmental assessments were also conducted for the purpose of property acquisiton and in support of litigation by the NYC Law Department.

Having read your mission statement and finding that I agree with the professionalism and work ethic you have chosen to present, I respectfully submit my resume for your consideration.

Respectfully yours,

Sergio Matos

APPENDIX ❦ IIB

DRAFT ALLOCUTION FOR GUILTY PLEA
TO VIOLATION OF CHAPTER 68 OF THE CITY CHARTER

1. You are pleading guilty here today to a violation of Section ___ of the City Charter. Is that correct?

2. The elements of that misdemeanor are:

_____

_____

_____

3. Do you understand the charge to which you are pleading guilty? Please tell me in your own words what you did.

4. Now, under Chapter 68 of the City Charter, the consequence of your plea today is that you will automatically lose your City [job][office][employment]. Section 2606(c) of the Charter provides:

> Any person who violates section twenty-six hundred four or twenty-six hundred five of this chapter shall be guilty of a misdemeanor and, on conviction thereof, shall forfeit his or her public office of employment.

Do you understand what this means? Have you discussed with your lawyer the consequences of losing your employment? If not, do you want an opportunity to do so? Please tell me in your own words what this means to you. Do you also understand that you will not be entitled to a hearing about the loss of your job at your agency as a result of your guilty plea? Do you understand that this automatic forfeiture of your job means that you will lose your City benefits such as health insurance and that if you wish to continue such insurance coverage, you will have to pay for it? And your pension and other rights may also be affected? Has your lawyer explained all of this to you? Knowing all of this, do you still wish to enter a plea of guilty to the Charter violation?

5. If I accept your plea of guilty, you will not able to withdraw the plea because you want to keep your job or for any other reason. Do you understand this?

APPENDIX ❦ A

Select Articles Recently Published by the ABA Section on State and Local Government Law

Federal Governmental Attorney-Client Privilege Decisions May Prove Significant to All Government Lawyers

Norman Redlich and David R. Lurie***

With its recent decision in *In re Lindsey,* 148 F.3d 1100 (D.C. Cir. 1998), *cert. denied,* 67 USLW 3318 (November 8, 1998), the District of Columbia Circuit became the second U.S. Court of Appeals to hold that the attorney-client privilege affords no protection against a grand jury subpoena issued to a government lawyer. Although neither the *Lindsey* precedent—nor the earlier Eighth Circuit decision in *In re Grand Jury Subpoena Duces Tecum,* 112 F.3d 910 (8th Cir.), *cert. denied,* 117 S. Ct. 2482 (1998)—concerned privilege assertions by state or local officials, the reasoning of these cases is of potentially crucial importance to all lawyers serving government officials and agencies.

In *Lindsey,* Deputy White House Counsel Bruce Lindsey refused to provide a grand jury with an account of communications he had with the President in rendering legal advice with respect to an Independent Counsel investigation. Independent Counsel Kenneth Starr then successfully moved to compel Lindsey's testimony, prevailing at both the District and Circuit Court levels. In rejecting the White House's privilege claim, the D.C. Circuit acknowledged that, in civil proceedings, federal officials (like their state and municipal counterparts) enjoy privilege protections as to their communications with the government lawyers that serve them. But, the Circuit Court held, "the attorney-client privilege dissolves in the face of a grand jury subpoena." 148 F.3d at 1119.

The D.C. Circuit grounded this holding on its "view of the proper allegiance of the government lawyer." *Id.* at 1109. That allegiance, the Court concluded, is owed first and foremost to the "public" and to the criminal justice system, not to the government agency or official the lawyer advises and serves. In reaching this conclusion, the Court relied upon the affirmative obligations that government lawyers undertake to uphold the nation's laws and even—under certain circumstances—to report instances of wrongdoing to law enforcement authorities. In light of these obligations, the Court reasoned, the "public's interest in uncovering illegality among its elected and appointed officials" trumps the interest of government officials and agencies in obtain-

---

*Dean Emeritus, New York University School of Law. Of Counsel, Wachtell, Lipton, Rosen & Katz, New York, New York.
**Associate of Wachtell, Lipton, Rosen & Katz, New York, New York.

ing fully informed advice from the lawyers that serve them. *Id.* at 1109. The Eighth Circuit followed similar reasoning in rejecting the assertion of the governmental attorney-client privilege in a grand jury proceeding. *See generally In re Grand Jury Subpoena,* 112 F.3d at 921.

Although these two recent decisions are limited to federal criminal proceedings, they are not confined to direct evidence or admissions of criminal conduct by government officials to their counsel. Rather, the courts held that the attorney-client privilege "dissolves" *any* time a grand jury seeks *any* evidence that it deems potentially relevant to a criminal inquiry. Since it is often difficult, if not impossible, for a government official to anticipate what information may in the future prove of interest to an investigator, they will have every reason to fear that counsel may become involuntary witnesses before a criminal tribunal and be forced to recount conversations that, at the time, appeared to be completely innocent of criminal taint. If allegiance to the "public" overrides traditional notions of attorney-client privilege, government officials will inevitably be deprived of the legal counsel that is so important to the proper functioning of government.

Although the recent Circuit Court decisions address only the scope of the privilege in the federal context, there is every reason to anticipate that courts will apply their reasoning to privilege claims by state and local officials (whether in state or federal criminal proceedings). The Supreme Court has denied review of both the Eighth Circuit and *Lindsey* decisions.

Ten Effective Strategies for Counseling Municipal Clients on Ethics Issues

Patricia E. Salkin

Government lawyers and local government officials often fail to pay attention to the subject of municipal ethics absent an allegation of unethical conduct or an outright crisis. Municipal attorneys should take the lead, however, in developing proactive strategies for ensuring the most ethical government possible by providing regular counsel on matters of ethics for municipal clients—even when not specifically requested to do so.

Although it may sound a bit peculiar to give the client what they did not specifically request, consider the circumstances. All involved in government, including full-time and part-time lawyers, have a responsibility to uphold the public trust and strive for integrity in government. It is incumbent upon lawyers to take primary responsibility for this trust since as a group, municipal lawyers may be "in the business" longer than elected local officials who may serve shorter terms of office. Lawyers are also educated and trained to uphold certain standards of ethics and professionalism as part of our formal and ongoing education process. Municipal officials are not granted a license to hold elective office contingent upon such formal prior or ongoing familiarity with public sector ethics issues.

Perhaps equally compelling, is the consideration that once a municipal client is accused of wrongdoing, whether based on fact or fiction, it becomes the job of the municipal attorney to counsel the official, interact with the media, and possibly defend, at a hearing and/or in court, the action(s) of the local official. As Senator Alan Cranston once pointed out, it is so easy to make allegations of unethical conduct, and so difficult to defend against the accusations. Municipal attorneys should consider appropriate steps to minimize municipal officials' exposure to potential allegations.

Effective Ethics Education Strategies

Although most municipal officials are well intentioned and honest, dealing with ethics issues can be tricky. While based in law through statutes, local laws, opinions of state attorneys general and comptrollers, and case law, ethics issues also involve lesser defined community standards and values which may be very difficult to precisely define or predict. Raise the subject of ethics education, however, and many times eyes glaze over and the "heard it already" syndrome overcomes the room. Municipal attorneys should consider employing a combination of different types of ethics education activities designed to provide ongoing sensitivity to ethics issues which may arise.

Select Articles Recently Published by the ABA Section on State and Local Government Law 297

1. ***Provide each newly elected and appointed municipal official with a compilation of applicable ethics laws, rules, and regulations.***

When a person is first elected or appointed to public office, they should be presented with a packet of applicable ethics laws and regulations that govern their conduct. This is often the first time that they are even made aware that a local ethics law exists or that a state statute governing their conduct is in effect. For others who may have been aware of the existence of "ethics laws," this may be the first time they have had an opportunity to actually read the text. Accompanying this compilation of laws could be a cover memo from the municipal attorney summarizing key provisions and highlighting key state and local ethics opinions of interest to the officials. This packet should be kept up-to-date and ready for distribution each January. Since no such packet is required by law, it will take the initiative of the municipal attorney to develop and implement this strategy.

2. ***Offer at least one annual ethics training session for elected and appointed officials.***

People typically do not enjoy the thought of attending ethics sessions. Either they believe they have heard it before, they know it all, or they believe it will be a boring lecture. Try a short interactive session with hypotheticals. Using facts from recent opinions of the attorney general or comptroller or from a governing state or local ethics commission is one way to command immediate attention. Not only are the "hypotheticals" not as fictitious as the audience might like to believe, but in discussing appropriate responses, municipal attorneys can draw upon the reasoning espoused by an official charged with interpreting certain ethics provisions. Some municipal officials who are under the jurisdiction of active ethics boards have been trained through role playing and/or games (modeled on board games such as *Trivial Pursuit* or game shows like *Jeopardy*).

3. ***Develop an ethics checklist for municipal officials.***

Design a short ten- or fifteen-question ethics checklist for municipal officials consisting of questions regarding potential family, business, work, and financial conflicts issues. Financial conflict-of-interest is the area where a great number of ethics allegations are lodged. By simply "asking the questions," even if all the attorney does is hand out the paper and request that everyone take it home for a "self-test," awareness is raised, and perhaps heightened scrutiny will prevail before the official takes an action that could present a potential conflict situation, such as passing upon an application involving a business associate or a relative.

4. ***Circulate clippings from current publications.***

Simply circulate clippings from local and regional newspapers and magazines to municipal officials with an "FYI" notation. No explanation is necessary for municipal clients to get the message that the media, citizen groups, political enemies, and others are lurking in the background waiting for an opportunity to catch an unsuspecting official dozing at the "ethics wheel." This type of subtle and relatively painless ethics education process is understated yet can serve as a powerful reminder of the impact of quick decisions absent ethical considerations.

5. Raise an ethics issue from a neighboring jurisdiction at a board meeting.

Although human nature may suggest that people do not want to hear about the ethics implications of their own actions, they love to hear the scandalous news about officials in other jurisdictions. This strategy is most appropriately used by simply raising the fact that an ethics allegation or inquiry was made in a neighboring jurisdiction. Use the occasion to discuss whether the conduct is reasonable, legal, or moral based upon community standards in your municipality. This is a comfortable way to discuss actions and situations which could just as easily arise "at home."

6. Encourage periodic review of the local ethics law.

Ethics laws are typically adopted following on the heels of a scandal or crisis, or enacted as a result of state mandate. Therefore, once these laws are enacted, they tend to sit on the books for long periods of time without review. But, like comprehensive land-use plans, these documents lose their shelf life as time goes on and community standards, ethics, and values change. Furthermore, new situations arise which were often not contemplated when the ethics law was under discussion, and over time, citizens, the media, and officials learn about provisions which may have been inadvertently overlooked (such as enforcement and penalties).

Be prepared to recommend a manner in which the review should be conducted. Who should be responsible for the review. (e.g., the local legislative body, an ad hoc public/private specially appointed body), who should be included in the review process, and the level of public participation should all be discussed. Consider inserting a provision in the local law requiring periodic review every five to ten years.

7. Recommend the appointment of an ethics officer.

Once an environment is created where ethics issues are on the forefront of officials' minds, there will likely be more questions asked. Although larger urban and suburban municipalities may have an ethics commission or board, most municipalities are without such an entity. Consider recommending the appointment of a municipal ethics officer who is charged with providing guidance to local officials. The municipal attorney may be the ethics officer, or some other employee may be designated. Regardless of who is appointed, it is important to make certain that this individual is vested with independence from the political process. Furthermore, consideration should be given to the precise functions and duties to be performed. For example, it may be best to grant an advisory function only as opposed to bestowing investigatory powers upon the individual.

8. Seek the appointment of a local ethics board or commission.

Where such a body does not exist, raise the discussion regarding the pros and cons of the creation of this entity. The powers granted to ethics boards and commissions are wholly controlled by the local government through the enacting legislation, and the establishment of these bodies can provide great protection for local officials. For example, where a local official is uncertain whether a particular action is appropriate, she or he can seek an opinion from the local ethics board. In the event that the board does not have any concerns with the proposed activity, the official may decide to proceed, with the comfort that if questioned by the media, she or he can produce an opinion from the local ethics board stating that no conflict existed. Issues of political appointments to the board, terms of office, independence, and powers granted to the board are matters for the local legislative body to consider.

9. Designate a board member as the "ethics guru."

Just as local boards and commissions may consist of committees, consider appointing an elected or appointed member of each local board or body as the "ethics guru" for that entity. They may serve as the municipal attorney's conduit for raising ethics issues in a proactive way before colleagues. They may also be the informal, "in-house" questioner of ethical conduct prior to actions being taken which may later be challenged in the media. This person may also be charged with attending special municipal ethics courses and bringing back information and training to the board.

10. Conduct an ethics audit.

Just as government law offices conduct preventive law audits of various municipal departments to determine where there may be exposure to municipal liability, consider conducting formal or informal ethics audits of municipal officials and departments for the purpose of helping to identify potential areas of concern. This may most effectively be accomplished through an interview process of key decisionmakers and policymakers.

Conclusion

In ensuring that ethics education and preventive law strategies are accomplished in a meaningful manner, municipal lawyers are limited only by our own creativity and innovation. Any one or more of these effective strategies if not already in place in localities represented would go a long way to helping preserve public trust and integrity in government. In our efforts to ensure the most ethical conduct on the part of municipal officials, attorneys must not lose sight of our own standards of ethics and professionalism.

"Pay to Play": The Debate Continues

Patrick K. Arey[*]

Background

In the early 1990s, reports surfaced in the news media concerning public finance professionals contributing to political campaigns in exchange for or in the expectation of receiving business from the governmental entities. This practice was not previously unknown and anecdotes had long circulated about certain politicians raising campaign funds from public finance professionals to whom the politician could direct business. This conduct was described as "pay to play," a shorthand expression for the making of political contributions in order to obtain or be considered eligible to obtain (that is, "short listed") public finance work. As a result, in June 1994, the Municipal Securities Rulemaking Board (MSRB) adopted and the Securities and Exchange Commission approved Rule G-37 in an effort to curtail this practice by broker-dealers and underwriters. However, because the MSRB has no jurisdiction over lawyers, Rule G-37 did not restrict political contributions by members of the legal profession.

Concurrent with the MSRB's deliberations, beginning in December 1993, representatives of fifteen law firms with the largest municipal securities practices met at the request of Arthur Levitt, chair of the Securities and Exchange Commission, to consider a voluntary ban on political contributions, similar to the ban adopted by investment banking firms in the prior year. After extensive discussions, this group was unable to reach a consensus to take any action, and reported that result to Chair Levitt. Shortly thereafter, in February 1994, the Board of Directors of the National Association of Bond Lawyers (NABL) adopted a policy statement on "pay to play" condemning this conduct, advocated hiring of bond counsel based upon professional qualifications, and endorsed disclosure of political contributions by firms engaged in a public finance practice.

In the summer of 1996, the Association of the Bar of the City of New York ("City Bar") proposed that the House of Delegates adopt a rule based upon Rule G-37 which would prohibit or restrict the ability of lawyers or law firms to contribute to political campaigns. This proposal was withdrawn in 1996 in order to permit further study of this issue and consultation with other inter-

---

[*]Patrick K. Arey is a member of the firm of Miles & Stockbridge in Baltimore, Maryland, and is Secretary of the Section.

ested entities within the ABA. The City Bar published its revised report in February 1997. Representatives of the State and Local Government Law Section were afforded the opportunity to comment on the report after its publication. Subsequently, the City Bar again presented its proposed rule for consideration by the House of Delegates in August 1997.

The City Bar's proposal, similar to MSRB Rule G-37, would bar lawyers engaged in a public finance practice from working for any issuer for a period of two years after the firm or lawyers in the firm contributed to the election campaign of officials of the issuer. The City Bar's proposal would allow public finance lawyers to make contributions up to $250 to candidates for whom they can vote. The City Bar's proposal exceeds the limits of Rule G-37 in at least two respects by prohibiting "soft money" contributions to political parties or organizations and extending the prohibitions on political contributions to all lawyers in the firm, not just those engaged in a public finance practice.

In response to the City Bar's proposal, Lawrence J. Fox, chair of the Section Officers Conference, appointed an ad hoc committee to develop an alternate proposal to the City Bar's proposal. This Committee offered an alternate proposal which, with the consent of the City Bar, was offered as a substitute for the City Bar's proposal. Officers of the State and Local Government Law Section played an active role in the drafting of the alternate proposal and its adoption by the House of Delegates on August 6, 1997.

The resolution adopted by the House of Delegates condemned "the conduct of lawyers making political campaign contributions to, and soliciting political campaign contributions for, public officials in return for being considered eligible by public agencies to perform professional services, including municipal finance engagements," conduct generally referred to as "pay to play." The resolutions further called upon bar associations, lawyer disciplinary agencies, and the judiciary to enforce, when applicable to prohibit this conduct, existing Rules of Professional Conduct, such as Model Rule 7.2(c), prohibiting a lawyer from giving "anything of value to a person for recommending the lawyer's services." Finally, the resolution created a task force to study the issue, to determine whether additional professional standards, laws, or procedures relating to political campaign contributions are necessary and desirable, and to report back to the House of Delegates in August 1998 its recommendations as to any additional professional standards, laws, or procedures, found to be necessary and desirable in the form of amendments to the Model Rules of Professional Conduct, aspirational ethical standards, or other appropriate measures.

The Task Force on Political Contributions was appointed by ABA President Jerry Shestack under the leadership of Jack Martin, general counsel to the Ford Motor Company. David Cardwell, a former Chair of the Section and its representative to the House of Delegates, was appointed to serve on the Task Force. In January 1998, the Section made a presentation to the task force at the ABA Midyear Meeting, urging, among other things, that "pay to play" should be viewed as an issue affecting all lawyers engaged to represent state and local governments and that the issue be addressed through the Model Rules of Professional Conduct, including, in particular, Rule 7.2(c).

Although the task force has not made its deliberations public, press reports have indicated that one proposal before the task force is a modified rule similar to that proposed by the City Bar which would limit the ability of individual lawyers to make political contributions to officials of jurisdictions for which the lawyer provides services. This proposal apparently departs from the City Bar's proposal in at least one important respect; it would apply to *all* lawyers engaged by state and local governments, not just those engaged for public financial transactions.

Despite the fact that "pay to play" is, at the time this article was drafted, under study by the task force, there are, nevertheless, important steps which the ABA can take to address "pay to play" without prejudging the report expected from the task force or detracting from any recommendations the task force may make. Moving forward on this issue at this point would maintain the momentum to eliminate "pay to play" begun at last year's Annual Meeting and encouraged by Chair Levitt in his remarks following the action taken by the House of Delegates condemning "pay to play." Of course, the question remains what actions can and should the ABA take with respect to regulating "pay to play," based upon a realistic and practical assessment of what actions it may effectively take with respect to this issue.

Two Steps Forward

Full and Effective Reporting and Disclosure of Campaign Contributions. In 1992, the House of Delegates adopted a policy concerning Fair Campaign Practices which called for "full, accurate, readily accessible and timely disclosure of campaign contributions and expenditures" and limits on campaign contributions. Such reporting and disclosure of campaign contributions will help to end "pay to play," especially where the pressure for contributions comes from persons running for elective office, their campaign committees, or political parties. One frustration expressed by critics of this approach is that such information is not readily accessible to the public. This approach, however, is premised upon making this information readily available. In addition, to the author's knowledge, the press has reported the extent of such contributions in New York, Maryland, and Virginia, suggesting that such information is available now to those who will take the time to assemble and collate it. The State of Maryland requires that persons or firms that do business with the state in excess of $100,000, including law firms and lawyers, report separately political contributions by such firms or persons.[1] This statute may serve as a model for other states in addressing "pay to play" through the disclosure of political contributions.

Competitive Procedures for the Selection of Legal Counsel. Another means of eliminating "pay to play" from selection of counsel is the use by governments of effective, open, and competitive procedures for the selection of legal counsel which emphasize experience, expertise, and professional qualifications. One significant concern regarding "pay to play" involves not just the making of a political contribution to receive business, but the perception on the part of law firms or lawyers that they will not be eligible for consideration for such business if they do not make political contributions to those who allocate such work. The making of political contributions either to obtain business or to be considered eligible for business are equally objectionable and should both fall within the definition of "pay to play."

The Section was active in drafting and promoting the Model Procurement Code, which provides procedures for state and local governments to insure open and fair competition in the procurement of both goods and services by governments. Similarly, both the Committee on Government Debt and Fiscal Planning of the Government Finance Officers Association (GFOA) and the National Association of Bond Lawyers (NABL) have recommended that governments employ a merit based competitive process for the selection of bond counsel.[2] The application of the Model Procurement Code or similar principles to the procurement of counsel would be a substantial step toward eliminating "pay to play" in the selection of counsel to represent state and local governments by separating the process of political contributions from the selection of counsel.

The Tough Nut: Regulating Political Contributions

While almost everyone agrees that "pay to play" should be eliminated, there is a wide gulf between those who would deal with the issue by regulating the political contributions of lawyers and those who would not undertake such regulation.

In the author's opinion, any rule which attempts to directly regulate political contributions by law firms or attorneys in the fashion of MSRB Rule G-37 is a market regulation rule which should be promulgated by an authority empowered to regulate markets on the national level, such as the Securities and Exchange Commission. This agency is charged with regulating the national securities markets and has been remarkably successful in regulating the national securities markets while at the same time allowing them the freedom to be the most open and successful in the world. A national market regulation rule would also have the benefit of being applied and enforced uniformly. On the other hand, any attempt by the ABA to introduce such a market regulation rule through its ethical rules would only lead to lack of uniformity, implementation, and enforcement. The adoption of such a rule by the House of Delegates would only be the endorsement of adoption of such a rule to the states or lawyer disciplinary agencies, each of which would have to adopt and enforce its own rule. The author's conversations with other lawyers on this subject suggest that, at best, such a rule would vary significantly from state to state, if adopted at all. The result would be more a trap for the unwary than any effective enforcement of a rule governing conduct in the securities markets. Such a lack of uniformity only flies in the face of recent efforts to bring greater uniformity to the securities markets on a national basis, such as the National Securities Markets Improvement Act of 1996 and recent legislative efforts to modify banking and the financial industry laws. Looking to the future, states and local governments are beginning to meet their capital requirements through the global financial markets, thus reinforcing the need for uniformity of market regulation within the United States.

This difficulty might be overcome, however, if the ABA were to adopt an interpretation of the existing Model Rules of Professional Conduct, particularly Rule 7.2(c). Model Rule 7.2(c) prohibits a lawyer from giving anything of value to a person for recommending the lawyer's services.[3] Model Rule 7.2 and its immediately related rules apply primarily to solicitation and advertising. Model Rule 7.2(c) is primarily designed to protect the public from for-profit plans to channel clients to certain lawyers under circumstances where the potential client will likely rely on such referral as an endorsement of the lawyer's competence, expertise, or integrity. These same principles apply to "pay to play" conduct designed to obtain business from state and local governments. However, given the context of Rule 7.2(c) and the lack of any decisions or opinions applying such rule to "pay to play," some specific action by the ABA is necessary and appropriate to make it clear to all lawyers and disciplinary agencies that this rule applies equally to "pay to play."

Either amending Model Rule 7.2(c), issuance of formal opinion to the effect that Rule 7.2(c) applies to "pay to play," or the adoption of a commentary to this rule expressly bringing "pay to play" within its scope will have the practical effect of providing uniform guidance to lawyers and disciplinary agencies in the application of this rule, thus avoiding the potential proliferation of different rules or levels of regulation of "pay to play" among the various states and their disciplinary agencies. This would not, of course, prohibit any disciplinary agency from adopting a specific rule regulating or prohibiting political contributions by lawyers engaged by state and local governments where the local circumstances warrant such a rule.

Summary and Conclusion

While lawyers debate the appropriate means of regulating "pay to play," almost all of them agree that "pay to play" is inappropriate and was properly condemned by the Association in 1997. This action by the House of Delegates should be viewed as a beginning of efforts to eliminate "pay to play," not a final resolution of this issue. Calling upon states and local governments to adopt full and effective systems for reporting and disclosure of campaign contributions and establishment of effective, competitive, and open procedures for selection of counsel, are steps which can be taken immediately to address this issue and over which there will be little argument.

The issue of limiting political contributions is tougher and often evokes an emotional response from participants in the debate. For the reasons noted above, the author believes that the most effective action which the Association can take is to express its belief that Model Rule 7.2(c) both encompasses and proscribes "pay to play" and to promulgate a formal opinion, amendment to the rule or commentary which specifically addresses "pay to play." Such action would promote the application of a uniform standard throughout the country when disciplinary agencies take appropriate action in cases involving "pay to play," thus avoiding the confusion inherent in attempting to implement a detailed market regulation-type rule which would likely vary in scope and application among jurisdictions and disciplinary agencies. While this solution may not satisfy those who seek a market regulation rule addressing "pay to play," in the author's judgment, such rules are best adopted and enforced by agencies with the expertise, interest, and authority to address such issues on a national level.

Endnotes

1. MD. CODE ANN. art. 33, §§ 30-1 through -3 (1997).
2. *See, e.g.,* the NABL publication SELECTION & EVALUATION OF BOND COUNSEL (1988), which is currently undergoing revision.
3. Rule 7.2(c) states:

> A lawyer shall not give anything of value to a person for recommending the lawyer's services, except that a lawyer may (1) pay the reasonable cost of advertising or written communication permitted by this rule; (2) pay the usual charges of a not-for-profit lawyer referral service or other legal service organization; and (3) pay for a law practice in accordance with Rule 1.17.

The similar prohibition under the Model Code of Professional Responsibility is DR 2-103(B), which provides that a lawyer "shall not compensate or give anything of value to a person or organization to recommend or secure his employment . . . except that he may pay the usual and reasonable fees or dues charged by any of the organizations listed in DR 2-103(D)." (DR 2-103(D) referred to legal aid and other legal services organizations.)

Municipal Ethics Check
for the Land-Use Lawyer

Patricia E. Salkin*

Lawyers involved in the land-use game, whether representing planning and/or zoning boards, applicants, or third-party interests in a community, should be aware of a host of ethical issues which may confront one or more players in any land-use decision-making process. This article focuses narrowly on the interplay of state and local government ethics in a land-use environment. For a more detailed discussion of ethical dilemmas presented to land-use lawyers under the Code of Professional Responsibility, as well as a discussion of who is the client of the government lawyer, see *Land Use Law & Zoning Digest* (May 1997).

The following questions highlight common scenarios found in jurisdictions across the country. May a lawyer who sits as a member of the planning board step down to represent a client before the board and then return to his or her seat after the matter is presented and/or resolved? A member of the planning board is also the local real estate agent for the largest realty company in the town. Is this an inherent conflict-of-interest? May he or she vote on proposed new housing developments when she is likely to earn a commission on any sale made within these developments? May members of zoning boards vote on matters involving their neighbors, friends, business associates, or anyone they know? When is disclosure enough? When is recusal appropriate?

Since land-use decisions may be valued in the multimillion dollar range, there is often a great deal at stake for applicants fiscally, and for the community in terms of quality of life, financial stability, and the natural environment. Therefore, these decisions are at times highly controversial, hotly contested, and very public. As a result, the decision-making process is often critiqued under a microscope by all interested parties as well as by the media. This, no doubt, contributes to heightened awareness by applicants and the public of potential conflicts-of-interest among and between the players, as well as other ethical dilemmas which may be present (such as the appearance of impropriety).

Earning the Public Trust

The public expects and deserves the highest degree of ethical conduct when it comes to government decision-making. Without this "public trust," our

---

*Patricia E. Salkin is the director of the Government Law Center of Albany Law School and the Section's publication director.

planning and zoning boards and local legislative bodies would lack the confidence and support of the people. This would undermine the public purpose behind local land-use decision-making and further complicate what may already be difficult and controversial situations.

One aspect of earning the public trust is the appointment of knowledgeable and interested people to serve on land-use decision-making boards. It is not uncommon to find planners who work in neighboring localities, architects, engineers, lawyers, realtors, and builders interested in serving in such a capacity. On one hand, their professional expertise is desirable, yet on the other hand, the public needs to be certain that these same people, whose earning potential may be tied to land-use planning and zoning decisions, avoid conflicts-of-interest, decision-making out of self-dealing, and even the appearance of impropriety. While these may prove (un)intentional disincentives to service, there are thousands of people on boards and legislative bodies who earn a living in a field related to land-use decision making, and questions of ethics are constantly on the horizon for them.

Government officials, elected and appointed, and those who interact with government are expected to avoid conflicts-of-interest and situations where there is potential for personal financial gain. More obvious issues like bribery and influence peddling carry criminal penalties, while conflicts-of-interest matters may yield to lesser civil fines. Perhaps most significant, lawyers and their clients would prefer to avoid headlines in the local newspapers making allegations of unethical conduct. Referred to as the "Newspaper Smell Test," prudence dictates that if you don't want to read about in the headlines of the local paper, then avoid the action.

Ethics Rules Applicable

Each state has a code of ethics or a code of conduct for public employees. While some states pay minimal attention to the issue of municipal ethics, other states have specific statutory provisions for local government officials. Furthermore, a number of states specifically authorize and/or mandate that local governments adopt their own codes of ethics. Some state statutes make specific reference to conflicts-of-interest in state and regional planning acts and laws. Attorneys who work for or in front of planning and zoning boards must be conversant with these rules for a number of obvious reasons: (1) under a statutory or local law definition, if the lawyer represents the municipality or the board, he or she may be bound individually by the law; (2) lawyers counseling local entities or individuals therein must be familiar with special ethical considerations in the public sector; and (3) lawyers representing applicants before the boards need to know the applicable standards of ethical conduct to best serve the interests of their clients.

In addition to the codes and local laws, state ethics commissions or boards and local government ethics boards also provide interpretations of the codes in the form of formal and informal opinions. Some state offices make their opinions available through online research databases, subscriptions services, and in some cases, the Internet. Opinions from local ethics committees may be more of a challenge to research.

The state attorney general and the state comptroller may also offer formal and informal opinions to municipal officials and municipal attorneys on a wide variety of ethics issues including conflicts of interests and compatibility of dual office holding. These opinions are published (and readily available online) and serve as a useful source of insight into the application and interpretation of constitutional, statutory, and common-law ethics principles.

Conflicts of Interest

Addressing the issue of local conflicts of interest for elected and appointed officials can be a daunting task. The rule of thumb is, with public as well as professional legal ethics, avoid even the appearance of impropriety. The public should be assured that local officials are able to exercise their best judgment free of any hint of self-interest, especially on issues such as controversial land-use permits. (*In the Matter of Stanley Byer v. Town of Poestenkill,* 1996 N.Y. App. Div. LEXIS 10546 (3d Dep't 1996)). The Attorney General of Arkansas explained that the conflict of interest theory is based "on the fact that an individual occupying a public position uses the trust imposed in him and the position he occupies to further his own personal gain." (*See* 1994 Ark. AG Op. 93-446 (Feb. 3, 1994), *citing City of Coral Gables v. Weksler,* 164 So. 2d 260, 263 (Fla. App. 1964)).

The difficulty or challenge for lawyers giving advice to local officials-clients is that a determination as to whether a conflict-of-interest exists is made on a case-by-case basis, and courts will look to the magnitude of the interest at issue. (*See In the Matter of Stanley Byer; also Matter of Parker v. Town of Gardiner Planning Board,* 184 A.D.2d 937, 585 N.Y.S.2d 571). So, for example, when a member of the planning board was appointed after he voiced public opposition to a proposed floating zone in a revision to the master plan, and subsequently has an opportunity to, and does, officially vote for a plan which does not contain the floating zone, an allegation that he had a conflict of interest based upon his own financial interest is insufficient since his personal opinion cannot be equated with his financial interests (*In the Matter of John Segalla v. Planning Board of the Town of Amenia,* 204 A.D.2d 332, 611 N.Y.S.2d 287 (2d Dep't 1994)). And, when it was alleged that a member of a planning board had, at most, a .15 percent financial interest in the gross sales for two years for a company requesting subdivision approval from the board, this amount of interest was *de minimus,* and it would be speculative as to whether it would actually influence the board member's judgment (*Matter of Parker*).

Some states have directly addressed the issue of conflicts-of-interest in their planning statutes. For example, while Idaho encourages the creation of diverse planning and zoning boards, section 67-6506 provides, "A member or employee of a governing board, commission, or joint commission shall not participate in any proceeding or action when the member or employee or his employer, business partner, business associate, or any person related to him by affinity or consanguinity within the second degree has an economic interest in the procedure or action." The provision goes on to require disclosure of any actual or potential interest in any proceeding, and makes violation of the section a misdemeanor. In applying this provision, a court recently held that where a member has an economic interest in the procedure or action, the section prohibits participation by that member, even if he or she will not vote. (*Sprenger, Grubb & Assoc. v. City of Hailey*, 903 P.2d 741 (1995).)

In Michigan, the failure of a zoning board member to disqualify himself or herself from a vote in which the member has a conflict of interest constitutes misconduct in office and is grounds for removal (Mich. Stat. Ann. § 5.2963(18)(4)). An opinion from the Attorney General's Office found that where a member of a township zoning board owns land within the township which is affected either directly or indirectly by a matter before the board, the member must disqualify himself or herself when the matter is considered. *See* Op. Mich. Att'y Gen., Sept. 8, 1980, No. 5774.

Compatibility of Office

The issue of compatibility of dual-office holding often arises in the land-use context. The question of whether one person may ethically be a member of two different planning or zoning boards in different municipalities is particularly troublesome. The reason for the dual-office holding may be that there is simply a lack of citizen interest in sitting on one or both boards. It could also be a calculated decision by a municipality to appoint a planning or zoning board member to the county or regional planning board so that this person can offer insight into the decision-making process in matters which come before the local board first. Whatever the motivation, the question is whether this presents a situation which triggers an ethical violation.

There is a split of opinion on the legality of such dual office holding. In 1991, after two fairly controversial Attorney General Opinions (89-36 Op. Att'y Gen. 112 (1989), and 90-56 Op. Att'y Gen. 1099 (1990)), the New York State Legislature stated that members of planning boards and zoning boards may serve simultaneously as members of a county or regional planning board (N.Y. Gen. Mun. Law § 239-b (McKinney 1997)). On the other hand, the Illinois Attorney General recently opined that the positions of township trustee and county board member are incompatible because, among other things, the two units of government are authorized (not required) to contract with each other and to enter into intermunicipal agreements. Therefore, it would be difficult to adequately represent the interests of both municipalities when trying to bring about such cooperation (1994 Ill. AG 94-008 (Mar. 24, 1994)). This issue is particularly important today in light of continued efforts to stress the positive impacts of inter-jurisdictional and regional land-use planning activities.

310   APPENDIX A

As mentioned in the introduction, jurisdictions often seek people with professional and/or business familiarity with some of the complex and technical issues which may come before a planning or zoning board. Attracting this volunteer expertise, however, may prove costly to board members. For example, a recent opinion of the Attorney General in New York determined that a licensed architect who sits on a zoning board should not represent an applicant before the local building department since a potential denial of the permit would bring an appeal to the zoning board (Op. N.Y. Att'y Gen. 94-51, Dec. 20, 1994). The Attorney General reasoned that disclosure and recusal was inappropriate in this situation since under New York's General Municipal Law § 805(a)(1)(c), " . . . a municipal officer or employee may not receive or enter into any matter for compensation for services to be rendered in relation to any matter before any municipal agency of which he or she is an officer, member or employee." The Attorney General opined that "[i]n representing applicants, the architect is creating the possibility of conflicts of interests, which are not unlikely to occur. A public official should not take actions which place him or herself in a position where recusal would likely be required."

Proactive Steps

While it is true that "sunshine is the best disinfectant," a seasoned land-use practitioner should be proactive and educate clients so that ethics allegations do not run rampant, resulting in loss of public confidence, diminished reputations, and added costs to a project. Ethics training should be a regular part of the attorney's work with the municipality. If you represent the municipality as a whole (including land-use matters), you may suggest a periodic review of the local ethics law to make certain that provisions are clear and unambiguous. This is a good first step toward avoiding unnecessary ethics allegations and violations. Too often, a municipality enacts a local ethics law and then rarely, if ever, does it go back to review its usefulness.

Conclusion

These issues merely begin to scratch the surface of a much needed continued study and dialogue on government ethics questions that confront land-use practitioners on a daily basis. It is incumbent upon those of us who advise and interact with the public sector to be more conversant with the nuances of public sector ethics. In addition to our duty to represent the profession, when we work in the public sector, we have a responsibility to preserve and protect public trust and integrity in government.

APPENDIX ❦ B

State Ethics Commissions/Agencies

What follows is a list of state executive agency ethics commissions or agencies charged with some oversight of executive agency public officials with respect to ethics laws and/or financial disclosure. Each agency listed is vested with differing authority, some much broader than others. Some states have additional ethics agencies charged with oversight for the legislature and for lobbyists.

Alabama
Alabama Ethics Commission
100 North Union Street, Suite 104
RSA Union Building
Montgomery, Alabama 36104

Alaska
Alaska Public Offices Commission
2221 East Northern Lights
    Boulevard, #128
Anchorage, Alaska 99508

Arizona
Arizona Commission on Judicial
    Conduct
1501 West Washington Street
    Suite 229
Phoenix, Arizona 85007

Arkansas
Arkansas Ethics Commission
1610 West Third Street
Little Rock, Arkansas 72201

California
Fair Political Practices Commission
428 J Street, Suite 800
Sacramento, California 95762

Colorado
Department of State
1560 Broadway, Suite 200
Denver, Colorado 80203

Connecticut
Connecticut Ethics Commission
20 Trinity Street
Hartford, Connecticut 06106

Delaware
State Public Integrity Commission
Tatnall Building, Ground Floor
PO Box 1401
Dover, Delaware 19903

311

312   APPENDIX B

Florida
Florida Commission on Ethics
2822 Remington Green Circle
PO Drawer 15709
Tallahassee, Florida 32317

Georgia
State Ethics Commission
2082 East Exchange Place, Suite 235
Tucker, Georgia 30084

Hawaii
State Ethics Commission
PO Box 616
Honolulu, Hawaii 96809

Idaho
Office of the Secretary of State
State House, Room 203
Boise, Idaho 83720

Illinois
Board of Ethics
100 West Randolph Street
   Suite 3-300
Chicago, Illinois 60601

Indiana
State Ethics Commission
402 West Washington Street
Room W 189
Indianapolis, Indiana 46204

Iowa
Ethics and Campaign Disclosure
   Board
514 East Locust, Suite 104
Des Moines, Iowa 50309

Kansas
Commission on Governmental
   Standards and Conduct
109 West Ninth Street, Suite 504
Topeka, Kansas 66612

Kentucky
Executive Branch Ethics
   Commission
Room 273 Capitol Annex
Frankfort, Kentucky 40601

Louisiana
Louisiana Ethics Administration
8401 United Plaza Boulevard
   Suite 200
Baton Rouge, Louisiana 70809-7017

Maine
Commission on Governmental
   Ethics and Election Practices
#135 State House Station, Room 114
Augusta, Maine 04333

Maryland
State Ethics Commission
300 East Joppa Road, Suite 301
Towson, Maryland 21286

Massachusetts
State Ethics Commission
One Ashburton Place, Room 619
Boston, Massachusetts 02108

Michigan
State Board of Ethics
Department of Civil Service
PO Box 30002
Lansing, Michigan 48909

Minnesota
Ethical Practices Board
658 Cedar Street, First Floor
St. Paul, Minnesota 55155-1722

Mississippi
Mississippi Ethics Commission
PO Box 22746
Jackson, Mississippi 39225

Missouri
Missouri Ethics Commission
221 East Metro
Jefferson City, Missouri 65109-1254

Montana
Commissioner of Public Practices
1205 Eighth Avenue
Helena, Montana 59620

Nebraska
Nebraska Accountability and
   Disclosure Commission
State Capitol Building
   Eleventh Floor
PO Box 95086
Lincoln, Nebraska 68509

Nevada
Nevada Commission on Ethics
Capitol Complex
Carson City, Nevada 89710

New Hampshire
Office of the Secretary of State
Room 304 Statehouse
Concord, New Hampshire 03054

New Jersey
Executive Commission on Ethical
   Standards
PO Box 082
Trenton, New Jersey 08625

New Mexico
Office of the Secretary Ethics
   Administration
State Capitol, Room 420
Sante Fe, New Mexico 87503

New York
New York State Ethics Commission
39 Columbia Street
Albany, New York 12207

North Carolina
North Carolina Board of Ethics
116 West Jones Street
Raleigh, North Carolina 27603

North Dakota
Office of the Secretary of State
600 East Boulevard
Bismark, North Dakota 58505-0500

Ohio
Office of the Secretary of State
30 West Broad Street
   Fourteenth Floor
Columbus, Ohio 43266-0418

Oklahoma
Oklahoma Ethics Commission
B-5 State Capitol
Oklahoma City, Oklahoma 73105

Oregon
Government Standards and
   Practices Commission
100 High Street SE, Suite 220
Salem, Oregon 97310

Pennsylvania
Pennsylvania State Ethics
   Commission
309 Finance Building
PO Box 11470
Harrisburg, Pennsylvania
   17108-1470

Rhode Island
Rhode Island Ethics Commission
40 Fountain Street
Providence, Rhode Island 02903

South Carolina
State Ethics Commission
PO Box 11926
Columbia, South Carolina 29211

South Dakota
Office of Secretary of State
500 East Capitol
Pierre, South Dakota 57501

Tennessee
Registry of Election Finance
404 James Robertson Parkway
  Suite 1614
Nashville, Tennessee 37243

Texas
Texas Ethics Commission
201 East Fourteenth Street
  Tenth Floor
Austin, Texas 78701

Utah
Office of Lieutenant Governor
203 State Capitol
Salt Lake City, Utah 84114

Vermont
Office of Secretary of State
109 State Street
Montpelier, Vermont 05609-1101

Virginia
Office of Secretary of
  Commonwealth
Old Finance Building
Capitol Square of Virginia
Richmond, Virginia 23219

Washington
Washington State Public Disclosure
  Commission
711 Capitol Way, Room 403
PO Box 40908
Olympia, Washington 98504

West Virginia
West Virginia Ethics Commission
1207 Quarrier Street
Charleston, West Virginia 25301

Wisconsin
Wisconsin Ethics Board
44 East Mifflin Street, Suite 601
Madison, Wisconsin 53703-2800

Wyoming
Legislative Service Office
213 Capitol Building
Cheyenne, Wyoming 82002

APPENDIX ❦ C

Select Bibliography

Adams, Mark A., et al. "Ethics in Government (Eighth Survey of White Collar Crime)." *American Criminal Law Review* 30 (spring 1993): 617.

Appleby, Paul H. *Morality and Administration in Democratic Government*. Baton Rouge, La.: Louisiana State University Press, 1952.

Bailey, Stephen K. *Ethics and the Politician*. Santa Barbara, Calif.: Center for the Study of Democratic Institutions, 1960.

Baker, "Political and Practical Ethical Problems of a City Attorney." Florida Municipal Attorneys Annual Conference, August 1990.

Barcott, Jane. "1990 Update on Ethics Legislation." Conference on Government Ethics Laws, September 1990.

Barsdate, Lory A. "Attorney-Client Priviledge for the Government Entity," *Yale Law Journal* 97 (1988): 1725.

Beauchamp, T., and T. Pinkord, *Ethics and Public Policy*. Englewood Cliffs, N.J.: Prentice Hall, 1983.

Bell, Clyde L. "Legislative Ethics: Ends and Means." *Popular Government,* spring 1975, 18–22, 26.

Bernstein, Marver H. "Conflicts of Interest in State and Local Government." Monograph. 21 January 1971.

Boling, T. Edwin, and John Demsey. "Ethical Dilemmas in Government: Designing an Organizational Response." *Public Personnel Management Journal* 10, no. 1 (1989): 11–19.

Bonczek, Stephen J. "Creating an Ethical Work Environment: Enhancing Ethics Awareness in Local Government." *Public Management,* October 1991, 19–23.

Bowie, N. *Ethical Issues in Government*. Philadelphia, PA: Temple Univ. Press, 1981.

Bowman, James S. "Ethics in Government: A National Survey of Public Administrators." *Public Administration Review* 50, no. 3 (May/June 1990): 345–53.

Bryce, Joseph C., Thomas J. Gibson, and Daryn E. Rush. "Ethics in Government." *American Criminal Law Review* 29 (1992): 315.

Burke, John. "Reconciling Public Administration and Democracy: The Role of the Responsible Administrator." *Public Administration Review* 49, no. 2 (March/April 1989): 180–85.

Buzak, Edward J., "A Guide to the Local Government Ethics Law," *New Jersey Law Journal* 128 (1991): 11.

Carpinello, George F. "Should Practicing Lawyers Be Legislators?" *Hastings Law Journal* 41 (November 1989): 87.

Carroll, James D., and Robert N. Roberts, "If Men Were Angels: Assessing the Ethics in Government Act of 1978." *Policy Studies Journal* 17 (winter 1988–89): 435.

Caylor, David. Ethics Section Report, National Institute of Municipal Law Officers Mid-Year Seminar, 1993.

Citizens League of Greater Cleveland. "Ethics in Public Business." *The Citizens League of Greater Cleveland (Newsletter)* 35 (May-June 1959): 1–4.

Civic Research Institute. *Ethical Conduct: A Model Code for Local Government.* Kansas City, Mo.: The Institute, 1962.

Clarke, James P. "Codes of Ethics: Waste of Time or Important Control." *Public Management* 49 (August 1967): 222–26.

Cody, W. J. Michael and Richard R. Lynn. *Honest Government: An Ethics Guide for Public Service.* Westport, Conn.: Praeger Publishers, 1992.

Coffin, Tristram J. "The New York State Ethics in Government Act of 1987: A Critical Evaluation," *Columbia Journal of Law and Social Problems* 22 (summer 1989): 319.

Cohen, Audrey C. "The Citizen as the Integrating Agent: Productivity in the Human Services." *Human Services.* (mono. series, n.p.) September 1978.

Commission on Government Integrity. Draft of Proposed Ethics Act for New York State Municipalities. New York State Commission on Government Integrity, 1988.

Committee on Standards of Official Conduct. *House Ethics Manual,* 102d, 2d Session. Washington, D.C.: U.S. Government Printing Office, 1992.

Cooper, Terry L. *The Responsible Administatror: An Approach to Ethics for the Administrative Role.* San Francisco: Jossey-Bass, 1990.

Cooper, Terry L. *An Ethic of Citizenship for Public Administration.* Englewood Cliffs, N.J.: Prentice Hall, 1991.

Cooper, Terry L., and N. Dale Wright, eds., *Exemplory Public Administrators: Character and Leadership in Government.* San Fransisco: Jossey-Bass, 1992.

Council on Governmental Ethics Laws. *The Guardian,* The Council of State Governments, February, April, June, August, October, and December, 1993.

Cox, Archibald. "Ethics in Government: The Cornerstone of Public Trust." *West Virginia Law Review* 94 (1991): 281.

Curran, Stephen J. "Government Lawyers and Conflicts of Interest." *Georgetown Journal of Legal Ethics* 3 (1989): 191.

Davies, Mark. "1987 Ethics in Government Act: Financial Disclosure Provisions for Municipal Officials and Proposals for Reform." *Pace Law Review* 11 (winter 1991): 243.

Davies, Mark. "Governmental Ethics Laws: Myths and Mythos." *New York Law School Law Review* 40 (1995): 177.

Davis, Gary F. and William E. Gressman. "The Office of Government Ethics' First Biennal Report: The State of Government Ethics in the Executive Branch." *Federal Bar and News Journal* 37 (September 1990): 380.

Dellay, Patrick J. "Curbing Influence Peddling in Albany: The 1987 Ethics in Government Act." *Brooklyn Law Review* 53 (1988): 1051.

Denhardt, Kathryn G. *The Ethics of Public Service Moral Dilemmas in Public Organizations.* New York: Greenwood Press, 1988.

Dixon, Thomas F. "Application of the Code of Judicial Conduct to Administrative Agency Proceedings." *The Colorado Lawyer,* June 1991, 1155.

Dobel, J. Patrick. "Integrity in the Public Service." *Public Administration Review* 50 (May/June 1990): 354.

Donahue, Anne Marie, ed. *Ethics in Politics and Government.* The Reference Shelf, vol. 61, no. 2. New York: H.W. Wilson Company, 1989.

Donahue, Keith W. "The Model Rules and the Government Lawyer, A Sword or Shield? A Response to the D.C. Bar Special Committee on Government Lawyers and the Model Rules of Professional Conduct." *Georgetown Journal of Legal Ethics* 2 (1989): 987.

Douglas, Paul H. *Ethics in Government.* Cambridge: Harvard University Press, 1952.

Duggan, Annis. "Ethics in Government." *American Criminal Law Review* 28 (1991): 473.

Eastland, Terry. *Ethics, Politics and the Independent Counsel: Executive Power, Executive Vice, 1789–1989,* Washington, D.C.: National Legal Center for the Public Interest, 1989.

Elefant, Carolyn. "When Helping Others Is a Crime: Section 205's Restriction on Pro Bono Representation by Federal Attorneys." *Georgetown Journal of Legal Ethics* 3 (1990): 719.

Federal Bar Association, Professional Ethics Committee. "The Government Client and Confidentiality: Opinion 73-1." *Federal Bar Journal* 32 (winter 1973): 71.

Feinberg, Harold. *Ethics, Incompatibilty, and Conflicts of Interest of Public Officials,* 6th rev. New Brunswick, N.J.: Rutgers University Bureau of Government Research and University Extension Division, 1969.

Fleishman, Joel, Lance Liebman, and Mark H. Moore, eds. *Public Duties: The Moral Obligations of Government Officials.* Cambridge: Harvard University Press, 1981.

Fox, Charles J. "Civil Service Reform and Ethical Accountability." *Public Personal Management Journal* 10, no. 1 (1981): 98–102.

Gutman, Amy and Dennis F. Thompson. *Ethics and Politics: Cases and Comments.* Chicago: Nelson-Hall, 1990.

Harlan, Danielle. "Conflicts of Interest: Government Attorneys." *Government Journal of Legal Ethics* 5 (1991): 133.

Hastings Center. Institute of Society and the Life Sciences. *Project on Legislative Ethics Progress Report.* January 1983.

Hays, Steven W., and Richard R. Gleissner. "Codes of Ethics in State Government: A Nationwide Survey." *Public Personnel Management Journal* 10, no. 1 (1981): 48–58.

Hobbs, E.H. "Ethics in Government." *Public Sector* 1, no.1 (September 1976): 1–4.

Informal Advisory Letters and Memoranda and Formal Opinions of the United States Office of Government Ethics, 1979–1988. Washington D.C.: U.S. Office of Government Ethics, 1989.

Hochman, Joseph I. "Post-Employment Lobbying Restrictions on the Legislative Branch of Government: A Minimalist Approach to Regulating Ethics in Government." *Washington Law Review* 65 (1990): 883.

Jennings, Bruce, and Daniel Callahan. *Representation and Responsibility: Exploring Legislative Ethics.* New York: Plenum Press, 1985.

Johnson, Graham E. "The Public Official and the Public Trust." Paper prepared for the Eighty-Second National Conference on Government, National Municipal League, Williamsburg, Va., November 1976.

Josephson, Michael S. "Ethics Legislation: Problems and Potential." *State Legislatures,* July 1989, 50.

Kass, Henry D. "Exploring Agency as a Basis for Ethical Theory in American Public Administration." *International Journal of Public Administration* 12, no. 6 (1989): 949–69.

Kellar, Elizabeth K. *Ethical Insight Ethical Action: Perspective for the Local Government Manager.* Washington, D.C.: ICMA, 1988.

Kent, Bruce W. "Ethics and the Government Lawyer." *The Journal of the Kansas Bar Association* 62 (February/March 1993): 30.

Koffsky, Daniel L. "Coming to Terms with Bureaucratic Ethics." *Journal of Law and Politics* 11 (spring 1995): 235.

Kreutzer, S. Stanley. "Codes and Conflicts in Big City Governments: A Look at New York." *Good Government* 83 (spring 1966): 7–8.

Lanctot, Catherine J. "The Duty of Zealous Advocacy and the Ethics of the Federal Government Lawyer: The Three Hardest Questions." *Southern California Law Review* 64 (May 1991): 951.

Lefkowitz, Louis J. Remarks before the American Society for Public Administration, New York Metropolitan Chapter, New York City, 25 October 1973.

Lewis, Carol W. *The Ethics Challenge in Public Service: A Problem-Solving Guide.* San Francisco: Jossey-Bass, 1991.

Lilla, Mark T. "Ethos, 'Ethics,' and Public Service." *The Public Interest,* no. 63 (spring 1981): 3–17.

Lombard, Eliot H. *Encouraging Integrity in Office.* New York: Citizens Union Research Foundation, Inc., 1964.

McBride, Ann. "Ethics in Congress: agenda and action (Symposium: Ehtics in Gov't)" *George Washington Law Review* 58 (February 1990): 451.

Madsen, Peter, and Jay M. Shafritz, eds., *Essentials of Government Ethics.* New York: Meridian, 1992.

Moore, Mark H., and Malcolm K. Sparrow. *Ethics in Government: The Moral Challenge of Public Leadership.* Englewood Cliffs, N.J.: Prentice Hall, 1990.

Mundhiem, Robert H. "Conflict of Interest and the Former Government Employee: Rethinking the Revolving Door." *Creighton Law Review* 14 (1981): 707.

National Academy of Public Admisitration (NAPA). "Ethics in the Public Service." Summary of a symposium held November 1975.

National Municipal League. *A Code of Ethics for Public Officials.* Proceedings of the Sixty-Sixth National Conference on Government, Mayflower Hotel, Washington, D.C., 16 November 1962.

Newman, Robert C. "New York's New Ethics Law: Turning the Tide on Corruption (A Symposium on Ethics in Government)." *Hofstra Law Review* 16 (winter 1988): 319.

New York State Commission on Government Integrity. *Raising Our Sights: The Need for Ethics Training in Government.* February 1990.

New York State Legislature Assembly Committee on Ethics and Guidance. *Ethics Manual for Members and Employees of the New York State Assembly.* Albany, N.Y.: The Committee, 1981.

Norton, Jerry E. "Government Attorneys' Ethics in Transition." *Judicature* 72 (February/March 1990): 299.

Obermaier, Otto G. "Legal Ethics 1990: What Every Lawyer Needs to Know about Ethical Obligations on the Government Lawyer." *Practicing Law Institute* 403 (October 1990): 411.

Office of Government Ethics for the Executive Branch. *Government Ethics Newsgram* 10, no. 2 (summer 1993).

Roback, Herbert. Memorandum to Tom Fletcher and Dwight Ink, 8 December 1975 (categorizes ethical issues in public administration).

Rohr, Jon A. *Ethics for Bureaucrats,* 2d ed. New York: Marcel Dekker, 1989.

Salkin, Patricia E. "Legal Ethics and Land-Use Planning." *The Urban Lawyer* 30 (spring 1998): 383.

Sanders, Maureen A. "Government Attorneys and the Ethical Rules: Good Souls in Limbo." *Brigham Young University Journal of Public Law* 7 (1993): 39.

Satery, Thomas J. "The Ethics in Government Act of 1978 and Subsequent Reforms: The Effect of Political and Practice Influences on the Creation of Public Policy." *Seton Hall Law Review* 13 (winter 1990): 243.

Sheeran, Patrick J. *Ethics in Public Administration*. Westport, Conn.: Praeger, 1993.

Sheppard, Harrison. "American Principles and the Evolving Ethos of American Legal Practice (Legal Ethics Symposium)." *Loyola University of Chicago Law Journal* 28 (winter 1996): 237.

Temporary State Commission on Local Government Ethics. "In Search of a Wise Law: Municipal Ethics Reform." State of New York Temporary Commission on Government Ethics, 20 March 1991.

Thompson, Dennis F. *Politics, Ethics and Public Office*. Cambridge: Harvard University Press, 1987.

Thompson, Dennis F. "Paradoxes of Government Ethics." *Public Administration Review* 52 (May/June 1992): 254.

Thompson, Dennis F., *Ethics in Congress from Individual to Institutional Corruption*. Washington D.C.: The Brookings Institution, 1995.

Torpey, William G. *Federal Executive Branch Ethics*. Alexandria, Va.: W. G. Torpey, 1990.

United States Office of Government Ethics. Government Ethics Newsgram, vol. 7, no. 2 (summer 1990); vol. 9, no. 1 (winter/spring 1992); vol. 10, no. 1 (spring 1993).

United States Office of Government Ethics. *Second Biennial Report to Congress*. U.S. Office of Government Ethics, March 1992.

Vaughn, Robert G. "Ethics in Government and the Vision of Public Service (Symposium Ethics in Government)." *George Washington Law Review* 58 (February 1990): 417.

Weisburg, Debra S. "Eliminating Corruption in Local Government: The Local Government Ethics Law." *Seton Hall Legislative Journal* 17 (1993): 303.

Worthly, John A. "Ethics and Public Management: Education and Training." *Public Personnel Management Journal* 10, no. 1 (1981): 41–47.

Zimmerman, Joseph F. "Ethical Behavior in the Public Service." Paper presented at the University of Nuremberg, Federal Republic of Germany, 25 June 1985.

Zimmerman, Joseph. *Curbing Unethical Behavior in Government*. Westport, Conn.: Greenwood Press, 1994.